DATE DUE

Singing a New Tune

Singing a New Tune

The Rebirth of the Modern Film Musical, from *Evita* to *De-Lovely* and Beyond

SINGING A NEW TUNE

The Rebirth of the Modern Film Musical, From *Evita* to *De-Lovely* and Beyond
by John Kenneth Muir

Copyright © 2005 by John Kenneth Muir

Editor and photo researcher: Michael Messina
Book design by Pearl Chang based on cover design by Mark Lerner

Library of Congress Cataloging-in-Publication Data:
Muir, John Kenneth, 1969–
Singing a new tune : The rebirth of the modern film musical, from *Evita* to *De-Lovely* and beyond / by John Kenneth Muir.
    p.   cm.
Includes bibliographical references and index.
ISBN-13: 978-1-55783-610-6
ISBN-10: 1-55783-610-8
1. Musical films—United States—History and criticism. I. Title.
PN1995.9.M86M85 2005
791.43'6—dc22   2005012606

British Library Cataloging-in-Publication Data
A catalog record of this book is available from the British Library

Applause Theatre & Cinema Books
19 West 21ST Street, Suite 201
New York, NY 10010
Phone: (212) 575-9265
Fax: (212) 575-9270
Email: info@applausepub.com
Internet: www.applausepub.com

Applause books are available through your local bookstore, or you may order at www.applausepub.com or call Music Dispatch at 800-637-2852

Sales & Distribution

North America:
  Hal Leonard Corp.
  7777 West Bluemound Road
  P. O. Box 13819
  Milwaukee, WI 53213
  Phone: (414) 774-3630
  Fax: (414) 774-3259
  Email: halinfo@halleonard.com
  Internet: www.halleonard.com

Europe:
  Roundhouse Publishing Ltd.
  Millstone, Limers Lane
  Northam, North Devon EX 39 2RG
  Phone: (0) 1237-474-474
  Fax: (0) 1237-474-774
  Email: roundhouse.group@ukgateway.net

Written with love for Frances Stallard Leftwich,
my all-singing, all-dancing Nana who loves those classic Hollywood musicals
. . . and does a hell of an Eric Cartman impersonation.

And

For Jay Cocks, because of Lindsay Anderson's *O Lucky Man!*
Joss Whedon because of *The Sky's the Limit*
and
James Lyons for *The Long Day Closes*

Contents

Acknowledgments

My utmost thanks goes to my agent June Clark, for getting the ball rolling again on a fantastic project. My special gratitude to Frances Leftwich and Peggy McGee—my classic movie musical experts in residence—who inundated me with everything from *Oklahoma!* and *White Christmas* to *My Fair Lady* and *Mary Poppins*. I would be nowhere without their video and DVD collections.

In Hollywood and beyond, my dearest appreciation goes to Michael Boretz, Katie Hands, and Cassidy Gering for so ably helping to facilitate the interviews that make this text special. And, as always, I appreciate the assistance of my sweet wife, Kathryn, a sounding board, proofreader, and fellow movie musical viewer.

And of course, my deepest gratitude goes out to the interviewees who selflessly and graciously undertook this study of the modern movie musical with me. In alphabetical order, these fine talents include Jay Cocks, Keith Gordon, Todd Graff, Dick Hyman, Todd Haynes, James Lyons, John Cameron Mitchell, Sir Alan Parker, Craig Pearce, and Joss Whedon.

Not Your Father's Razzle-Dazzle

Film scholars and historians across the globe have frequently pronounced the movie musical a dead art form, all "laid out to rest" with "hands across its chest," to paraphrase lyrics from Fred Zinnemann's *Oklahoma!* (1955). Even worse, the film musical, suggests prominent film critic Kenneth Turan, remains "the one Hollywood genre that never manages to sustain a comeback."[1]

This is a particularly lamentable state of affairs given the form's proud and unique heritage. After all, the movie musical is renowned as a "peculiarly American concept" according to genre historian Richard Barrios, as well as one he describes as "alternately loved and derided."[2]

Half a century ago, in the 1950s, the genre was well loved indeed. It was the tops at movie houses, the toast of Tinsel Town, and a guaranteed victor in the all-important box office sweepstakes. Yet, in the overcrowded pop culture landscape of the twenty-first century, the old-fashioned, toe-tapping musical is more or less scorned. No longer does it remain "precisely," to quote Rodgers and Hammerstein's *The King and I*, America's "cup of tea."

Still, reports of the movie musical's demise are greatly exaggerated. And frankly, the genre's long medical history suggests that there have been flat lines before, or at least arrhythmia. Over the course of the twentieth century, the format endured several body blows.

For example, the musical format almost collapsed in its formative years, during the early 1930s, suffering from overkill. Watching their fortunes fall precipitously, desperate theater owners displayed marquee signs promising musical-weary audiences that their new weekly fare was *not* of the genre. Of course, the musical survived this hardship, and its best days were yet to come, thanks to artists, including Fred Astaire, Stanley Donen, Gene Kelly, and Vincente Minnelli.

In the 1950s, movie musicals again faced a challenge, this time from that newfangled and infernal contraption called television, and hand-wringing critics worried that audiences would no longer attend theaters. Instead, movie musicals just got better, and the 1960s proved to be one of the genre's most fascinating—and popular—decades, featuring classic films such as the award-winning *West Side Story* (1961), *Mary Poppins* (1964), *The Sound of Music* (1965), and *Oliver!* (1968).

And lest the naysayers forget, it wasn't so long ago that the MGM musical compilation film *That's Entertainment* (1974) was regarded both inside the industry and out—rather prematurely—as "Hollywood's own eulogy to the end of an era in which song and film were united."[3]

But again, there was a reversal of the movie musical's gloomy fortunes. Before musical fans could mourn, or for that matter, count "five-six-seven-eight," the musical leapt once more into the forefront of popular culture imagination with disco decade blockbusters such as John Badham's Bee Gees spectacle, *Saturday Night Fever* (1977), the John Travolta and Olivia Newton-John crowd pleaser, *Grease* (1978), and one of the most influential and revolutionary musicals of any decade, Bob Fosse's electrifying and autobiographical *All That Jazz* (1979).

The musical genre, like Fosse's much harried protagonist in that film, Joe Gideon, may have suffered open-heart surgery in the seventies, but wasn't exactly dead, either.

Even the conservative tableau of the 1980s demonstrated cautiously positive signs presaging the format's eventual recovery. British playwright Dennis Potter reinvented elements of the old formula in *Pennies from Heaven* (1981) and his landmark BBC television miniseries starring Michael Gambon, *The Singing Detective* (1984).

The dawn of the MTV age also promised to bring music into American households twenty-four/seven, even as popular dance musicals such as *Flashdance* (1983), *Footloose* (1984), and *Dirty Dancing* (1987) heralded a new age of cinematic riches, albeit with wild new flourishes including music video-style editing, aerobic dance moves, and fashionably torn sweatshirts.

But then arrived yet another near-crushing brush with mortality in the early 1990s. A trio of expensive studio flops, *For the Boys* (1991), *Newsies* (1992), and *Swing Kids* (1993), signaled the early warning signs of a catastrophic stroke that would strike full bore in 1994. This was the year that director James L. Brooks, mastermind of award-winning entertainments such as *Terms of Endearment* (1984), *Broadcast News* (1987), as well as the much-admired TV series

The Simpsons (1990) and 2004's *Spanglish*, directed a thirty-million-dollar musical extravaganza for Columbia Pictures entitled *I'll Do Anything*, starring Nick Nolte and Albert Brooks.

During *I'll Do Anything*'s routine preview test screening, something that wasn't so routine occurred. One hundred audience members leapt from their seats and hoofed it out of the auditorium when the musical numbers—composed by Sinead O'Connor, Prince, and Carole King—commenced. The result of the disastrous screening was an infamous first in Hollywood: every musical interlude in the film, save one featuring a child (Whittni Wright), was cut out before release.

That's right, song and dance were surgically excised from *I'll Do Anything*, like an unwanted appendix or other vestigial organ. Deemed "unnecessary" by the modern body pop culture, scalpel-wielding film editors performed the operation under the supervision of director Brooks himself. More damagingly, the all-too-public failure of this would-be musical had a ripple effect on the genre.

To wit, in 1995, *The Fantasticks*, an adaptation of the popular and long-running, Off-Broadway stage production, was euthanized outright. Directed by another esteemed Hollywood talent, the late Michael Ritchie, *The Fantasticks*, like *I'll Do Anything*, suffered a negative test screening and because of studio trepidations, apparently merited a mercy killing. It gathered dust for five years before an extremely limited release in the year 2000.

For the musical genre, one day it was kicks, the next it was kicks in the shin, as *New York, New York*'s (1977) chanteuse Francine Evans might put it. The result of this dramatic audience hostility and studio disdain for the movie musical soon caused the emergence of something unique and rather ironic: the first new screen prohibition of the most permissive era in cinema history.

"In the movies these days you can show almost anything," observed journalist Moira McDonald, "but there's still one big taboo. Singing in the old-fashioned, let's-put-on-a-musical kind of way."[4]

In other words, the movie musical really *did* appear dead this time. Empirical evidence (i.e., studio test cards) indicated it was so disdained a format that you couldn't get arrested making one.

Of course, musicals had bombed in earlier eras. *Lost Horizon* (1973) leaps immediately to mind, but this time there was a distinction. In the mid-1990s, filmmakers couldn't even get a *release date* if their actors were to break into song.

It was a new and sad nadir for the once-thriving genre that had introduced the world to Fred Astaire, Ginger Rogers, Judy Garland, Gene Kelly, Barbra Streisand, Liza Minnelli, Julie Andrews, and, er, John Travolta.

But what were the reasons for the hostility evidenced so strongly against *I'll Do Anything* in 1994, and by extension, the genre itself? Why now were American moviegoers so dismissive of a form their parents and grandparents had cherished? Why was the format deemed such a guaranteed loser that studios would rather shelve musicals and take a loss, rather than roll the dice and release them?

"The musical started to lose its popularity once people embraced modern idioms," wrote journalist David Thomson of *Sight and Sound*, clarifying the matter for us.[5] And what, pray tell, are those modern idioms? First and foremost, naturalistic acting and dialogue, as opposed to the more overtly theatrical style that dominated the ages of Astaire and Kelly.

Perhaps more to the point, one critical modern idiom is a concentration on sexually oriented material. Right up into the 1960s, movie musicals represented coded reflections of romantic love and sexual desire. Everybody recalls that old proverb about movie musicals, that when a man and a woman sing in one, they're in love. When they dance in one, they want to have sex.

In the world of Brittany Spears and Paris Hilton, such beating around the bush is quaint at best—and at worst, obsolete. If audiences in the era of *I'll Do Anything* felt the need to be tantalized by sex, they could view *Basic Instinct* (1992), *Sliver* (1993), *Indecent Proposal* (1994), *Body of Evidence* (1995), or *Showgirls* (1995). In the world of a more freely sexual cinema, the musical format's greatest, long-standing metaphor no longer contained significant currency.

Another modern idiom might simply fall under the umbrella descriptor of *realism*. By the 1990s, audiences demanded more realism from their entertainment, and the epoch of reality TV had begun in earnest with programs such as *Cops* (1989) and the emergency reenactment docudrama, *Rescue: 911* (1989). Even television's best new fictional dramas became considerably more realism obsessed, with programs such as Steve Bochco's butt-exposing *NYPD Blue* (1993) and NBC's frenetic *ER* (1994) often deploying hand-held, shaky cameras to foster immediacy, anxiety, and realism, three seeming hallmarks of our modern national mood.

And, as utterly charming and delightful as the great movie musicals surely remain, no one in his right mind can ever accuse them of being realistic.

"I was never taken by the idea of the fabric of drama suddenly ripped asunder as people break into song," opined journalist Christopher Sharrett in *USA Today*, a viewpoint reflected by a great many other viewers too.[6] Even long-time genre admirers and contributors are occasionally taken aback by the "unreality" of this old movie musical convention.

For instance, Jay Cocks, Oscar-nominated screenwriter of diverse films including *Age of Innocence* (1993), *Strange Days* (1995), *Gangs of New York* (2002), and also the recent musical biography of Cole Porter, *De-Lovely* (2004), recalls his response when first seeing a musical production on stage. "I go back to my first reaction as a kid," he remembers. "We had the Broadway cast albums of three Rodgers and Hammerstein shows: *Carousel, Oklahoma!,* and *South Pacific,*" he describes. "We played them over and over again. My parents finally took me to my first Broadway show, and I remember what it was. It was a revival at City Center of *Oklahoma!* Well, I looked at these cowboys in these satin shirts and I thought to myself, 'Cowboys don't sing! I don't get this!'"

For some contemporary viewers, movie musicals suffer from this same fatal "realism" disconnect. "You would see the old Busby Berkeley musicals, and [now] they're kind of weird," Cocks weighs in. "I was not into camp, then or now. It's hard to put it together, what's going on."

Beyond the artificiality inherent in the format, there are other reasons why movie musicals were ailing in the nineties. The only successful genre examples landed in theaters via the auspices of Walt Disney Studios: dynamic animated flicks such as *Beauty and the Beast* (1991), *Aladdin* (1992), and *The Lion King* (1992).

Though these incredibly successful and delightful movies were gratefully received by fans, the very fact that they were animated, rated G, and aimed at children under ten seemed, perhaps, to undercut the validity of the genre. Apparently, it was okay to watch singing and dancing candlesticks or lobsters, just not live-action human beings.

Many scholars also propose that cable network MTV and its ubiquitous music videos "ransacked" the form and rendered it "aesthetically exhausted" by the mid-nineties.[7] This is a valid concern, because with a twenty-four-hour cable station broadcasting music videos, why spend eight hard-earned dollars on a movie musical? It's easier to stay on the sofa and surf with the remote control!

"The MTV-ization of the culture has made it so that people have gotten out of the habit of seeing musicals that were not commercials for the actual song, as opposed to [songs used] as a storytelling device [in a narrative]," elucidates Todd

Graff, director of the independently produced movie musical *Camp* (2003), "so you're up against that."

"Until the recent success of *Chicago*, I would have said the public has not had enough of them [movie musicals] to accept the form anymore," advises Dick Hyman, a composer and the musical arranger of Woody Allen's *Everyone Says I Love You* (1997).

"Some of the responses we had to *Everyone Says I Love You* indicated that younger people in the audience didn't understand the musical premise [i.e., the nature of the singing in a film]. They hadn't been exposed to the basic operatic convention, which is that characters burst into song. However, I was pleased to see the success of *Chicago*. It certainly worked, so maybe we've seen the future. I hope so."

The reasons the musical failed to thrive in the mid-1990s are legion, and perhaps, coalesced into a perfect storm that rendered adult, live-action representatives of the genre (like *I'll Do Anything*), either laughable or insipid. The simplest answer may be that American audiences, having suffered through the traumas of the Gulf War, Waco, the Oklahoma City bombing, and the O. J. Simpson trial, felt more cynical about life than even a decade previous.

And in the incarnations most familiar to moviegoers—whether via the exuberant *Singin' in the Rain* (1952), the treacly and heart-warming *The Sound of Music* (1965), or even the fun-loving, 1950s-era romp, *Grease* (1978)—the movie musical seemed out of step.

But again, a note of caution; critics shouldn't don their black jackets and mourn the death of the movie musical just yet. Even in the dark days of the early nineties, the form waited patiently to resurrect itself, remembering, as Mary Poppins might conclude, "that forbearance is the hallmark of its creed."

Accordingly, since the closing months of 1996, there's been a slow and steady rebirth of this beloved and classic American form. It is the movie musical's battle to climb, scratch, and claw its way out of the grave that forms the heart of this survey, a close examination of a most unusual period in the movie musical's long, up-and-down history.

How and why did the musical resurrect itself in a decade that had thus far proven its worst in movie history? The seeds of this rebirth were actually planted in the most unexpected soil imaginable, in another unique movement in modern cinema.

While mainstream Hollywood seemed intent on dishing out ever more expensive and banal fare, like dueling volcano movies in 1996 and dueling asteroid movies in 1998, a new independent film culture in America also sprang up, with dedicated practitioners like Kevin Smith, Richard Linklater, and Edward Burns.

These "guerilla" filmmakers utilized new tactics to make their films, spent less cash than Hollywood peers, and realized critical and financial success via the backdoor world of film festivals. This was a universe where, in the twenty-first century, musicals could once again compete, in part because, put bluntly, the financial stakes were lower. Although this new brand of musical looks markedly different than its golden age cousins, returning in "forms that Fred Astaire, Busby Berkeley, and Vincente Minnelli would scarcely recognize," the movie musical nonetheless thrives in the indie film venue.[8]

"Generally, if you're going to experiment at all with form or content, whether it's dealing with the dark nature of human behavior in a film like, say, *In the Bedroom* (2002), or playing with form like *Dancer in the Dark* (2000) or *The Singing Detective* (2003), it's going to have to be in the indie world because the people in the studios, probably rightly from a business point of view, don't want to be in that business," suggests Keith Gordon, director of *The Singing Detective*.

"I think it's terrible from an artistic, cultural point of view that they don't [want to be in that business], but these are not people who really care about whether the movies they make are good. They care about whether they make a lot of money, because that's how they keep their jobs. I mean, I don't hate the studio folk—they're just trying to eat—but the problem is the way that economics have evolved, you can't make *The Singing Detective* for fifty million dollars. It would be insane, so for at least the foreseeable future, anything that is experimental, whether it is musicals or Richard Linklater using animation in *Waking Life* (2001), is going to have to come out of the indie world. It's the only place people are spending small enough sums of money and can afford to take those chances."

Gordon's analysis is spot-on. In the mid-to-late-1990s and early years of the twenty-first century, the independent film came of age and was offering A-list actors a new venue to practice their craft in more meaningful ways than the average studio film could permit. Also, like *Chasing Amy* (1997), *The Blair Witch Project* (1999), or *Open Water* (2004), the movement offers ample opportunity for a small film to break out as a mainstream hit, given the right "buzz" and marketing.

Thus independent filmmakers were suddenly afforded access to hot new stars (like Katie Holmes, Ewan McGregor, Robert Downey Jr., Alicia Silverstone, and Edward Norton) as well as the potential of financial glory. Considering these bonuses, the indie world represented a logical place to make room for a genre believed to be in decline: the movie musical. It was there, under the radar, that the genre took its first wobbly steps back to the mainstream.

Accordingly, in the years from 1996 to 2003, a bevy of musicals evolved in this fashion, including Woody Allen's *Everyone Says I Love You* (1996), Todd Haynes's *Velvet Goldmine* (1998), Kenneth Branagh's *Love's Labour's Lost* (2000), Lars von Trier's *Dancer in the Dark* (2000), Todd Graff's *Camp* (2003), and Gordon's own *The Singing Detective* (2003).

Not every one of these films turned a profit to be certain, but each was artistic, energetic, and unique, just the sort of production that reenergizes a format perhaps too steeped in the past. Artistry and experimentation inevitably precede mainstream acceptance, and these films set the pace for the next decade.

"There are musicals out there," agrees Anita Monga, the film programmer for San Francisco's Castro Theater. "They just aren't in the unabashed form they used to be."[9] In other words, according to American music historian Michael Feinstein, the genre is now in a state of "constant evolution."[10]

Joss Whedon, the creator of the popular TV show *Buffy the Vampire Slayer*, composed eleven songs for that series' musical episode, "Once More with Feeling," and also directed the landmark episode. A little known fact is that he's also a virtual encyclopedia of musical film history. And Whedon doesn't regard the current conjunction of independent film and movie musicals as a strange marriage in even the slightest.

"Because, you know what? Let's put on a show," he suggests. "We'll use the old barn . . .

"A musical doesn't need that much behind it, and if you have the big machine behind it," Whedon continues, "it's going to be very hard to get off the ground. There are people today who want to make musicals. There will *always* be people who want to make musicals, and if I get to make a musical, chances are, it's not going to be the biggest budget I ever get to work with. More money is always more money, and it's never to be scoffed at, but a musical doesn't need it more than any kind of picture does. If you're trying to create a more beautiful world, go shoot on someone's better-looking lawn.

"It's actually a pretty good time for someone who wants to do something a little more outlandish," Whedon considers. "And if it hits, if it works, if it strikes a chord, and it costs all of six million dollars to make—or even half that—because the risks are smaller, [the rewards] can be bigger."

Delightfully, the movie musical revival traced throughout this text has actually been a multifront resuscitation, not limited to independents. In our span of study, a few brave Hollywood studios have also poured considerable sums of cash into bigger budget, glossy musicals in the cause of jump-starting the genre.

Since 1996, audiences have witnessed Sir Alan Parker's sweeping epic, *Evita* (1996), Trey Parker and Matt Stone's comic masterpiece, *South Park: Bigger, Longer & Uncut* (1999), Baz Luhrmann's dazzling *Moulin Rouge* (2001), and Rob Marshall's razzmatazz of motion, the Oscar-winning *Chicago* (2002). All achieved "hit" status during their theatrical runs, thereby smashing the movie musical's financial losing streak of the mid-1990s.

"To me, *Chicago* and *Evita* were fairly old-fashioned," Keith Gordon notes. "They weren't really experimental. They were experimental in the sense that 'Okay, it's a musical,' but they were both safe bets because they were both based on massive hit plays, with massive audience interest based on that, and then done in a fairly conventional style, comparatively.

"*Moulin Rouge* is the one where I look at it and say, 'This is a truly experimental film,'" Gordon continues. "God love whoever said, 'We'll throw the money into making this,' and even then, it was much less expensive than it should have been for a studio movie. I think if it had been made by a more traditional director in a more traditional way, it would have cost a hundred million dollars, and it didn't."

Considering these examples, the movie musical appears to be taking significant strides in a return to health. It stands at the vanguard of personal cinema in the independent movement, reaps mainstream success with the big-budget format in the case of *Chicago*, and even pushes its own long-standing boundaries with revolutionary, all-singing, all-dancing fare, such as *Moulin Rouge*. All in all, the prognosis for this so-called dead art form is much more upbeat now than it was ten years ago.

Perhaps the most important fact to keep sight of in this quasi-revival is that mass audiences are again seeming *receptive* to the musical film, especially after *Moulin Rouge.* "It's a genre we miss,"[11] *Moulin Rouge* star Nicole Kidman declared in 2002, and *Singin' in the Rain* legend Cyd Charisse echoed the same sentiment following *Chicago*, noting that today's public is "starved for something entertaining."[12]

Why? Because, according to Oscar-winning composer Elliot Goldenthal, the musical, despite its many ups and downs over time, remains "something that we really crave as another form of cinema."[13]

John Cameron Mitchell, director of *Hedwig and the Angry Inch* (2001) believes that's certainly the case. "I think they [audiences] are [becoming more receptive.] It's just a matter of subject matter and style that is relevant," he says. "You could say that *Chicago* is an old-fashioned musical. It has the darker themes of Bob Fosse, but it's still a very traditional musical, and it did very well.

"And things that are unconventional, like *Moulin Rouge* and *Hedwig*—and even *Dancer in the Dark*—have their audiences, for sure," asserts Mitchell. "All of those were successful."

"For today's audience, it's very much about the *contract*," emphasizes *Moulin Rouge* screenwriter Craig Pearce. "This isn't the 1930s, where we just accept that the movies are a magical land and people sing and dance. We don't just accept that convention. We have to make a case-by-case, film-by-film specific contract with the audience, whether it's *Chicago, Moulin Rouge,* or *8 Mile* (2003). It's very much about how you are going to use music, and what the contract will be with audiences.

"Today's audiences are really savvy; they're really smart, and they're really media literate," Pearce continues. "They have their camcorders, and they edit their movies on the computer, so we all understand that media is manipulation. It's just how well and how satisfyingly the storyteller does it these days that's important."

The trick in keeping the movie musical pirouetting through our cinemas for years to come thus seems to be the pinpointing of inventive and acceptable ways to seal this contract with the audience. It may be something bold and new, like *Moulin Rouge*, or ironically, it may be something so old and outmoded that it simply *feels* new to young audiences.

"There's no reason why you can't still do the old-fashioned book musical where people break into song out of dialogue," says Graff, "but it's not my taste as a filmmaker or a writer, and so to me, I would rather try to figure out new ways to do what a good book musical does—where the numbers move the story along—but without actually having book numbers."

Or to put it another way: "These story forms are resilient," concludes Thomas Schatz, a professor of radio, TV and film at the University of Texas at Austin, "and will be reinvented constantly—good filmmaking is always about reinventing convention—taking the familiar and making it strange."[14]

Since, as *Evita* and *Dancer in the Dark*'s choreographer Vince Paterson has declared, "It's okay to dance and do musicals again,"[15] we've got the green light, and so the mission of this book is to examine the daring and different movie musicals forged during the strange "rebuilding" years from 1996 to 2004, often with the testimony of the very filmmakers who brought them to us.

In documenting this fascinating new age of movie musicals, *Singing a New Tune* reveals the multitude of challenges and choices made by moviemakers crafting genre films today, and analyzes how the various efforts from this span not only helped the musical spark stay ignited, but also pushed it to a new crescendo.

Along our journey, the book gazes back at landmark movie musicals of the past, so as to more completely understand how the genre has developed over the decades. It also reflects briefly on the manner in which cinema's little sister, television, has contributed to the new vitality of this uniquely American art form, and prepped a generation of audiences for a genre on the ascent.

With the aid of several expert interviewees, including Sir Alan Parker, Todd Haynes, John Cameron Mitchell, Jay Cocks, Keith Gordon, Todd Graff, Dick Hyman, James Lyons, Craig Pearce, and Joss Whedon, we're at last ready to begin our beguine.

It's showtime, folks!

PART I
Music in the Air

CHAPTER ONE
The Old Razzle-Dazzle

A History of the Movie Musical through the 1980s

The complete, total, and unabridged history of the movie musical has filled many volumes before, thanks to authorities in the field, including the late, great Stanley Green.

However, that's not why we're here.

It is *not* the purpose of this chapter to describe every single movie musical produced from the late-1920s to the 1990s, rather only to survey and summarize the genre as a whole and to hit the hot spots, as it were. To do any more, we'd never get to the heart of today's musical, and in the end, that's the mission of this study.

Instead, this chapter serves as a sketch of the genre's long life, enunciating many of the form's dramatic ups and downs, both its evolutions and revolutions. As is often the case, history remains the best indicator of the future, so to thoroughly understand the context of the twenty-first-century movie musical, one must necessarily, as *The Fantasticks'* El Gallo might say, "try to remember" how the genre looked before; how it—and the arts of singing and dancing on film—have evolved across the span of nearly a century.

The titles you'll see explored in the following pages represent both the classic and the notorious and serve as guideposts along our Yellow Brick Road, critical junctures in our understanding of the directions the movie musical has taken and in fact, may next take.

Along this odyssey, the very writers and directors behind today's most memorable movie musicals often discuss their favorite productions and inspirations, serving as our tour guides, or more appropriately a Greek chorus, through eighty years of tripping the light fantastic.

ON WITH THE SHOW: THE 1920s AND THE DAWN OF THE MUSICAL

The movie musical was born a mere two years shy of the catastrophic stock market crash that plummeted the United States into the Great Depression. On October 6, 1927, the extravaganza called *The Jazz Singer* premiered at the

Warner Theater in New York City, effectively driving a spike through the heart of the silent film era.

Widely acknowledged as both the first "talkie" and the first musical, this effort from producer Darryl F. Zanuck and Warner Bros. was adapted from the stage by author Alfred Cohen and directed by Alan Crosland. It starred vaude-villian Al Jolson (1885–1950) as an aspiring singer hoping to make it big in the music world, and also evidencing an oversized affection for his dear old mum.

Part silent, part talkie, the film featured limited dialogue, including the immortal introduction to sound in film, "You ain't heard nothing yet," courtesy of the newly developed Vitaphone sound system. Despite the technology's limitations, Jolson immediately emerged as the movie musical's first star. He belted out "Toot, Toot, Tootsie," Irving Berlin's "Blue Skies" (last sung in the movies, of all places, by Brent Spiner's android character Data in *Star Trek: Nemesis* [2002]), and finally that syrupy Mother's Day card, "My Mammy." Audiences ate it up.

More significant than the film's overall quality, which has been roundly debated for almost eighty years, was its impact on Hollywood. *The Jazz Singer* sparked a tidal wave shift in the industry, causing panic as studios, actors, and writers evaluated the way business had been done. Although critics were "dubious" of sound film, and moviemakers were "secretly skeptical," appropriately it was the audience, the "buying millions" who determined the course of history, according to film historian Terry Ramsaye.[1]

Hollywood promptly decided sound was the way to go, and it became incumbent upon film artists to incorporate the new technology. In the process, filmmakers were forced to evolve "a whole new grammar of film," according to historian William K. Everson.[2]

In 1928, theaters across the nation rapidly retrofitted their auditoriums for sound broadcast, and studios accommodated the development of recording technologies. Hollywood learned to "do mixing and dubbing," the studio orchestra was mated with "the soundtrack in post-production," and most importantly, "singers could rerecord the numbers they breathlessly mimed during athletic dance numbers."[3]

Yet many popular silent stars also faced a veritable career apocalypse. Some didn't survive the transition to sound simply because their voices didn't fit their established image. Others couldn't adjust to the fact that acting styles had to develop with the advent of sound, moving away from a world of grand theatrical gestures and eye-popping reactions and nearer a more restrained realm of subtlety, inflection, and tone.

The Jazz Singer symbolized a second beginning for movies, and follow-ups like *The Singing Fool* (1929) returned Al Jolson to the limelight for popular songs like "Sonny Boy." However, it was the 1929 film *The Broadway Melody* that really stoked the hot new trend of movie musicals.

This film was advertised as being "all" talking, singing, and dancing, which meant that the age of the talkie had indeed arrived. But *The Broadway Melody* was important for other reasons. For one, it is considered the first musical to boast an original score (by Nacio Herb Brown and Arthur Freed), and, for another, it was a backstage musical, meaning that personal dramas offstage intertwined with musical numbers performed onstage.

This formula became the *de rigueur* style of musicals in the early 1930s, almost to the point of absurdity, and has never really been absent from the screen for long in intervening decades. The backstage musical has been revived as recently as *Waiting for Guffman* (1997), *A Mighty Wind* (2003), and Todd Graff's *Camp* (2003). Sometimes the stage in question is Town Hall, sometimes a community theater, and in few cases, even at summer camp. The format remains the same.

Produced by Irving Thalberg for MGM, *The Broadway Melody* proved a tremendous hit and spawned fifty similar movie musicals (either Broadway-style revues or backstage musicals) in the next two years alone![4] Its success also paved the way for an onslaught of films in a series, including *Broadway Melody of 1936*, *Broadway Melody of 1938,* and *Broadway Melody of 1940*.

The Roaring Twenties went out with a musical bang thanks to films like *The Broadway Melody*, which was the first sound movie to win an Academy Award for Best Picture. Other backstage musicals (like 1929's *On with the Show*), as well as narrative-free revues (like *The Hollywood Revue of 1929*), filled out a decade of remarkable transition, but the best was definitely yet to come.

GOING HOLLYWOOD: THE 1930s

The 1930s began and ended on disturbing notes. The Depression impacted cash-strapped Hollywood studios at the beginning of the decade, impeding the deluge of movie musicals, and World War II took a toll on the lighthearted format as the forties neared. But between those bookends, the musical format strutted its stuff in high style, thanks to the efforts of some unique and legendary individuals.

Prime among these talents was a choreographer and, later, a director named Busby Berkeley (1895–1976). Watching his films today, with their incredibly elaborate and geometric dance numbers, and near military-style symmetrical precision, it isn't difficult to fathom that this artist arose from the ranks of the U.S. Army, where he directed big-scale parades. In the twenties, Berkeley had some success on Broadway before heading west, but it was in Hollywood that he became a behind-the-scenes star of the genre for his innovative—and frankly, bizarre—visions.

Though Berkeley's films often featured the same sort of predictable "backstage" dramas that were popular at the time, he was nonetheless a film pioneer who pushed the musical format forward with his unique understanding that the movie frame was not merely a stage. Busby comprehended that it was not enough merely to grab a Broadway show and restage it number-for-number, eye-level, as a strip of celluloid. In the big movie revues preceding him, that's often precisely what occurred.

Instead, Berkeley frequently incorporated innovative camera motion and demonstrated unique camera placement, effectively going where no camera had gone before, and thereby interpreting dance numbers in a revolutionary fashion. He once famously carved out a hole in a studio ceiling so as to position his camera far enough above his subjects for a particularly steep high angle shot.

"He really freed the camera, and freed the musical number from the proscenium, so that you could go above," comments *Velvet Goldmine* editor James Lyons. "I love [those films], how can you not? The amazing craziness that you would give a hundred girls violins with neon bows . . . the extravagance of that is amazing."

Berkeley's ingenuity and inventive nature was on full display in *Gold Diggers of 1937*, a film based on the play *Sweet Mystery of Life*. The movie concerns the misadventure of Dick Powell's hapless insurance salesman Rosmer Peek and his stenographer girlfriend Norma (Joan Blondell). They sell a life insurance policy to a flamboyant theatrical producer, J. J. Hobart and then somehow end up getting embroiled in the making of an elaborate musical production. As might be expected, the film culminates with the requisite—and elaborate— production number, in this case to the tune of "All's Fair in Love and War."

The theme of this particular song is the neverending battle of the sexes, and Berkeley runs wild with the concept, stretching it to the limit. A brief description:

> While a male cast member tap dances on a *Land of the Giants*–sized rocking chair, a female dancer in crisp military uniform lights a bomb beneath it, an act of sexual terrorism which precipitates a trippy ten-minute interlude of bizarre imagery.
>
> The rocking chair explodes into tiny wooden fragments, and promptly reforms into a cannon aimed right at the camera. Without warning, this piece of artillery then fires cannonballs directly at the audience, over which are superimposed the smiling faces of the gorgeous women dancers.
>
> From this spiky visual, two armies (both garbed in immaculate white) emerge at either end of the black stage, one male and one female. The men open fire with rifles, and the women return fire with wafts from their perfume bottles that, when they strike, look like the detonations of chemical weapons from the First World War.
>
> As the two armies connect at the frame's middle, the men wave white flags indicating their surrender, and a veritable army of women in uniform marches across the stage to form a vast phalanx. They move from arrowhead formation to a single line that spans the frame, and then, before you know it, the female warriors are vetting elaborate and perfectly synchronized flag work.
>
> A wall of billowing flags approaches the camera directly, and then— just when you think it can't get any stranger—the images suddenly reverse and audiences see the cannon reforming into the atomized rocking chair. Then, finally, we're reacquainted with the lead actors. Before viewers can take a breath over the sheer, outrageous spectacle of the thing, the curtain falls and the movie is over, no explanations, no coda at all.

The whole blooming climax of *Gold Diggers of 1937* lasts several minutes, exists outside the film's hokey, antique "backstage" narrative, and beautifully expresses the central conceit of the song, that men and women are always in battle . . . and that the women frequently win!

Sometimes, as in *Gold Diggers of 1937*, Berkeley's trademark sequences involved over a hundred dancers. Sometimes, they involved swimming. Sometimes there was elaborate wirework. But inevitably, they were scrupulously staged and shot with a style of martial precision that was oft-imitated, but never equaled. Even more amazingly, Berkeley's numbers weren't just about formation, but *information*, as they often vetted a ministry in and of themselves, separate from the often tepid narratives concerning backstage rivalries and romances.

This is an important development, because the age of Busby Berkeley built on the advances of the 1920s. It pushed the musicals further in a fresh artistic direction, one where song and dance were expressive of themes and ideas, not merely pleasant renditions of then-popular tunes.

A new paradigm in visualization was not the only distinction of the 1930s. This was the Golden Age in which some of the greatest songwriters in modern history arrived in Hollywood and composed songs that have, no doubt, become the soundtracks of our lives.

Jerome Kern composed the music featured in *The Cat and the Fiddle* (1934), *Music in the Air* (1934), *Sweet Adeline* (1934), *Roberta* (1935), *Show Boat* (1936), *Swing Time* (1936), *High, Wide, and Handsome* (1937), and *Joy of Living* (1938).

Cole Porter contributed music and lyrics to such films as *Born to Dance* (1936), *Anything Goes*, and *Rosalie* (1937), while Irving Berlin was the maestro of *Top Hat* (1935), *Follow the Fleet* (1936), *On the Avenue* (1937), *Alexander's Ragtime Band* (1938), *Carefree* (1938), and *Second Fiddle* (1939).

George and Ira Gershwin (*Shall We Dance* [1937], *A Damsel in Distress* [1937], *The Goldwyn Follies* [1938]), and Richard Rodgers and Oscar Hammerstein II also composed during this memorable era, and Hollywood was fortunate to have every one of them.

These artists composed beautiful, catchy, and frequently witty and thoughtful songs that have withstood the test of time and also the onslaught of new musical genres, including bebop, rock'n'roll, disco, and hip-hop. Today, most people don't necessarily remember the movies titles, but they certainly remember the tunes. Who can forget Berlin's "Cheek to Cheek" (*Top Hat*); Porter's "I Get a Kick Out of You" (*Anything Goes*), "I've Got You Under My Skin" (*Born to Dance*), and "In the Still of the Night" (*Rosalie*); Berlin's "Let's Face the Music and Dance" (*Follow the Fleet*); Kern's "The Way You Look Tonight" (*Swing Time*); or Gershwin's "Let's Call the Whole Thing Off" (*Shall We Dance*)?

Each of these tunes is instantly recognizable and, more to the point in this particular study, has also informed the musicals of succeeding generations. Artists of today—including Woody Allen (in *Everyone Says I Love You*), Kenneth Branagh (*Love's Labour's Lost*), and Irwin Winkler (*De-Lovely*)—have resurrected these compositions for audiences who weren't even alive seventy years earlier. The ultimate compliment, perhaps, came from Branagh, who decided for *Love's Labour's Lost* that the only music in history which could stand cheek-to-cheek with the words of the Bard were these amazing 1930s compositions of Porter, Kern, Gershwin, and Berlin.

The 1930s also introduced the world to a troika of remarkable and dynamic screen couples: Nelson Eddy (1901–1967) and Jeanette MacDonald (1903–1965) in MGM fare like *Maytime* (1937) and *Rosalie* (1937); RKO's Fred Astaire (1899–1987) and Ginger Rogers (1911–1995); and MGM's Mickey Rooney (1920–) and Judy Garland (1922–1969).

The Astaire-Rogers team remains the most highly regarded today, for a variety of solid reasons, virtually all of them related to the immortal spirit of dance. As a young man, Nebraska native Astaire (né Frederick Austerlitz) began his professional career as a vaudeville performer alongside his sister, Adele, and went to RKO studios in 1933, where he was quickly dismissed by executives as being something less than handsome.

However, Astaire persevered. His talent on the dance floor didn't just shine, it glowed. Regarded far and wide as a consummate professional and perfectionist, Astaire eventually teamed with the lovely dancer Ginger Rogers in 1933, and together this duo danced their way through ten films and into the history books. She was elegant and smart; he was refined, sophisticated, and often depicted in top hat and immaculate black tux.

Their first film together was *Flying Down to Rio* in 1933, but Astaire and Rogers are probably best remembered for three great films: *The Gay Divorcee* (1934), *Top Hat* (1935), and George Stevens's *Swing Time* (1936). Though opinions vary, *Swing Time*, the story of "Lucky" John Garnett, is generally regarded as the finest example of their partnership as well as one of the great musicals of the decade.

As is typical of Astaire-Rogers fare, *Swing Time*'s plot is as light as a feather, with Astaire's lucky man leaving behind a fiancee and jumping on a train to New York. It is there, after an altercation on a busy street intersection, where he promptly falls in love with Ginger Rogers's no-nonsense dance teacher, Penny Carrol, a so-called screwy dame.

Tantalized, Garnett pursues the teacher to Gordon's Dancing Academy and pays for a lesson. After first pretending to have two left feet, Garnett dazzles Carrol and her boss with his fancy footwork. From there, the duo undergo various amusing difficulties—including the winning and losing of a deed to a nightclub—before finally confessing their love for each other and casting aside their romantic rivals, including a hard-hearted band leader with good humor and laughter.

Essentially a confection, *Swing Time* is a fantasy piece about success on the dance floor, in gambling, and of course, in love. Realism never got within five miles of the movie, and the central characters lived in a fancy hotel, wore marvelous clothes, and didn't seem to work for a living, or worry much about the way of things.

Shot on sound stages, *Swing Time* today feels somewhat simpleminded. But that's a compliment, for when Fred Astaire and Ginger Rogers take to the floor and start to dance, the film triumphs as an expression of pure *joie de vivre*. It's magic.

Filmed in very long takes and in long shots with camera motion at an absolute minimum, the Astaire-Rogers dances were works of art and always the focus of the frame. Cutting too much or too frequently would have only disrupted their rhythm, so *Swing Time* and the other Astaire-Rogers team-ups feel like bravura showcases for the performers. The couple's work in film thrived not merely on their talent and fluid grace—nor did it depend on the restraint of editors—but on that rare and valuable quality known as charm.

"I think what made them special," considers writer Craig Pearce, "is that, in a strange way, they represented the Every Couple. But of course they were a fantastical, glamorized version. Even though he was a beautiful dancer and incredibly skilled and charismatic, Fred Astaire wasn't that good-looking. He wasn't Rock Hudson, just this guy who had an incredible gift.

"In a sense, it's the same way with Ginger Rogers, even though she was fantastically talented. There was something very ordinary about her at the same time, and I mean that in a good way, not a bad way. Even when they wore tux and top hat and beautiful ballgowns, you could imagine them lounging around the house in cardigan and housecoat, so I think that was their attraction. They presented a very accessible fantasy."

"When Fred Astaire is sad because Ginger Rogers doesn't want to dance with him, it's a very beautiful sad," adds movie editor James Lyons. "It's a quite cheerful sad."

"I believe all film in the history of cinema aspires to be Fred Astaire," considers Joss Whedon. "I think he is the single greatest phenomenon in the history of film."

And he isn't talking about Astaire's performance in *The Towering Inferno*, either.

"The airiness, the transcendence, the delight, the absolute authority . . .," Whedon muses. "This was a guy where you would be confused when he suddenly broke into dialogue. He was built to dance."

In 1939, a very different kind of screen couple, the youthful Mickey Rooney and Judy Garland, headlined *Babes in Arms*, directed by Busby Berkeley. It was a significant production not just because it was incredibly popular and launched a number of films with the duo, but because it was the first venture created under the supervision of producer Arthur Freed's unit at MGM, who was later responsible for some of the finest musicals ever created.

Babes in Arms concerns wily and wild teenagers—at least by thirties standards—Mickey Moran (Rooney), son of a vaudevillian, and Patsy Barton (Garland), who join forces to "put on a show" and thereby avoid a work farm. Adapted from a 1937 Broadway property, the movie featured songs including "You Are My Lucky Star" and the title piece, "Babes in Arms."

Finally, an enduring masterpiece arrived in theaters in 1939 on the heels of the amazingly successful Disney animated musical, *Snow White and the Seven Dwarves* (1937). After purchasing the rights to the children's book by L. Frank Baum for the princely sum of seventy-five thousand dollars, MGM commenced production on *The Wizard of Oz*, which starred the sixteen-year-old Garland and boasted amazing sequences lensed fully in color.[5]

"As with many musicals, it had a long gestation period," remembers Craig Pearce. "It had a couple of directors, and it nearly killed a couple of people because the creators were trying to find a style to express Baum's books, which were popular and much loved. How do you take the essence of that and express it in film, and in a musical and dance?" he wonders.

Those answers came from director Victor Fleming (and an uncredited King Vidor) and in the form of the splendid music by Harold Arlen and lyrics by E. Y. Harburg. What eventually emerged was a high-caliber fantasy film of the first order. *The Wizard of Oz* featured amazing (and vivid) tornadoes, terrifying talking trees, monster monkeys, flying witches, and gleaming emerald citadels.

The tale of a girl seeking to return home from an alternate world called Oz, meeting colorful friends like the Scarecrow, Tin Man, and Cowardly Lion along the Yellow Brick Road, and battling a Wicked Witch has become an acknowledged classic not just within the genre, but in film history. Its most memorable tune, "Over the Rainbow," is a paean to youthful longing, and the desire to transcend present circumstances. Recognized in every corner of the world, the song is merely one delightful element of this beloved musical.

"I love it," enthuses Pearce. "It's the quintessential 'quest' film. It's the quest to find the way home, and also a quest for a heart, a brain, and courage. It is about all these individual characters [Dorothy, Scarecrow, the Tin Man, and Cowardly Lion], but ultimately they just represent part of us.

"We all should have courage; we all should have a brain; and we all should be able to find our way home," says Pearce. "No matter how far we travel, we always want to feel like we have a home—that we know where it is—and that we can go, if we need to. That's the beauty of *The Wizard of Oz* and why it is so loved today—by every generation."

The Wizard of Oz indeed influenced generations of filmmakers. The "fantasy" musical genre, which includes magic, mystical lands, and strange creatures (à la the Munchkins), is one that has been with us ever since, in films as diverse as *Mary Poppins* (1964), *Willy Wonka and the Chocolate Factory* (1973), and even the urban remake *The Wiz* (1978).

Capped off by this landmark fantasy, the thirties symbolized a remarkable era of growth and expansion for the movie musical. From Shirley Temple to the Marx Brothers, from Busby Berkeley to *The Wizard of Oz*, from Fred Astaire and Ginger Rogers to Judy Garland and Mickey Rooney, it was a decade of musical thrills and evolution, and one of the most important decades in the genre's long history.

"Musicals have always been about the dream of a person: 'I'm gonna be a big star,' or the kids sing 'If Momma was married,'" suggests James Lyons, "but it's also about an *ideal*. In the 1930s, musicals were made while the country was in terrible financial straights, and yet there were these beautiful art deco sets and gorgeous women wearing white. It was a fantasy of what people *could* be, and their grace and charm."

The movie musicals of the 1930s were mostly filled with simple, straightforward plots, feeding the need for audiences to escape the doldrums of an unpleasant reality, and yet that wasn't exclusively the case, either. Some films of the period did explicitly reference the economic troubles of the time.

"There's no Depression," an insurance salesman deadpanned in *Gold Diggers of 1937*, "don't let your prospect talk about it!" In one of the film's songs—"With Plenty of Money and You," which was performed twice—lead actor Dick Powell viewed happiness as having his girl (Joan Blondell) plus "plenty of money." Cash may have been the "root of all evil," as well as "strife and upheaval," by the lyrics, but it could also, apparently, buy security and happiness.

In another case, 1933's *42nd Street*, a landmark film starring Ruby Keeler, there was an acknowledgment of a different sort, of theater's dark underbelly. It was a facet that would be played up more frequently in decades to come.

"I love *42nd Street*. It talks about the underworld in musical terms," says James Lyons, "but it's not that far from *New York, New York* (1977), which is saying that you can have these extravagant [musical] gestures, and talk about real things, like there are prostitutes and drug addicts in our world." So even as far back as the "golden" thirties, the seed for the future development of musicals had already been planted.

STRIKE UP THE BAND: THE 1940s

The 1940s commenced with a continuation of the musical's big-screen domination, and audiences essentially got more of the same. Judy Garland and Mickey Rooney reteamed for variations on their *Babes in Arms* formula in *Strike Up the Band* (1941) and *Babes on Broadway* (1941). *Broadway Melody of 1940* followed up on another 1930s franchise, but this time featuring Cole Porter songs and star Fred Astaire. Even Disney was back with more musical animated offerings, doing what the studio did best with the controversial classic *Fantasia* (1940). An interesting wrinkle of the decade saw director Busby Berkeley's production numbers featured in full-on Technicolor for the first time, in films like *The Gang's All Here* (1943).

The first years of the decade also introduced America to new stars like Betty Grable in *Down Argentine Way* (1940), *That Night in Rio* (1940), and *Moon Over Miami* (1941), as well as comedians Bob Hope and Bing Crosby in their comic musicals *Road to Singapore* (1940) and *Road to Zanzibar* (1941).

But with Europe enmeshed in an all-consuming war, it was only a matter of time before the musical format once again began to morph. On December 7, 1941, Japan attacked Pearl Harbor, and America was officially at war.

Legendarily, on December 8, 1941, James Cagney began filming the first overtly patriotic musical, *Yankee Doodle Dandy*. Though the film is actually a biography of famous Broadway song-and-dance man George M. Cohan (1878–1942), a prolific writer of musicals and plays, it also celebrates Americana, pausing to note, importantly, that Cohan was "born on the Fourth of July."

Yankee Doodle Dandy featured such hit songs as "Over There," "You're a Grand Old Flag" and "The Yankee Doodle Boy," and the film won Cagney an Oscar. It also set off a miniboom of nationalistic "war" musicals. *The Star-Spangled Rhythm*, an all-star revue that included Mary Martin, Veronica Lake, Bing Crosby, Bob Hope, and Dick Powell, premiered in 1942.

Others from this school included *Stage Door Canteen* (1943) and *Hollywood Canteen* (1944). Another notable example, *This Is the Army*, marched into theaters in 1943, highlighting music and lyrics by Irving Berlin. It included an unforgettable rendition of "God Bless America" by Kate Smith, and even an appearance by an aspiring young actor named Ronald Reagan.

Yankee Doodle Dandy was actually advantageous for two 1940s trends in musicals, not merely one. Since the patriotic film was such a hit, the musical biography was suddenly in vogue. Cohan had his day of glory in *Dandy*, and afterwards came the story of George Gershwin in *Rhapsody in Blue*, a sanitized version of Cole Porter's life in *Night and Day* (1946), and even the Jerome Kern story in *Till the Clouds Roll By* (1946).

Today, the musical biography remains a staple of American cinema, and audiences, in 2004 witnessed a more accurate take on Cole Porter's life in *De-Lovely*, Taylor Hackford's full-throated and dynamic bio of Ray Charles, *Ray*, and, in *Beyond the Sea*, the story of crooner Bobby Darin. Some tunes, it seems, get played again and again and never get old.

The year 1944 saw the birth of yet another landmark movie musical, and one of the most financially successful films of the decade. Directed by Vincente Minnelli, *Meet Me in St. Louis* was based on a series of short stories by Sally Benson published in *The New Yorker*. The pieces recounted the tale of an "American family" planning a move from St. Louis, and the film, produced by Arthur Freed, starred Judy Garland, Mary Astor, Tom Drake, June Lockhart, Margaret O'Brien, and Hugh Marlowe.

Set over the span of a year from 1903 to 1904 and the turning of the seasons (a storytelling device dusted off and put back to work in Woody Allen's 1997 musical comedy, *Everyone Says I Love You*), *Meet Me in St. Louis* featured the memorable tune "Have Yourself a Merry Little Christmas."

"One thing that's really wonderful about that film is that it doesn't have a strong narrative, but rather a beautiful one," says James Lyons. "It's about the family, and how they deal with the idea that they're going to move from St. Louis over the course of the seasons. That's it. It has quiet moments on the different holidays, and it's a remarkable, gorgeous film in the subtlety of characterization and the wonderful nature of Judy Garland and the songs.

"It's important to remember that *Meet Me in St. Louis* is the epitome of what's supposed to be classical Hollywood filmmaking," Lyons continues. "And that film is a long, quiet dream. It's not a driving thing. It's not *Moulin Rouge*, where you have another idea, another idea. What Minnelli did there was a meditation, and I don't know when anyone is going to feel the freedom to do that in this [today's] climate."

"One of the greatest musicals I ever saw was *Meet Me in St. Louis*," affirms Jay Cocks regarding the sentimental, heartfelt picture. "It's hard to beat that."

Critics and audiences concurred, and since imitation is the sincerest form of flattery, perhaps it is no surprise that Hollywood soon produced a raft of "American family"–style movies, including *State Fair* (1945) and *Centennial Summer* (1946).

An important musical of vastly different stripe arrived on American shores in 1948, courtesy of Great Britain, and proved a great influence. *The Red Shoes* depicts the story of a ballerina named Vicky (Moira Shearer) who must decide between a career in dance and her love for her husband, composer Julian (Marius Goring). Her passion for dance is symbolized by "The Ballet of the Red Shoes," a work based on a (creepy) fairy tale by Hans Christian Andersen. Torn by loyalty to the man she loves and another who can help her achieve stardom, Vicky eventually arrives at an unhappy end, thanks to the red shoes, but not before plenty of ballet is performed onscreen.

The Red Shoes blends tragedy, melodrama, fantasy interludes of an expressionistic nature, and never slights the presentation of dance on film. In fact, it relishes the art, and all the dance is staged with an almost Berkeley-like aplomb. Danny Peary writes about the film in his landmark text, *Cult Movies*:

> *The Red Shoes* is simultaneously romantic and expressionistic, a daydream and a nightmare, a psychological drama and a fairy tale. As Thomas Elsessor wrote of Powell and Pressburger's other expressionis-

tic dance film, *The Tales of Hoffmann* (1951), *The Red Shoes* is "a pure meditation on the cinema, in its dual aspect of intimate art and mass-medium, of emotional reality and perverse illusion."[6]

Despite the film's value, film executives were worried they had an expensive bomb on their hands. Ballet in a major motion picture? An unhappy ending? A running time over two hours? *Sheesh!* Try to sell that in Peoria!

The Red Shoes clearly represented a style determinedly different from Hollywood's usual approach, thanks to writer Emery Pressburger and director Michael Powell. Although studio suits held their breath, *The Red Shoes* proved a sensation in both the United Kingdom and the States. It was a box office hit and even won two Oscars (for Best Music and Best Art Direction). In addition to nabbing nominations for Best Picture and Best Writing, *The Red Shoes* also had a tremendous impact on Hollywood.

In the 1950s, at least two MGM films—*An American in Paris* (1951) and *Singin' in the Rain* (1952)—culminated in elaborate, splendidly choreographed ballet numbers, each lasting more than ten minutes each. High art collided with commercial art in Hollywood, and America liked it!

"It's lovely," says Joss Whedon of *The Red Shoes*. "I wish more of it was dancing and less of it was people talking, but I find it bizarre and wonderful. I feel like it did what I never felt comfortable with in *An American in Paris*. [In *The Red Shoes*] the ballet took over the movie, and I was quite emotionally involved as to what was happening. And in *An American in Paris*, the conceit didn't quite work in the same way for me. I think it didn't have enough insanity. Which is an amazing thing to say about a movie with Oscar Levant in it."

The year 1948 also teamed dancer Gene Kelly, Judy Garland, and director Minnelli (now Garland's husband) in Arthur Freed's MGM adaptation of a 1942 stage epic by S. N. Behrman called *The Pirate*. The satirical story concerns a girl named Manuela (Garland) who is infatuated with the mythical pirate Macoco, despite her engagement to Don Pedro Vargas (Walter Slezak). When a traveling actor named Serafin (Kelly) falls in love with Manuela, he claims to be Macoco, but the object of his desire isn't pleased to learn the truth.

"It's regarded as a failure, and an arty, overstuffed extravagance," considers Jay Cocks "[but] it's a terrific movie with a great score by Cole Porter. He wrote this whole score, which contained this great song 'Be a Clown.' That song contains my favorite nugget of show business advice of all time: 'Jack, you'll never lack if you can quack like a duck.' That's all you'll ever need to know about show business."

Not coincidentally, given Cocks's affection for the song, Kevin Kline's Cole Porter performs the memorable "Be a Clown" in *De-Lovely*, with MGM's Louis Mayer singing and dancing at his side.

The 1940s culminated with the first Astaire-Rogers partnership in almost a decade, 1949's *The Barkleys of Broadway*, and another classic animated Disney musical, *Cinderella* (1949).

Overall, the decade represented a time in history when some of the greatest singing, dancing, writing, producing and directing talents aligned. Arthur Freed at MGM, with the likes of Gene Kelly (1912–1996) and directors Stanley Donen (1924–) and Vincente Minnelli (1903–1986), was ready to marshal these resources and inaugurate the next phase of musical evolution (and in glorious color to boot).

Not surprisingly, MGM dominated the next decade. The studio was so successful, according to historian John Kobal, because their directors "could create a unity of expression through song and dance."7

"I always liked musicals that had a much more dramatic underpinning or a stronger comic underpinning, and that's why I prefer the MGM musicals of Kelly and Donen and Minnelli," says Cocks. "Those are the musicals that really made a difference to me."

Even though the days ahead promised to be bright, also looming at the close of the forties was a new crisis. Like the transition from silent movies to talkies in the late twenties, it was an issue that would affect the entire movie industry, not just the musical genre. In this case, all the fretting was over a little invention called *television*.

"As the decade drew to an end, TV's continuing grip on audiences resulted in a sharp decline in cinema audiences," writes Clive Hirschhorn in his history, *The Hollywood Musical*. "The situation was aggravated by the McCarthy Communist witch hunts, which did nothing to help the prestige of an industry already humiliated by TV."8

Once more, change was in the air, and scholars were mourning not merely the end of the musical, but the potential end of cinema.

WITH A SONG IN MY HEART: THE 1950s

As forces beyond the movie industry conspired to curtail movie attendance, the musical productions of the 1950s retaliated by simply being better than ever.

"Unquestionably the most professionally scripted, designed, choreographed, danced, sung, acted, orchestrated, photographed, edited, and directed, the 1950s musicals still cast the unmistakable glow of glamour on the screen, and stand as permanent tributes to the genius who guided them from inception to release," write genre historians Richard Fehr and Frederic G. Vogel in *Lullabies of Hollywood: Movie Music and the Movie Musical, 1915–1992*, putting a fine point on the assertion.[9]

Prime among these finely crafted pictures was the 1951 MGM/Freed effort *An American in Paris*, which boasted a screenplay by Alan Jay Lerner, and the music and lyrics of the Ira and George Gershwin catalog. The film starred (and was choreographed) by Gene Kelly and was directed by Vincente Minnelli.

An American in Paris is the tale of Jerry Mulligan, an ex-GI living in Paris as a starving artist, a painter. During the course of the film, Jerry must choose between a wealthy patron (Nina Foch) and Lise (Leslie Caron), a romantic young girl with whom he has fallen madly in love. Complicating matters, the delicate young swan plans to marry Mulligan's friend, a Frenchman named Henri (George Guetary).

Shot in Culver City (not Paris) and featuring dated optical effects, *An American in Paris* culminated in innovative fashion, with Kelly's seventeen-minute ballet, which took a month to shoot, cost $542,000 to create, and featured Mulligan dancing his way through a dreamscape reflecting the work of painters like Renoir and van Gogh.[10]

Although it was difficult to imagine the robust, athletic (and well-fed) Kelly as a dedicated starving artist, *An American in Paris* reveals this actor at his glorious best. In today's vernacular, Kelly is the Jackie Chan of his age. Willing and able to perform amazing and precise dance moves and stunts requiring total control over every muscle in his body, not to mention extraordinary timing, Kelly is the real deal.

In *An American in Paris*, whether dancing atop a piano or successfully navigating the obstacle course of his overdecorated garret, Kelly is nothing except extraordinary. And then, of course, there's that ending, perhaps inspired by *The Red Shoes*, in which Kelly slips effortlessly into the grandeur of ballet, revealing his comfort with a so-called high art as well the more macho, athletic style for which he is known and loved.

But the amazing thing about *An American in Paris*, even today, is how deftly the film utilizes dance to express the internal doubts, desires and dreams of a character, in this case Mulligan. When Kelly must decide about a future with or without Lise, the audiences "goes inside" his thoughts, and the ballet exposes his state of mind and plays out his feelings. In the modern age of movie musicals, both *Dancer in the Dark* and *Chicago* have drafted this conceit of song and dance as the representation of a character's inner voice and life.

This sequence in *An American in Paris* occurs against lovely and intentionally artificial, expressionistic backdrops of Paris which are reflective of the character's vocation as a painter. In a more conventional, naturalistic film, the pace could not slow down to express something as simple and human as a decision or a mood. However, in a movie musical and within the artistry of dance and set to music, anything is possible.

"If you see *An American in Paris* it suddenly transforms into a ballet, [and] that's surely the proper way to express falling in love with a girl. That's great!" notes James Lyons. "*An American in Paris* is a good example of places where the narrative just opens up to music and color and glorious idealizations of a woman, and you don't need to have a narrative there. That's an inspiration to everybody—and it was a huge commercial hit, which should be remembered. There's a long tradition in musicals that make individual sequences and scenes a pleasure unto themselves. A lot of the rules of keeping the plot moving forward don't apply . . . and shouldn't."

And, like so many movie musicals of past ages, *An American in Paris* does not concern itself with reality. All the characters seem relentlessly upbeat, even though they don't have money. Henri gladly surrenders Lise, realizing, apparently, that he shouldn't stand in the way of true love. And life itself apparently consists of sitting in an outdoor café and dancing with little French children to the tune of "I Got Rhythm."

Yet these comments are not criticisms, only observations. *An American in Paris* expresses the notions of longing and desire through dance; it revels in these emotions and exists in that rarified state where dance can tell us more about what a character feels than declaratory dialogue. And it pauses—when necessary—to let us swoon at the intensity of such feelings.

In 1952, Arthur Freed produced another film with MGM and Gene Kelly that would rival the artistry of *An American in Paris*, and in many ways surpass it. Codirected by Kelly and Stanley Donen, *Singin' in the Rain* is not only a great musical, but perhaps one of the ten greatest films ever made.

The best movie musicals ever made, in any era from 1929 to 2004, are those that in some fashion utilize the musical format to reflect truths about show business, theater, movies and the genre itself. They are self-reflexive exercises, concerned as much with themselves and what they represent, as the onscreen story they yet.

In the modern era, *Velvet Goldmine* concerns the rise and fall of a pop star, *Moulin Rouge* focuses on the production of a bohemian fantasy about love, truth, and beauty, and uses pop music from today to do it. In *Dancer in the Dark*, the heroine, Selma, is obsessed with musicals, particularly *The Sound of Music*, and her life is depicted in stark contrast with that fantasy of what this genre represents.

In *De-Lovely*, an angel visits Cole Porter and stages Porter's life as a musical. In *Chicago*, murderous Roxie sees herself as a star and visualizes her life as jazz acts. In *All That Jazz*, Joe Gideon's life and even his death are mirrored as spectacular production numbers.

Singin' in the Rain remains the paradigm for this self-reflexive structure. It dramatizes the tale of Donald Lockwood (Gene Kelly), a former vaudevillian and stuntman who is a big star at the end of the silent era in film history. The film opens in 1927 at the premiere of Monumental Pictures' *Royal Rascal*. As talkies emerge, Lockwood realizes that life will soon change drastically, especially for his onscreen partner, the vain and despicable Lina Lamont (Jean Hagen), who talks like she just hopped off a bus from the Bronx.

Because of Lina's inappropriate diction and suddenly behind-the-times style of film emoting, the couple's latest flick threatens to be a disaster and laughed off the screen. But with his friend Cosmo's (Donald O'Connor) help, Lockwood plots to salvage the production by transforming it into an all-singing, all-dancing musical extravaganza. The only concern is that Lina can't sing well either, which means that Don's real-life love interest, young Kathy (Debbie Reynolds) must dub Lina's voice *and* her songs. Lina, who isn't ready to see the "Lockwood and Lamont" movies go the way of all flesh, takes steps to hide Kathy's identity and destroy her career in Hollywood, but not if Don has anything to say about it.

Constructed around producer Arthur Freed's considerable song catalog, *Singin' in the Rain* is rife with great tunes, including "All I Do Is Dream of You," "Good Morning," and of course, "Singin' in the Rain." But more importantly, these songs are staged in a manner that exhibits a *joie de vivre* uncommon in film history. Bursting with energy, the *Singin' in the Rain* numbers have become iconic, especially Kelly's tromp through the puddles on a back-lot city street after saying goodnight to his lady love. Equally impressive, however, is

O'Connor's insane, almost self-destructive routine to "Make 'Em Laugh," which is nearly gasp-provoking in its pace, intensity, and sheer physicality.

The only sour note around "Make 'Em Laugh" may be the song itself, which boasts something of an unusual history, as writer and historian Jay Cocks reveals. "Stanley Donen and Gene Kelly came to Arthur Freed one day, and said, 'We're doing this, and we need a comic song in this piece, and we don't have one.' And Arthur Freed said, 'What do you boys have in mind?' And they said, 'Something like "Be a Clown" from *The Pirate*.' So he said, 'Oh yeah, okay.'

"So three hours later, he showed up on the set with this new song, 'Make 'Em Laugh.' Stanley Donen told me this story himself. He looked at Gene Kelly; Gene Kelly looked at him; and they both said, 'This is "Be a Clown" . . .' and then, 'Ah, fuck it!' So they staged the whole thing, and it's a great number. It's a fantastic number.

"But when they were staging it—and I only found this out recently— Irving Berlin was visiting the set, and they started the playback of the song. Irving Berlin said, 'Wait a minute! What is this?! Who wrote this song?' He got all pissed off and really indignant, and went and yelled at Arthur Freed. But when Cole Porter found out about it, he just laughed. He laughed because, hey, he's Cole Porter and he's got a lot of other things. I'm not sure I would have thought it was so funny.

"But also, Cole Porter was very pragmatic, and Arthur Freed was the single greatest producer of musicals in music history, so Cole Porter probably thought it wouldn't be too practical if he really rained down too heavily on this guy, and he just kind of shrugged it off," Cocks continues.

"You know that great line in *The Red Shoes*? 'It's worse to have to steal than be stolen from?' I'm not sure I believe that, but I'm not as creative as Cole Porter! I don't have as many good ideas to spare as he did. With one pragmatic eye and one philosophical shrug, he just let the whole thing blow by him. But, yes, 'Make 'Em Laugh' is a blatant, naked copy of 'Be a Clown,' so comparison is inevitable."

Although this behind-the-scenes story reveals that Freed didn't always live up to Don Lockwood's stated mantra of "Dignity. Always Dignity," nor does it take away from *Singin' in the Rain* as an awesome and singular moviegoing experience. The film is clever in referencing an early era in film history, and genuinely funny with its many one-liners, outrageous stunts, and amusing depiction of Lamont. Jean Hagen's performance as the villainous Lamont is grossly underrated, and her character's stupidity and selfish actions balance the picture's optimism, and keep it moving forward like a locomotive. By concerning movies themselves, and stardom and celebrity too—topics Americans still love—*Singin' in the Rain* remains amazingly relevant in the twenty-first century.

"The thing about *Singin' in the Rain* is that it successfully marries the screwball comedy style with a break-into-song musical," says Craig Pearce. "The best musical films of that period do that. It has a great screwball comedy kind of patter . . . and a satisfying story with a beginning, middle, and end. The songs actually move the action forward, and it's *A Star Is Born* kind of story."

"Besides the fact that it's gut-bustingly funny, it would be a great movie if nobody ever sang a note," considers Joss Whedon. "I recently watched it again, and realized that a lot of the songs, [coupled] with the extraordinary choreography and beautiful filmmaking, take the idea of why we love to sing and dance, or love to watch singing and dancing, why it moves us, and then amps it up to its most primal element.

"I have an infant son, and I watch him dance. He just hears music and starts to move, and if you look at the number 'Singin' in the Rain,' it goes from elegant, intricate dancing to jumping in puddles. You look at 'Make 'Em Laugh,' and he's [O'Connor] lying on the ground, running around in circles laughing like a hyena. You look at 'Moses Supposes,' and they [Kelly and O'Connor] end up piling things on top of their teacher. It's just unbridled joy. A musical number is such an exciting thing that it makes them fall apart and turn into children. It reveals the very essence I think of what makes musical numbers so exciting. Just one of the four thousand reasons why *Singin' in the Rain* just can't be beat."

"It's Aristotelian," concludes Todd Graff. "I think *Singin' in the Rain* is virtually a perfect film. Just as a writer, I kneel at its altar . . . . It has all the elements that a well-made story should have. Not that every story has to obey those rules, but if you are making a story in that way, you're just never going to see it executed better than this. It's so delightful and irreverent, and it's sprinkled with a kind of movie magic."

Some of that movie magic has a name too: Gene Kelly. Renowned in the industry as a perfectionist, this talent is responsible for some of dance's finest moments in the history of film. Kelly's professional career was filled with ups and downs, but he accomplished a very basic and important mission: to "present dance to as wide an audience as possible, to point out that dance is a form of athletics as well as art, to keep trying to film dance in new ways," says Robert Trachtenberg, director of an *American Masters* documentary on the artist.[11]

In addition to offering the world two undisputed classics in *An American in Paris* and *Singin' in the Rain*, the 1950s was important for another reason. It was in this era that musical theater and film saw a more complete fusion than ever before (or since), with a group of book musicals adapted directly from the works of Richard Rodgers and Oscar Hammerstein II. These films included *Oklahoma!* (1955), *Carousel* (1956), *The King and I* (1956), and *South Pacific* (1958).

A generation of moviegoers love these films for good reason, though—at the risk of sounding snobbish—they seem to evidence neither the intense artistry of *An American in Paris*, nor the well-rounded, fast-paced entertainment value evident in *Singin' in the Rain*.

By today's standards, these films feel slow-paced. *Oklahoma!*, for instance, squanders its weighty 140-minute running time on a single event, pondering whether cowboy Curley (Gordon MacRae) and Laurey Williams (Shirley Jones) will attend the social together. Rod Steiger's Jud is the film's foil, who also has a thing for Laurey, and the film features fantastic songs, such as "Oh, What a Beautiful Mornin'" and "The Surrey with a Fringe on Top," the latter probably most famous to contemporary audiences for its appearance in the 1989 Rob Reiner film *When Harry Met Sally*. It all just feels a bit inconsequential for the hefty running time.

"For historical value, *Oklahoma!* is hugely important because it's really the first book musical, but outside of that and [the fact that] it has beautiful, beautiful songs in it, [all it's about] is will Curley take Laurey to the social?" agrees Todd Graff.

The King and I is certainly a better film, but not necessarily a great one. Starring Yul Brynner, who took home an Oscar for Best Actor, the film concerns the king of Siam (Brynner) and the new schoolteacher seeing to his brood of children, the English Anna Leonowens (Deborah Kerr). She sings the delightful "Getting to Know You" before a roomful of Siamese tykes (who like Brynner, speak in pidgin English), and mourns for her dead husband, Tom, while developing a respect and affection for the king.

Shot in Cinemascope (a new technology in 1953), the popular film is lush in its sets and coloring, but essentially *The King and I* is the same story as Rodgers and Hammerstein's *The Sound of Music*, and that film adaptation, produced in the 1960s by director Robert Wise, remains more cinematic and features, arguably, a more memorable score.

One such similarity in music is "I Whistle a Happy Tune," which Kerr (dubbed by the ubiquitous Marni Nixon) sings to her fearful son early in the film. It's a suggestion about what to do when feeling bad or afraid. The much-improved version of that song is "My Favorite Things" in *The Sound of Music*, which also advises one on how to become happy when feeling sad.

Other Broadway-to–silver screen adaptations of the 1950s, though not by Rodgers and Hammerstein, included *Brigadoon* (1955), *Hit the Deck* (1955), *Silk Stockings* (1956), and *The Pajama Game* (1957).

The musicals of this era also spotlighted some interesting new players, who have since become cultural icons. Gorgeous Marilyn Monroe appeared in *Gentlemen Prefer Blondes* in 1953. Elvis Presley, the King himself, shimmied and twisted his way through rock'n'roll ventures like *Rock Around the Clock* (1956), *Love Me Tender* (1956), and *Jailhouse Rock* (1957). Strangest of all, perhaps, the Broadway adaptation *Guys and Dolls* (1955) included the unlikely appearance of method actor Marlon Brando.

"What motivates song is a big question in musicals," considers James Lyons. "In the Hollywood musicals, the characters were fictional constructs and they would start singing, and you could buy it. But . . . when Brando did it in *Guys and Dolls*, people didn't like it. He couldn't really sing that well, and it didn't work."

Some films of the 1950s revealed a great deal of depth, including 1955's *It's Always Fair Weather*, produced by Arthur Freed for MGM. Codirected and chore-ographed by Stanley Donen and Gene Kelly this film was an unofficial sequel of sorts to 1949's *On the Town*, which concerned sailors on twenty-four-hour leave from the Navy. *It's Always Fair Weather* recounts instead the story of three soldiers reuniting ten years after the end of World War II. What they discover by rejoining, however, is nothing less than a midlife crisis.

"It's about the emotional texture, that piece," suggests Jay Cocks. "It's about the scene. This is *The Best Years of Our Lives* (1946) with music, and Donen and Gene Kelly were genius book writers."

The last years of the 1950s saw the advent of at least one more great Arthur Freed production, the delightful *Gigi* (1958). With music by the legendary

Frederick Loewe, screenplay and lyrics by Alan Jay Lerner, and direction by Vincente Minnelli, the film was based on a story by Colette, and one that probably couldn't be remade in today's politically correct world.

The story involves a rich, easily bored man named Gaston (Louis Jordan) who falls unexpectedly in love with the childish and tomboyish, but rapidly blossoming, young girl named Gigi (Leslie Caron). Throughout the film, Gaston seeks advice from Maurice Chevalier's character, his uncle Henri, who sings "Thank Heaven for Little Girls" and who today would promptly be arrested for the sentiment.

Other tunes include "I Remember It Well," and the film is considered a hallmark because it is the first Hollywood musical (mostly) shot on location in Paris, a far cry from *An American in Paris*'s stock footage, rear-projection, and Hollywood reconstructions.

What's remains a bit shocking about *Gigi* is its frank sexuality. "Do you make love all the time?" Gigi innocently questions Gaston, and for those who believe that the movie musical is always a chaste thing, with little reference to sex outside the context of song and dance, this stands as evidence to the contrary. Gaston's song about his cheating woman, "She Is Not Thinking of Me," also walks right up to the line of explicitness . . . in a most delightful way, of course.

The late 1940s and 1950s represent a time in American cinema when the colorful musical movie was in its prime. It was bold, vibrant, disarming, and most of all, giddy. This emotional euphoria may have been a reflection of America's new dominance in the post–World War II world, or a willful ignorance of America's problems, like the Cold War and McCarthyism. But the toe-tappers of the decade oozed with artistry and joy.

"Either how *Slaughter on Tenth Avenue* (1957) is a three act play within one number or [the ballet] in *An American in Paris*, it's really difficult to capture joy on film," notes Graff. "It's hard anywhere, but it's particularly hard on film, because the camera is so merciless, and joy is so far behind your eyes when you're an actor, and people are complex. So to be able to create a world where you're just sort of celebrating, like *Anchors Aweigh* (1945), that's not easy to do."

The enduring gift of the 1950s is that Donen, Kelly, and Minnelli just made it look that way.

THE SOUND OF MUSIC: THE 1960s

The 1960s opened with a bang and a shot of adrenalin when *West Side Story* (1961), a contemporary "gang" retelling of Shakespeare's *Romeo and Juliet*, took America by storm.

Robert Wise and choreographer Jerome Robbins codirected a screenplay by Ernest Lehman, with music contributed by Leonard Bernstein and lyrics by Stephen Sondheim. Working on his twenty-eighth film as director, Wise was responsible for the "book" portions of the film and Robbins the musical and dance parts. However, more than halfway through production this accommodation was altered when the studio removed Robbins and left Wise to complete the movie.[12]

Shot at authentic locations in New York City, erected on the foundation of intense rehearsal that reportedly stressed the youthful cast to the breaking point, and featuring story elements regarding ethnicity and even racism, *West Side Story* symbolizes yet a further plank building the bridge between more realistic movie musicals and the old-fashioned, artificial, back-lot, Hollywood format of old.

West Side Story concerns two modern street gangs, the Caucasian Jets and the Puerto Rican Sharks, and how lovers Tony (Richard Beymer) and Maria (Natalie Wood) are literally caught in the crossfire of a turf war. The film immediately declares its intention to be seen as contemporary and cinematic by Wise's use of gritty, location footage. The film opens with a spectacular high angle view of modern New York that gazes down on bridges, ports, skyscrapers (including the Empire State Building and United Nations building), and then zooms ever closer on a basketball court, where the Jets are itching for trouble and snapping their fingers to the beat of the film's first number.

"I was the one who insisted that we open in New York," director Wise told interviewer Harry Kreisler at uc Berkeley in 1998. "I knew I had to deliver New York some way . . . And I started to wonder what the city would look like from a helicopter just straight down."[13]

Wise's curiosity resulted in the film's famous opening sequence of New York's urban landscape, and served as the realistic preamble before a full-on leap into musical convention, with tough gang members strutting their stuff at street level. The first five minutes of the film are quite extraordinary as, for the first time in history, the musical format blends with graffiti, alleys, fire escapes, and other settings that would never have been utilized in the 1930s.

With gang members stalking the streets, often galloping towards the camera (and the camera often moving backwards in a visual retreat), the film's opening confrontation is literally a ballet of violence as the Jets confront the Sharks. There is very little dialogue (besides "Beat it!") and the effect is a total immersion in this new world.

The remainder of the film is also inventive, reframing the famous balcony scene in Shakespeare's *Romeo and Juliet* on an alley fire escape. And rewardingly, Wise's new integration with reality also requires the story to deal with the notion of racism. One song, sung by the Puerto Rican Sharks, is called "In America" and beautifully lays out the positive and negative aspects of our so-called free and open society. Potently, the film also deftly explores, especially for a musical, the concept of how racism emerges from fear.

Viewers will either love Wise's approach in *West Side Story* or hate it, depending on their sensibilities, because the film is neither a deliberately hyper, heightening of reality (*Moulin Rouge*) or a stab at stark realism (*Dancer in the Dark*), but rather an interesting balancing act. Wise accomplishes the same nimble feat in *The Sound of Music*.

Although the music in *West Side Story* is terrific and memorable—especially "I Feel Pretty," "Tonight," and "There's a Place for Us," and Rita Moreno remains a knockout as Anita, the girlfriend of the Sharks' leader, Bernardo—*West Side Story* may just represent the demarcation point for the modern film musical and audience acceptance. One will either get the deal—or contract, as Craig Pearce might term it—and accept it, or shakes one's head in disapproval and move on.

"I struggled with *West Side Story* the first time I saw it," remembers *The Singing Detective* director, Keith Gordon, "though I've come to really love that movie."

The Academy Awards however, had no issue with *West Side Story*, and the film won ten Academy Awards upon its release. This is still a record for the movie musical, even in 2004.

"*West Side Story* kicks ass!" Joss Whedon enthuses. "*West Side Story* did something that had snuck into other musicals, but had never been understood, which is the glory of the juxtaposition of reality with musicals. To see a bunch of toughs walking on the street, and one of them suddenly does some beautiful arabesque or something, is just breathtaking. And it is because you mix those two worlds. If you do it wrong—let's say you take 'cops' and you take 'rock'— it might not work so well.

"You're also into that confluence between fighting and dancing, which *West Side Story* pioneered, pretty much. It works beautifully, and absolutely introduces a new era, because all of the sudden, the cold strange world is a musical place. And that doesn't necessarily make it a good one."

More traditionally, in 1964 Audrey Hepburn starred in the Lerner-Loewe *My Fair Lady* after a young Julie Andrews lost the part because she was not yet an established star and the movie apparently needed marquee credentials. The film was based on the Broadway production from the mid-fifties (which featured Andrews), the Greek Pygmalion myth, and George Bernard Shaw's own version of it.

The movie adaptation stars staid Rex Harrison as Professor Henry Higgins, and Hepburn is his callow student, whom, as part of a wager to fool the aristocracy, he schools to become a proper English lady (and eliminate her Cockney accent). After phonetic speech coaching and forays into the world, Hepburn is eventually transformed into a brilliant and charming girl, and Professor Higgins discovers he can't resist her, just in time for a happy ending.

Hepburn's songs were dubbed by Marni Nixon, but nobody seemed to care. The film was a great critical success, earning a whopping eight Oscars for Best Picture, Best Actor (Rex Harrison), Best Direction (George Cukor), Cinematography, Art Direction, Sound, Score, and Costume Design. The film was a financial winner too, and history had great things in store for Hepburn's runner-up, Ms. Andrews.

"I think the greatest musical film I've seen is *My Fair Lady*," suggests composer Dick Hyman. "Although there is much spoken dialogue preserved from the original play, the music, while light, really aims toward the operatic. It is through-composed. That is, one song refers to another, and they all reflect the composer's total concept.

"I recently read the original play, *Pygmalion*," Hyman continues, "and was struck by how faithful the adaptors were to Shaw's basic text. And I thought all the performances were touching."

In broad strokes, the story of the 1960s movie musical is very much the story of a talent named Julie Andrews. The actress lost out to Hepburn in *My Fair Lady*, but was cast instead in the Walt Disney fantasy musical, *Mary Poppins*, which also premiered in 1964.

Like so many musicals of this age, the story of Mary Poppins concerns a nanny/governess/teacher coming to care for unruly, spoiled children, and helping them find discipline and self-respect. This off-the-shelf character also teaches the parents (whether a banker, the king of Siam, or a German ship captain) to discover the glory of love for family.

In *Mary Poppins*, all the action begins on Cherry Tree Lane in London when the misbehaving Banks children, Jane and Michael, get lost in a nearby park, and their anxious nanny quits out of frustration. Mr. Banks (David Tomlinson), a strutting, pompous banker, believes he should select the next nanny and hires a cheery lass by the name of Mary Poppins, who, unbeknownst to him, flies in off a cloud.

Mary Poppins escorts the children on a wondrous adventure in the park (and through other dimensions) with a one-man band, chalk artist, and chimney sweep named Bert (Dick Van Dyke). Eventually, the children wreak havoc at Mr. Banks's office, and the management fires him. Realizing that it is more important to fly a kite with his children than work at a job, Banks softens and earns the love of his kids, which results in Mary Poppins's departure, her job now complete.

Based on the *Mary Poppins* books by P. L. Travers, the film was directed by Robert Stevenson from a script by Bill Walsh and Don Da Gradi. Brothers Richard and Robert Sherman composed the music, which included the Oscar-winning "Chim Chim Cher-ee" and the immortal "Supercalifragilistic-expialidocious." The latter, like "I Whistle a Happy Tune" in *The King and I* and "My Favorite Things" in *The Sound of Music*, serves basically as a coping mechanism for kids when times get hard and they don't know how to get by. These were the days, remember, before Ritalin.

Mary Poppins is a latter-day *Wizard of Oz*, though perhaps without such a strong narrative, and a fantasy film musical that, like its star, is "practically perfect in every way." A truly imaginative work of art, it boasts characters jumping into drawings, taking flight, dancing with animated farm animals, and flying about on carousel horses broken loose from a merry-go-round. There's a show stopper where Dick Van Dyke dances in near-perfect synchronicity with a raft of cartoon penguins, and the sequence with the chimney sweeps dancing on the London rooftops is exhilarating.

The film also includes some gorgeous cinematography. In one scene, George Banks walks down a picturesque road surrounded by trees. The film is shot in color, but this is a beautiful image of grays and blacks surrounding him. At this point in the tale, he's lost his job and feels rudderless, that the future is bleak, so the colorless, sullen image captures his mood and contrasts strongly with the optimism on display from Ms. Poppins. Watching the film today, forty years after its premiere, one still can't help but feel deep satisfaction.

"You kind of discount it," Joss Whedon reflects. "Because when you've been through years of therapy because of Dick Van Dyke's bad British accent, and you think, 'Well, kids . . . and it's clichés . . . and it's Julie Andrews . . . ,'" he jokes. "But what a good movie it [actually] is! It's a really solid flick. The numbers are invigorating and catchy. [In college] I saw a Technicolor print and it was just gorgeous. It was just when musicals were about to become really ugly. It was the end of the gorgeous era, and I just think it's a delight."

Mary Poppins was a huge hit in the sixties, and inspired the course of musicals over the remainder of the decade. Fantasy became a primary ingredient of the genre. *Doctor Dolittle*, played by Rex Harrison, talked to the animals in 1967, and *Chitty Chitty Bang Bang* saw Dick Van Dyke pilot a flying old car in 1968.

Importantly, *Mary Poppins* also begat the nearly decade-long dominance of its charming star, Julie Andrews. In the span of just a few years, she headlined a variety of hits, including the classic *The Sound of Music* (1965), and *Thoroughly Modern Millie* (1967), as well as expensive misses, such as Robert Wise's *Star!* (1968) and Blake Edwards's *Darling Lili* (1969).

In the eighties, the actress was fronting musicals of a different sort, including the cross-dressing *Victor/Victoria* (1983). Andrews declined to be interviewed for this book, her agent noting that she wanted to save all the juicy stories of these movie musicals for her own memoirs. So that's something to look forward to.

The year 1965 brought a number of musical treats to theaters. One of the strangest, perhaps, was Columbia's Western/comedy/musical *Cat Ballou*, directed by Elliott Silverstein from a screenplay by Walter Newman. Based on a serious western novel by Ray Chanslor, the film was a flat-out spoof of the genre (before *Blazing Saddles* [1974]) and starred twenty-eight-year-old Jane Fonda as Catherine "Cat" Ballou, a school teacher in the Old West who takes matters into her own hands when her rancher father is murdered by the villainous Tim Strawn (Lee Marvin). She plans her revenge, and hires the legendary cowboy Kid Shelleen (Marvin again) to help execute it. The only problem is, he's a drunk . . . and so's his horse.

What makes *Cat Ballou* of interest to musical fans is a narrative framing device in which Nat King Cole (in his last performance) and Stubby Kaye portray wandering minstrels. Acting as a kind of musical Greek chorus, these most unusual cowboys sing "The Ballad of Cat Ballou," a tune which describes the outlaw Cat as the wildest girl in the Old West since Calamity Jane. The ballad featured lyrics by Mack David and music from Jerry Livingston and was nominated for an Academy Award. *Cat Ballou* was actually nominated for five Oscars, and Lee Marvin took one home for his unusual dual role.

The Sound of Music, or "The Sound of Mucus" as star Christopher Plummer once famously called it, also arrived in 1965 and the world has never been the same.[14] From the first shot, Robert Wise announced his intention to build on the style of *West Side Story* and bring the movie musical into the more realistic realm of the sixties.

Famously, *The Sound of Music* begins with a gorgeous aerial shot of snow-covered mountains laden with fog. Wind blows on the soundtrack, and in a series of gorgeous exterior shots, the camera lowers irrevocably towards trees and rivers—until we seem to be zooming over sky, land, and water, our glorious earth—across a green plain. Then, in one of the most magnificently staged shots in cinema history, arrives the film's trademark image, a solitary Julie Andrews spinning in dance as she utters the famous Rodgers and Hammerstein lyrics "the hills are alive with the sound of music."

One might think that after such an auspicious start, there would be nowhere to go but down, but *The Sound of Music* never falters, and virtually every song in the film is a winner, including "Sixteen Going on Seventeen," "Do Re Mi," "My Favorite Things," "Edelweiss," "So Long, Farewell," and of course, "Climb Ev'ry Mountain." It's an incredible and rousing set of tunes, and each one materializes at just the right time to prevent an overdose of maudlin emotions.

In broad strokes, *The Sound of Music* tells the same story as *Mary Poppins* and *The King and I*. Sort of. A nun named Maria (Andrews) is ordered by her convent to become the nanny of the von Trapp family, including a gaggle of seven unruly children. Making matters worse, von Trapp himself (Christopher Plummer) is a military martinet and strict disciplinarian. Summoning his children by elaborate codes blasted out on a whistle, he makes life utterly miserable for everybody, including Maria. But unlike *The King and I* or *Mary Poppins*, the nanny and the daddy eventually fall in love and marry. Even more impressively, the film's climax is actually rather suspenseful, as the von Trapps flee their home in Austria to escape Nazi pursuit and are nearly discovered by a turncoat local. How often can musicals make that claim?

The Sound of Music gathers much steam not just from beautiful exterior locations—the European castles and villages—but from the characterizations. Andrews is enchanting as Maria, what with her penchant for saying "whatever comes" into her mind, in other words, honesty. And Christopher Plummer's heart seems to melt at just the right pace, and even keeps tension from leaking out of the romantic love story. In all, this film is impossible to resist. Even if you want to.

"I love it like a kid," Todd Graff admits. "I think that it's sentimental, and I'm not usually a giant fan of holocaust stories where it's about the triumph of six people rather than the extermination of millions. But it has a beautiful score, obviously. And Julie Andrews is Julie Andrews, and you can't help but love her because she's so lovable. It's a machine that works."

"*The Sound of Music* is a phenomenon," adds Craig Pearce. "In every culture in the world, from every village in Central Asia to the depth of the South American jungle, I'm sure you can find *Sound of Music* fans. It's the most successful musical ever.

"It works against all the odds," he continues. "In one way, it is quite naturalistic in the way the characters relate, and it has a larger serious issue which you deal with, which is Nazism. But then it's got this really amazing collection of songs. Slam dunk hit after hit after hit, and it manages to marry all these elements together just so fantastically well.

"It's always enjoyable to watch. It's on TV every year at least. But you turn it on anyway, and it sucks you in. It's just really, really well made."

"We had no idea it was going to go through the roof like it did," director Robert Wise reported in 2002. "It's still one of the highest-grossing musicals of all time."[15] In fact in the year 2003, the American Film Institute included three tunes from *The Sound of Music* ("The Sound of Music," "My Favorite Things," and "Do Re Mi") on their list of top one hundred movie tunes, at positions ten, sixty-four, and eighty-eight. Quite a showing for a thirty-nine-year-old film.

Besides Julie Andrews, other musical stars were born in the 1960s too. Foremost among these was doubtless Barbra Streisand, who, prepolitical activism phase, demonstrated tremendous screen presence, not to mention powerful lungs, in a variety of droll musicals.

After playing Fanny Brice on Broadway, Streisand took the role to the screen in 1968's *Funny Girl*, and costarred with Omar Sharif. The film was so successful that Streisand was selected for the lead role of Dolly Levi in *Hello,*

Dolly! (1969) over several more mature and experienced actresses, including Julie Andrews. The film was an opulent comedy and represented Gene Kelly's last directing gig on a musical film.

Unfortunately, *Hello Dolly!* like many of the musicals that closed out the decade, proved to be a financial failure considering its high budget of nearly thirty million dollars. It thus joined the ranks of such nonstarters as *Star!*, *Darling Lili*, the disastrous adaptation of *Camelot* (1967), choreographer Bob Fosse's directorial debut, *Sweet Charity* (1969), and Andre Previn's *Paint Your Wagon* (1969). These films failed to grab audiences, and studios were starting to pay attention.

Once more, the musical format found itself tap dancing to a crossroads. There were some enormously positive signs for continued survival, no doubt. In particular, efforts like *West Side Story* and *The Sound of Music* updated hackneyed old formulas and fostered increased realism, and Julie Andrews was certainly a star to rival Judy Garland.

Optimistically, the decade ended with another Oscar-fest, *Oliver!* (1968), which earned five Academy Awards (including Best Picture) after being nominated for eleven. Based on Charles Dickens's *Oliver Twist*, the film was shot in Britain over a period of half a year and featured Ron Moody as Fagin and young Mark Lester as the titular tyke, Oliver.

The Beatles also made a couple of highly unusual and popular films during the sixties, from the magnificent and self-reflexive *A Hard Day's Night* (1964) and ludicrous James Bond–like *Help!* (1965) to the animated fantasy *Yellow Submarine* (1968).

But could even the popularity of that group bring youngsters back to a formula that was beginning to feel increasingly archaic? More importantly, could musicals continue to fill theater seats in a world populated by the likes of futuristic fare like *2001: A Space Odyssey* (1968) and *Planet of the Apes* (1968)? Or more relevant "personal" contemporary visions like *Easy Rider* (1969)?

Only time would answer that question, but there was another issue of concern too. The old Hollywood musical guard didn't have much juice left by the sixties. The facts were telling: Fred Astaire made his last musical, *Finian's Rainbow*, in 1968. Bob Hope and Bing Crosby went on the road for the final time when they visited Hong Kong in 1962. Cole Porter died in 1964. The era of the Freed unit at MGM had ended with *Gigi* in 1958, and Kelly was no longer making musicals by the 1970s.

If there was going to be a musical revival in the decade of disco, it would have to arise from a new aesthetic, and a new band of artists. The challenge was accepted.

THERE'LL BE SOME CHANGES MADE: THE 1970S

If the 1970s had been at all like the 1960s, the world might have been treated to a decade brimming with dozens of musicals constructed on the myriad successes, achievements, talents and other foundations evident in the previous decade. But that didn't happen; at least not in the ways the industry, and perhaps audiences, expected.

Director Robert Wise, who had accomplished so much to enliven the genre in the sixties with *West Side Story* and *The Sound of Music*, didn't direct a single musical in the seventies, concentrating instead on the in vogue genres of science fiction and horror with *The Andromeda Strain* (1971), *Audrey Rose* (1977), and *Star Trek: The Motion Picture* (1979).

He wasn't alone, either. Stanley Donen closed out the decade directing a horror film set in outer space about Kirk Douglas, Farrah Fawcett, Harvey Keitel, and a homicidal robot. It was called *Saturn 3* (1980).

And what of the magnificent and charming Julie Andrews, the undisputed champion of the 1960s musical? She was MIA in the seventies. The actress did not appear in a single movie musical from 1970 to 1979.

So was the sound of music dimming to a whisper? Had the razzle-dazzle fizzled?

Not really.

The old-school style was still there to be found and enjoyed, but the musical was also, for the first time in a long while, really blazing new and different trails too. It is this decade, the turbulent 1970s, which has actually formed the basis for the current resurgence in the genre in the early twenty-first century. Many of the musicals from this era are more challenging and more unusual than what had come in the previous forty-five years, and perhaps more flawed too, but there is nonetheless a new aesthetic at work.

But we'll get to that soon.

One of the few established acting talents who survived the 1960s unscathed was Barbra Streisand. As the sixties closed, despite the financial failure of *Hello, Dolly!*, the chanteuse was still considered one of the biggest draws at the American box office. Streisand made a variety of films during the new decade, including *On a Clear Day You Can See Forever* (1970), the sequel to *Funny Girl*, entitled *Funny Lady* (1975), and the powerhouse 1976 remake, *A Star Is Born*.

Of these three, critics will quibble about ranking, but Vincente Minnelli's *On a Clear Day You Can See Forever*, a film produced by Alan Jay Lerner, is no doubt among the most underrated. It features Barbra Streisand as Daisy Gamble, a woman who wants to stop smoking, but who discovers instead, via hypnosis, that she has lived previous lives.

Obsessed with paranormal notions such as reincarnation, the movie over-comes a flat performance by romantic lead Yves Montand, and again showcases director Minnelli's thorough mastery of cinema imagery. A superstar talent in the world of musicals, he is often championed for his "sweeping scope," "lavish visual style," and "judicious use of color," and those qualities are as evident in this film as in acknowledged classics like *An American in Paris* and *Gigi*.[16]

"Vincente Minnelli is the beginning and the end of musical directors," suggests Joss Whedon. "I think that's exemplified in the number in *Brigadoon*'s 'Waiting for My Dearie,' which I could watch four hundred times. He could do more with a very little bit of movement in a very small room, than [other] people could do with a stadium.

"If you look at Cyd Charisse's big numbers in *Silk Stockings*, and then just the simplicity that's going on in 'Waiting for My Dearie' you realize just what extraordinary mastery Minnelli had. I don't think all of *Gigi* works, but what works does so because he understands space and that terrible sadness that comes with the exultation of being able to be in the world of the music."

In the specific case of *On a Clear Day You Can See Forever*, the film's visu-als play delicately and stylistically with the notion of time's passage, and the ongoing and perhaps repetitive nature of human life. It's not a perfect film by any means, and was only moderately successful with audiences.

Beyond Streisand's continued presence, there were two interesting and contradictory trends at play in the decade of Nixon, Ford, and Carter. The first involved the continuation of the status quo, the presentation of old formulas already rendered antique by the rapid social changes of the 1960s. Oppositely, a series of directors also toiled to propel the genre into new territory, accommo-dating the new idioms of the hippie generation.

On the former front, Hollywood offered a new version of Frank Capra's classic *Lost Horizon* (1973), based on a work by James Hilton. This time, Charles Jarrott served as director, and the film's visuals were accompanied by an original

Burt Bacharach soundtrack. The film was shot on the then-considerable budget of six million dollars at the Columbia back lot. The choreography of the musical numbers, including "Living Together, Growing Together," was directed by Hermes Pan, a veteran of Hollywood who had worked with Fred Astaire.

The tale of Western foreigners stranded in the mythical Far East of Shangrai-La, the film stars luminaries of the day like Peter Finch, John Gielgud, Liv Ullmann, Sally Kellerman, and Michael York, but their efforts were ultimately for naught. The film met with savage reviews, and became one of the decade's biggest bombs, derided in some corners as *Lost Investments*. The film appeared on many "worst film of the year" lists, and critics were exceedingly cruel.

Patrick Gibbs, writing for the *London Daily Telegraph* noted that it was "dreadfully old fashioned in the rigid handling of song and dance routines," and that a major trouble was that "few of the cast can sing, and the songs have lyrics of awful banality and tunes to match."[17]

Another old-fashioned style musical that didn't quite cut it was *Mame*, a remake of the popular 1958 film, *Auntie Mame*. It didn't fare much better with audiences than *Lost Horizons* when it was released a year later, in March 1974. Directed by Gene Saks, this adaptation of the play about a wealthy and eccentric woman who unexpectedly becomes guardian to her nephew, saw the plum role of Mame Dennis go to past-her-prime TV star Lucille Ball, though Angela Lansbury had played the role successfully on Broadway in the sixties.

Ball endured a lot of brickbats for her less-than-stellar singing voice and range, but how can anyone seriously find fault with Lucille Ball? She was a delightful presence, even if *Mame*'s story seemed hopelessly mired in the world of previous decades, not in the "new" truths evidenced by the personal cinema of the 1970s.

Another failure of the early 1970s also featured a faded TV star. In this case, the film was a Florence Henderson vehicle called *Song of Norway* (1970), a flaccid regurgitation of the successful *The Sound of Music*. Andrew L. Stone directed this musical biography of composer Edvard Grieg, and proved concretely that the old-fashioned musical format had little currency in the decade of the ERA and Whip Inflation Now buttons.

"This movie is of an unbelievable badness," wrote Pauline Kael in the *New Yorker*. "It brings back clichés you didn't know you knew—they're practically from the unconscious of moviegoers . . . it seems to have been made by trolls."[18]

Much more successful than *Song of Norway* was Norman Jewison's stunning *Fiddler on the Roof* (1971), a spectacular adaptation of Sholom Alecheim's tale of a poor Jewish milkman, Tevye. Set in prerevolutionary Russia in 1910, in the town of Anetevka, the film was based on the popular Broadway show that had starred Zero Mostel.

Shot in Yugoslavia and starring a then-unknown actor named Topol (*Flash Gordon* [1980], *For Your Eyes Only* [1981]), *Fiddler on the Roof* was packed with unforgettable songs (arranged by John Williams) that have remained in the pop culture lexicon ever since, including "If I Were a Rich Man," "Tradition," "Matchmaker," and "To Life."

Fiddler on the Roof is a traditional musical in the sense that it concerns the hopes and aspirations of a likeable, down-on-his-luck fellow and expresses them in song and movement, but Jewison's effort is also, like the oeuvre of Robert Wise, incredibly cinematic and naturalistic, with authentic locations augmenting the reality of the piece in a way that could never have been managed on stage or in the early decades of the format.

Jewison conducted extensive research prepping the film, and the fruits of his labor are impressive, as one number after the other leads audiences deeper into the world of Jewish religious rituals and tradition. In all, it's a stunning three-hour entertainment and was a genuine success too, making more than fifty million dollars against a budget of less than ten.

Despite the success of *Fiddler*, it was clear in the 1970s that the directors of movie musicals needed to push the envelope as far as it could possibly go if they were to create meaningful and relevant films. In 1972, choreographer and legend Bob Fosse directed Joel Grey and Liza Minnelli, daughter of Judy Garland and Vincente Minnelli, in the stunningly different *Cabaret*, an intimate tale of one stage performer's life and career in pre-Nazi Germany on the eve of World War II. Billy Wilder and Gene Kelly turned down offers to direct the film, and the project went to Fosse, which turned out to be a good thing, given the tendency in his work to go dark.

Based on the play by John Van Druten and the musical by Joe Masteroff, with music by John Kander and Fred Ebb, the film introduces the moviegoing world to Joel Grey's decadent Master of Ceremonies at the Kit-Kat Club, and escorts viewers into the tumultuous life of Sally Bowles, an American (British in the play) cabaret performer at the club in Berlin.

She falls in love with an English tutor named Brian (Michael York), but he thinks he may be gay. Sally and Brian eventually share an intimate relationship, but then a new man enters the picture, a wealthy German named Maximillian (Helmut Green). This couple grows into a ménage à trois, and eventually Sally discovers she's pregnant. When she decides to have an abortion, Brian realizes it is time to go home to England, and Sally, all alone and hopeless now, returns to the cabaret.

With cinematography from the unparalleled Geoffrey Unsworth, who later shot *Superman: The Movie* (1978), the film is both stark and dark in its visualizations, and mature and forthright in themes, which include homosexuality, a ménage à trois, abortion and other screen taboos that don't often appear in movie musicals.

The film's songs by Kander and Ebb are utilized in a unique fashion. On one hand, they are utterly cynical, bemoaning the role and power of money in society ("Money Makes the World Go Round"), and on the other, they are randy and raunchy, even laughingly mocking threesomes and other matters of sex with "Two Ladies."

Finally, the climactic song is "Cabaret," and it is utterly sad and devoid of hope, describing a universe, where "life is a cabaret." But the film has already revealed Sally's life to be something quite different than a show. It is totally despairing, lonely, empty, and teetering on the verge of the fascist holocaust that swept Europe. "Cabaret" is a brilliant capper to the film, and sad counterpoint to the story the audience has just witnessed.

In addition to his undisputed skill with dancers, Bob Fosse remains a master film editor and his mise-en-scène in *Cabaret* is powerfully, almost harshly constructed. He never shies away from the artistic equation dictating that form should reflect content, and in one memorable instance, onstage theatrical antics are cross-cut with scenes of Nazi violence offstage to craft a dramatic point.

Another key and powerful moment, Grey's introduction in the picture (to the tune "Wilkommen"), involves an intentionally distorted visage in the mirror, which alerts audiences that this Master of Ceremonies symbolizes a twisted reflection of his context and culture, and perhaps even his audience too, both in movie houses and in the Kit-Kat Club.

Cabaret remains a film of tremendous power, and one that proved how serious topics like sexual orientation and politics could be vetted in the heretofore conservative, traditional, musical form.

"And what that picture did was, it suddenly signaled the end of a certain kind of musical convention . . . [that] said . . . we don't have to separate movie sex and music anymore," reported Scott Simon on National Public Radio.[19]

"We looked a lot at *Cabaret* when we were making *Moulin Rouge*," reveals Craig Pearce. "It's very much an Orpheus story, because it's about an underworld: the world of the Kit-Kat Club, the world of bohemian Germany in the early thirties in the Weimar Republic. There's a whole lot going on in the under-world, and the stakes are very high, because they are personal stakes. It's about love and relationships and identity and sexuality, but it's a really great illustra-tion of an underworld, because in the upper world, much bigger forces are taking hold. It was the rise of Nazism before the Second World War, so it's a great metaphor for an underworld.

"What's really interesting about *Cabaret* is that it was made in the 1970s, when there was this really naturalistic style to film," Pearce continues. "It's heightened and realistic at the same time. The numbers in the Kat-Kat Club are heightened, and you have a license to make them that way because you're in a nightclub in the 1930s. But the musical numbers never break the fourth wall into the body of the film. They're like a Greek chorus, commenting on what's come before, or what is about to come afterwards in the story. It's a really inter-esting device that works very, very well in this instance. Often it doesn't work well in a musical, but it's very clever the way Fosse engineers that.

"The only time there is actual singing outside the nightclub is when Sally and Brian go to the country with Maximillian and stop at that restaurant in the country, and the choir is there and it starts singing 'Tomorrow Belongs to Me' [a Nazi anthem.] And it's absolutely chilling, but it doesn't break the fourth wall."

"Bob Fosse is amongst the most amazing interpreters of the musical on film," suggests director Todd Haynes. "I just think that it's hard to do anything more interesting than *Cabaret*, which *Chicago* owes a great deal to."

A masterpiece of the musical format, but told within the context of early 1970s cinematic techniques, meaning naturalistic and personal filmmaking, *Cabaret* eventually picked up eight well-deserved Oscars, though it lost the Best Picture Award to Francis Ford Coppola's *The Godfather*. Still, Liza Minnelli and Joel Grey both went home with Academy Awards, and the film is today acknowledged as a classic. Historian David Zinman writes that it is "far supe-rior to any other musical of its time," and that it is "a brilliantly evocative, unconventional movie that brings to the screen a fast-paced, boldly filmed story that keeps us mesmerized right from the colorful opening sequence."[20]

Another fantastic musical film came out of the early 1970s, but alas, many historians don't even consider it a musical because it plays so much within the traditional form. This experiment is *O Lucky Man!*, directed by the late Lindsay Anderson (1923–1994). The film is a sprawling, three-hour satire-cum–fairy tale that begins with the legend "once upon a time" and proceeds to parody virtu-ally every aspect of modern Western society and, in particular, British society.

O Lucky Man! stars Malcolm McDowell as a man named Travis who is the central figure in a modern-day odyssey. Hired by the Imperial Coffee Company as a salesman, Travis is sent to run the northeast sector where the former salesman, Oswald, has mysteriously vanished. Travis performs this job ably for a while, partying with the locals in his spare time, but then his life takes an odd turn when another sales assignment lands him in Scotland and he is (mistakenly) detained as a spy at a top-secret military facility.

After his brief incarceration (and torture) Travis survives what appears to be a nuclear blast, wanders out into a pastoral setting, and is nursed back to health via the bosom (literally) of a saintlike figure in a church. He hitchhikes back to London, but is waylaid at the Millar Research Facility, where doctors seek to experiment on him and transform him into some kind of chimera. He escapes captivity again, and winds up in the van of a rock band. Travis remains with the group for a time, and romances a groovy groupie played by Helen Mirren.

When he learns that Mirren's father (Ralph Richardson) is the richest, most notorious business man in the world, Travis ingratiates himself with the old man and becomes his assistant. He fully immerses himself in the corrupt corporate world. However, Travis is soon framed by the old man and made the fall guy for an international crime. He is sentenced to jail for five years of hard labor. When he is released, Travis is promptly mugged and attacked by the poor, some of whom he has sought to help through charity work. Beaten and bruised, Travis finally ends up at an audition for a movie, and wins a part in a film.

As the preceding summary probably indicates, this is a wild and dynamic film that travels many places and tries to achieve many things. It's a movie that, by Jay Cocks's assessment, "bursts with wit, rage, enterprise, stylistic audacity, and social agitation."[21]

Uniquely, the same troupe of actors, including Richardson, reappear over the course of the film, essaying different roles, and part of the picture's interest is a result of seeing how these characters are reflections and echoes or contrasts of one another. Despite the huge shifts in locale, tone and characterization, one constant throughout *O Lucky Man!* is indeed music.

In particular, composer Alan Price (formerly of the rock band, the Animals) appears throughout the film, both within the narrative as a band member, and outside the story, during real recording sessions for his songs. The film thus occasionally "breaks" and reveals him singing tunes such as "Poor

People" or "Sell, Sell," and all of his music comments in some fashion, usually ironically, on the episode unspooling on screen.

"It has an original score by Alan Price, and it's one of the greatest scores ever written for a movie," enthuses Jay Cocks. "It's three hours long, and Anderson went a step or two further than *De-Lovely*. He not only integrated the music, he not only used it as counterpoint, and as a way of getting into the scene and moving the story along, [but] he integrated the performance of the music by the composer into the actual movie.

"This thing is stunning. Of course, it was a big flop. But you see this, and it will change your idea of what musicals can be, and what they should be. It's got all kinds of things going on in it. Just one of the greatest movies ever, a true masterpiece."

"*O Lucky Man!* was an influence on *Velvet Goldmine*. Totally!" James Lyons reports. "*O Lucky Man!* is one of those movies that we [Todd Haynes and Lyons] would have seen at midnight, and it starred Malcolm McDowell, who was another cult figure from *A Clockwork Orange* (1971) and *If* (1968).

"And what's interesting is that how I connect to that film is as an editor, in its cutting style. At that moment in time, the British filmmakers, particularly Nicholas Roeg were really investigating this elliptical way of putting together a narrative. You could say it came from drugs, and maybe it did.

"It [*O Lucky Man!*] refuses to resolve," Lyons continues. "It has satirical moments in it. That's a great, amazing movie, and it's totally in the spirit [shared by *Velvet Goldmine*] of 'There's a world that needs to be changed.'"

The same year brought another unusual effort to the screen, Norman Jewison's adaptation of the Tim Rice stage musical, *Jesus Christ Superstar*. The show had run in London since 1969, and went to Broadway in 1971, but director Jewison put an incredible visual spin on the material by shooting the film on location in Israel, often in the blazing heat, and gracing it with a modern sensibility.

Although the film occurs during the last week of Jesus's life, it blends eras in a strange fashion. Jesus Christ is sometimes referred to as "J. C.," Roman soldiers wear contemporary-style military uniforms, and there's even a twentieth-century bus on display. Jesus is played by Ted Neeley, and Judas (Carl Anderson) is depicted as a black man. The songs all have Christian connotations including "The Last Supper," "Gethsemane," and "Crucifixion," but the vibe is pure pop culture. It's a film that infuriated some, and stimulated others. Like Sir Alan

Parker's *Evita* (1996), all of the dialogue is sung in opera fashion, which alone makes the film a curiosity.

The year 1975 saw the release of several challenging and different movie musicals which have all earned places in the history books, though for various reasons. Surveying these titles alphabetically, the first film was director Peter Bogdonovich's experiment, *At Long Last Love.*

The film stars Burt Reynolds and Cybill Shepherd, and includes the music of Cole Porter in what is essentially, a modern-day version of the charming 1930s musicals beloved by previous generations. What makes the film such an experiment is that none of the featured cast can actually sing or dance very ably, making it the forerunner to such nineties films as *Everyone Says I Love You* and *Love's Labour's Lost.* Even more interestingly, Bogdonovich demanded that all the singing be accomplished live on set. This was something that was not even done in the 1950s.

Upon release, *At Long Last Love* was so poorly received by critics and audiences that eventually Peter Bogdonovich sent letters to the press apologizing for what he detected as his personal folly in trying to include live musical performances, warts and all.

"*At Long Last Love* is regarded as the great white elephant catastrophe of its time," considers Jay Cocks, "but it's not bad, because he [Bogdonovich] does interesting things with people who can't really sing or dance."

The next movement in the bizarre film trilogy of 1975 was *The Rocky Horror Picture Show*, which concerns a white-bread couple (Susan Sarandon and Barry Bostwick) who, on a dark and stormy night, seek refuge in the gothic mansion of a mad scientist, Dr. Frank'N'Furter (Tim Curry), a self-described Transylvanian transvestite transsexual. The film is simultaneously a musical and a parody of B-movies, and the songs, many by the then-popular artist Meat Loaf, who appears in the film, drive the story to its bizarre, but strangely inclusive and tolerant ending.

In its day, the film was considered a bomb, but by the late 1970s and early 1980s, *Rocky Horror* transcended its unimpressive theatrical performance and came to define the "midnight film" phenomenon. Adapted from a play by Richard O'Brien, the movie was directed by Jim Sharman and has today grossed more than $150 million worldwide.

Ken Russell is the auteur behind the third and final musical mutant of 1975, the British rock opera known as *Tommy.* This is the story of a deaf-mute

(Roger Daltrey) who becomes the Pinball Wizard of the universe. "Your senses will never be the same," the ads promised, and they were correct. This movie is wall-to-wall music, with songs serving as dialogue, and Pete Townsend, Elton John, and Eric Clapton providing the tunes. It's a bizarre kaleidoscope of music and imagery, but one that fits in perfectly with the envelope-pushing nature of musicals in the 1970s.

Whatever one may think of *O Lucky Man!*, *Jesus Christ Superstar*, *At Long Last Love*, *The Rocky Horror Picture Show*, or *Tommy*, there could be no denying that the movie musical was trying on a new (top) hat in the 1970s, and going for broke stylistically. There were failures in this regard, but also successes.

Traditional in some fashions, and actually quite dark and fresh in others was Martin Scorsese's *New York, New York*, released in 1977. This impressive movie stars Robert De Niro as saxophonist Jimmy Doyle and Liza Minnelli as singer Francine Evans, who fall in love in the 1940s after V. J. Day, and then suffer through a tumultuous, eventful relationship across the years. Although as a sax player he "blows a barrel full of tenor," Jimmy is also a self-hating, self-destructive lout who cheats on Francine, snorts cocaine, and eventually abandons their child all together.

Fortunately, Francine finds "Happy Endings" for herself by becoming a movie star, and by deciding, in the film's final frames, that she has had quite enough of the mercurial, temperamental Jimmy. Along the way, Minnelli croons "Just You, Just Me," "You Are My Lucky Star" and the song that Jimmy and Francine have composed together, the Kander-and-Ebb warhorse "Theme from New York, New York."

Produced by Irwin Winkler (*De-Lovely*), *New York, New York* featured many great old tunes from yesteryear by the likes of Arthur Freed, Nacio Herb Brown, the Gershwins, Richard Rodgers, and Lorenz Hart. It also showcased gorgeous, old-fashioned filmmaking. Down to its very film stock, it seemed to authentically evoke the 1940s.

Several exteriors in the film appear patently false, and sound stages were decorated with mauve-and-apricot-colored skylines, which gently reminded viewers of movies of the 1940s and 1950s and their strangely welcoming and lustrous artificiality. These lovely period touches were then contrasted by the nature of the narrative itself, which was nothing if not modern and hardcore. De Niro's amorous and aggressive character nearly kills pregnant Francine during one harrowing night sequence, and the destructive power of his jealousy, fear and self-loathing is almost tangible throughout. When the long-suffering Francine achieves success away from Jimmy, the audience breathes a sigh of relief. He's a dark, dark fella.

In its initial release, a critical production number called "Happy Endings" was deleted from *New York, New York*. In subsequent releases (and on video and DVD) the number has been restored, and it is difficult to imagine the film without it. Watching it today, one can detect how closely Scorsese has studied old film musicals.

This sequence involves a screening of Francine's new film (titled *Happy Endings*), and like a latter day Busby Berkeley, Scorsese's camera escorts the audience right "into" the film for a deluxe, ten minute fantasy sequence that includes everything from high-angle, Berkeley-style choreography to Marilyn Monroe–style, *Gentleman Prefer Blondes* fantasy in the "Aces High" interlude.

The "Happy Endings" number represents an almost perfect mirroring of the last ten minutes of *An American in Paris*, or the "Broadway Melody" number at the climax of *Singin' in the Rain*. It is self-contained and valuable on its own terms, telling the complete tale of an usherette (Minnelli) who is discovered by a Broadway producer, becomes famous, and then—when he abandons her— faces loneliness.

Not only does this elaborate sequence function splendidly as a self-contained musical universe, it is also an ironic reflection of Francine's "real" life. In this version, there is indeed a happy ending in store for her, and she wins not merely fame and fortune as a Broadway star, but eventually Mr. Right too. In Scorsese's rain-soaked New York, the film's other reality, there is no such traditional closure or happy denouement. Again, the artifice of the upbeat movie musical has been subverted to contrast a more naturalistic, ambiguous world.

Notably, *New York, New York* also pokes around the issues surrounding a "creative marriage," the business/music partnership of Francine and Jimmy that results in so much stress in their personal lives. They not only have different temperaments, but different artistic tastes. In one sequence, Jimmy even mocks Francine for the lyrics she has written out for his new composition.

"That's a duality that you see in many movies about music," notes James Lyons. "You have the saxophone player who wants to play bebop, and you have Liza Minnelli, who turns into some version of Judy Garland/Peggy Lee. When they meet and they write 'New York, New York,' it's this wonderful synthesis, but then they split irrevocably. Maybe that happens in pop culture."

While musicals searched for their identity in the mid-1970s, trying on new hats and new ideas that included political commentary (*O Lucky Man!*), and more candid views of sexuality (*The Rocky Horror Picture Show*), a new form of popular music swept the nation, and for that matter, the world.

That form was disco.

Derided by some, especially hardcore rock enthusiasts, disco represented a new trend on nightclub dance floors, and beneath glitter balls. The disco ethos was superficial, experiential, and hedonistic. Its adherents donned hot pants, halter tops, and platform shoes, and the music of the time came from Earth, Wind & Fire or Donna Summers. As a cultural movement, disco was flashy, hot, and very, very sexy.

In the year 1977, one movie accurately captured the texture of this new world. *Saturday Night Fever* starred *Welcome Back Kotter* (1975) breakout John Travolta as Tony Manero, a kid from Brooklyn who, like the hoofers of previous ages, just had to dance. By day he was something of a loveable loser, but by night—and in the clubs—he knew how to *strut*. In his element on the dance floor, Tony was a god of motion and music, and the soundtrack of his life was informed by the Bees Gees and their hits "Stayin' Alive," "More Than a Woman," "How Deep Is Your Love," and "Night Fever."

Not entirely unlike the stories of the Fred Astaire–Ginger Rogers movies of ages past, *Saturday Night Fever* concerns the all-important quest to win a dance contest, with the surly and macho Manero partnering with a more upscale woman than those from his neighborhood, the remote Stephanie (Karen Lynn Gorney). Of course, Fred Astaire was never depicted having sex in the backseat of his car, nor dealing with unsympathetic parental figures and uncouth buddies, but what can you say? Times change.

Electrified by its contemporary music, and deeply resonant because it tapped the zeitgeist of the age, *Saturday Night Fever* was not a familiar-style musical. The characters never sang nor expressed their emotions through song. Boy, did they dance, and the soundtrack was composed of songs that reflected not just the age, but the emotion of the individual scenes. This new approach, which some authors have called "dance-icals" or dance musicals, worked marvelously, and *Saturday Night Fever* emerged as one of the highest grossing films of the 1970s.

"I love that movie. I think it's fantastic," says director Todd Haynes. "It's so much about class, and this amazing ability to transform and ascend from our limited lives in the world through music and dance."

Directed by John Badham from a screenplay by Norman Wexler, the film made a bonafide star of John Travolta, spawned a rip-off disco TV sitcom *Makin' It* (1979), not to mention a dance contest program, *Dance Fever*. A sequel directed by Sylvester Stallone followed in 1983, *Staying Alive*, but more to the point, the dance musical became the new, accepted method of crafting a movie musical in Hollywood.

From the early 1980s right into the present, the industry has leaned heavily on this format in the films *Flashdance* (1983), *Footloose* (1984), *Dirty Dancing* (1987), *Swing Kids* (1993), and *Save the Last Dance* (2001).

The final years of the 1970s witnessed the arrival of two more stage-to-screen adaptations, and each seemed to capture the magic of an age, but this time it was the 1950s and the 1960s, respectively.

The first effort was *Grease* (1978) and it starred John Travolta as Danny Zuko and Olivia Newton-John as his summertime, high school girlfriend, Sandy. Travolta was a greaser and Newton-John a square good girl, and, basically, peer pressure kept them from getting together. A retro treat, *Grease* became the top-earning musical of the decade featuring a bevy of hits from the Broadway musical, including "Summer Nights," "Hopelessly Devoted to You," "Greased Lightning," and the anthem of high school triumph featured during the climax, "We Go Together."

The other movie musical adaptation from the stage was the Milos Forman effort, *Hair*, which in some ways was a far more substantive film than *Grease*, but also, alas, much less successful. It didn't evoke nostalgia, but instead recaptured the turbulence of the hippie era and late 1960s. The film featured brilliant choreography by Twyla Tharp, and dramatized yet another love story about unlikely lovers, this time a society girl (Beverly D'Angelo) and a farm boy (John Savage), who has been drafted to serve in Vietnam. The film's Master of Ceremonies is played by a young Treat Williams, who effortlessly holds the film's center of gravity and is sacrificed in an unhappy finale.

The tunes were just as catchy as those featured in *Grease*, including "Aquarius" and "Let the Sun Shine In," but general audiences were apparently not yet in the mood to revisit recent national traumas like the Vietnam War.

Finally, the 1970s culminated in splendid fashion with *All That Jazz* (1979), an autobiographical musical by Bob Fosse. Roy Scheider of *Jaws* (1975) and *Blue Thunder* (1983) starred as the frazzled and overworked, but brilliant and sensitive choreographer Joe Gideon who is struggling to edit a movie, choreograph a show, and assemble the failed pieces of his personal life, which include a girl-friend, an ex-wife, and his adoring young daughter.

Keith Gordon, now a successful director in Hollywood, was cast in the film as young Joe Gideon, and was on the set for a little more than a week, as opposed to the longer stints he worked on *Dressed to Kill* (1980) and *Christine* (1983). Gordon recollects that Fosse was a director who worked more like a choreographer, instructing the performers with a high level of specificity, down to when in a scene an actor should lift his head or how he should hold his hand.

"He was that sort of person who was the complete controller that you have as a choreographer more than a director of naturalistic modern acting," Gordon reflects. "Most directors work much more from a sense of, 'Well, as long as the feel of the scene is right.' They're not obsessing about each tiny detail. Fosse approached filmmaking like he approached the specifics of the dance. I was absolutely thrilled to do whatever he wanted. Yes, it was micro-management, but I didn't care. If a Bob Fosse or a Stanley Kubrick says, 'This is how I work,' you do it the way they work. If Picasso paints a certain way, that's great, that's how he paints. You don't start questioning it.

"I think *All That Jazz* is one of the great films," Gordon says. "[Working on the film] was also a bit of a creepy experience because I was seventeen years old, practically a virgin, and here I was doing this very sexual scene with three women—one of whom was actually a guy. Another was actually a real stripper and who, I think, was pretty drunk and kept propositioning me between every take. In a way, it was probably good for the scene, [because] I was definitely a little freaked out by the whole thing.

"Fosse was sort of notorious for directing actors by using manipulative tricks to get them in a certain state. He got some amazing performances that way, but sometimes it would be weird to deal with. The thing that he did with me was—in the midst of this—when we were doing the part of the scene where the strippers were molesting me, he came over and said, 'It would be really good if you could actually get hard.' Talk about having a button pushed and having your manhood challenged! I can tell you there's nothing less sexual than having these three rather creepy figures grabbing at you, with a camera pushed up your nose at the time.

"Looking back, years later, I realized that he was trying to get a certain level of panic and upset in me, not really worrying what was sexually going on. As time went by, I heard from other people that this was typical Fosse and vintage Fosse, and he would do that. There was a famous story where he told one actress that her father had died. That he had just heard that. Then they shot the scene and he told her afterwards 'No, I was just telling you that,' and apparently she walked off the set for several days. But also, it was the best work she had ever done on film. He was known for doing that kind of thing."

However Fosse accomplished it, *All that Jazz* emerged as a serious Oscar contender and a modern musical masterpiece. Though Scheider, in an interview on the film's DVD, referred to the plot as "the old familiar" tale of the struggling artist, in this case it was the manner in which Fosse vetted his story that felt so energetic, so electrifying. From Gideon's oft-seen morning ritual—cigarettes, contact lenses, pills, and a shower—to the stunning dance numbers themselves, Fosse edits the film in a sizzling, fast style that reveals the hectic, frenetic pace of this man's life.

The editing in *All That Jazz* seems to be racing against a ticking clock somewhere, and that's an appropriate metaphor for Gideon, who is clearly living on borrowed time, and destined to die after open-heart surgery. Fosse actually took his cameras to film a real cardiac surgery and this footage represents a shocking right turn in the film's narrative style. Actually, the whole film works in that fashion, with surprising pieces and clips folded into a spectacular, exhilarating and diverse whole.

Another scene perfectly captures the anxieties of Joe Gideon, and the skill of Bob Fosse as a director, while exposing his personal lack of confidence. The scene involves a read-through of his latest show, and as always Gideon is nervous that the actors, choreographers and producers won't like what he has created. Fosse artfully dials down the dialogue from this sequence, so that background sound effects become paramount. The audience hears people breathing, the ticking of a clock on the wall as it enters the frame, and other usually unnoticed noises of everyday life. By bringing the volume up on these distractions, and removing the positive response of those conducting the read-through, Fosse reveals to us how Gideon literally can't hear the forest through the trees; can't receive the praise, only fear the criticism.

All That Jazz is self-reflexive, brilliantly dealing with the world of film through movie-centric dialogue such as Gideon's discussion of his life, "This is only a rough cut." There are also allusions to Fosse's previous films, particularly a *Cabaret*-style threesome (though with two women and one man), and even ironic use of tunes like "Bye, Bye Love" and "There's No Business Like Show Business," which illuminate Gideon's life and death as the final curtain call.

The opening sequence, a cattle call audition on stage for Gideon's stage show, is a textbook example of how to successfully edit dance in the modern film idiom. There is an abundance of short cuts which often capture different pieces of some motion, and which, assembled by this genius, puts truth to the long-held belief that spirit and movement can't be captured on film in a collection of tiny pieces. The fact is, there are two ways to shoot dance. Astaire's films do it one way, and Fosse another. Both are brilliant.

"The opening five to seven minutes of *All That Jazz*, the audition scene, is worth all three hours of *A Chorus Line*," suggests Jay Cocks. "And I'll throw in *Dreamgirls* too. It is so brilliant, that opening. It is about the process of theater, the process of selection, and it says it with dance, and says it dramatically. It's just genius.

"You know the moment when Roy Scheider walks up to that dancer and puts his hand on his hip and is thinking whether to cut her or not?" Cocks asks. "And then he looks at her and just shakes his head and smiles? And she smiles back? That's the essence of show business. I've been to a musical audition. On the one hand, if you have that frame of mind, it's hilarious, like *The Producers*. On the other hand, it is so heartbreaking. You just want to curl up into a ball. You cannot help but love actors—pains in the ass though they may be in other ways—for going through something like this time and time again. I just love them for that, and that one moment in *All That Jazz* captures that so brilliantly."

Still, this praise doesn't necessarily mean that Cocks is ready to sign off on the whole enterprise. "*All That Jazz* is fantastic when it's about show business," he considers "but when it's about philosophy it tends to get a little dodgy. It tends to get a little top-heavy, is what I would say."

Referencing everything from *Cabaret* to Fellini's 8½ ("Jessica Lange in a white dress in *All That Jazz* comes from Claudia Cardinale in a white dress," Cocks reminds us), *All That Jazz* is like a synthesis of the 1970s movie musical format. It's brilliant in explosive fits and starts, surprising for a spell, and unceasingly bold and experimental. The totality, as Cocks suggests, may not exceed its individual pieces, but *All That Jazz* reveals that the musical format—at least in the hands of a master like Bob Fosse—indeed had a future.

Much of the 1970s was about experimentation. From *At Long Last Love*, which gazed back, to *The Wiz* (1978), which re-set classical Oz inside the modern, urban wonderland of New York City and featured an African American cast, the musical was in search of those elusive new idioms. Gritty realism found expression in films like Robert Altman's brilliant *Nashville* (1973), but extravagant flourishes and a heightened reality still won the heart and dazzled the eyes in films such as *All That Jazz*.

"For me," notes director Sir Alan Parker with simplicity, "Bob Fosse was the best."

No discussion of cinema in the 1970s would be complete without a mention of George Lucas's watershed space opera, *Star Wars*. A colorful and exciting epic about galactic swashbucklers, the film captured the imagination of America in 1977, and the movie business has never really been the same. From *Star Wars* on, Hollywood cinema has increasingly been concerned with cranking out blockbusters, not the kind of personal films just gaining traction in the sixties and early 1970s.

For all intents and purposes, *Star Wars* was the first real special effects movie of a new age, one in which technicians and their masterful achievements rendered a totally acceptable and hence believable new reality. Giant creatures called Wookies might live on far-flung planets, but to millions of viewers, the costumes and special effects made these and other flourishes, like tractor beams and light sabers, seem so real that the fantasies created by Lucas were gleefully accepted. It was a paradigm shift. The impossible could seem real thanks to prosthetics, motion-control cameras, highly detailed miniatures and the like.

Musicals and the fantasies they encouraged, by contrast, were no longer afforded the same degree of leeway. The musical was a genre not based on new technology or special visual effects, but rather on elements straight from the heart. Like songs. Like the beauty, elegance, and simplicity of dance. Audiences permitted themselves to believe in droids, trash compactor monsters, and TIE fighters, but as soon someone broke into song during a movie, there were titters of disbelief.

In this new world, musicals would find it increasingly difficult to compete with the more technologically driven blockbuster films, and this change in the movie business would have a definite impact on the 1980s and beyond.

HOLDING OUT FOR A HERO: THE 1980s

As the 1980s commenced, it was bombs away at the box office as a series of expensive and formulaic musical flops dotted the pop culture battlefield. Making matters more dire, while these efforts misfired at the box office, a stealth attack was being prepared from the musical format's crafty old nemesis: television.

In 1980, Steve Guttenberg starred in *Can't Stop the Music*, playing a struggling composer whose incredible songs could only be done justice by a new and amazing band called . . . the Village People, which according to this film's story, he formed. *Can't Stop the Music* was a fictionalized account of the band's early days, directed by one-time musical performer Nancy Walker, and it received the some of the worst reviews in film history. The movie won a spate of Razzies (including worst director, worst movie, and worst screenplay) and earned back less than 10 percent of its twenty-million-dollar budget.

Xanadu, starring Olivia Newton-John as a muse named Kira, was much more entertaining, but neither audiences nor critics appreciated Newton-John's musical follow-up to *Grease*. Gene Kelly appeared in the film as one of Kira's old flames, and Michael Beck played Sonny, her new beau who dreams of opening the ultimate night club. Culminating in a roller-skating disco number, *Xanadu* is packed with tunes from Newton-John, including the memorable hit "Magic," but also a bevy of songs from ELO. No, that isn't the name of a terrorist organization, but the very synthetic-sounding Electric Light Orchestra.

Reviewers actively disliked *Xanadu*'s notion of melding 1940s big-band music with disco numbers, and the box office results were poor. Still, the film is considered a camp classic and boasts adherents to this day. Whether one likes it or not depends, perhaps, on the age at which you saw it. For young people who saw it during its original release, it holds a place in the heart not far removed from *Grease*.

And the losers just kept coming.

Grease 2 introduced the world to actress Michelle Pfeiffer in 1982, but that proved small consolation for a lackluster musical that featured neither John Travolta nor Olivia Newton-John. Instead, Patricia Birch's *Grease 2* picks up at Rydell High in 1961, just two years after the events of the original film, and tells the story of new teen loves, Stephanie (Pfeiffer) and Michael (Maxwell Caulfield). The big twist this time is that it's the male who is the clean-cut kid and Stephanie the "greaser."

In a tenuous attempt to link the sequel to the original, Michael happens to be the English cousin of Newton-John's Australian character, Sandy. Though the ads promised that "Grease is still the word," the film was hard-pressed to repeat the incredible business of its 1978 progenitor, which grossed more than three hundred million dollars worldwide. By contrast, *Grease 2* grossed about six million.

Much better than any of these films was Alan Parker's incredible and rousing 1980 effort *Fame*, originally known as "Hot Lunch." Featuring music by Michael Gore (who later worked on Todd Graff's *Camp*), this energetic film is a backstage musical of sorts, with a screenplay by Christopher Gore that revolves around the High School of the Performing Arts in New York City, and the loves and labors of the students who attend. They were there to "make it happen," regarding stardom, and they had to pay their dues "in sweat!"

All the stock "theater" types one had come to expect attended *Fame*'s school, only they were brought up-to-date for the 1980s. There was the dedicated musician, prodigy Bruno (Lee Curreri); shy-girl Doris (Maureen Teefy); proud African American dancer Leroy (Gene Anthony Ray); the token homosexual, Montgomery (Paul McCrane); the haughty ballerina and the singer Coco, played by Irene Cara, who longs to be a star.

Despite such stereotypes, the dynamic film skillfully represented the new realities of the 1980s, including a deeper concentration on realistic teen issues of the time, including drugs and sex. Though some saw the film as over-the-top, especially with its quasi-spontaneous dance numbers spilling over into city streets or threatening the cafeteria, it nonetheless rung true with its target audience.

Fame instantly became the favorite movie of every aspiring teenage dancer and singer in America, and the film was a substantial enough hit to generate a TV series in 1982 that saw Curreri and Ray stay back as students, and Debbie Allen and Albert Hague return in their roles as instructors. The series was a big hit too and lasted for five seasons before cancellation. There have also been several stage adaptations of the film though, one hastens to add, without the input or consent of Sir Alan Parker.

"I know we started a fashion in leg warmers around the world," notes Parker. "It's interesting that *Fame*-type schools have opened all over the world. The film was about the flip side of the American dream. It was as much about failure as success. The TV series made me puke, but it was a big hit in sixty odd countries in syndicated television. I tried to make the music come out of the dramatic situations."

"I love that movie," states Todd Graff, who counts *Fame* among his inspirations for the movie, *Camp*. "And when I rewatched it after not having seen it for a long time, I realized it was grittier than I remembered . . . one character gets an abortion, one character gets sexually exploited, [and] one is gay. It had all kinds of stuff in it, and that was really inspiring more than anything else. That within this fun musical I was trying to make [*Camp*], I could still make the kids have real issues and deal with their sexuality, their body issues, and stuff that they were able to do so well in *Fame*.

"I dug that film when it came out," remembers Todd Haynes. "It's also a kind of preposterous, crazy movie, with these outrageously talented kids leaping [around]. It's interesting when the musical decided to combine an element of grittiness with the surreal nature of the musical form. There are other examples of that. *West Side Story*, at the time, seemed kind of gritty because it was on location. Just to start shooting musicals on location was a different direction than the past, and *Fame* is in that tradition, but there is an element where it's kind of funny, because they're trying to bring naturalism into something that you can't make natural."

In 1981, American audiences got their first taste of British playwright Dennis Potter's most challenging, satirical material in the Steve Martin musical vehicle *Pennies from Heaven*. Produced by MGM, the film was an expensive remake of a TV program on the BBC, but the story remained the same.

This is the odyssey of a sheet music salesman named Arthur Parker (Martin), a man who feels "empty" inside, and fills his head with the happy tunes of his time, Chicago of 1934. Saddled with an unhappy marriage to a frigid, repressed woman, Joanie (Jessica Harper), Arthur seeks sexual comfort while on the road, hooking up with a shy teacher named Eileen, played by the Broadway musical star Bernadette Peters.

Arthur abandons Eileen to run his own record store back at home, but she is desperate, now pregnant with his child. With few alternatives, she becomes a prostitute called "Lulu" and seeks help from a pimp, played by Christopher Walken, in acquiring an abortion. Everything ends badly when Arthur is arrested and hanged for the murder of a blind girl he encountered once, even though the real culprit is actually "The Accordian Man," a hobo he bought dinner for on a single occasion.

Despite being made in the 1980s, *Pennies from Heaven* is one of the truly great, classic Hollywood musicals. The costumes by Bob Mackie and sets by Ken Adam accurately evoke the age of the Great Depression, and the musical numbers employ everything from Busby Berkeley high-angles to thirties-style flourishes like wipes, and the iris in/iris out. But it is for the use of thirties tunes, all lip-synched by the actors, that this film remains so powerful. It is constantly ironic, playing the upbeat, out-of-date music as direct contrast to the events in Arthur's life.

When Arthur visits a bank to get a loan and is refused with an emphatic "no," he immediately jumps into a number, "Yes, Yes," wherein he is inundated with cash bags and silver coins. This tune and others tell him how life *should* be. "Songs tell the truth," Arthur insists. But do they really? The film answers that question by creating a dichotomy between dusty-brown Midwest highways and, in the "Pennies from Heaven" number, glittering coins of gold and silver. To quote former vice presidential candidate John Edwards, it's really "two Americas."

The movie features other joys, including the climax, wherein Martin and Peters step into the shoes of Astaire and Rogers in a stunningly accurate re-creation of *Follow the Fleet* (1936). Christopher Walken also tap dances his way through Cole Porter's "Let's Misbehave" in expert fashion. What's a pleasure about all these numbers is that director Herbert Ross has selected not merely the music of the thirties, but the filming style too, relying on long master shots, and not cutting into the dances every five seconds. As a result, Martin and Walken in particular are revealed to be incredible dance talents with tremendous dexterity and powerful physical presence.

Shot with style to spare by cinematographer Gordon Willis, *Pennies from Heaven* is another example of an experimental musical, and therefore one that may have been better made in the 1970s. It challenges the precepts of what a musical can achieve, and doesn't shy away from evoking unhappy or ambivalent feelings in the audience. The soundtrack may be determinedly (and relentlessly) upbeat, but in the mouths of these lost, confused characters, the tunes play as devastating counterpoint. Perhaps not surprisingly, the film bombed at the box office, though it won over many critics.

"In America, the bad people have to do the bad things," Dennis Potter said of the film in 1988. "And the good people have to do the good things and [the viewers] couldn't deal with Steve Martin doing bad things."[22] In other words, *Pennies from Heaven* didn't live up to the popular perception of movie musicals as happy, lightweight, and ultimately free of troubling ideas.

"It's just a great film," describes James Lyons. "Steve Martin is wonderful in it. It's a very good example of how you can use music, and the most corn ball, melodramatic feelings that someone has, and use them for what they honestly are, and then put them on a landscape of what life honestly is. That's a great movie, and it's totally underappreciated."

"I think *Pennies from Heaven* is one of the most important musicals ever made," agrees Joss Whedon. "It's incredibly underrated. The heart of this is in the songs. It's so much about what people can't express, and how they look to a musical world to solve their problems when they can't even live through this one."

The year 1982 brought something completely different, thanks again to Sir Alan Parker. It was this year that one of the strangest, most impressionistic musicals was released: *Pink Floyd: The Wall*. Advertised with the tagline "The Memories. The Madness. The Music. The Movie . . . ," this feature concerned just about everything, from creativity, drugs, the music business to totalitarianism. It starred Bob Geldof as a strange cat named Pink, and his odd, psychologically fragile existence was punctuated by a terrific, pounding sound track from Pink Floyd's Roger Waters.

In *Pink Floyd: The Wall*, the music and the images told a dazzling, almost psychedelic story with an expressionistic narrative, and it pointed precisely to the genre's stylistic future. It was much more than a music video, but it pioneered many of the shots and flourishes that would become *de rigueur* in that form.

"*Pink Floyd: The Wall* has become a cult movie," Parker acknowledges. "It was very different from my other films. All the music was recorded—they'd sold eleven million albums already. In a way, it's an experiment in cinematic language. The parameters were never set, and creatively, that can be a wonderful freedom. The whole film was like the image of Bob Geldof lying amongst the debris of his trashed room: the pieces put back together to create a weird and wonderful work of art.

"To be honest, we made it up as we went along. Day by day and shot by shot. I don't mean that in a disparaging way, because it was a very creative environment, and more than a touch anarchic, considering the dollar bills being burned. The challenge was to tell a story with just music and images."

A much more traditional musical arrived in 1983, and was set back in 1934 like *Pennies from Heaven*, the sexual identity comedy *Victor/Victoria* starring Julie Andrews, Robert Preston, Lesley Ann Warren, and James Garner. It is the tale of a female singer, Vicki (Andrews) who pretends to be a female impersonator at a Parisian nightclub.

Mistaken identities abound as both men and women seek to demonstrate affection towards the hapless lass. Henry Mancini wrote the tunes and Leslie Bricusse provided lyrics. The film was an amusing farce that captured the attention of Oscar with numerous nominations, including one for Julie Andrews for Best Actress. Oddly, this sexual identity story arrived right around the same time as another, the nonmusical Dustin Hoffman vehicle, *Tootsie* (1982).

The summer of 1982 also saw proof positive that musicals were no longer strong competitors in the marketplace. While audiences thrilled to *E.T.*, *Poltergeist, Firefox,* and *Star Trek II: The Wrath of Khan*, they stayed away from the film adaptation of the play *Annie*, a fifty-million-dollar production. The story of this orphan living in the Depression starred Albert Finney as Daddy Warbucks and Aileen Quinn as the redheaded sprite. The picture was directed by the late, great John Huston, who was roundly criticized in many circles for his direction that some regarded as leaden.

That was also the criticism lobbed at Richard Attenborough's 1985 feature, *A Chorus Line*, starring Michael Douglas. Another stage-to-screen adaptation, this big budget feature was based on the hugely popular 1975 Broadway show that ran for fifteen years. The film was an expensive purchase for Universal— nearly six million dollars—but director Attenborough's studied approach was perhaps too grounded in reality to please the critics. Slow-paced and lugubrious, the film won few fans or admirers.

The next year saw the release of another big-budget musical stage-to-screen adaptation, the twenty-five-million-dollar effort, *Little Shop of Horrors* (1986). Based on an Off-Broadway show (which in turn was based on a low-budget 1960 Roger Corman film), the property is a horror movie spoof concerning a loser named Seymour (Rick Moranis) who befriends, if that's the correct word, a monstrous, maneating plant named Audrey II (after his girlfriend played by Ellen Greene) at Mushnik's Flower Shop.

Steve Martin appears in a delightful cameo as Orin, a sadist/dentist, and Bill Murray makes for a memorable patient/masochist. The songs from Howard Ashman and Alan Menken, a staple of Disney animated musicals in the nineties, are nothing less than extraordinary. Directed by Frank Oz during a year-long shoot at Pinewood Studios in England, the film bucked the trends of the eighties, as one of its producers William S. Gilmore described to *Cinefantastique*:

Here we have an old-fashioned book musical in the traditional sense with fourteen visual vocalists singing on screen . . . I know this type of film is out of vogue, but essentially, it's the music and lyrics that tell the whole story. Unfortunately, modern day kids think a musical means a film like *Flashdance* or *Footloose*.[23]

Little Shop of Horrors garnered terrific reviews, but like other musicals of the eighties wherein people actually sang (rather than just danced to rock tunes), the film was a flop. Instead, it was the "other" kind of musical, the ones that Gilmore described, that were the successes of the decade.

While the 1980s saw very few winning musical films in the traditional break-out-into-song opera style, matters were actually more dire even than that. A new player entered the entertainment arena in August 1981 and, thanks to the proliferation of cable TV access in the U.S. over the next few years, was soon reaching a large and engaged demographic.

MTV—the first music network—was born. The inaugural video the new station aired was, appropriately, "Video Killed the Radio Star" by the Buggles, and that was just the beginning of the assault. Very soon, MTV popularized the new medium of music videos, or "clips" as they are sometimes termed. The new musical stars of the 1980s, from Duran Duran to Michael Jackson to Madonna, had no need to develop exciting new musical film properties to show off their skills, but could instead rely on the video format and free air time too. This resulted in changes to the music and film industries still being felt today.

Almost immediately upon MTV's birth, there were complaints from social critics that the network catered mainly to the attention-impaired with its three-minute music videos. Film historians worried that MTV was ransacking the imagery of the musical film and leaving that genre dead in its wake. Still, there were opposing voices who believed that the ascent of MTV could only be a good thing, as the network was resurrecting the notion of song and dance fused in a thematic storytelling device, albeit a very short one.

"I think both of those things are true," suggests James Lyons. "That's how it always is with art. Stuff gets ransacked, and the sacred art gets torn down and ripped apart, and used for different things. A genre gets codified, and then as soon as it is codified, people want to fuck it up and screw around with it."

"I did *Pink Floyd: The Wall* before the advent of the music video, and I wish I had a dollar for every shot I've seen stolen on MTV," laments Sir Alan Parker.

"MTV *has* stolen everything," Lyons emphasizes. "Every single, strong stylistic device that has come up in the history of movies is being plundered, and maybe that's how it should be. But . . . the way to understand MTV is through the history of advertising. The techniques developed in advertising were applied to making musical sequences, which before were only done in films. All those techniques that people are angry about come from a *commercial* background. This is how they sell stuff. It's attested to in the market place."

Not that Lyons is judging MTV as either a good or bad thing. "All forms can be good," he suggests, "and all forms can be used for evil."

Joss Whedon doesn't believe MTV should be used as the scapegoat for why musicals are unpopular. "MTV has little skits all the time," he reminds us. "People are now more used to seeing people singing songs they listen to than they ever have been in the history of music because of MTV. And yet people say audiences won't accept people bursting into song. It's because they think of it as an inherently hokey paradigm. They're thinking about a particular kind of music and they're thinking about a particular kind of filmmaking. The fact of the matter is, if the music speaks to people and the moment is right and every-thing comes together in the right way, they'll accept it completely. They accepted *Chicago*, [though] it had a conceit that things were happening in Renée Zellweger's mind, and some of it was onstage.

"On *Buffy*, I cheated. I used the in of 'Isn't it weird when people break into song?' which is great fun, and was an easy way for me to let the audience feel comfortable. You have to find your way to do that, and it's definitely possible, and it's different for every movie," Whedon suggests. In other words, we're back once more to Craig Pearce's notion of the contract with the audience, the deal that makes a musical acceptable to the masses.

It wasn't long after the rise of MTV in America that Hollywood musicals morphed once more. The stories tended to be similar: the backstage musical, or the tale of the dance contest, but now the musical numbers were framed in a much different, more aggressive fashion. There was quicker cutting, more dynamic, overtly stylistic angles, and less concentration on seeing the human form in its entirety, or in motion. In fairness, this had also been the style of Bob Fosse in films including *All That Jazz* in 1979, so perhaps it is unfair to pin this trend on MTV. And besides, this style isn't necessarily bad or inferior, merely different.

One of the first films to capitalize on the MTV-ization of the culture was Adrian Lyne's *Flashdance*, which premiered on Tax Day in April 1983 with the ad line "What a Feeling." From a screenplay by Joe Eszterhas and Tom Hedley, Lyne fashioned a modern day fairy tale (aimed directly at teenage girls) filled with sound and fury—and energy.

Flashdance tells the high-voltage tale of a welder by day, exotic dancer by night (played by Jennifer Beals), who desires to attend a prestigious ballet school and also hook-up with Mr. Right in the person of Michael Nouri. In plain description, with a few tweaks, this could be the plot of *The Red Shoes*, or any "star is born"–type film, wherein a protagonist fights big odds to achieve a dream.

However, *Flashdance* is a little different from the old razzle-dazzle. For one thing, it is more frankly sexual than any old-fashioned Hollywood film. One number, "He's a Dream," involves a dancer dousing herself in water onstage, while not wearing much. For another thing, the musical numbers are shot and edited like videos with a distinct beginning, middle, and end, accompanied by a pop soundtrack. These video moments are dazzling, brilliantly cut, and fast-paced, but they embody the spirit of dance in a new way, less about the body as a whole, or even skill, than about the fitness and sexuality of the dancer.

Again, it ain't bad, just different. Though a twitchy Paramount reportedly sold something like a quarter of its stake in *Flashdance* before the film's release, it nonetheless went on to become a monster hit. The soundtrack sold more than five hundred thousand copies in the first two weeks of release, the film's musical numbers (especially the one with water . . .) were parodied endlessly, and Jennifer Beals's casual fashions in the film, including a ripped sweatshirt, became required gear for a generation of teens.

In 2003, twenty years after *Flashdance*, Jennifer Lopez shot a video for her song "I'm Glad" that re-created shot-for-shot, in almost fetishistic fashion, the climactic audition dance from *Flashdance*, succinctly pointing out that, to this generation at least, the film does stand shoulder-to-shoulder with the likes of *Swing Time* or *Singin' in the Rain* or other classics. The old guard may not appreciate that assessment, but there's more than one way to skin a cat, and the name of the game in crafting movie musicals is discovering the new idioms, the new vernacular. *Flashdance* accomplished precisely that feat. No need to be a snob about it.

"*Flashdance* is really of its time," Craig Pearce considers. "Again, you find that successful musicals are generally about really simple, mythical big ideas, and *Flashdance* is an 'overcoming impossible odds' story in many ways. I remember it was one of those films where I thought ahead of time, 'This is going to be crappy.' But it's well-made and because of that you get caught up in the story. I remember really enjoying it when I saw it as a kid."

An extension of *Saturday Night Fever* and the dance musical format, *Flashdance*, with a little inspiration from the MTV ethos, dominated the direction of the decade's remaining years. *Footloose*, another dance musical starring Kevin Bacon followed promptly in 1984. As did *Breakin'*, a film concerning street break dancers struggling to make it big.

As late as 1987 and the nostalgic hit *Dirty Dancing*, starring Patrick Swayze and Jennifer Grey, the formula was firmly cemented. Find two attractive stars; add great soundtrack; include lots of sexy dancing. Stir together and whammo, you've got a hit.

The problem wasn't that the dance musicals were bad. Indeed, most of them (from *Saturday Night Fever* through *Dirty Dancing*) are loads of fun, but their dominance in the latter part of the 1980s moved the emphasis in the musical away from the form it had taken for decades.

"Those movies are of their time," declares Joss Whedon. "They're touching on something I care about [dance], but it's not like *Footloose* is good. Kevin Bacon can't dance. And I get crabby about that. Those movies have a place . . . but it ain't my place. The best filmed musical numbers in terms of dance that I can remember seeing in a long while are in *White Knights* (1985), and that's a very silly movie, and quite long. But the opening is gorgeously filmed and stunning to look at," Whedon considers. "But you have to wade through two hours of anti-Russian politics to get there."

Where had the old fashioned musicals gone? The ones where the characters didn't just dance to Top 40 hits, but also belted out their deepest feelings, dreams and desires in song? Alas, audiences no longer sought that connection with the sound of music.

Indeed, very few musical stars were born in the 1980s cinema, because what *Flashdance* and its ilk proved rather dramatically was that dancers were no more than stunt doubles for the lead performers. Because the human form was only being depicted in pieces and quick cuts—a split here, an elbow there—the important body part could belong to anyone. Fred Astaire, Gene Kelly, and others became stars because viewers could actually *connect* to them and their feats; could actually *observe* them doing the hard work and making it look so magnificent. In the 1980s, the actors were only needed for their sweaty close-ups, and so anybody could have played those roles. Sleight of hand in the editing room had replaced physical achievement on the set. The only people who were achieving something miraculous were the film editors.

In this shift to a time when, to paraphrase Ginger Rogers, the young people tried to dance with their faces, a gentle and sweet genre inevitably suffered.

And a Hollywood tradition faded.

THAT'S ENTERTAINMENT!

The multidecade history of the musical reveals how the genre has always been inexorably tied to changes and influences in the culture. Musicals began when the silent era ended, and were part-and-parcel of the new "talkie" film revolution in the twenties. Movie musicals soothed a nation in distress during the Great Depression and World War II. When America became a dominant world power after the Second World War, the format blossomed into glorious color.

More than that, the Eisenhower era of prosperity lent itself to a renaissance, to an age of true cinematic artistry—a blend of distinct schools like comedy and dance—and this was reflected in the Minnelli and Donen-Kelly pictures from MGM. The musicals of the 1960s like *West Side Story* and *The Sound of Music*, while remaining true to their grand heritage, began to accommodate the ethos of a more realistic, more personal cinema with authentic locations instead of studio back lots and painted backdrops.

In the seventies, the modern age overtook the musical, and the format responded with films that were challenging, experimental and funny. Bob Fosse, Lindsay Anderson, Peter Bogdonovich, and others sought to preserve the essential format of the song-and-dance show, while making their films more realistic, more daring, and even topical.

Finally the 1980s, post–*Star Wars*, represented the beginning of the blockbuster era when book musicals couldn't compete. The rise of MTV, love it or hate it, again provided the movie musical a new format to first compete against and then emulate. In line with the increasing tendency in film towards realism and naturalism, fewer and fewer films were willing to break into song.

And then came the 1990s.

CHAPTER TWO
The Razzle-Dazzle Fizzles?

The Early Nineties

As the Reagan era became the Bush I era in the late 1980s, the movie musical was a format in free fall. In the mid-1980s, even the ever-dependable Disney Studios had abandoned musicals, creating its first PG animated feature with no songs whatsoever, the dark fantasy epic *The Black Cauldron* (1985). The film was a tremendous failure, grossing only twenty million dollars in release, less than half its budget.

However, by 1988, Disney got back on track in a clever way. The mid-to-late-1980s was a time punctuated by a string of excessively violent and adult action-hero films like *Rambo III* (1987) and *Cobra* (1987), and many moviegoers in America started complaining about the dearth of family films populating the local multiplexes. With the election of George Bush Sr. and his conservative vice president, Dan Quayle, "family values" were again at the forefront of pop culture discussions, and in 1989 Disney reestablished its musical dynasty with *The Little Mermaid*, a picture that cost ten million to make, raked in over two-hundred million, and won Oscars for its composers, Alan Menken and Howard Ashman. Menken's score was a winner, and so was their song "Under the Sea."

You could almost sense the nation at large sighing with relief. Parents finally felt confident taking the kids to the movies again, the film was witty enough for the adults to stay tuned, and the flick made serious dough. Everybody emerged a winner.

Almost immediately, Disney revved up with a series of similar initiatives, including *Beauty and the Beast* (1991) and *Aladdin* (1992), both featuring award-winning scores from Menken. By 1994, the formula was set in stone and *The Lion King* (with score by Elton John and lyrics by Tim Rice) perfected the formula. *The Lion King* grossed nearly eight hundred million dollars, and that impressive figure didn't even account for all the receipts from sales of plush Nala and Simba toys.

Each of these Disney endeavors represented wonderful heartfelt entertainment, filled with singing and dancing little creatures (like the undersea denizens of Ariel's world in *A Little Mermaid*), yet it quickly became accepted wisdom in Hollywood that the only movie musicals which could succeed in the market-place had to be cartoons aimed at the kiddies and filled with monsters and other fanciful figures. The era of the fantasy musical was once again upon the world, and longtime musical fans were glad to cheer the wonderful Disney efforts, even though many lamented the absence of live-action pieces.

In 1991, it was Bette Midler, ingenue of 1979's *The Rose*, who accepted the challenge of creating a new live-action, backstage-style musical entitled *For the Boys*. Produced by her All Girl Productions company, the film recounted the story of entertainer Dixie Leonard (Midler) and her costar on stage, snappy Eddie Sparks (James Caan). This duo fought, laughed, and cried together as USO entertainers for forty years, through World War II, the Korean War, and Vietnam.

For the Boys was a melodrama filled with great musical set pieces from vari-ous decades in American history, including "Billy-a-Dick," "For All We Know," the Lennon-McCartney tune "In My Life," and Diane Warren's "Every Road Leads Back to You." Directed by Mark Rydell, the period musical resembled the life story of Bob Hope and Martha Raye (who allegedly threatened to sue . . .) and was rated R for some of its more adult moments. The then-king of musi-cals, Disney, passed on the project, leaving Fox to finance the film for a stagger-ing forty-million-dollar price tag.

Shot at the Citadel in South Carolina and in Los Angeles, *For the Boys* was a big gamble and represented something of an epic, the sort of Hollywood "event" film that isn't frequently made anymore. Advertised with the slogan "Laughter and Tears. Triumph and Tragedy. They Lived It All. For the Boys," the musical drama opened on thirteen hundred screens the weekend of November 22, 1991.

Disappointingly, *For the Boys* grossed only six million dollars during its opening weekend, the long Thanksgiving holiday. And even as Midler picked up accolades (including a Golden Globe Award and an Oscar nomination), the film failed to attract large audiences, eventually grossing less than twenty million dollars against its investment.

Overlong at two hours and forty minutes, the problem was that the film's (admittedly fine) music just didn't appeal to young audiences. A survey showed that only 15 percent of ticket buyers on opening weekend were under age twenty-five.[1] Film executives, who prize the under twenty-five demographic above all, widely concluded that a movie musical, even one with tremendous production values and headlined by a star, couldn't necessarily cut it in the 1990s.

Despite the commercial failure, *For the Boys* is no embarrassment. As always, Midler is terrific, and the film itself is a sprawling and supremely entertaining motion picture in the classic Hollywood school known as *melodrama*. It is corny, oversentimental, and pompous at times (in the same manner as such recent Oscar nominees as *Seabiscuit* [2003] and *A Beautiful Mind* [2001]), but in the final analysis, a somewhat touching film.

Next from the gate was another lavish live-action musical called *Newsies*, this one from Disney Studios and featuring songs once more by the amazing Alan Menken. Directed by choreographer Kenny Ortega (*Dirty Dancing* [1987]) and written by Bob Tzudiker and Noni White, the film starred eighteen-year-old Christian Bale and a bevy of adolescent boys, including Gabriel Damon and Max Casella, as put-upon newspaper carriers in 1899 New York who are forced to go on strike when their boss, legendary newspaperman Joseph Pulitzer (Robert Duvall), attempts to cut their take by a tenth-of-a-cent.

Ann-Margret played the newsies' confidante, a dance-hall madame, and Michael Lerner portrayed a villainous circulation manager. The songs in the film included the anthem "Carrying the Banner," "Seize the Day," "My Lovey-Dovey Baby," "Strike Action," and "Santa Fe."

Like *For the Boys*, *Newsies* was not some fly-by-night operation, but rather a big budget effort with outstanding production values. Described in the press as an "American *Oliver*"[2] and advertised with copy that read "A Thousand Voices. A Single Dream," *Newsies* cost twenty-five million to produce, and, if nothing else, that investment was certainly up there on the screen. Production designer William Sandell gloriously re-created turn-of-the-century New York using three different studios, including Universal's New York street set,[3] and the kids starring in the film were well prepped for their routines after attending a rigorous ten-week dancing and martial arts boot camp.[4]

Although a pre–*Batman Begins* Christian Bale was apparently wary of singing and dancing and reported that, "in general," he didn't "like musicals," he nonetheless did a fine job in the leading role, in no small part because of the boot camp's "severe" rehearsals.[5]

Unlike *For the Boys*, which had pretty much limited the musical numbers to onstage renditions by the main characters (uso singers entertaining the troops), *Newsies* delved whole hog into the book musical tradition, featuring moments where characters stopped chatting and sprung forth joyfully into song and dance. Heralded as an old-fashioned musical, the film was promptly labeled "risky" by the *Wall Street Journal* and Michael Patrick, president of the Carmike Cinemas chain announced the terrain of the battle: "Anybody that's playing a musical has an uphill battle ahead of them."[6]

As it turned out, Disney had ample reason for concern. When *Newsies* was released in early April of 1992, it fared worse than even *For the Boys*. Although Disney resorted to previewing the film with free showings of *Beauty and the Beast*, *Newsies* very quickly emerged as the lowest grossing live-action movie in Walt Disney Studios' history.

At the box office, *Newsies* suffered from the bluesies. It grossed less than three million dollars against its considerable budget, and the critics were quite unsympathetic. "No *Newsies* is good newsies,"[7] quipped Ralph Novak for *People*, and *Entertainment Weekly's* Owen Gleiberman wrote that "the movie stands as a text demonstration of 'why they don't—and probably shouldn't—make 'em like they used to.'"[8] Writing for the *Chicago Sun-Times*, Roger Ebert awarded the film only one-and-a-half stars out of a possible four.

"We saw it in the theater, okay?" Joss Whedon admits. "We were among the ten. At that point I was working for Disney. I think the greatest musicals—with the exception of *South Park*—that have come out of the American cinema in the last ten or twenty years have all been Disney musicals. Menken and Ashman were like gods to me, so I went to see *Newsies*. What it did right is very simply the idea. There are some songs in there that aren't bad, actually. If you listen to the score, you forget why you hated the film, and then you watch it again and go, 'Oh yeah, right.' And what it did wrong is almost everything else. It's not well directed, and it's kind of crappy in a lot of ways. It's not believable.

"But the idea of an actual historical event, the newsies strike at the turn of the century, is a perfect idea for a musical," Whedon contends. "It makes sense, but people forget that directing a musical is the single hardest directing there is. Directing a movie—which is something that almost no one can do well—requires at least some basic understanding of every kind of skill. You have to have some feeling for everything you're putting on the screen, or be brilliant at hiring people who do. With musicals, the things you have to understand just doubles. It's a really hard thing to pull off. It [*Newsies*] had a first-time director, [and] the script was a little all over the place. [But] it's not irredeemable."

The twin failures of *For the Boys* and *Newsies* in two years seem like more than plenty to sour any studio on big budget musicals, but lo! and behold, in

1993 came along another quasi-musical production of considerable expense, entitled *Swing Kids*.

Starring Christian Bale (again!) as an impressionable lad named Thomas, and Robert Sean Leonard—the actor with three first names—as the rebellious son of a deceased Nazi resistor, *Swing Kids* was a dance musical in the tradition of *Saturday Night Fever, Flashdance, Footloose, and Dirty Dancing*. But it dramatized a serious story against the backdrop of near-constant music, and importantly, dance. *

In this case, *Swing Kids* concerned a group of boisterous German teenagers who were aficionados of American jazz in Hamburg during the Nazi regime of the 1930s and 1940s. Known as "Swing Kids," these adolescent agitators allegedly numbered in the hundreds and were inspired by Hollywood movies of the era like *Born to Dance* (1936) and *The Broadway Melody* (1929).

According to historian Michael Kater, author of the book *Different Drummers: Jazz in the Culture of Nazi Germany*, the swing boys "wore long hair and custom-tailored suits, and carried rolled umbrellas for a British flair," while the girls sported "short skirts and silk stockings."[9] The adults in *Swing Kids* were represented in the film by Barbara Hershey as Leonard's sympathetic mother, and a thoroughly evil (and charming) Kenneth Branagh as a gestapo officer with an unseemly interest in Hershey, and therefore her rebellious children.

Swing Kids filmed in the Czech Republic, in Prague, during freezing temperatures in 1992. Thomas Carter, who later helmed the hit Julia Stiles flick *Save the Last Dance* (2001), directed the picture from a screenplay by Jonathan Marc Feldman. Advertised with the tagline, "In a world on the brink of war, you either march to one tune or dance to another," *Swing Kids* opened in March 1993 and promptly bombed, never grossing more than six million dollars.

Critics didn't much care for the film either, with Leah Rozen of *People* magazine noting that the film often resembled "little more than Hamburg 90210."[10] *Entertainment Weekly* was more caustic, questioning why on earth *Swing Kids* was made in the first place.[11]

Of all the early nineties attempts to revive the movie musical, *Swing Kids* remains perhaps the most objectionable, given the serious nature of its tale. The film failed, in part, because it played uncomfortably like a more dramatic version of Kevin Bacon's *Footloose*, only with kids battling Nazis rather than restrictive parents and John Lithgow's repressive, right-wing reverend.

Swing Kids was also woefully heavy-handed in its approach. This was nowhere more obvious than during the film's climactic scene, wherein swing kid

Robert Sean Leonard is beaten up by his former friend played by Christian Bale, now transformed into a Nazi Brownshirt. As Bale's vicious blows land on the wounded Leonard, director Carter cuts down to our hero's feet, and we see them triumphantly mimic the fancy footwork of swing. It's a ridiculous and overblown coupling of images, violence and music, and one that overemphasizes the film's main point that even physical force cannot supersede the freedom of self-expression.

It doesn't help that this valedictory moment is followed immediately by the film's ostensible resolution, as Leonard is hauled away to a concentration camp and his little brother—now taking up the worthy cause—shouts victoriously and encouragingly after him, "*Swing Heil!!!*" Alas, this is a place where a little subtlety might have been in order, but instead the film just hammers obvious points (repression = bad; freedom = good) in such creaky solemnity that it seems laughable.

Another moment in *Swing Kids* is perhaps too ambiguous. Leonard, Bale, and another friend race to the rescue of a swing kid being attacked by a Nazi, only to discover he is a Jew. The swing kids then express anger about the fact they made a mistake. The film thus raises the specter of prejudice in an awkward manner and just leaves it floating there in the atmosphere. Were the swing kids willing to accept the exploitation and abuse of the Jews, so long as they had their beloved music and hip fashion? This weird moment, like so many others, works against the film's overall purpose, and reduces the Hamburg swing resistance to just another adolescent cry of defiance.

Swing Kids was most effective as an entertainment, and as a musical, when the director cut loose with the music, most often in the Bismarck Club where the kids danced. Carter's camera prowls the dance floor with penetrating, panning cameras, and the wild dance steps it records reveal a frenzy and wildness that feels gravity-defying. The jazz music is fun to listen to, the swing moves are athletic and never less than astonishing, and indeed, a new swing craze swept the nation in 1998 thanks to Gap jeans commercials and bands like Cherry Poppin' Daddies and Squirrel Nut Zippers. However, that fad came five years too late to be of benefit to the ham-fisted *Swing Kids*.

"Hey, Swing Heil, buddy!" Joss Whedon salutes. "For my thirtieth birthday, my wife made a swing to put in our yard, and on the bottom is painted 'Swing Heil' as a joke, because we both laughed so hard [in *Swing Kids*.] But you know, I loved what there was to love about *Swing Kids*. The juxtaposition of

The classic Hollywood movie musical at its apex: The poster for *An American in Paris*, trumpeting Technicolor and stars Gene Kelly and Leslie Caron.

An American in Paris (1951)

BELOW Gene Kelly—the Jackie Chan of the 1950s and a movie musical icon—faces a deluge of umbrellas in a publicity shot from one of the ten best movies ever made, *Singin' in the Rain*.

Singin' in the Rain (1952)

OPPOSITE PAGE

TOP Oh What a Beautiful Mornin': A cowboy named Curly (Gordon MacRae) croons to his prospective lady love, Laurey (Shirley Jones), in the Rodgers and Hammerstein movie adaptation *Oklahoma!*

BOTTOM "Do you make love all the time?" Gaston (Louis Jordan) and Gigi (Leslie Caron) connect in *Gigi*, the colorful end of the Arthur Freed era, shot on location in Paris.

Oklahoma! (1955)

Gigi (1958)

BELOW Practically perfect in every way, it's Julie Andrews—the musical star of the more naturalistic 1960s—testing for her role in Robert Wise's *The Sound of Music*.

OPPOSITE PAGE One lady from the Kit-Kat Club: Liza Minnelli is Sally Bowles in Bob Fosse's dark-minded *Cabaret*.

LADIES
WARDROBE
PICTURE G-09 Date 4-8-64
TITLE SOUND OF MUSIC
DIRECTOR R. WISE
ACTRESS JULIE ANDREWS
PART OF MARIA
CHANGE No. 10
EXt. TERRACE
INT. BALLROOM
"SO LONG
FAREWELL"
SCENE No. 47
Designer DOROTHY JEAKINS x10

The Sound of Music (1965)

Cabaret (1972)

For the Boys (1991)

ABOVE For the birds or *For the Boys*?
Eddie (James Caan) and Dixie
(Bette Midler) entertain the troops
in the expensive 1991 misfire.

OPPOSITE PAGE

TOP Got the bluesies? Try *Newsies*.
That's future Batman Christian
Bale (center) strutting his stuff.

BOTTOM Swing Heil: Even though
Nazis are on the march, German
teenager Thomas (Robert Sean
Leonard) just wants to dance to
American jazz in *Swing Kids*.

Newsies (1992)

Swing Kids (1993)

I'll Do Anything (1994)

ABOVE Song-and-dance men who neither sing nor dance: Struggling actor Matt Hobbs (Nick Nolte) and cynical movie producer Burke Adler (Albert Brooks) star in the movie musical without music, *I'll Do Anything*.

those guys and their form of rebellion and dancing in Germany worked great, but the movie didn't work at all."

FAR FROM HOLLYWOOD

Ironically, the most interesting movie musicals of the period from 1991 to 1993 were made far, far away from Hollywood, and on a minuscule budget to boot.

In 1991, the fledgling decade had seen another hit from Sir Alan Parker, whose reputation with movie musicals was rapidly becoming unimpeachable. This time out, the vet directed a backstage musical-type venture involving a populist Irish rock band in Dublin. The film was called *The Commitments*, which was also the name of the world's hardest working band, as featured in the movie. A rollicking blend of rock music and family drama that earned an Oscar nomination for best editing (for Gerry Hambling) and a Golden Globe nomination for best picture, *The Commitments* was great fun that featured songs including "Mustang Sally," "Chain of Fools," and "In the Midnight Hour."

"I saw *The Commitments* as a dramatic film first and foremost—that was about music," Parker describes. "We approached the music very differently to *Evita*. Because the Commitments were singing directly into a visible microphone, we were able to shoot all the vocals live. Firstly, we laid down the basic tracks for the twenty-four chosen performed songs. We used a new system for shooting and recording the music, which had never been used before on film.

"Most film music from *Singin' in the Rain* to MTV uses prerecorded tracks and vocals which are played back as the camera takes up different positions with the artists miming," he explains. "I wanted to capture the reality of the rehearsals and performing by recording the vocals live onset. This is very difficult, as modern film requires different angles to be covered and a constant soundtrack is needed in order for the finished, edited scene to match cut-by-cut.

"We used a new system of out-of-phase speakers which enables us to play the prerecorded constant backing tracks at maximum volume onset to give us a live performance atmosphere for the vocalists to sing to. Each vocal was then recorded live onto a twenty-four track recorder that was onset with us. Because of the out-of-phase speakers, the vocals could be recorded cleanly, as they were filmed for remixing later. This allowed us the technical precision needed for a complicated cut, but gave us the truth, energy and spirit of a live performance. It also enabled us to interweave dramatic dialogue with songs. Again we were only able to do this because they were singing directly into visible micro-phones."

Another independently produced success story came from a director whose name would one day be associated with the musical genre because of *Moulin Rouge*. In 1992, Baz Luhrmann directed *Strictly Ballroom*, the first of his Red Curtain trilogy, and a tale, not unlike *Flashdance* or *Saturday Night Fever*, about a guy who just has to dance. Based in part of Luhrmann's own experiences in the apparently cutthroat and highly dogmatic world of Australian ballroom dancing, *Strictly Ballroom* emerged out of an amateur production Lurhmann had staged a decade before making the movie.

The film details the story of young Paul Mercurio, played by Scott Hastings. He's a dancer who wants to do things his own way and invent his own style and steps. Unfortunately, Paul's imaginative dance moves and unwilling-ness to conform to traditional dance values cause him strife. He loses a dance partner, and faces the disapproval of the Ballroom Federation, headed by a fella by the name of Barney Fife(!) Eventually, Paul teams with a new partner, Fran, and competes in a major international contest to prove once and for all the value of his innovations.

Strictly Ballroom won a whopping nine Australian Film Institute Awards including Best Film and Best Screenplay (an award shared by Luhrmann and his cowriter, Craig Pearce.) It became a sensation in the United States in the late summer of 1992, and represented the latest dance musical in the genre.

Pearce recalls the film's development, and the style it evoked. "It's about a world that is both our world and not our world. It's a little bit heightened. It's got particular rules that came to the world of the story. In *Strictly Ballroom*, it's a world where people dance all the time. They fall in love—they're dancing; they're having an argument—they're dancing; their lives are falling apart—they're dancing. They're having a fight—they're dancing; they're rebelling—they're dancing. That was the convention of that film.

"Ultimately, it's an allegorical story; it's a fairy tale," Pearce describes. "It's about ballroom dancing, but it's not about ballroom dancing. It's a David-and-Goliath story mixed with an Ugly Duckling story set in the world of ballroom dancing. Basically, it's about overcoming impossible odds. Had it been in outer space, it would have been *Star Wars*. Had it been in Roman times, it could have been *Gladiator*."

Although they captured the delight of classic Hollywood musicals better than their modern counterparts, *The Commitments* and *Strictly Ballroom* were not necessarily viewed by Hollywood as musicals at the time. Still, it was a moment of some success prior to the musical format's death knell in the mid-1990s, even if it originated far from Tinsel Town.

I'LL CUT ANYTHING

The movie musical's latest death blow struck in 1994 on a project that by rights should have actually revived the format, James L. Brooks's *I'll Do Anything* starring Nick Nolte and Albert Brooks. Conceived as a musical that would closely examine (and skewer) Hollywood life, much like the classic *Singin' in the Rain*, *I'll Do Anything* tells the story of a struggling actor named Matt Hobbs (Nolte) as he navigates the treacherous landscape of Tinsel Town relationships.

At the same time he gets a job driving a neurotic producer (Brooks) to movie test screenings, Matt must cope with his young daughter (Whittni Wright) from a previous marriage. Like Robert Altman's *The Player* (1991), and Brooks's own *Broadcast News* (1987) or even his animated series *The Critic* (1995), *I'll Do Anything* was sharply satirical. But like Brooks's *Terms of Endearment*, it was also meant to be heartfelt and true.

And that's where the music should have entered the picture.

"I thought the musical form would get me to more of the truth," James L. Brooks noted in the press. "For example, I wanted to make a sad ballet out of the table hopping in Hollywood."[12]

To aid him in his quest to reach the truth, Brooks hired a top-notch team of songwriters, including Prince, Sinead O'Connor, and Carole King. The choreography was arranged by none other than Twyla Tharp. All signs were that Columbia Pictures had a winner on its hands, and the studio scheduled the thirty-five-million-dollar picture as its "event" Christmas release.

But something funny happened on the way to *I'll Do Anything*'s debut. Life imitated art, and eerily like Albert Brooks's producer in the movie, director James L. Brooks found his work unexpectedly hung up in the testing process, at a screening in Culver City in August 1993.

The entertainment media was quick to pounce on reports of what *Entertainment Weekly* termed "mega-bad buzz."[13] But even that colorful descriptor didn't quite convey the whole ugly picture. When faced with the two-and-a-half-hour cut of *I'll Do Anything*, audiences *blanched*. One hundred audience members walked out of the preview when the songs began,[14] others noted on their opinion cards that they hated the songs, and there were reports that "everyone cracked up as soon as the characters opened their mouths and began to sing."[15]

It was a disastrous preview, but could the press be exaggerating? Really . . . how bad could a screening be? That's precisely the question Albert Brooks asked his director, and James L. Brooks came back to the actor with an honest reply. "Well, half the audience walked out."[16]

With disaster percolating and industry insiders already comparing *I'll Do Anything* to the previous summer's Arnold Schwarzenneger–John McTiernan bomb, *The Last Action Hero*, drastic action was deemed necessary. In a strange way, *I'll Do Anything* pulled the same gimmick as the one depicted in the classic musical *Singin' in the Rain*, only in reverse. Whereas characters in that film attempted to save a project by *adding* music sequences, *I'll Do Anything* adopted the opposite route and music was *subtracted*.

Accordingly, all musical numbers but one were cut, and Columbia pumped an additional ten million dollars into the production, bringing the film's budget up to a whopping forty-five million. Then, the film's release date was delayed two months, so that Brooks could reshape the material, sans song and dance. Not surprisingly, the director found the reediting process a little difficult, lamenting a "ripple effect" that drove him crazy, and that caused a "tidal wave" of alterations in the final cut.[17]

Producer Polly Plat spun the bad news by telling *Entertainment Weekly* that the extraordinary changes were necessary simply to strengthen *I'll Do Anything*'s "narrative flow."[18]

While James L. Brooks recut like mad to reframe *I'll Do Anything* as a conventional comedy-drama, the message from the unfortunate preview screening was not lost. Audiences disliked the film because they were unwilling to sit through a musical; too impatient to appreciate the fantasy of characters singing their desires and dreams instead of expressing them directly and realistically. What those preview cards revealed was a total dismissal of the musical, and more than that, open hostility.

The Hollywood musical was officially dead. Or, as *Newsweek*'s Marc Peyser and Mark Miller noted, *I'll Do Anything* officially represented "the first nonmusical musical."[19]

When *I'll Do Anything*, "a skeleton of a former musical"[20] in the words of critic Stanley Kauffmann and a "flat-footed gelding"[21] according to Ty Burr, finally premiered in the winter of 1994, only one song remained intact. In this case, it was little actress Whittni Wright's Carole King ditty, "You Are the Best," that survived the massacre. Wright's character, Jeannie, sang the song to her despondent father (Nolte) in a touching moment midway through the film.

I'll Do Anything did not receive particularly caustic reviews, given the circumstances, and Siskel and Ebert both awarded the film unreserved thumbs up. Still, the loss of the original musical sequences was a terrible sacrifice which left the film feeling uneven, almost unfinished. All the satiric barbs about Hollywood were quite smart and snappy, but many scenes seemed to just cry out for a song and dance to push the whole enterprise to the next level.

Overall, musical removal surgery and all, *I'll Do Anything* was not lacking charm, yet audiences still stayed away from it, making the whole ugly recutting exercise for naught. The movie earned back only about ten million dollars.

The score card for musicals in 1994 was telling. For the fourth time since 1991, a big-budget, live-action Hollywood musical had very publicly self-destructed in theaters. In the case of *I'll Do Anything*, studio executives were quick to take note of audience disdain for musicals, and *I'll Do Anything* had a ripple effect.

(NOT SO) FANTASTICK

The next musical to come down the pike after *I'll Do Anything*, Michael Ritchie's *The Fantasticks* (1995) wasn't even granted the dignity of a theatrical release. Instead MGM opted to save money, write the bloody thing off, and leave it sitting on the shelf for five years.

Again, this was a rather stunning decision, in many ways even more detrimental to the survival of the movie musical than the *I'll Do Anything* debacle. For *The Fantasticks* wasn't some unknown (or even little-known) property. On the contrary, the story of two lovebirds, their nosy fathers, and a mysterious carnival come to town was a highly marketable and popular venture that had succeeded on television and Off-Broadway for a generation.

Created by Harvey Schmidt and Tom Jones, *The Fantasticks* was the epitome of success over the last four decades of the twentieth century. Since its debut at New York's Off-Broadway Sullivan Street Theater in 1960, virtually every stage actor of note from Richard Chamberlain and the late Jerry Orbach to Elliott Gould and Liza Minnelli had appeared in the production. It had been staged in Japan, the Middle East, and virtually every corner of the earth, a universal and populist hit because of its truths about young love, and several interesting allusions to Shakespeare's *Romeo and Juliet*.

In 2002, the play finally closed after forty-two years and more than seventeen thousand performances, but by then it was already a permanent fixture of the pop-culture landscape, having provided at least two memorable tunes, "Soon It's Gonna Rain" and the melancholy and haunting "Try to Remember." The Hallmark Hall of Fame produced a well-remembered TV version of the material in 1964, and so *The Fantasticks* was probably as well known to middle America as *Cats* or *Annie*.

A movie version should have been a no-brainer, especially given the talent involved with it. A longtime admirer of the Off-Broadway show, director Michael Ritchie (1938–2001), jumped aboard the project already a veteran of such impressive features as *The Candidate* (1972) starring Robert Redford and the crowd-pleasing *Bad News Bears* (1976). He described his passion for the project and enunciated succinctly the appeal of a *Fantasticks* film adaptation: "Big screen, big emotion, big orchestra."[22]

For the role of Mr. Bellamy, Luisa's meddling father, Ritchie retained the services of the remarkable and legendary Joel Grey, thus marking the actor's return to movie musicals for the first time since his electrifying star-turn in Fosse's *Cabaret*. Ritchie also cast a former *Tiger Beat* star, young Joe McIntyre of the defunct boy band New Kids on the Block, to play naïve Matt to Jean Louisa Kelly's wistful Luisa. Behind the scenes toiled one of the best cinematographers in the business, Fred Murphy.

Under Ritchie's direction and Murphy's eye, the film was crafted to resemble a Thomas Hart Benton painting, with strong touches from *The Wizard of Oz* and *Oklahoma!* in the mix as well. Adding to the authenticity of the piece, most of the songs were performed live on the set, with only a modicum of post-production tinkering.[23]

"The trick was taking it out of the theater and lending it a movie-based reality, in this case 1920s America," Ritchie commented on the dazzling and impressive look of his film, which featured wide-open skies, neverending roads, and fine period detail.[24]

It seemed like a surefire thing, especially since *The Fantasticks* was no *For the Boys, Newsies,* or *I'll Do Anything* in terms of budgetary concerns. The feature was modestly produced for ten million dollars.

But the *I'll Do Anything* fiasco had rattled an entire industry, MGM was up for sale, and another musical bomb wasn't going to reflect very well on the company. Although a Thanksgiving 1995 release had been announced, a preview screening went badly (again) and the studio suits got cold feet. So *The Fantasticks*—a beautifully photographed version of the popular stage play—was destined to remain hidden from sight, not even granted the dignity of a limited release.

At least one person wasn't surprised. "*The Fantasticks* has never been a normal property," cocreator Schmidt lamented in 1997, even as the film gathered dust in a vault somewhere.[25]

It was not until the year 2000 that *The Fantasticks* returned to the public consciousness. Now under new ownership, MGM undertook an earnest attempt to release some of its failed projects that hadn't yet seen the light of day. New MGM board member Francis Ford Coppola accepted the assignment of reediting two of these aborted productions, the sci-fi thriller *Supernova* (2000) starring James Spader and Angela Bassett, and Ritchie's troubled *The Fantasticks*.

On the latter, Coppola trimmed twenty-five minutes from the piece, and reduced the film to a scant eight-six minutes in length. He concentrated on what advance screeners had complained so vociferously about: the film's resemblance to a stage musical. Coppola thus eliminated some of the movies "more theatrical" and "stagey" moments.[26] He also slashed whole musical numbers from the proceedings, including the delightful "Take a Radish." He even went so far as to tinker with the film's structure.

For instance, "Try to Remember" had originally appeared as a bookend piece in the movie, starting and finishing the film with the rakish El Gallo (Jonathon Morris) singing it on the road, and thus granting the reprise a different and deeper resonance at the climax. Coppola removed the song from the beginning of *The Fantasticks*, in the process undoing some of its worth, heft and thematic value. It remains the most memorable song in the feature, both vocally and visually, as the caravan of Fantasticks heads to the horizon against a nostalgic American landscape.

Despite the changes, Ritchie professed satisfaction with the new cut, feeling that his own version had been "too reverential" to the play, and that he had failed to reconceive the film as a movie, "as it should have been."[27]

Finally, in a new (and aborted) form, *The Fantasticks* appeared perched to make the not-so-fantastic voyage straight to home video. However, Harvey Schmidt and Tom Jones had a unique stipulation in their contract stating that the film had to be released in theaters before skipping off to the secondary markets. Accordingly, the film was released in four cities starting late September 2000.

Regarding the curtailed release of *The Fantasticks*, Jones noted that it was "the sensible thing to do when there's apparently no audience for movie musicals."[28]

So, after five long years on the shelf and an extensive cut job, *The Fantasticks* emerged in 2000 to little fanfare. Looking at the film today, one detects that maybe, in some version, it was something rather special, an old-fashioned musical wherein the old codes are still in effect. We get a wishing, longing ballad out of Luisa, and Matt and Luisa's duet expresses their desires well. And of course, the film offers a kind of diabolical ring-leader and commentator in the charismatic El Gallo, seemingly referencing characters as diverse as Grey's *Cabaret* Master of Ceremonies and even Che in *Evita*. The vibrant, beautiful vistas of the American West remind one of Zinnemann's *Oklahoma!* and the audience is privy to jokes about Shakespeare and even the theatricality of musicals in "Theatrical Abductions," the movie's replacement for the out-of-date "The Rape Song."

Though brief and at times even abrupt, Ritchie's *Fantasticks* features a nice twist on old musical concepts too. Here the happy ending—the joyful joining of Matt and Luisa—comes about half way through the film and leads to a quite unhappy realization, that longing and desire are sometimes more fulfilling in love than the aftermath, the so-called happy ending of togetherness and marriage. Once the romantic hurdles in a relationship are crossed, what is left to pine over? The bills?

This is one of the few musicals that recognizes how romantic relationships can represent a long, slow anticlimax after the thrill of the chase and the excitement of forbidden passion. Take away the painted sunset, the sense of drama, the blue lagoon, the tinsel sky, and the golden moonbeam, and what are you really left with? *The Fantasticks*, even in so abbreviated a form, acknowledges this theme with a degree of wit.

But any appreciation (or disdain) for *The Fantasticks* arrives post-2000. For the purposes of this chapter, *The Fantasticks*—made in 1995—represents the epitaph for the musical format. In the first half of the nineties, three attempts at various musical formats bombed (*For the Boys*, *Newsies,* and *Swing Kids*), one musical (*I'll Do Anything*) was totally eviscerated, and another (*The Fantasticks*) was locked away like Rapunzel in her tower, because there was no longer an audience for the form. At the end of the day, fans of the musical film were left in 1995 with what they began with in 1989 and 1990: more Disney cartoons.

How had the genre that dominated the thirties, forties and fifties fallen so far from grace?

"Well, first of all, what we're basically saying is, 'How come there's no more musicals?'" suggests Joss Whedon. "It works on a number of levels. For one thing, vaudeville is dead, which is not news. Vaudeville was a time when people who trained to be actors [also] trained to be singers and trained to be dancers. There were always people out their like Dan Dailey or Van Johnson, who you didn't associate with song and dance, who could—do I dare say it?—bust a move at any time. Because that was just a part of coming up in Hollywood. That doesn't really exist anymore.

"I looked at *Singin' in the Rain* recently and I was like 'These people—these three people [Kelly, O'Connor, and Reynolds] are movie stars because they could do something nobody else could do.' Not just be pretty, which they were. Or be funny, which they were. But because they were physically capable of doing something that looks impossible. And again, that simply does not exist, or people aren't looking for it, and people aren't training for it in the same way. So you don't have the same level of performer. Or at least you don't have it as the norm, and you don't have people looking for it. And so you get things like *The Company* (2003), where Neve Campbell pretends to be a ballerina. And word to the wise: if you're going to do that, don't surround yourself with the Joffrey. It's just a different standard."

Whedon also suggests that the difficulty of creating movie musicals is a critical part of the format's slow decline. "All it really takes is really good music, really good lyrics, really good singing, and acting, and dancing, and really good filmmaking. Any one of those is hard to come by in a movie. Musicals are simply the most difficult kind of movie to make. They require the biggest number of skills, but I don't think people have ever really been turned off. They just need a different vernacular in which to speak. Somebody in the fifties watching *Sunny Side Up* (1929) would find it laughably old-fashioned. Then they could watch *The Band Wagon* (1953) and think it was a normal, modern film. Someone watching *Hair* (1979) in the eighties could do the same thing."

So don't cry for the musical just yet. As Whedon and the others suggest, the truth is . . . it's never left us. And during the next period of film history, from 1996 to 2004, a group of dedicated artists including Sir Alan Parker, Woody Allen, Todd Haynes, Trey Parker, Kenneth Branagh, Lars von Trier, Baz Luhrmann, Rob Marshall, Todd Graff, Keith Gordon, and Irwin Winkler began hunting in earnest for Whedon's new musical vernacular. In many cases, they found it.

And now, on with the show . . .

PART II
Get Back to Where
You Once Belonged

CHAPTER THREE
From Evita to Moulin Rouge

1996–2001

SANTA EVITA

In 1996, all hopes for the musical's future seemed to rest squarely on the shoulder pads of a single popular property. "The future of movie musicals will be affected by how well the new movie *Evita* sells," predicted Nigel Andrews in the *Financial Times*. "No major musical has succeeded since *Grease* in the 1970s, and the only major hit before that was *The Sound of Music*."[1]

Considering the gravity placed on it, Sir Alan Parker's *Evita* seems an ideal production with which to began an investigation of the rebirth of the modern movie musical. Had the film failed on release in the mid-nineties, only God knows how long it would have been before any Hollywood studio mustered the courage to attempt another genre production. And, because it did succeed, perhaps, there was at least one recent victory on the scorecard that movie executives could point at.

"*Evita* was made when musicals were less popular," Sir Alan Parker, director of the film, acknowledges. "Musicals became unpopular because of the music explosion and the glut of so much, so different music. The film audience (very young) was listening to different music from the tunes banging out on the Broadway stage (mostly for older audiences), hence the divide. Also a night out at the theater is a different experience than going to your local cinema. We are more forgiving when it's live. Also, over the years, a lot of very poor films were made from very good stage shows, which led the audience to fall out of love with the form."

Rescuing an entire genre is a tall order for any production, but *Evita*, at least, had good genes. Nearly twenty years earlier, in 1976, composer Andrew Lloyd Webber and librettist Tim Rice had fashioned their musical biography, *Evita*, about Argentina's controversial (and deceased) first lady, Eva Duarte Perón (1919–1952).

After the release of an album first, and then a well-received beginning on stage in London, where Elaine Page essayed the titular role, the stage show emigrated to America and became a smash hit on Broadway in late 1979. Patti LuPone played Evita in the States, and Mandy Patinkin was her opponent of sorts, the bitter revolutionary, Che.

Wife of Juan Perón, Argentina's president, Eva Perón, or Evita, as she was known, was either a sinner or a saint, depending on one's perspective. The subject of some thirty biographies just in Spanish alone, Eva Perón was often revered as a quasi-mythical figure who, by some accounts, may have been a miracle worker. Some forty thousand letters were sent to the Vatican describing her incredible deeds, in hopes of acquiring her a sainthood.[2]

However, in Hollywood, the miracle surrounding Evita Perón was simply getting the film produced in the first place. As far back as 1981, an assortment of talents sought to transfer the musical from stage to screen without success. Actresses including Charo, Barbra Streisand, Pia Zadora, Raquel Welch, Liza Minnelli, Diane Keaton, Cyndi Lauper, Olivia Newton-John, and Meryl Streep had all been considered for the role.

As late as 1994, *Grease 2* alumna Michelle Pfeiffer was reported to have cinched the part,[3] but she had to surrender it after recording a few demos for Oliver Stone, due to the advanced state of her pregnancy.[4]

Potential directors included Francis Ford Coppola, Herbert Ross, Richard Attenborough, Ken Russell, Michael Cimino, Glenn Gordon Caron, and Oliver Stone, and the project seemed to bounce ping-pong-like from studio to studio, from Carolco to Disney, and then finally into the hands of producers Robert Stigwood and Andrew J. Vajna.

Eventually the project landed in the lap of a director who knew a thing or two about musicals. In the 1970s, Sir Alan had directed the unusual *Bugsy Malone* (1976), a gangster musical starring teenagers. In the eighties, he had given the world a phenomenon known as *Fame*, and the trippy cult movie *Pink Floyd: The Wall*. By the early 1990s, he had directed the highly successful backstage musical, *The Commitments*, so Parker boasted the perfect genre credentials to create what in essence was an old-fashioned book musical.

Ironically, Parker had actually been offered *Evita* as a film project (by producer Robert Stigwood) as early as 1981, but right after directing *Fame,* felt it unwise to jump right back into another genre film. It was a decision he always regretted. Or, at least for fifteen years . . .

Madonna, who had not proven so bankable on screen lately with a string of bombs including *Who's That Girl* (1987) and *Body of Evidence* (1993), lobbied hard for the role of *Evita*. She sent Parker an impassioned, four-page handwritten letter (and music video) to augment her case. Eventually, she persevered. The pop diva was so enamored of the role that she reportedly accepted a pay cut, earning one million dollars for her performance. She didn't even take a percentage of the film's profits.[5]

"People see Eva Perón as either a saint or the incarnation of Satan," she told *People* magazine. "I can definitely identify with her."[6]

When crafting *Evita*'s screenplay, Alan Parker went all the way back to the 1976 album (featuring singer Julie Covington), the format that had preceded the stage show and landed "Don't Cry for Me, Argentina" at the number one slot on the British pop charts. In fact, as he reports in his essay *The Making of Evita*, he loved the album so much that he actually sought to create the film as far back as that bicentennial year. He was informed at the time, however, that the property was bound for the stage first.

"I actually wrote my screenplay on my own. Oliver Stone had written a script some years earlier which I never read, but the Writers Guild is strict about this, hence his credit with mine on the screenplay," Parker reports. "The great challenge for me was that I had agreed with Andrew and Tim that it would be a sung-through piece, an opera.

"This meant that the complicated story had to be told with images and recitative only. I had seen the stage show a couple of times, but went back to the original music. It was the original album that I had originally been inspired by. There were also a number of cast albums of different subsequent productions and I culled different ideas from those.

"On film, I was particularly concerned about clarity, hence the new music, and indeed the new song ['You Must Love Me.'] Also, I rejiggled the songs a bit. I gave 'Another Suitcase' to Eva instead of the Mistress because this is an odd character you see briefly in the story and never again, and she has one of the best songs, so I gave it to Madonna. In the end," Parker stresses, "film inhabits a real world, and the suspension of disbelief that is easy to achieve in live theater is not acceptable to a film audience."

Adapting a property from stage to screen, as the last sentence indicates, is no walk in the park. Parker expertly lays out the specifics of the equation for us to better understand it:

In the theater, you're enjoying the theatrical moment, you're applauding the performance that exists for that night only. The fundamental difference is one of focus. In a theater, even if you're in the front row, you're always separated from the actors. You take in the whole prosce-nium arch all the time. Film has editing. Close-ups. And [film] tells the story from every angle and point of view. Theater sees things only from the front. A different set of rules exists in the theater, which has to be discarded on film. Film gets inside of things and this can be a blessing and a difficulty, because in the end, in real life, people don't stop to sing to one another.

And that is an important point. In *Evita*, there is little or no spoken dialogue. All the language is communicated through song. "Different manifestations of the film script over the years did flirt with using the spoken word," Parker says. "I always wanted it to be an opera. That was the challenge for me. Andrew and Tim preferred it. Only the film studios ever brought up conventional dialogue. Presumably because large sums of money were involved (fifty million dollars) and no one was ever sure that we could pull it off.

"*Bugsy Malone* was a pastiche of the classic thirties Hollywood musical, and so the musical numbers came out of nowhere with no nod to reality. With *Fame*, the music always came out of the story—we never suspend belief," Parker continues. "Dancing on top of the taxicabs on 46th Street obviously is pushing reality to the extreme, but although it might not happen in real life, there's always a chance that it *could* happen.

"With a sung-through opera," Parker contrasts, "your biggest concern as a director is the forward linear energy, hoping that the audience is staying with you for the ride, and that the narrative is easily understandable."

With the screenplay fashioned by Parker, Jonathan Pryce was cast as Juan Perón, and *Desperado* (1994) star Antonio Banderas came aboard as the Greek—or rather Argentinian—chorus, Che. Production soon commenced on an A-list musical that would come to cost over fifty million dollars. It was Hollywood's biggest gamble in years.

In preparation for the film, *Evita's* cast underwent four months of rigor-ous vocal training, and Madonna took "intense" singing lessons with coach Joan Lader to strengthen her voice.[7] Beginning on October 2, 1995, the rehearsals stopped and the process of prerecording the songs with an eighty-four-piece orchestra began at CT Studios in Wembley, England.

In his essay on the making of the film, Sir Alan Parker refers to that first day of recording as "Black Monday" because it went so poorly. During this period, the cast and crew of *Evita* toiled for seven days a week to prepare for the whopping forty-nine musical sections of the film that would be required for playback on the set.[8]

Evita's principal photography began in Buenos Aires, where the cast and crew were promptly greeted with boos by protesters. Placards and signs read "Fuera Madonna" [Piss off Madonna] and "Death to Alan Parker and your English Task Force," according to the director.

Meanwhile, Parker had personally lobbied the president of Argentina, Carlos Menem, to film at Casa Rosada, or the Pink House, the Perón's official residence. This would represent a major coup, so to speak, if it worked out, because the residence had never been committed to film before on any production. But even though he was granted permission to film at Casa Rosada, Parker decided to take no chances. His production designer, Brian Morris photographed every square inch of the residence, and there were secret plans to construct it in its entirety at Shepperton Studios in England, should things fall through in Argentina.

They didn't. *Evita*'s crew was afforded access to Casa Rosada, thanks to some additional—and timely—diplomacy by Madonna, and Parker counts the two nights on the balcony there as the production's most difficult days, but also his personal best. The scenes were filmed with four thousand extras on the street below.

From there, *Evita*'s production high-tailed it to Budapest, Hungary, in late March 1996, where Eva Perón's impressive state funeral was subsequently lensed, a scene that also required four thousand fully costumed extras.

One of the many complexities in shooting *Evita* involved the creation of the epic and memorable musical sequences, which often encompassed several locales per song, both indoors and exteriors. "It was very complex," Parker acknowledges. "Everything was well planned beforehand. The better you prepare a film the easier the shoot. Our days were very busy and we shot very fast. Probably because we weren't in the comfort of a Hollywood sound stage but in real streets, we were a giant mobile film studio and consequently had to be very organized and swift of foot. Only when we got back to Shepperton Studios did we seem to relax."

Filming was completed near the end of May 1996, and Parker began to edit the picture in mid-June, revving up for a Christmas release. "A lot of credit should be given to my editor, Gerry Hambling, who cut together so brilliantly all the disparate pieces I shot," says Parker. "He is acknowledged by his peers to be the greatest cutter of film to music—he also cut *Fame, Pink Floyd: The Wall, The Commitments,* and *Bugsy Malone* for me."

An elaborate, globe-trotting production, which in the end included more than forty thousand extras,[9] *Evita* also contended with Madonna's surprise pregnancy during production. These and other unanticipated twists and turns made the film a near-impossible one to shoot quickly. Here was Parker's own tally from his essay, *The Making of Evita*:

> We had filmed eighty-four days, shooting in three different countries, involving over six hundred film crew. We had done 299 scenes and 3,000 slated shots on 320,000 feet of film with two cameras. Penny Rose's costume department, with a staff of seventy-two in three different countries had fitted forty thousand extras in period dress. Over 5,500 costumes were used from twenty different costume houses in London, Rome, Paris, New York, Los Angeles, San Francisco, Buenos Aires, and Budapest.[10]

"It was difficult on every level," Madonna acknowledged to Larry King on CNN,[11] not just because of her condition, not just because she had to endure something like eighty-five costume changes during production, but because of those vast, impressive crowd scenes, and even the controversial nature of the film's subject, a divisive political figure if ever there was one.

"Madonna really understood the character and did her homework," reports Parker. "In the fifties, Eva was the most famous person in the world. When we made the film, the same could be said of Madonna. Although Madonna isn't known for her philanthropy, she certainly has had her detractors around the world. Understanding celebrity on this global scale, she didn't need to act it, she was living it. Also never underestimate how hard she [Madonna] worked on the part."

Another factor *Evita* had in its favor was a reunion of the play's creators. After a decade-long professional separation, Parker brokered a peace treaty between Andrew Lloyd Webber and Tim Rice, and they joined forces to compose a ballad for *Evita*, the stirring "You Must Love Me." It eventually won the duo an Academy Award for Best Original Song.

As *Evita* neared its release date of Christmas 1996, the film was touted with the ad-line "The Most Anticipated Motion Picture Event of the Year," and promotion ratcheted-up into overdrive. The presence of Madonna in the picture, wearing 1940s fashions, was expected to spark a "style revolution," and indeed, according to Kal Ruttenstein, Bloomingdale's fashion director, that's precisely what occurred, with customers coming in and "saying, 'I want to look like that.'"[12]

Among the products directly related to *Evita* were a five-strand pearl necklace by Carolee, an Estee Lauder makeup called the Face of Evita, and forties-style garments by Nicole Miller, Victor Costa, and Elie Tahari. Not to mention Ferragamo shoes, apparently the favorites of the late Ms. Perón.[13]

"You Must Love Me" also went out on the radio in October of 1996, well in advance of the film's holiday release, and appeared on over 110 Top 10 play lists. It was the highest debuting cut on *Billboard*'s "Hot 100" air play chart the first week of release, stoking the fire for the film's premiere.[14] Advance buzz reached such a fever pitch that Madonna's asking price for a film jumped into the five- to six-million-dollar range.[15]

When *Evita* premiered on Christmas Day on just two screens, America was primed, and the film grossed a record-breaking amount: over seventy-one thousand dollars in just those venues.[16] The movie went on to become a solid hit in the United States, but an absolute phenomenon worldwide, eventually grossing more than $140 million. For the first time in more than a few years, a big-budget Hollywood musical had earned its way into the "plus" column.

For the most part, *Evita*'s reviewers were rather impressed. Writing for the *Chicago Sun Times*, Roger Ebert gave the film a rating of three-and-a-half stars. "You must watch her," insisted *Time*'s Richard Corliss, "and to find the soul of the modern musical for once on the big screen, you must see *Evita*."[17]

Others were on the fence. "What a tantalizing, frustrating movie this is: you yearn to be drawn inside its seductive surface and never get there. Instead of deepening with Evita's amazing metamorphosis, the movie remains opaque," suggested *Newsweek*'s David Ansen.[18]

Writing for *Macleans*, Brian D. Johnson seemed to share that perspective, declaring that "*Evita* is an impressive but empty exercise in hyperbole. For once, however, Madonna is not to blame."[19]

"The glorification, for that is what it is," considered John Simon, "of Evita Perón was in bad taste on Broadway, and remains so now."[20]

Director Parker has clearly thought a great deal about this character, the drama, and the nature of his film's unusual protagonist, even as critics questioned her true nature: "Eva was a multifaceted character. Once again, depending on people's points of view, I either glamorized a fascist or denigrated a saint. I suppose I should be flattered that the film could effect people in such diametrically opposite ways. Musicals don't usually tackle politics and nationalism on this scale. Most film versions of musicals are stage bound and never escape the restriction of the proscenium arch and the theater walls.

"Personally," he continues, "I think she was an opportunist who had good intentions regarding the poor of Argentina, but became intoxicated by her own celebrity, causing her to become a not-so-nice person. If she had lived longer, she would have probably become even more autocratic and fascistic.

"Her life (and dying) was pure melodrama. Depending on who you ask in Argentina, she is either thought of as a bitch and a whore or a benevolent saint. She had many enemies, but she was undoubtedly adored by millions. The love story with Juan is also important from a dramatic point of view (and hence the new song to reiterate this). In the end, it's the woman's contradictions that make for a more interesting drama."

Alan Parker's sweeping 1996 epic, *Evita*, begins in Buenos Aires in 1952, as the death of Argentina's adored first lady, Eva "Evita" Perón (Madonna) is announced in a theater where the former actress's movies once lit up the silver screen. Following the announcement, an angry young agitator named Che (Banderas) reveals her life story, commencing with her youth as the illegitimate child of a middle-class adulterer, and her terrible experience of being turned away from his funeral, all because of class.

A tango dancer by age fifteen, Evita begins her long ascent up the ladder of show business, becoming a photographer's model, then an actress—and finally, the consort of a general. Always realizing when to trade up, Eva Duarte, "the greatest social climber since Cinderella," soon romances an up-and-comer in the military, General Juan Perón, and takes her place at his side after his release from prison.

Once in power, Evita becomes a divisive figure—a saint to some, a sinner to others. She travels Europe as a goodwill ambassador, only to be labeled a whore and a fascist. Meanwhile, our guide, Che, decries the lack of progress made in Argentina since Perón's coup, noting "that little has changed" for the peasants on the ground . . . even as Evita drops hints that she should be the country's vice president.

With nowhere to go but down, Evita finally cements her legacy by dying young, at thirty-three. Her state funeral draws crowds in the hundreds of thousands, flags fly everywhere at half-mast, and mourners line the streets to view her body in its glass-top coffin. Although Evita always implored Argentina not to cry for her, this time it weeps . . .

By a freak coincidence, this author viewed *Evita* in preparation for this book on the same weekend in which former U.S. President Ronald Reagan passed away, and was pleasantly taken aback by just how "right" director Alan Parker gets the details. Theater and politics, we must remember, are one in the same. *Evita* is a spectacular meditation on that very subject.

"No, you make a good point," says Parker. "So much of politics is theater. Remember, Perón learned from Germany and Italy in the thirties and saw how they could 'put on a show.' He was smart to realize Eva's popularity with the people, and so his 'show' also had a female lead. Reducing politics to theater and the shallowness of the subsequent exploitation is obviously one of the themes of *Evita*. It's not far from the glitz of American political conventions and the relentless road shows that accompany elections."

Considering this theme, *Evita*'s potentially most inaccessible quality, that all the dialogue is sung, opera-style, actually works for the film rather than against it. Though it seems a bit strange in today's climate to witness performers like Madonna and Pryce belt out tunes about unions, the upper class, and would-be presidents, this is the nature of the beast. *Evita* is and always has been a tale about one politician's rise to power and the consequences—for good or ill—of that rise, so it's not wrong for the film to exist in a kind of heightened, theatrical reality. The fate of a nation rests with these people, and the material is downright Shakespearean, so why not make it as grandiose and big as possible?

Alan Parker directed *Fame* with a careful eye towards balancing naturalism and theatricality, and he navigates the same delicate line with precision here. The film's period detail is remarkable, the settings and locations nothing short of awe-inspiring, and Parker stylishly sets some of *Evita*'s best scenes to the hard-driving, rock cadences of the Webber score.

In "Oh! What a Circus," the number builds to a fevered pace just as violence erupts. Fast-cutting dominates this sequence as windows are shattered and fires rage. There are high angle views of armies and protesters clashing, and citizens on the run, and the imagery is epic. On one hand, this is the *Doctor Zhivago* (1965) of musicals in regards to scope, but on the other, there is nothing stately about this scene. It is rock and roll pandemonium, and in these and similar moments, *Evita* expresses the notion that rock is the music of anarchy, of passions unleashed. The form of the music reflects the content of the narrative.

The same song also explains Eva Perón's charismatic magic in a sense, specifically with the lyrics, "She didn't say much, but she said it loud." What *Evita* *truly* stood for is somewhat of a mystery, but the noise surrounding Evita, even after death, is deafening.

Some critics have complained that *Evita* is a failure because it never provides the audience with an "in" to understanding Eva Perón. What does the film really feel about her? reviewers wonder.

The presentation of "Don't Cry for Me, Argentina," in particular, answers this query. Evita stands regally atop the balcony at Casa Rosada and begins to speak in generalities about her journey. Parker's camera pans across a crowd of rapturous faces during her utterances, and a point about Evita's rise to power is made succinctly. The movie is really less about who she is than who *we* are. Like those people in the streets, we all want to be saved by someone else. We want our leaders to be immortal, to rescue us, to raise us up. If they can't do it with their actions, then their oratory, their rhetoric will suffice. At least for a while.

This point is powerfully made through images and song, as Evita recounts her life story to the masses. It is clear that it is her very biography itself that appeals to these people, not the specifics of what Eva believes, or more importantly, what she will do now that Perón has attained power. Indeed, Evita's answer to Argentina's social and economics problems seems to be: "I love you and hope you love me." It's as simple as that.

The stillness on the street below in the shots throughout this sequence evidence a sense of rapture. The crowd is spellbound, and its near paralysis visualizes the power of Evita's biography, and the reason why so many people loved her. When the masses begin to hum back the song she sings to them, tears glazing their eyes, they are mirroring her journey, buying into the attractive, packaged fantasy she presents them.

Another song, "Waltz for Eva and Che," also symbolizes the relationship and bond between charismatic leader and hopeful people. Matters have not improved in Argentina after Perón's rise, and the people (represented by Che), want to know what Eva is going to do about poverty and the like. They are asking explicitly for a reason to continue to love her . . . any reason.

Entrenched power (represented by Evita) responds that, well, at least she's trying. There are no solutions, she warns, even if she were to live "a hundred years." In other words, just enjoy the ride because there are no answers to the dilemmas that effect humans, only rhetoric and the momentary glory reflected by individual leaders.

The waltz, this dance for two, explicitly positions Evita and the people of Argentina as entangled partners, both lovers and enemies. On one hand, the people are lured to her image, her legend and biography. On the other hand, she has not helped them . . . yet she continues to seduce them, feeding off their love and responding to their need to believe in someone.

"Mmm. The greater metaphor I leave you to explain," says Parker. "For me, the problem [with that dance] was keeping everyone in synch over many different locations. The dance was choreographed as one continuous piece on the rehearsal stage, and then I chopped it up to shoot in sections. Once again, her [Madonna's] dress had to be let out, as she got bigger with her child as the waltz was shot over a two-month span."

One of the most poignant moments in *Evita* arises from a song not present in the Broadway show, the award-winning "You Must Love Me." In this composition, the audience learns the price of being a legend, an icon like Evita. Though Eva wins in a sense by having the masses adore her, she also loses, because as a political animal and legend she can never really know how Perón, her own husband, feels about her. Their rise together was mutually advantageous and convenient. Her continuance at his side is a result of the fact that she is beloved and popular. But inside, she wonders, does he really love her? Is their relationship merely one of political expedience?

"Why are you at my side?" the lyrics ask. "How can I be of any use to you now?" These are the questions of a woman who has sacrificed too much, perhaps, to be a public figure. She is high-flying, adored, all right, especially by the people, but Eva's life is such grand theater that she has no emotional barometer when it comes to her own husband and his feelings. She is insecure in this love, though supremely confident in public.

Considering these examples, *Evita* is a movie musical unlike any other. It asks the big questions about politics, our leaders, and the price paid to achieve power and to hold it. Evita herself is not really the point; but our image and perception of her is. Through the competing songs of Eva and Che, and even through their waltz, Parker allows the viewer to see all sides of this public figure, without reducing her to clichés. There is no overt judgment in *Evita*, and that may be distancing for some, but rewarding for others who realize just how ambiguous life can be.

Happily, *Evita* also fulfilled a mandate beyond the call for an artistic movie musical. It accomplished the mission that critics and observers had so ambitiously established for it. Simply put, it kept the musical format alive.

"A lot of *Evita*'s success was down to the personal popularity of Madonna, and this opened the musical up to a whole new audience which helped the films that followed to be made," Parker considers. "Also, it made some money, which gave courage to the money men in Hollywood who had become wary of the success of the musical, considering they are not inexpensive to make."

Parker is gracious to credit the hard-working Madonna, yet it was also his experience as a director of successful musicals across the span of decades that helped the complex film to traverse its many built-in difficulties.

"My mentor Fred Zinnemann once said to me that his worst film was *Oklahoma!* I said, 'Why?' He said, 'I have no rhythm,'" Parker reveals. "I think musical films are the most difficult to shoot. So much has to be conceived before you start. Technically it's demanding and restricting, but also exhilarating—playing music very loud on a set inspires everyone, right down to the guy who pushes the dolly. I'm not a musician but I understand music and I can cut [it] in my head, which is important."

JUST YOU, JUST ME

The prolific Woody Allen, who was once described rather astutely as "the most musically sensitive of modern directors," embarked on his first full-fledged film musical in the mid-1990s with the delightful *Everyone Says I Love You*.[21] It was Allen's twenty-fifth feature, and one based on a concept he had devised nearly two decades earlier, while crafting Oscar-winner *Annie Hall* (1977).

Although the flick was actually released shortly before *Evita* on December 6, 1996, that was only to qualify *Everyone Says I Love You* for awards. The film went into general release in early January 1997, hence its placement here.

When word of *Everyone Says I Love You* first got out, many people laughed at the notion of the neurotic, comic Woody Allen directing an all-singing, all-dancing musical, but on closer examination, it really isn't such a strange notion. Allen is an artist who has always been attracted to the romantic decades of the twenties, thirties, and forties, and for many audiences those decades still represent the heyday of the form, so it makes sense for Allen to honor them.

In addition, Allen's preferred shooting style relies heavily on long master shots to build a sense of rhythm and pace, thereby echoing the old-style musicals of RKO and MGM to at least a modest extent. When the masters deployed this technique, it wasn't just because Fred Astaire's contract demanded it, but rather because a master shot and a steady camera most beautifully revealed the fluidity of the dance, and could build excitement at the skill on display. When Allen utilizes this approach, it's for different ends, to achieve a kind of parry and thrust, a comedic and verbal ballet of give and take, but the ethos is not wholly dissimilar. Comedy and dance both depend on timing, rhythm, and pacing.

Woody Allen is also considered highly knowledgeable about music history, and that too probably made the musical form irresistible, and a good fit for him. "I have a reasonable good knowledge of songs from 1900 to 1950," he explained to reporter Gary Susman. "That's my ear, the Porter-Kern-Gershwin era. I find those songs—and this is my own personal taste—the most beautiful of all American songs."[22]

It is appropriate then that the musical Allen would envision, *Everyone Says I Love You*, involves those very musical standards of the 1930s that he adores, including the work of Bert Kalmar, Harry Ruby, Richard Rodgers, Lorenz Hart, and Cole Porter. Even the title comes from a tune that had been performed in the Marx brothers' film, *Horse Feathers* (1932).

However, in keeping with an oeuvre that includes several angst-filled, comic examinations of love and relationships, including *Annie Hall* (1977), *Manhattan* (1980), *Hannah and Her Sisters* (1984), and *Husbands and Wives* (1992), Woody Allen also wanted his new musical to remain firmly grounded in his New York reality, and therefore identifiable to today's realism-obsessed audiences.

"I wanted to do a musical, but not for real singers and dancers," Allen explained to *Time*'s Richard Zoglin. "I wanted people who could just act, and who would sing with all the emotion of people who are doing the best they can, but it's heartfelt."[23]

In other words, the director hoped the actors would first and foremost embody their characters (as actors do in naturalistic film), and their singing skills were secondary to him, because he wanted to capture some essential and universal aspect of life: that belief that deep inside all of us there lives a song.

However, Allen didn't share his unusual intent with his prospective actors during the casting process, and the director was hunting pretty big game too, including Hollywood heavyweights like *Pretty Woman* (1989) star Julia Roberts and *Scream*'s (1996) Drew Barrymore.

"I'm not above tricking my actors," the auteur admitted, concerning the casting process. "I didn't want them to think that they'd be in a musical. It didn't matter to me if they could sing or dance. I just wanted natural, spontaneous reactions as they'd glide from dialogue into melody . . . then they could sing with all the warts and scars showing without any preparation."24

Composer Dick Hyman, an artist who once served as the musical director for Arthur Godfrey and has released over one hundred albums under his own name, has collaborated with Woody Allen on several films, including *Everything You Always Wanted to Know About Sex* But Were Afraid to Ask* (1972), *Manhattan* (1980), and *Zelig* (1983). Known for his jazz piano improvisation, Hyman reports that a high level of secrecy is actually par for the course with this director.

"Woody is perfectly pleasant to deal with, and if he has one characteristic, it's my impression that he doesn't tell people more than they need to know. I've written music for scenes for which I really had no context. I might have been given a few pages of the script, or perhaps not—maybe just the video of the scene. I believe he works with actors on the same need-to-know basis. He casts people carefully and expects them to establish their characters. In the course of things, in terms of music and acting both, naturally, he'll step in and make suggestions and modifications. But he's given me considerable latitude to be creative, and there have been times when I was able to introduce certain uses of music which had not occurred to him."

In this situation, as the arranger and composer for the film, Hyman was for once in a position to "need-to-know" a great deal about the assignment. "In this case, I knew more about what it [the movie] was in total, and it was unprecedented, but I was given the entire script. So I knew what the whole was about, and was able to integrate the music in that fashion, and we worked from that. I have said that I thought that myself and Susan E. Morse, whose role was more than film editor—she sometimes assumed the duties of an assistant producer—and Roy B. Yokelson, the audio-engineer, were the equivalent of the entire MGM music department on this film."

Ed Norton, director of *Keeping the Faith* (2000) and star of such films as *American History X* (1998) and *Fight Club* (1999), was among the surprised performers who didn't realize he had been hired for the stealth musical. A month before filming was to commence, Norton was informed by telephone that he would soon "be sent sheet music," and that remark was his first notification of the film's genre.25

To their credit, the actors didn't balk at the prospects of singing in a major motion picture, though having nonsinging actors did pose a great hurdle for Hyman.

"Well, the unique challenge was that all these people were expected to sing!" he declares. "This was a revelation to many of them, who hadn't ever done this professionally. Sandy [Susan B. Morse] broke the sometimes unsettling news and arranged to record each person, singing, say, 'America the Beautiful,' so that I could learn their range and vocal characteristics. Then I sketched out the arrangements for the various songs Woody had decided on and Derek Smith, my piano-playing alter ego, and I rehearsed each performer. Some knew how to sing more or less, while others needed some basic instruction and encouragement."

As it turned out, of the main cast, which included Julia Roberts, Alan Alda, Lukas Haas, Natalie Portman, Natasha Lyonne, Tim Roth, Edward Norton, Goldie Hawn, Drew Barrymore, and Allen, only Barrymore ended up being dubbed, although the decision wasn't based on cowardice. "My voice didn't match with Skylar's," the actress reported, noting that her singing voice was unusually throaty, not light and airy like the character.[26]

"All except Drew Barrymore turned out to be capable," remembers Hyman, "but she told us at the beginning that she was unable to carry a tune. At our first meeting, we found that this was indeed the case, so we eventually had her singing voice dubbed by Olivia Hayman. Olivia is the daughter of Richard Hayman, the fine arranger and harmonica player (remember *Ruby*?), who is, by the way, a colleague with whom I've often been confused."

Apparently Woody Allen encouraged little vocal training in terms of the film's singing, and in fact, sought to make certain the actors wouldn't come across as *too* polished.[27] "We actually recorded a few takes which, modesty aside, I did my best Sinatra, and they sounded good, and we didn't opt for those," reported Ed Norton. "He said, pull it back a little, make it a little more like a guy singing on the street."[28]

Hawn also reported that her singing voice was tempered so as not to "show up" the other cast members.[29] Both Hawn and Alda revealed skills that were a pleasant surprise for Hyman. "Alan Alda sang in musicals, I believe, and Goldie Hawn's original background was as a singer. In fact, I understand that Woody felt he needed to advise her to sing less professionally in order to match the other voices."

Allen's approach with song and dance mirrored his approach with performance. He kept things loose and improvisational, and for some actors, this was difficult. "There was so much improvisation," Natalie Portman reported on her official website, "and I just couldn't do it."[30] In fact, the young actress apparently considers this film her worst screen performance for just that reason.

But if some elements of *Everyone Says I Love You* needed to appear spontaneous, there were others that had to be well prepared. For instance, the song "I'm Through with Love" was adopted as the movie's central theme and metaphor. Because Allen, Roberts, Alda, Portman, Norton, and Hawn would all sing it, this involved a number of arrangements.

"That was Woody's idea," notes Hyman. "Then, of course, there's [also] the rap version. That was Woody's idea too. So I wrote a draft of that, and he said he wanted it to be more obscene. So, I did more in that direction, and we engaged some professional rappers who ultimately became my cowriters, and they put some important things in it and also used some standard rap devices.

"It turned out very well, but in the end, Woody did not want it on the cast album," Hyman admits. "I have the full version of it . . . somewhere."

Then there was the arrangement of another tune, "Cuddle Up a Little Closer," which involves one of the film's jokes. "Woody's very funny idea called for a Hindu taxi driver to burst into an unlikely old time song in his native tongue, the passengers joining in at the ending," Hyman explains. "Well, first of all, the lyrics of 'Cuddle Up a Little Closer' had to be translated into Hindi. We found a young man at Yale named Sanjeev Ramabhadran who was able to do that, and then asked him to record the song, performing with piano only . . . The actor playing the driver was actually lip-synching."

Regarding the shooting of the musical numbers, Hyman relied on a tried and true technique: prerecording. "Most of the songs were prerecorded with voice and piano alone. Then, when we got a good take—and we often edited a couple of performances—we replaced the piano with the orchestra in a subsequent recording session. That is, I conducted the orchestra to accompany the already recorded vocal track.

"On the other hand, we used a full orchestra and chorus for Grandpa [Patrick Cranshaw] for 'Enjoy Yourself,' which he sings postmortem in the funeral home, and we recorded it the old way—everyone playing and singing it at the same time. Woody's performance of 'I'm Through with Love' was done the same way, basically, although he sang after the orchestra had recorded the accompaniment."

One beautiful and charming moment in the film involves Alan Alda serenading Goldie Hawn at a piano to the tune of Cole Porter's "Looking at You."

"Of all the songs that people talk to me about in that film, that's the one that seems to reach them the most," reflects Hyman. "It was a comparatively little known Cole Porter song, and it's very charming in its way."

"We didn't, in that case, replace my own piano playing [which] I had done with Alda when he sang it in the studio just the two of us. I used that, and it became the basis of the arrangement. In time-honored fashion, I brought in the orchestra after eight bars. That's the way they used to do that kind of thing."

After a shooting schedule that transported the cast to Paris and Venice, and then back to Manhattan, Woody Allen began cutting together the film, and to keep it lively and well-paced, removed several numbers in the process. Five songs were excised from the film, including the entire role of comedian Tracey Ullman.[31] A cameo by Liv Tyler was also reportedly removed before the film premiered.

When *Everyone Says I Love You* debuted, it received some of the best reviews of any Woody Allen film in years. Roger Ebert suggested the film might be the best in the director's long career, and many of the critics detected exactly how carefully and lovingly Allen had crafted a movie musical that, while grounded in the present, reflected an older, perhaps more gentle and sentimental era.

"This kind of movie escapism recalls the screwball comedies with which Hollywood distracted audiences during the Depression. It's a world where no one has to work and everyone has too much money," noted critic Joseph Cuneen.[32]

"Allen is using music the way it was used in the thirties and forties when actors like James Stewart, Joan Crawford, and Clark Gable were occasionally pressed into musical service despite their limitations," opined Jack Mathews in *Newsday*.[33]

"Woody Allen's new film has charm," raved Stanley Kauffmann in the *New Republic*, "*Everyone Says I Love You* is warm from its first moment, and almost all the time thereafter, it glows."[34] The film also landed on the "Year's 10 Best Lists" of *Time* magazine, the *Chicago Sun-Times*, the *Los Angeles Times*, *Good Morning America,* and others. It seemed audiences concurred with the critical assessment, and *Everyone Says I Love You* proved a modest hit, a more financially successful picture than Woody Allen's other ventures in the nineties. Not exactly a blockbuster, but again, it may be important to note that the movie musical was again earning money, not losing it.

Everyone Says I Love You is the story of a hip, young New Yorker named D.J. (Lyonne) as she recounts a year in the life of her most unusual blended family a gaggle of upscale Manhattan liberals. This includes D.J.'s bleeding heart mother, Steff (Hawn), and stepfather Bob (Alda), who are worried about their son, Scott (Haas), who has mysteriously begun to espouse conservative talking points.

Meanwhile, another child, Skylar (Barrymore), prepares to wed a young lawyer named Holden Spence (Norton), despite her "white knight" syndrome and reservations that he is not particularly romantic.

On vacation in Europe, D.J. assists her biological father, a neurotic writer named Joe Berlin (Allen), to get over the failure of his latest romantic relationship, despite his protestations that he is "through with love." As the seasons change, Joe romances a beautiful woman named Von (Roberts) in Venice, exploiting D.J.'s ill-gotten knowledge of Von's therapy sessions as ammunition to win her affections.

Back in Manhattan, Skylar and Holden break up when Skylar dates a dangerous ex-convict named Charles Ferry (Roth), and the whole family mourns when Grandpa (Cranshaw) passes away, his ghost imploring everybody in the family to "enjoy themselves" because it is later than they think.

As the eventful year ends, D.J.'s family gathers in Paris for Christmas. Von and Joe have broken up, Scott is his liberal self again, and the marriage of Holden and Skylar is a go. On Christmas Eve, after a party in which the guests are costumed as the Marx Brothers, Joe and his first wife, Steff, steal a moment to share a romantic dance on the banks of the Seine.

As this synopsis reveals, *Everyone Says I Love You* is as light as a feather, and appears to intentionally invoke the structure of the 1944 hit, *Meet Me in St. Louis*, the Judy Garland picture which also concerned a "year in the life" of an American family, and was punctuated by the turning of the seasons. The difference here is that Allen's extended family is very liberal, very dysfunctional, and very 1990s.

One interesting thing about the film is how Allen starts right off with a song, "Just You, Just Me," thereby short-circuiting any rocky sense of transition from dialogue to musical production number. From frame one, without preamble, explanation, or disclaimer, this film is a real musical, and within seconds, Allen builds on that notion to add comedy to the movie's formula.

We see not just Holden and Skylar crooning away, but other denizens of New York too, including women out with baby strollers, a nurse and her ward, and then finally, we get the punch line. An unkempt homeless man on the street collects money in a can, and, of course, he's singing about love too.

This comedic image immediately bursts any bubble of pretension, and suddenly the film is really off to the races, marshaling humor and music in tandem to forge a comment about people swooning with the music of love.

The core tenet of *Everyone Says I Love You*, and one that is brilliantly fostered by Allen's unusual decision to have nonsingers and nondancers play the major roles, is that everybody in this world carries a tune in their heart. The lyrics of the song "Everyone Says I Love You" reinforce that stance, and perhaps it is the image of the homeless man, the nurse, the crook, the taxi driver, or the jewelry store salesman, which stays with us most powerfully. Each one of these people is more or less a component of our daily life and when they burst into song, they mirror some essential quality in the human spirit that we recognize. If that guy on the corner can do it, we can too.

"All they can manage is a wistful croak or an awkward shuffle," wrote *Time*'s Richard Schickel. "This is very funny and it is often very poignant. For which of us has not dreamed those sweet little dreams of transcendence—sung a love song under our breath, done a silly little two-step on the way home from a musical when we guessed nobody was looking?"[35]

That is precisely the magic chemistry of Woody Allen's engaging and heartfelt film. "Talent is not the point; desire is the point," emphasizes critic David Denby,[36] and that translates into an interesting notion about humanity, and how we each carry internal radios tuned directly to our emotional ups and downs.

Watching Edward Norton sweetly and haphazardly fumble his way through complex dance steps in "My Baby Just Cares for Me" is some kind of revelation in movie musical history, and perhaps in comedy history too. This talented actor falls over a desk, is overpowered by the other (professional) dancers in the scene, and yet there he proudly stands, up front and center in his own musical fantasy, not permitting his lack of grace to stop him or even slow him down for one second.

There's something really empowering about that image.

This is a different dynamic than *Pennies from Heaven*, where Steve Martin or Bernadette Peters imagined themselves warbling with perfect pitch to the cheery tunes of their time. There, the musical numbers were ironic counterpoint; cynical and sinister reflections of the characters' reality.

In *Everyone Says I Love You*, the notion of actors awkwardly singing their own internal tunes makes the characters (and the performers) more human, loveable, and endearing in a way that feels fresh and invigorating. It is not the fantasy land evoked by the splendor that is Fred Astaire. It is not the spectacle and grandeur of *Evita*, but something wholly its own, and totally sweet.

Everyone Says I Love You is just the kind of movie that musical purists will likely despise. For really avid theater and musical aficionados, desire probably doesn't count when it comes to singing, yet for the average moviegoer, and for an American populace out-of-practice with understanding and interpreting the musical form, this effort presents a near perfect reintroduction.

Still, the Allen approach is a controversial one.

"I really think that asking nonprofessionals to sing limits what you can do in a musical," suggests Hyman. "The results may be amusing, interesting, even charming, but at best they are amateurish. Of course, I am aware that even in *My Fair Lady*, Audrey Hepburn's voice was replaced by Marni Nixon's. And that Rex Harrison hardly sang at all but declaimed the lyrics. So they had some problems too."

In the final analysis, music is—and should be—democratic. It's for the butcher, the baker, the guy who sings in the shower, and the opera star too. Everyone loves music and everyone says I love you, and Allen's film links these commonalities. That's his vernacular, his contract, and it's an efficient one.

And besides, the dance moves of the professionals are certainly well-choreographed by Graciela Daniele, and the music is beautifully orchestrated by Dick Hyman, so even for "high art" fans, there is pleasure to be unearthed here. What may be most refreshing about the film is the grace with which Allen has staged it. This is the fashion in which critic Brian D. Johnson described Allen's camera work, and his words captures the feel of the film beautifully:

> Allen still shoots and edits with unparalleled fluidity and grace. By following the dialogue with a moving lens instead of piecing it together in the cutting room, he gives his actors a rare creative freedom that they visibly relish. This is also the most postcard pretty film that the director has ever made. When his camera is not cruising Venetian canals or ogling the Eiffel Tower, it is flashing Central Park's spring blossoms and fall's colors. The screen glows with old-fashioned opulence.[37]

Over the last decade or thereabouts, especially since the Mia Farrow scandal, Woody Allen has been viewed more frequently as a filmmaker outside the mainstream, one who appeals only to a liberal, intellectual elite. What *Everyone Says I Love You* reestablishes rather handily is Allen's connection to the mainstream audience, his capacity to craft a deft fantasy that is accessible to every demographic.

A perfect example of this accessibility is the film's climactic number, which features Goldie Hawn and Woody Allen dancing together on the bank of the Seine. The water shimmers gently behind them, and the cityscape of Paris is bathed in soft, lovely gold. Woody stretches out his hand and effortlessly lifts the elegant Hawn high into the black night sky, reminding us we all feel as light as air when we're in love.

This sequence is so romantic, beautifully shot, and vividly executed, that it is instantly identifiable to anybody who has ever felt that euphoric flush of romantic love. It's glorious, and it really doesn't matter a whit that Allen can't dance as nimbly as Fred Astaire or as athletically as Gene Kelly. What does matter, perhaps, is that he feels the same joy in his heart, and that means that as an audience, we experience it too. Love, passion, sophistication, and music needn't be reserved for the figures we see on the silver screen. Cue the music—and watch us dance too.

Woody Allen's method of blending song, dance, and comedy serves as an efficient, if highly unorthodox way to slide the movie musical right back into view on American movie screens. In the same era, other filmmakers were attempting analogous alchemies.

For instance, comedian Christopher Guest, master of the so-called mockumentary format also presented an unusual musical in 1997, *Waiting for Guffman*. Like all the Guest films, *Guffman* is a movie with an improvised script, but based on an extensive outline he cocreated with actor Eugene Levy. As in his other low-budget pictures from Castle Rock Entertainment, there's a climax that culminates with some fashion of performance, whether it is a competitive dog show (*Best in Show* [2000]) or a folk music revue (*A Mighty Wind* [2003]).

In the case of *Waiting for Guffman*, the film's denouement is the presentation of a community theater production, a musical play entitled "Red, White and Blaine." The revue has been created by one Corky St. Clair (Guest) to celebrate the town of Blaine's sesquicentennial anniversary. Corky is a flamboyant high school drama teacher who was once shunned on Broadway, and has now escaped to the Midwest to more fully express himself and his creative drives. Performing's in his blood, and the same is true of his inexperienced but enthusiastic cast, which includes dentists, the local Dairy Queen hottie and a couple of travel agents.

During the performance of "Red, White, and Blaine," the film's wacky characters, played by Fred Willard, Catherine O'Hara, Eugene Levy, Parker Posey, and Guest, perform a variety of bizarre and very funny songs, including the hilarious World War I effort called "Penny for Your Thoughts," which sees an intentionally clumsy Posey and not-very-limber Guest attempt a delicate ballet.

Another terrific song in *Waiting for Guffman* is the immortal "Stool Boom," which concerns Blaine's reputation as the (foot) "stool capital of the world." Actor-comedian Harry Shearer composed this ditty with Guest, and spoke about it in this author's *Best in Show: The Films of Christopher Guest and Company*:

> Chris came over and he said, "There's this premise about the town of Blaine," and that stools were "the big thing." So we were sitting at the bench of the piano in my house, and the phrase "Stool Boom" came out. Chris had a melody already, which came out being the B-part of the song. I was playing, and just sort of came up with the vamp, and a little magic stuff happened. You put yourself in the right mood and the song comes through you, even if it's a jokey song like that.[38]

Waiting for Guffman is a comedy that explores how everybody, even those blessed with only a modicum of talent, is moved, even transfixed by the thought of stardom and performance. These enthusiastic amateurs give every song their absolute best—even if it isn't very good—and the comedy is both gentle and sweet, because we all recognize these types and identify something of ourselves in them. *Guffman* is also a wickedly funny film, and a unique example of the backstage formula that has walked hand-in-hand with the genre since its very inception.

Another backstage movie musical released in 1997 is one the world probably should have been spared. I refer to the Bob Spiers's pop-music extravaganza known as *Spice World*. For those who have mercifully forgotten it, the British pop group ("band" is probably too strong a descriptor here) the Spice Girls were an international sensation in the mid-1990s.

The group's first single, "Wannabe," became the "biggest selling debut single ever" and ascended to the number one slot in the charts in thirty-two countries. Impressively, the Spice Girls' first album sold more than fifty million copies within a year of its release.[39]

The once-popular group consisted of five female performers: Baby, Ginger, Scary, Sporty, and Posh Spice, and their popularity made it inevitable that they would eventually appear in a film. With a script fashioned by scribe Kim Fuller, the writer who gave the world *From Justin to Kelly* in 2002, the film is actually an insubstantial homage to the classic Beatles film *A Hard Day's Night* with its heady blend of music, fantasy, and reality.

The film concerns the Spice Girls, who play themselves, as the group endlessly circles London in their oversized, fully equipped bus, which, like the TARDIS in *Doctor Who*, is apparently dimensionally transcendent: larger on the inside than out. The girls are in the employ of a mysterious benefactor, played by former James Bond, Roger Moore, and soon they clash with a nasty tabloid editor out to destroy their reputations, and also hear incessant movie pitches from an American producer played by George Wendt. Alan Cumming is in the movie too, playing a hapless filmmaker who is shooting a documentary about the girls that aspires to "crash through the show business wall."

Any way you want to tart it up, *Spice World* is a charmless, stitched-together film that connects a number of light fantasy moments so as to provide the group the opportunity to perform several of their cookie-cutter, distinctly unmemorable musical hits. In one such fantasy, all the girls imagine that they're pregnant. In another sequence, they meet up with extraterrestrials while in the forest taking a pee. The aliens just want their autographs, of course.

Another videoesque music sequence reveals the Spice Girls at an elaborate photo shoot, and they dress up as iconic characters, including Wonder Woman, Marilyn Monroe, Olivia Newton-John in *Grease*, and Honey Rider from *Dr. No* (1962).

Spice World tries hard to be something along the lines of *A Hard Day's Night* meets *Austin Powers* (1997), but the personalities and charisma of the Spice Girls are limited at best and interchangeable at worst, and for a movie that's supposed to be about girl power, it's strange that this force of feminine nature is powered by a male chief (Moore). Mostly, the Spice Girls come across as whiners and slackers, and the only scene that might have evidenced some charm—featuring the group in its early "hungry days"—is instead a desperate grasp for legitimacy, as though the Spice Girls are all about their music and not merely a commercial product packaged for mass pop-culture consumption.

"When you're feeling sad and low," suggests one of the signature Spice Girl tunes, "spice up your life!" The movie could have heeded that advice. With fewer outrageous flourishes, and a bit more substance, it might have been all right. And about any future comparisons between the Spice Girls and Beatles? Well, I've seen *A Hard Day's Night*. I've reviewed *A Hard Day's Night*. Believe me, girls, *Spice World* is no *A Hard Day's Night*.

PERFECT AND POISONOUS

While humorous movie musicals like *Everyone Says I Love You*, *Waiting for Guffman*, *Spice World*, and *South Park: Bigger, Longer & Uncut* (1999) dominated the final years of the century, the independently produced ode to the age of Glam Rock, 1998's *Velvet Goldmine*, represented something entirely different. The project began in the mid-1990s with a unity of purpose among its collaborators, cocreators Todd Haynes and James Lyons. The duo had worked together on several films previously, including *Poison* (1991) and *Safe* (1995), the latter starring Julianne Moore, but their new project was a more personal one in some ways.

"On my side, it [*Velvet Goldmine*] came out of an idea I had in college," reports Lyons. "I knew a kid, a local rock musician, who had literally run away from home. He ran away from his repressive Westchester house to come to New York City and be in a rock band. And he fell in with that rock band, and I was always going to write a story about that [experience]. That character turned into the Christian Bale character [Arthur]. So there was always that line, that there would be a kid [in the story]. But there was also the idea of making something about glitter rock, and what an incredible thing it was."

Glitter or glam rock, as it is alternately known, is a phenomenon of the early 1970s, and one created by music icons including David Bowie, Iggy Pop, Lou Reed, and Marc Bolan of T-Rex. It was a movement in pop culture that arrived "between Woodstock and disco,"[40] wherein the old lines of sexuality were blurred, along with male and female fashions. It was especially popular in Great Britain.

"I was raised in Los Angeles, and my orientation through much of elementary school was still classic sixties media imagery, which I was very interested in and attracted to," *Velvet Goldmine's* director, Todd Haynes, sets the scene. "But then something else began to emerge around the time I was going to junior high school. *This Bowie figure.* This Alice Cooper phenomenon. And to me it was actually scary at first. It was really off-putting and otherworldly and strange, and I'm sure all of that could easily explain a deeper fascination or attraction to it, as well.

"[It was] something suggestive to me that maybe I wasn't able to confront at the time," he continues. "And those were extreme images. The androgyny was harsh and in your face, and there was a real assault on the public with these images, I think—purposefully and brilliantly—and a concerted attempt to over-turn a lot of the sixties. So that's where it [*Velvet Goldmine*] generates a lot of its energy."

But even more than the in-your-face element of glam rock, there was another fascinating component of this age. A new voice for sexual equality, tolerance, and even experimentation emerged, perhaps not quite consciously, from glam rock, and it deeply affected many young people of the period. This movement was called "an important watershed for gays who were inspired by their cross-dressing heroes to come out of their closets."[41]

This facet of the trend was represented in *Velvet Goldmine* by the charac-ter of Arthur, who comes to an understanding of his own sexuality and views Brian Slade and Curt Wild as figures of identification. In particular, in one fantasy sequence Arthur sees them on TV and exuberantly informs his zombie parents, "That's me! That's me!"

"That was a central part of it," Haynes acknowledges. "There were these brazenly bold statements by David Bowie. Some people refute them today as false. [But] it didn't really matter [if they were true], when an androgynous pop star is on television saying, 'Yes, I'm bisexual. I sleep with boys, I sleep with girls, it's all the same to me,' and was that brazenly casual.

"What's funny is that everybody can identify with Bowie in different ways," Haynes says. "Everybody was drawn to that image. It wasn't exclusive to boys who had gay feelings. Girls were obsessed with Bowie, and straight boys were strangely lured to this image, because it was available to them as a kind of safe, homoerotic fantasy because he was so feminine-looking. Everybody had a safe access to him, even though it all felt dangerous and exciting at the same time."

"When we were growing up . . . a band like Queen, which was so obvi-ously gay, was not seen as a gay band," editor Lyons points out. "It was so wonderful. Everybody could like them, and it really led to a blending of straight and gay, particularly for guys, because guys always want to be guitar heroes. I was thrilled with it when I was a child. It wasn't even that those musicians were models; they were just these fascinating objects. I needed to have everything . . . I needed to have all the Bowie stuff."

In conjunction with the era of glitter rock, the seventies also represented a period of experimentation in the American and British cinemas, and in musicals specifically, and the new cinematic freedoms impacted the genesis of *Velvet Goldmine* in the mid-to-late 1990s.

"When I was growing up in the 1970s, there was this big thing where you could go and watch midnight movies and see *Pink Flamingos* (1972) or *2001: A Space Odyssey*. It's gone now," Lyons laments. "The main thing was rock concert movies. I saw *Pink Floyd: Live at Pompeii* (1972) or the Led Zeppelin movie— all those things. At that point, every rock band had a movie, and you'd watch them at midnight, and then get really stoned."

"I saw *O Lucky Man!* when I was very young," Todd Haynes recollects. "I loved it. I loved *If*—which is a little different. I would see all these films, as well as obsessively view all the European art cinema, and all the great revival films that you could see at that time. It was such a treat. I dug *Phantom of the Paradise* (1974). I liked Ken Russell's films, everything from his sober *Women in Love* (1969) to the weirder ones, like *Tommy* (1975) and *Lisztomania* (1975). They're crazy, and so radically inventive and giddy. They are inspiring, because anything seems possible in them."

It was a rude awakening, however, when Lyons and Haynes attended college in the late 1970s and early 1980s only to discover that the cultural moment of experimentation had pretty much passed them by.

"We grew up wishing that we had been part of the hippies of the sixties, so that by the time we got to college, we were looking around. '*Where is that counterculture?*'" says Lyons. "We could still smell the idea of a counterculture that people once believed was going to change everything."

The two artists may have missed that aspect of American life, which eventually gave way in the eighties to a narrow-mindedness and anti-intellectual strain that remains with the nation today, but while working on *Velvet Goldmine*, the two writers hoped to evoke the golden age they never got to enjoy.

"We didn't think we were making a musical for our time, we thought we were making a head musical," establishes Lyons. "Todd used to sometimes say,

'Take out your joints now!' I'm not a big proponent of drugs, but that was a way, in the 1970s, to see movies. You would ritualize the movie; you'd get a little high from the movie, and it would be more intense.

"We were celebrating what we saw as the freedom of that time to experiment with your body. Which included drugs. There was a feeling that you could have an experience, and that experience itself was a value, whether you tried cocaine for the first time in your life, or you're a guy, and you kiss a man for the first time in your life. Those values were there in the 1970s, and they're gone.

"That's a big impulse of the film," Lyons acknowledges, "that it should come back. Life is an adventure, if you're brave enough to seize it, and that [also] goes for stylistic flourishes!"

Not coincidentally, the often flamboyant age of glam rock also proved the perfect subject for a musical, an art form that was known for its dynamic nature and bold colorations.

"I love the stated artifice and celebrated sense of artifice—also an attack on sixties naturalism—that was part of the glam rock generation," Haynes describes. "I wanted to apply that very artifice and sense of creating oneself as a fiction, and apply it to the narrative style so that I wasn't going to stick to any one style. In many ways, the most surreal, unnaturalistic, the most imaginative and free form in film is the musical."

"We picked a moment in show business that was colorful and theatrical," Lyons acknowledges. "I don't know how you would make a movie musical about Joni Mitchell, James Taylor, or Carole King, those earnest singer-songwriters. I don't know how you'd make a musical about Nirvana and Kurt Cobain, because they were so earnest. Not that I don't love music from those periods, but in both cases it was like, 'I am an artist and I am sincerely expressing my emotions, and it's personal.' Musicals are, by their very nature, artificial. They go through artifice and through color and costume and things that are patently fake."

In other words, glam rock and musicals were a match made in heaven. Now the trick would be to craft a story that could reflect the essence of the glam rock era and its dynamic stars without actually being a biography of any specific real artist or personality.

"I definitely wanted to break out of a lot of the different presumed categories that we think of, especially dealing with the star story genre, which often tries very hard to peek at the highs and lows of a celebrity's career, and sprinkle it with the appropriate songs from their career to dramatize them," describes Haynes. "But usually, the songs are contextualized in a stage setting so that it has a naturalistic framework that you depend on as the truth as to what happened to this character. Of course they always fall short of any sense of objective truth, as all movies do, and in some ways, the fun is in the discrepancies between what we remember and what we love about those performers."

Armed with the intent to revisit an age passed, it was time to focus on the specifics of *Velvet Goldmine*, which Lyons originally wanted to title *For Your Pleasure*. "We did a lot of research," notes Lyons. "We read everything that we could about Bowie, and the music itself. I never really made it all the way through, but Todd read this giant biography of Oscar Wilde."

Oscar Wilde (1854–1900)? Why was this nineteenth-century Victorian dramatist, poet, and author of *The Picture of Dorian Gray* (1981) important to a musical production about glam rock set in the early 1970s?

"For me it seemed inevitable, and a relatively obvious connection to make, once you entered the world of English tropes and the twentieth century, and arguably before that, Beau Brummell, the dandy," describes Haynes, "the self-professed connoisseur of artifice and inverter of values based on the real.

"Basically, people who attacked the notion of the real. And often there's a link to sexuality and identity that fueled that. And Oscar Wilde used language so brilliantly. I think his examples rise to the top in his literary work, but I definitely saw a continuum there."

"We wanted to make the claim for a spirit that is not necessarily a gay spirit, but who had been there all along, and who has often been associated with gay people," considers Lyons. "It [this quality] comes from somewhere that we don't understand, and goes somewhere else, and it's magical and wonderful, and as many times as you try to kill it, it will come back. Ideas like that. There's always gonna be a guy who wants to wear eyeshadow, and you can't do anything about it."

Another element of *Velvet Goldmine*'s structure involved the layering of the plot in a format highly reminiscent of Orson Welles's 1941 masterpiece, *Citizen Kane*. That film's narrative includes a reporter seeking to learn more about the recently deceased newspaper magnate Charles Foster Kane and his opaque life. Through a series of interviews, the reporter attempts to assemble the man's biography and arrive at some conclusion about who his subject "really was." Of course, *Citizen Kane* ends with a missing piece of the puzzle the reporter was never privy to, Kane's childhood toy, a sled named Rosebud, which alludes to Kane's final utterance in this mortal coil.

"To me, *Citizen Kane* is a very profound movie, and one of the many profound things about it is that framing device," suggests Lyons. "You're investigating a person. And by the end of it, you find only that you don't know who the person is. You end up knowing a lot about Kane, but not everything. Welles shows you the sled, Rosebud, which the reporter never sees. Even knowing that it's a sled doesn't explain a man's life.

"To us, the idea was that you can investigate a man's life and never really know anything. And so our main figure, Brian Slade consciously obfuscated any attempt at knowing him. We wanted him to be a figure like a Bowie or a Dylan, so that was a reason to reference the *Citizen Kane* structure, to have that inquiry."

For director Haynes, there was another motive to mirror *Citizen Kane*'s famous narrative structure. "One thing I felt pretty certain about, and Jim and I talked about this a lot while we were developing the ideas—a lot of which did erupt from his original concept—was that I knew it was going to be a film more about the fan than the artist. I wanted a distance from these artists.

"I was never comfortable with the biopic tradition that's all about 'What really happened behind closed doors,' and 'What did David Bowie really say to Lou Reed in that room?,' things we can never know. It always feels a little cheap to be spending so much time trying to construct these missing narratives, when, in fact, what they did produce publicly—the illusion of wild, campy, androgynous sex and radical expression—was so strong that there was almost nothing that could have happened in real life that could have matched it. And who needs it, when that [aspect] is fully documented and completely available to us today? So I wanted it to be filtered through the fan, and have there still be an element of mystery about these artists.

"The *Citizen Kane* structure is the classic one that sets up the series of mysteries and veils between the investigative source and the subject, and it was an excellent and baroque reference in the history of cinema to equate with this particularly baroque period in rock'n'roll too."

Another facet of this *Kane* homage was that it granted *Velvet Goldmine*'s creators the opportunity to fashion a tale that took place across multiple time periods. One time line involved the ascent of glam rock and the heyday of Brian Slade. The other, involving Arthur as investigator, was set well after the form was dead, in a kind of hopeless, Orwellian 1980s.

"I'm not sure that Miramax ever understood this, but we always wanted the film to be melancholy, to have this big sense of loss for the time that was gone," Lyons notes. "Even though it was only a few years later (the eighties), it seemed to make sense to have a present day that was a bit drab, and look back at this golden age. The structure provided that too.

"What's funny about the eighties in the movie is that they aren't really the 1980s that we know," suggests Haynes. "It's more the product of a fictionalized, doomed future that was projected in the 1970s, which is one of the reasons why Bowie was fascinated by Orwell. His [Bowie's] frivolous decadence began to turn into a kind of degenerative, apocalyptic future in records like *Diamond Dogs*. So that was already in their vernacular, and of course, we've retreated in so many different ways from the radical spirit and sense of possibility that people must have felt at the end of the sixties and early seventies. And today's administration is just more extreme than anybody could have imagined."

In re-creating the world of glam rock for *Velvet Goldmine*, Haynes and Lyons were quickly advised that the film would have to begin with a disclaimer. The point of contention was that some folks (Bowie, Reed, Iggy, and Bolan, among others) might claim the film was about them—and litigate.

Accordingly, *Velvet Goldmine* opens with a title card advising viewers that the film is a work of fiction, but that it should nonetheless be "played at maximum volume." This suggestion has many sources, from Scorsese's rock performance movie, *The Last Waltz* (1978), to ones even more relevant to the glam experience.

"That's on *Sticky Fingers*, the Stones album," notes James Lyons.

"On the *Ziggy Stardust* record, it literally says on the record that it should be played at 'maximum volume,' so we slipped that in," adds Haynes. "But really, it was a legal disclaimer that we were encouraged to introduce the film with for legal purposes, to emphasize that this was fiction. I just had to do it in a way that was a little more fun and dressed up in the style of the movie to come, [rather] than a bland legal disclaimer at the beginning. That was my version of the legal disclaimer."

"We were not trying to portray David Bowie. We were not trying to portray Lou Reed," Lyons emphasizes. "We mixed up elements from all the different stars that we read about, so that the character [who] people associated with Bowie had elements of Lou Reed, and the character that people associated with Iggy has elements of other people. Our lawyer said 'You have to make that statement in the very beginning; that this is fiction.' Of course, how could you not know it's fiction?"

With a screenplay fashioned, casting *Velvet Goldmine* was the next step in the process. "Ewan McGregor was somebody I knew I wanted in the film right away after seeing *Trainspotting* (1996)," remembers Haynes. "But it took longer to find the best Arthur for the film, and the best Mandy for the film. And with the role for Brian Slade, because of specific requirements—the whole androgyny and thinness and beauty that was required for the character—that narrowed it. Once I met Jonathan [Rhys-Meyers] I was pretty set. It was hard to match him in that.

"We probably looked the longest and hardest for Mandy. This is a very strange character who is this hybrid American-Brit girl, whose accent would wane purposefully in and out of an American and English accent. Some people think that was a mistake, but it's completely purposeful. There are people like that, and apparently Angela Bowie was like that.

"But more than that, Mandy was that Sally Bowles, extravagant feminine persona," says Haynes. "A lot of girls that age don't have that example anymore. All those airs, and that kind of female faggotry that we associate with a character like Sally Bowles was just no longer present in our contemporary culture. It was wiped away. Girls aren't supposed to act all fluttery and fabulous, and 'darling' this and 'darling' that. It was very hard for American actresses to even say the word 'darling,' let alone pull it off comfortably. It was hard, because I read some great people who interpreted it in different ways."

But Haynes was more than satisfied when he met Australian star Toni Collette, Muriel in *Muriel's Wedding* (1994) and recently, Carla of *Connie and Carla* (2004). "Toni Collette can just do anything. Australian culture was interesting because you could sort of understand American culture and English culture as an outsider and incorporator of both, in her own native Australian culture. So that was the key, aside from her being brilliant and super intelligent."

Christian Bale, the future Batman, returned to the musical format in *Velvet Goldmine* after his less-than-successful stint in the genre in early nineties films including *Newsies* and *Swing Kids*. They were all joined by English comedian Eddie Izzard as Slade's money-hungry agent, Jerry Devine. Those producing the film included Killer Films' Christine Vachon (*Hedwig and the Angry Inch*, *Camp*), and R.E.M. singer Michael Stipe.

Ewan McGregor reported preparing for his role by researching the era and watching tapes of the age's real stars. In particular, he viewed footage of "Lou Reed and Robbie Robertson in *The Last Waltz* to try to get that fucked-up, groggily rock and roll voice."[42] This was critical for the role of a loose cannon, and genuine American rocker, like his character, Curt Wild. Collette prepped rigorously too, in part by reading Angie Bowie's autobiography "to figure out what she must have gone through."[43]

On a budget of approximately seven million dollars, *Velvet Goldmine* commenced principal photography in early 1997, shooting in London and Manchester. To Haynes's best memory, the shoot was not longer than forty-five days. "It was super tight," he recalls. "It was a really tough shoot for me, just because of the money and how incredibly demanding the script was, and how many little, short scenes in different locations—let alone different eras—we had to accomplish.

"It was hard to shoot in London," the director continues. "That was one of the best things about it, to be in London and really delve into it and use British crews, but just to move around in that city, and to move from place to place with the whole crew was hard, because it's a really congested city."

Complicating matters, the film was a musical, and that meant elaborate production numbers had to be staged with extremely limited time, and on a narrow budget. Added to that mix was a component of live performance, and sometimes four hundred extras were required for scenes.

"We did different things for different scenes as they were required," Haynes explains. "We did as much rehearsal as we could, but that was still pretty sparse, given our timetable. But it depended on the performance. When Ewan McGregor performs his two songs I wanted him to sing live on camera, so we had a back-up track prerecorded, an instrumental track that the musicians would pantomime to, but he would sing live in his master takes. He was actually singing live on film, which is not the way it's usually done.

"The other [musical numbers] were almost all prerecorded. Jonathan may have sung 'Sebastian,' but for the most part he would prerecord his own voice on certain songs and lip-synch to it, or other people supplied his voice for other numbers, including Thom Yorke from Radiohead, who did several Roxy Music covers.

"But the live scenes required a kind of planned improvisation, where we always tried to have several cameras [going] at once. Sometimes [we'd use] two 35 mm cameras and one 16 mm camera, so we were able to catch as much spontaneous and simultaneous activity as possible. That meant strategizing placements of the camera so you wouldn't cover each camera in the other, literally, in the frame, and that you were getting a good, rounded coverage for a particular performance, so the actor wouldn't have to keep doing it and matching it. The goal would be to maintain the spontaneity and have it on film, covered in enough angles that you could intercut."

Todd Haynes also notes that it was "hard to strike a balance" sometimes in the vetting of the material. *Velvet Goldmine* is an interesting hybrid, both a grounded, naturalistic film, and one that reaches for the artificial heights of old-fashioned musicals. It was an uneasy and revolutionary blend, and the director considers himself blessed that his cast related to and understood the material so well. "I was amazed how well all of them did in the end," he says.

Editing *Velvet Goldmine* turned out to be a difficult task, especially for James Lyons, who does the job for a living. Part of the problem, he says, is that there was just such a high degree of personal attachment to the material. "I loved the ideas and the images. Todd came up with spectacular images. I'm usually really good about knowing that you can't put everything into a film, [but] I'm really in love with the ideas, images and characters."

"It was hard," agrees Haynes, "but I really enjoyed the process. I was ready, after a grueling shoot, to be back in a room just with Jim, who I had a long creative relationship with . . . whom I really trusted. And [I] felt like we could really zero back in on what this was all about, together, without the distractions of production."

And, as it turned out, the director and editor shared a mantra about the film's eventual form. "We had an aesthetic rule we were trying to keep, which said 'more is more,'" describes Lyons. "In this case, put on more mascara, put on more sequins, more eyeshadow, more feathers. That's the nature of this kind of work, it's Oscar Wilde. Another *bon mot*! Just keep piling it on, and that's true of musicals. You can never go over the top, and we were very attracted to that idea, so that was a challenge."

Unfortunately, there were others who had a very precise notion of how, exactly, *Velvet Goldmine* should look, and what should be omitted from the final cut. Miramax paid more than two million dollars for the North American distribution rights, and had some notions about the film.[44]

"Miramax really only picked it up. They only had the rights to distribute the film," Lyons sets the scene. "Their promise of distributing it made sure that the film could be made, but they didn't put money into the actual making of the film, and that's an important distinction. It was lucky for us, because they would have recut the whole thing.

"We went to a meeting where they did that," Lyons reveals.

"All I remember is that they asked me to come into a meeting and without telling me, they just turned on a recut version of several scenes," Todd Haynes describes. "I just found it to be an offensive way to make suggestions. It felt like meddling. It's not the way I've ever really worked before, so I was not happy. We just left. It wasn't something I wanted to sit through."

"One thing they wanted to take out was the 'white and gold' scene where they [Brian Slade and Curt Wild] were having the press conference," Lyons recalls. "There's a white set, and all the different characters are in white and gold, [and there are] very arty references. They're all being asked questions by the reporters, and they answer in these different aphorisms that we collected from Wilde and art history, which we loved."

The folks at Miramax didn't feel the same way.

"It didn't 'move the story along.' It was 'too weird.' That's what they said," Lyons remembers. "It was also very faggy, and purposefully so. We tried to make it explicitly faggy.

"I don't think Harvey Weinstein is dumb. He gets the idea. But his idea is a commercial idea," Lyons specifies. "He probably wouldn't admit it, but he understands art history, it just doesn't mean anything to him. His argument is that you will reach more people if you don't have scenes like that which stop the narrative. And if you reach more people—and that adds up being more bucks for him—there is a sort of missionary aspect to the film. You really are beaming it out to the world, hoping that fourteen-year-old Jim will see that.

"His point is that if you want to reach people, have less weird shit. But we were like, 'No way!'" Lyons recalls. "There was no way Todd would ever let it go. No way I would. No way Christine [Vachon] would, thank God. They [Miramax] could ask us to get rid of it. They could show us it done, because they had copies of the dailies, but they couldn't make us do it."

"Miramax was a small company, once devoted to small films that would never have gotten seen any other way than behind their hard-driving campaigns," Haynes considers. "And then, once they reached phenomenal success with certain independent titles, it changed some of their goals. We coincided with one of the most extreme years, where they were after a sort of super-mainstream success, and received it. It was the year of *Shakespeare in Love*, and it was the year of *Life Is Beautiful*, so that was not the year to really hope that they would have any energy or time or money left over to deal with a very unique film like *Velvet Goldmine*, which isn't your typical movie. Unfortunately, the mentality is always to try to squeeze anything different into a form familiar to the audience in trailers and posters."

In this case, that meant an ad campaign which made *Velvet Goldmine* look and sound a lot like a murder mystery. "What happened? Who did it? And why?" asked the trailer's voiceover artist, in regards to the "murder of Brian Slade." As these interrogatives were made, the trailer quick cut to flashes of Mandy, Arthur, and other prominent characters, as though they were actually suspects in an Agatha Christie mystery.

"Ultimately, that became deceitful with *Velvet Goldmine*, because it wasn't a detective-mystery movie and it wasn't really anything you could really point to. And that was its strength," considers Haynes. "In many ways, what happened with *Moulin Rouge* proved that a film as adventurous and out there and otherworldly as *Velvet Goldmine* could really have found a larger audience with more support. I mean, it's a very different film from *Velvet Goldmine*, but it's very radical, very different, and it really takes the musical and turns it on its head."

Although Miramax wanted to make changes in the film and advertised it in a way that didn't come close to capturing its essence, the film began to receive very positive notices. At the Cannes Film Festival that year, *Velvet Goldmine* came extremely close to winning the Gold Palm, but instead took home a special prize for artistic achievement. Martin Scorsese was on the judge's panel that year.

"Scorsese really loved our film and in many ways it is similar to *New York, New York* in that we wanted to have these grand gestures in the spirit of it [the musical], even if we couldn't come close to replicating the Hollywood studio system," explains Lyons. "We wanted to have these very intimate moments of emotion. We wanted to have moments of genuine acting and tenderness, and by genuine, we meant a texture that is like what you saw Marlon Brando come up with, or De Niro or Meryl Streep, who are fascinated with and beautifully replicate the tiny elements of behavior and make you feel like you see a really full person. Which you don't see with Fred Astaire or Leslie Caron."

When *Velvet Goldmine* premiered in June 1998, many critics indeed felt that the film had achieved all those goals, and more. *Variety* noted that "the filmmaking is expansive and creative,"[45] while *Newsweek* raved that it was filled "with music, spectacular costumes and orgiastic revelry," declaring it "a brainy three-ring circus."[46]

While the *Advocate* had some quibbles about the film's "confounding time structure," it noted that the "flamboyant form" of the film "honors the content."[47] Stuart Klawans at the *Nation* was a little less forgiving, while still generally upbeat. *Velvet Goldmine*, he said, was "so often magical, inventive, rousing and smart" that he "winced at each loss of brain, heart or courage."[48]

Velvet Goldmine picked up a raft of other honors, including an Independent Spirit Award for cinematographer Maryse Alberti, and nominations for Best Feature and Best Director. The picture was also honored with an Academy Award nomination for Sandy Powell, the film's costume designer. Still, these accolades did not, in the end, make the film a box office hit.

"It didn't do well in its theatrical release. I don't know if it was well-explained to the filmgoing audience," says Haynes. "I think *Velvet Goldmine* is an unwieldy kind of film. It's a very hard film for people to see just once. It's too much. And you don't really know how seriously to take the plot changes, and how much to worry about them. Most people want to follow that on a first viewing of the film, and that removes a lot of the pleasure of it. Once you get a sense of what it's doing on the second or third viewing, it just starts to open up to people.

"That, in the market of contemporary film, is a harder proposition for people," Haynes considers. "I'm very happy that the film seems to have this amazing afterlife in exactly the places that I hoped, primarily among teenagers and girls and boys who are discovering the glam thing on their own. And there was an explosion of web sites that followed the film's release on DVD that was so amazing to Christine and me. These people were so into it!

"I was inspired to make a film for exactly that age, because I loved those movies that came out of the late sixties, like *Performance* (1970) and the Kubrick films," says Haynes. "And so many films came out of drug culture, and radical culture that were aimed at young people and kind of trippy, and a little bit hard to pin down, and full of layers that you could analyze with your friends, and see over and over again, and play the music, and really enter into these unknown worlds that shouldn't be completely visible on the first viewing.

"It should have layers and passages and secret trapdoors that lead you through them," Haynes suggests. "That was what I wanted *Velvet Goldmine* to be, and for a certain group of people, that's exactly what it is, and that's so cool. They just don't make movies like that anymore."

"I never thought of it as a musical, but I guess it is," considers John Cameron Mitchell. "In the way that *The Rose* (1979) is, though it's definitely more inventive. Todd Haynes is a friend of mine, and I'm a huge fan of his. We both shared notes on the development of *Hedwig* and *Velvet Goldmine*, which was simultaneous. I was a big glam rock fan when I was a kid in elementary school when I lived in Scotland [so] that's a film that's very close to my heart."

The fascinating and unusual *Velvet Goldmine* begins to weave its tale of glam rock in Dublin in 1854, as an alien spacecraft leaves behind a baby on a doorstep—a being destined to be the world's first "pop idol," the poet Oscar Wilde. A glowing green medal worn by young Oscar Wilde then passes down to another young boy several generations later—Jack Fairy. Fairy matures to become one of the originators of the 1970s movement known as glam rock.

Later in the 1970s, another up-and-comer on the music scene steals the unusual emerald pin from Fairy, and soon becomes famous himself as the glam rocker Brian Slade (Rhys-Meyers) and his extraterrestrial, onstage alter ego, Maxwell Demon. With the help of his wife, Mandy (Collette), Slade becomes a huge worldwide phenomenon and inspires fans with his music, bold sexuality, and flamboyant costumes. He even very publicly takes a male lover—American rocker Curt Wild (McGregor)—perhaps to enhance his image. But then, one day, Brian Slade stages his own too-public assassination, only to have it outed as a hoax. His record sales plummet following the publicity stunt, he becomes enmeshed in a cocaine scandal, and the age of innocence and glam rock comes to an abrupt end.

Ten years later, in the Orwellian world of the conservative 1980s dominated by President Reynolds, a young journalist named Arthur (Bale) who once idolized Brian Slade, is assigned by his editor to pen a story about "what really" happened to the glam rock pop star after his fall from grace. Arthur commences an investigation and a series of interviews, including one with Mandy, to learn, finally whatever became of his former role model. The answers prove elusive, until, with the help of Curt Wild, Arthur uncovers Brian Slade's strange and disappointing reinvention.

"*Velvet Goldmine* should be read as a fantasy," wrote *New Statesman* critic Jonathan Romney, "and like the best fantasies, it's fabulously superficial at first sight before revealing hidden depths and resonances."[49] Romney's suggestion represents a good way of first gazing at this multifaceted film, which, as Haynes suggests, opens up more and more on repeat viewing.

Velvet Goldmine unfolds with an effective conceit, that the genesis of glam rock and, indeed, the birth of Oscar Wilde is something almost "otherworldly," something born of the fantastic. Appropriately, the film begins with a view of a night sky, and after a shooting star intersects the frame, the camera seems to swoop lower, down through cottony clouds, until a flying saucer arcs past our view. It is this fairy-tale craft that carries the first pop star to earth.

Next, we meet young Jack Fairy, the heir to Wilde's legacy, symbolized by a green (alien) pin. After he is beaten up in a school yard, Jack discovers this jewelry in the mud. The very next shot involves a long composition of young Jack walking down a fairy tale–style road (a matte painting or other optical effect) that appears blatantly artificial, not unlike a view of the Yellow Brick Road in *The Wizard of Oz*. It is a mystical-looking landscape of gnarled trees on either side, a crooked road stretching off into the distance, and a low glowing sun hangs over the horizon as the viewer's implicit destination. When we next see young Jack, he has traveled over the rainbow indeed, and is applying lipstick and admiring the results.

We're not in Kansas anymore.

From the UFO to the evocative special effects shot and moment of self-discovery, the message of *Velvet Goldmine* seems plain: this is a magical journey, one filled with allusions. The film will do many things and go many places, but *never* will it feel like a traditional biography picture.

"We wanted the sequence to be beautiful, and to be charming, and to be stunning, and to be sad like that," notes James Lyons. "And so the purpose was simply to have a mysterious opening."

The fantasy aspects of the movie subtly tell us what we need to know about the film's *dramatis personae* and their journeys. In his first concert, for instance, Brian Slade, the next heir to Wilde after Fairy, sings explicitly about his spaceship and its "view screen," connecting right back to the opening images of the UFO. When Slade is shot on stage, slow-motion photography extends the moment of terror, as if seen through young Arthur's horrified eyes.

All through this sequence, white feathers fall across the frame like snow, a deluge. Again, this dousing of the audience is an appropriate image, not just given Slade's own peacocklike garb, but considering the fantasy. This world, at this moment (before the fall), is like Camelot, and even the forces of nature must bow before Slade. It rains feathers for him, the King of Pop and Rock.

The depiction of the 1980s is also fantasy, though of a very different kind. As Haynes has revealed, these visuals are meant to convey an idea of what the 1980s *might* look like from the vantage point of the 1970s. Hence, this is a world of slate gray skies (no ivory feathers) and overpowering architecture. Homeless, jobless people literally line the streets, their faces filled with despair and hopelessness.

A giant outdoor view screen, (a mirror of the lyrics in Slade's first song) is seen at the front of a gray, monstrous building, broadcasting a transmission from current pop idol, Tommy Stone. On other occasions, this screen is no doubt a point of broadcast for the propaganda of President Reynolds, and so this image immediately calls up the specter of Big Brother and George Orwell's *1984*, where government is big and intrusive, and individual freedom is lost.

This portion of the film is a "dark" fantasy, to be certain, but again, Haynes communicates his story in the imagery of that genre, not the more traditional biography. This is an appropriate selection, since we have seen in our history how so many musicals are indeed fantasies, from the explicitly refer- enced *The Wizard of Oz* to *Mary Poppins* and beyond.

Why is fantasy an important entree to the wild world of *Velvet Goldmine* and an effective way to vet the tale of Brian Slade? Again, as Haynes has noted, this is a story more concerned with the fan than about the artist. And fans often do live in a kind of fantasy world. They dress like their idols; they buy merchan- dise by their idols; they read obsessively and endlessly about their idols. They imagine themselves in the world of those they adore, whether that world be Tatooine, Vulcan, or that of Maxwell Demon (Slade).

The audience sees this concept in play specifically with the character of Arthur, who purchases Slade records and adoringly slaps posters up on his bedroom wall. We also see that Slade becomes the objects of Arthur's deeper fantasies, his sexual desires, which heretofore have not found a point of identi- fication in pop culture imagery.

The fantasy, and reality, of Brian Slade very much represents the terrain of *Velvet Goldmine*. For what is this story, really, but one of a boy who loves some- thing produced by a commercial mass culture not necessarily for what it represents to its creators and sellers, but for what it means to him personally, on the personal and fantasy playing field? Arthur is an unhappy character in the 1980s because his fantasy world and its prime inhabitant, with whom he so strongly identified ("That's me! That's me!") disappointed him, and ultimately left him, like everybody else living in the Orwellian 1980s of the film, rudderless. Thus *Velvet Goldmine* is very much about the fantasy of a fan, and how he shapes pop culture to suit his particular, personal struggle.

Popular culture thrives by selling fantasy to millions of people, asking them to buy into Britney Spears; or before her, Madonna; or before her, David Bowie; and before him, the Beatles. One of the most unique aspects of *Velvet Goldmine* is how Haynes depicts his musicians/fantasy figures. Jack Fairy is "the one everybody stole from," and hence a point of legitimacy. Curt Wild is a loose cannon, a firecracker who lives life to the fullest and exemplifies personally the wildness and freedom of his music. But really, who is Brian Slade?

The reason *Velvet Goldmine* merits repeat viewing is that there are all kinds of answers to that question. Slade is a man who steals (the emerald pin); who cuts loose anyone who can no longer help him (Mandy and his first manager); and who stages his own death as a publicity stunt. In the end, when the Maxwell Demon persona is no longer viable commercially, he disappears, abandons the fans, and reinvents himself, as the more acceptable 1980s icon, Stone. Slade does all of these things to remain popular; to be the (notorious) pop idol that Oscar Wilde dreamed of becoming. Why? Does he buy into the glam rock scene at all, or is it merely his route to the top? Is he really gay, or is his orientation merely another useful prop? Notice that Arthur and Curt—two very genuine characters—are depicted making love, but all we see of Brian and Curt (beyond kissing) is the two of them in bed together naked. We're left to draw our own conclusions on the real nature of their relationship, but it could be staged even to sell Brian's image in much the same fashion as the 'white and gold' press conference.

The bedroom scene with Brian and Curt references a situation Angela Bowie once described, upon finding Mick Jagger and David Bowie naked in bed. But on the other, it maintains the veil between the audience and Slade, and even makes one question his true motives.

"What Mandy says about that [situation] is exactly what Angie Bowie said in her book," Lyons notes. She discovered them in bed together naked, but not actually having sex. Their deportment, according to Lyons "makes a strong case that they've had sex, but both those guys are so tricky. Maybe they didn't have sex. Maybe they just went to bed naked, and that's all they did."

To *Velvet Goldmine*'s credit, that question, like many, isn't answered. The film rigorously follows the example set by *Citizen Kane*, and never truly or fully lifts the veil between the audience and its primary protagonist. In fact, *Velvet Goldmine* reveals even less than *Citizen Kane*, since there is no "Rosebud" to connect us to some facile answer about Slade's childhood yearnings.

Todd Haynes, for one, thinks that viewers, perhaps, shouldn't be too hard on Brian Slade for the compromises he makes in his persona. "I think it's hard to be a performer at the level of someone like a Brian Slade or David Bowie. Bowie is someone who was always extremely forthcoming about how he saw himself as an interpreter of the culture around him, as a 'human Xerox machine,' he said, who literally collected all the traces of what was in the culture, and brilliantly put them together. This is evident not only in his work, but in what a great producer he was of other people's work at that time.

"He was really a conceptual artist. In a weird way, it was a movement away from authentic communication and emotional directness that had come out of the folk era, the direct communication that was supposed to be real and true. But that very soon became a problem by even people like Bob Dylan, who epitomized that moment, but then moved on from it and plugged in electric— and freaked everybody out, entering into this sort of suspicious mainstream form of music.

"But Bowie was already moving in that direction toward a conceptual sort of expression. It wasn't really about some true intimate emotion. That doesn't mean it was wrong. It was driven by his own particular instincts and point of view and desires and emotions, but I don't think it was a direct expression of them. I think it was always filtered through an intellectual and conceptual understanding of his era and where we were headed. That puts him in a different category, but none that I would have a pejorative relationship to. You do see it shifting with the times and maybe starting to reflect the times in a way that you start to wonder what the core element is throughout. And he himself, who always, I think, was interested in an element of pop stardom, is the first to refute his period in the eighties as being some of his less creative or inspiring work. But I think he's someone who's always had a foot in superstardom and a foot in the artistic traditions and conceptual traditions of art-making.

"Slade is someone who isn't really provoked by the same guttural, emotional drives that have characterized American music and American tradition," suggests Haynes. "I think what they [English traditions] bring to the table is something much more theatrical and much more conceptual, and not as instinctive. And I think you see Brian Slade starting there brilliantly, and creating images that everybody is seduced by, and everybody falls in with him, but then he gets very caught up in the stardom and alienation that ensues. I wouldn't place him in any absolute position, but I do think he loses himself, and he loses everybody around him as a result. And there's something's less successful, but more grounded about where Curt ends up, and where Arthur seems to end up, even if there's a lot of loss and a lot of regret and a lot of pain in the process. Maybe Brian is protecting himself from those dangers."

The point is perhaps, that at the film's close, Slade remains a mystery, fantasy figure. The search for who and what he represents has been fruitless and he remains an enigma "of his time." It is not impossible to believe, in fact, that children of the 1980s will revere Stone in the same fashion as youngsters of the seventies loved Slade. He is the personification of the star who obfuscates his reality and instead gives the audience fiction. And often, that's precisely what the audience desires: the fantasy.

In so many ways, *Velvet Goldmine* represents the missing link, or perhaps the bridge, to a film like *Moulin Rouge*. Todd Haynes's film operates like a fantasy, taking us down that Yellow Brick Road. And its form reflects content, a re-creation of the fan-star nexus that is so prevalent in today's pop culture world, a fantasy of both participation and adulation. Like *Moulin Rouge*, *Velvet Goldmine* is colorful, extravagant, magical, dotted by pop culture allusions, and unfailingly clever.

The music and the images actually serve to deliver a subtle message about the culture watching the film, as do the songs in *Moulin Rouge*. In the latter, the songs emerge straight from the collective pop culture unconscious, our way of expressing true emotions like love. In *Velvet Goldmine*, the songs ask us to understand how a song, how a celebrity, can bring us right back to our childhood or teenage years, an age we always imagine as golden, and if we're lucky, even revive our youthful fantasies.

SUPER! (THANKS FOR ASKING)

Trey Parker and Matt Stone, the creators of the Comedy Central TV sensation *South Park*, ventured into musical terrain long before their 1999 animated theatrical hit, *South Park: Bigger, Longer & Uncut.* In the early 1990s, while big musicals like *Newsies* and *Swing Kids* were taking dives at the box office, this inventive (and raunchy) duo created a low-budget comedy/horror/musical known as *Alferd Packer: The Musical,* but now entitled for the ages *Cannibal: The Musical.*

Cannibal, we learn from its informative opening card, was originally released in 1954, but the movie was quickly upstaged by the more popular *Oklahoma!* and promptly forgotten, at least until the original negative was unearthed and then "painstakingly restored" to its present condition, using state-of-the-art techniques.

Nothing in that preceding paragraph is true, of course.

Cannibal is an independent flick made in 1993 for approximately seventy-five thousand dollars, while Parker was an undergraduate at the University of Colorado at Boulder. It is purportedly based on the "true story" of a most hapless pioneer, Alferd Packer (Parker), who in 1873 sets out with his beloved steed, LeAnn, and a team of prospectors to reach the Colorado Territory. But the travelers takes a number of wrong turns, winter falls, and, well, before long Alferd and his buddies resort to cannibalism. Years later, Alferd stumbles out of the wild, is promptly arrested, and nearly hanged for his crimes. In the process of this grisly misadventure, he finds love with a feisty reporter named Polly.

Shot on location in Colorado, Parker and Stone's first film is packed with grand vistas, flowing rivers, and monolithic mountains and canyons, but it mimics much more than just the "great outdoor" looks of Zinnemann's pictur-esque *Oklahoma!* Rather pointedly, the film's first song finds Packer on his horse in pure Curly style, singing not "Oh, What a Beautiful Mornin'," but, "Shpadoinkle." This tune describes *another* beautiful day, one wherein "the sky is blue and all the leaves are green," and Alferd sings that the sun is "as warm as a baked potato." It's a spot-on, drop-dead funny parody of Rodgers and Hammerstein, and it's only the first number in the film.

Another of Parker's disturbingly catchy tunes, "Let's Build a Snowman," proves so annoyingly upbeat that the lost prospectors kill one of their own party rather than hear another verse of the blasted thing. And finally, the movie climaxes in wonderful fashion with the rousing "Hang the Bastard," which not only includes a cowbell solo, but reveals scores of happy (if bloodthirsty) town folk dancing around their gallows and cheerily singing to send the doomed Packer straight to hell. Just when it can't get any more delightful, the film ends with a graphic decapitation and a disclaimer that reads: "Due to the graphic nature of the film, it should not have been watched by young children."

Packed to the gills with bloody gore, dismembered limbs, and even featuring an all–Asian–Native American tribe *Cannibal* didn't quite make the cut at Sundance in 1994, as was the intent of the filmmakers, but nevertheless the property was acquired by Troma, the genre company behind *The Toxic Avenger* (1985) and its sequels.

Troma released *Cannibal* on video in 1999, once *South Park* was already popular on TV, and it quickly became a midnight movie sensation and "a cult classic for the post-*Simpsons* generation,"[50] because of the gleeful and bloody way in which it dissected genre tropes, including the ubiquitous "yearning ballad" (here titled "That's All I'm Asking For").

Perhaps not surprisingly, the critics who bothered to review it really liked *Cannibal*. A lot. In fact, they ate it up. "Trey Parker and coconspirators prove that many time-honored conventions of the American musical theater—sappy ballads, bursting into song-and-dance under duress and employing the most idiotic similes with a straight face—are just as strange as any episode of *South Park*," wrote Lisa Nesselson in her review for *Variety*.[51]

Since its release, *Cannibal: The Musical* also has been performed across this grand country by ambitious theater companies hoping to have a sphadoinkle day. And given *Cannibal*'s musical proclivities, perhaps it shouldn't come as a surprise that there was more mad music to come from the film's originators.

In 1998, Trey Parker and his coconspirator, Matt Stone began to incorporate unique songs onto their cable TV series, which concerns four potty-mouthed third-graders in Colorado. One holiday-themed episode early in the series' run included a "yearning ballad" of its own, as one of the youthful characters, Kyle, sang about being "a lonely Jew on Christmas." Another character, Eric Cartman, the "big-boned" antihero of *South Park*, sang a very funny song called "Kyle's Mom's a Bitch" in the same episode. Isaac Hayes provides the voice to the kids' adult friend, Chef, and this character is always singing a tune that's way too sexually suggestive, like the ditty about his favorite delicacy, "salty chocolate balls."

When it came time to adapt the series to feature length, Stone and Parker would again cast their eyes upon the musical format for inspiration. To that end, Parker cowrote with Marc Shaiman eleven new tunes, and even resurrected the crowd-pleasing "Kyle's Mom's a Bitch."

Creating the animated *South Park* feature took eleven months from start to finish, and eventually came to include some three thousand separate shots.[52]

One of the film's dramatic set pieces involved a descent to hell by one of the four boys, the hapless Kenny, a sequence created at Blur Studio in Venice, California, on software called Dust Devil. The goal was to establish, in a fashion different from the primitive visuals of the TV series, "the 'grandeur' of hell," according to animation director Eric Stough.[53]

As it turns out, making an animated feature (on a budget of approximately twenty million dollars) turned out to be a whole lot easier than getting it past the Motion Picture Association of America (MPAA). One of the main motivations for making *South Park* into a film in the first place was to gain access to the world of humor beyond the PG nature of basic cable. But the MPAA didn't see things that way, and the film was twice slapped with the ratings' kiss of death, an NC-17.[54]

What had the MPAA so irked was not any depiction of violence or graphic sex, but merely the use of "scatological dialogue."[55] This complaint was an odd mirror of the movie's central theme, in which the mothers of middle-class America wage war on Canadian "smut," because the MPAA says deplorable, horrific violence is okay . . . but you shouldn't talk ugly.

The irony wasn't lost on Trey Parker, who described the film's premise in this fashion: "You could say *South Park* is about the struggle for basic inalienable freedoms in the face of oppression, but you'd sound like a jerk."[56]

When *South Park: Bigger, Longer & Uncut* debuted in two thousand theaters nationwide on June 30, 1999, the film did strong business, eventually earning close to eighty million dollars. But more to the point, critics loved the film—both as a musical and as a comedy. "Clearly, Parker and Stone spent more time than is healthy rehearsing productions of *Guys and Dolls* and *On the Town* in high school, because for all intents and purposes this film is a musical, and a damn good one at that," wrote Leslie Felperin, for *Sight and Sound*.[57]

"Wise (or at least wise-assed) about everything from pop culture to male sexual ignorance, from the demonization of Saddam Hussein to the digestive problems of fifth-graders," wrote Stuart Klawans, "*South Park* is the film against which all others this summer must be measured."[58]

Raves also poured in from the *Wall Street Journal*'s Joe Morgenstern, *Rolling Stone* reviewer Peter Travers and also the *New York Times*, which described *South Park* as the year's funniest comedy, and the best movie musical in years. *Time* ranked the film as the third best of the year (tied with Disney's *Tarzan*), and praised it as "devilishly, hummably funny."[59]

The *South Park* feature also picked up some notable honors. The crazed Terrence and Phillip song "Uncle Fucka" won an MTV Award for Best Musical Performance, but more importantly, the anthem "Blame Canada" was nominated for an Academy Award for Best Original Song. On the night of the telecast, Robin Williams performed the ditty with spirit, but the song lost out to a number by Phil Collins for the umpteenth Disney musical. But that's okay, the *South Park* gang soon had sweet revenge. On a follow-up episode of the TV series, one sequence featured Phil Collins with a gold statuette rammed up his ass . . .

As the curtain goes up in *South Park: Bigger, Longer & Uncut*, the audience meets third-graders and residents of South Park, Stan, Kyle, Kenny, and Cartman. The boys lie to their parents and buy tickets to see a new R-rated movie, *Asses of Fire*, which stars Canadian icons Terrence and Phillip and features their new hit single, "Uncle Fucka."

The Terrence and Phillip movie is laced with profanity, and the boys return to school repeating it. This leads to remedial counseling, and eventually Kenny's unfortunate death after he attempts to light a fart on fire as he saw Terrence and Phillip do. Now the boys' parents are even more outraged and "blame Canada" for the inappropriate behavior.

America's military seizes Terrence and Phillip during a taping of *Late Night with Conan O'Brien*, and prepares to execute them for crimes against America's youth. This precipitates a full-scale war with our neighbors to the north. Meanwhile, in hell, Satan has struck up a romantic relationship with Saddam Hussein, and realizes that if Canadian blood is spilled on American soil, the End Days will arrive, and he will rule the world.

Kenny befriends Satan down below, while on earth, foul-mouthed Cartman is fitted with a V-chip, a brain implant meant to curb his swearing. Wondering "What Would Brian Boitano Do?" Cartman and the others form La Résistance and hatch a strategy to free Terrence and Phillip during a USO show. It doesn't come off quite as planned.

Director Todd Graff describes *South Park: Bigger, Longer & Uncut* as "a work of pure genius. It was a perfect musical. It was structured within an inch of its life, it was built like a brick shit house, the numbers were hilarious, and the whole movie was hilarious and irreverent and original, but it obeyed all the rules of the musical genre. They recontextualized it by making it animated and potty mouthed and political, so it was great."

Indeed, the charms of *South Park* arise not just in its witty story about censorship or politics, but its deliberate lampooning of certain movie musical standards. "Anyone who's seen *Beauty and the Beast*'s Belle describing her provincial life will recognize the roots of 'Mountain Town,' and even Satan gets a yearning ballad wondering about life 'Up There,' à la *Little Mermaid*'s 'Part of Your World,'" wrote *Entertainment Weekly*'s Chris Willman.[60]

And that was only a sliver of the fun. "Cartman's perky 'Kyle's Mom's a Bitch' echoes *Chitty Chitty Bang Bang* with choruses in fake Chinese, Dutch, and French," observed *Time*'s Richard Corliss. "Saddam could be an Arabic fiddler on the roof as he struts his seedy charm in 'I Can Change' . . . There's a dexterous quartet of musical themes, à la *Les Mis*. And though a song whose refrain is, more or less, 'Shut your flicking face, Uncle Flicka' would seem to have little room for musical wit, ace arranger Marc Shaiman turns it into an *Oklahoma!* hoedown with kids chirping like obscene Chipmunks."[61]

And that's just for starters. Parker and Stone parody hip-hop music, BET style with their reprise of "Uncle Fucka" as a music video tie-in to *Asses of Fire*. The funky video features the Canadian duo Terrence and Phillip decked out in sunglasses, donning silver body suits, proffering piles of cash, and surrounding themselves with African-American female dancers in tight outfits, in all a perfectly observed vision of our slick music video culture.

"Kenny's Space Odyssey," in which the recently deceased boy floats about outer space between heaven and hell, is a trippy reflection of 1970s head musicals like *Tommy*, all dreamy and serene one moment, then hard-driving and pulse-pounding the next.

Saddam Hussein's ballad, "I Can Change" is not only a clever parody of *Fiddler on the Roof*, but more precisely, an ideal number for the wily former dictator. Saddam, who after the Gulf War pledged to disarm Iraq, here states that he can learn to keep his promises, he "swears it." Unlike President Bush (II), however, Satan buys the lie and gives him one more chance.

Beyond the mere cleverness of the songs, and the surgical precision with which they torpedo long-standing clichés, *South Park* is unremittingly clever for the manner in which it deploys its toe-tapping arsenal. "What Would Brian Boitano Do?" is not only the "best (and only) song written in praise of Brian Boitano,"[62] it is the turning point of the entire film, as the boys decide to strike back against the war-mongering moms. In this one song, the audience not only understands the crises of Cartman (the V-Chip), Kyle (his fear of confronting his mother), and Stan (his lack of self-confidence with women and quest to discover the clitoris), but learns how the boys intend to strike back and resolve these issues. The song is an upbeat anthem that ends happily with the boys hopping towards the horizon—in freeze frame—the battle engaged.

Other songs express yearning ("Up There"), compare and contrast the goals of the various groups in the films ("Medley") and even poke fun at Busby Berkeley's outrageous staging ("I'm Super"). Although *South Park: Bigger, Longer & Uncut* is packed wall-to-wall with obscenity, not to mention pot shots at God, christians, Brooke Shields, Saddam Hussein, Nickolodeon, political activists, homosexuals, Barbra Streisand, and Conan O'Brien, it is also, perhaps, the ultimate millennial musical. It has struck upon an outrageous vernacular in which the genre speaks clearly again, a stew of raunchy comedy, pop culture references and hysterically funny tunes. In some ways, this chemistry of foul language, over-the-top humor, and political satire is more potent than what any other genre film in the decade managed to conjure.

Old school musical fans may find their delicate and not-so-delicate sensibilities offended by the volleys *South Park: Bigger, Longer & Uncut* lobs at the genre and the audience. However, one should remember this is precisely the film's agenda; to strike at the viewer's beliefs and pretensions; to slap 'em across the face, make them question it all, while keeping toes-a-tapping all at once. It works beautifully, if only a viewer can approach it with no thought or regard for political correctness. Viewed in the right frame of mind, and with an appreciation for the musical clichés it eviscerates at warp speed, *South Park* is a barrage of laughs, and one of the funniest, most clever movies to come out of Hollywood in the last decade.

Returning to form, Parker and Stone spiced their latest flick, the 2004 puppet adventure movie *Team America: World Police* with funny musical moments too. Although the film is notorious for its scene of explicit puppet sex(!), musical lovers will find much to appreciate, including a performance of the play *Lease* (a parody of *Rent*) and a new anthem of liberty called "America, Fuck Yeah." *Team America* also included a new yearning ballad, this time for North Korean dictator Kim Jong Il, entitled "I'm So Ronery"; a parody of patriotic country music ditties by the likes of folks such as Toby Keith ("Freedom Isn't Free"); and a jaunty jab at movie clichés, entitled "Montage."

In 1999, the same year as the *South Park* feature, another movie also utilized music in a fashion that wasn't quite the norm for its vintage. Paul Thomas Anderson, who had directed perhaps the best film of 1997, the extraordinary *Boogie Nights*, made a return to cinemas with a three-hour film called *Magnolia*. An Altmanesque narrative consisting of interlocking vignettes and packed with dozens of characters (including ones played by Tom Cruise, Julianne Moore, the late Jason Robards, William Macy, and *Chicago*'s John C. Reilly), *Magnolia* isn't really a musical by standard definition.

However, at the two-hour-and-twenty-minute point in the film, as the dramatic emotions run high, every character in the film suddenly pauses and begins to sing the tune "Wise Up" with performer Aimee Mann, the tune's composer. It's a moment of cohesion that weaves the diverse characters and multitudinous stories together through song, and in the best tradition of the musical format, communicates their innermost feelings. This sequence is no accident or twist of fate, no music video "inserted" awkwardly into the film's narrative. On the contrary, Aimee Mann's compositions are the bedrock gestalt of *Magnolia*, and in fact, represent Anderson's very impetus to create the film in the first place. He felt that Mann's songs fit in exactly with the theme he wanted to explore in a screenplay, particularly "emotional rescue."[63]

Considering this collaboration, it is not a stretch to view Anderson as the book writer for Mann's tunes, and *Magnolia* dynamically showcases eight of her original and memorable compositions, including "Momentum," "Build That Wall," and "Save Me." Though "Wise Up" is the only song actually sung by the cast in *Magnolia* in old-fashioned opera style, the film nevertheless deserves a mention not just for its inspiration in the artistry and music of Mann, but for its boldness in including a full-on musical number in such a dramatic and strange film.

OH NO, THEY CAN'T TAKE THAT AWAY FROM HIM

By age forty, director and actor Kenneth Branagh had already been dubbed "our greatest living interpreter of Shakespeare"[64] and, between 1989 and 1999, brought the world three amazing screen adaptations of the Bard's work. These films were all of vastly different color and tone. *Henry V* (1989) was a spectacular and gritty war story, *Much Ado About Nothing* (1993), a buoyant comedy, and Branagh's fantastic four-hour version of *Hamlet* (1996) was something beyond compare or rival.

In 1999, Branagh set out on a quest that proved perhaps the greatest challenge of his distinguished career. He sought to adapt *Love's Labour's Lost*, a so-called minor Shakespeare comedy, to the silver screen. Making matters dicier, he envisioned the material as a musical.

William Shakespeare's *Love's Labour's Lost* was first performed in 1594–1595 and published in 1598. It seems fair to state that the material represents nobody's favorite Shakespeare comedy. The play was long viewed as one of the Bard's least effective early works, though that perception changed somewhat after a successful production in postwar European theater. Why such love loss for *Love's Labor's Lost*? Part of the problem was the density of the text itself. Not many average theatergoers could easily understand the language. In fact, not many critics can either, no matter what they may claim.

"*Love's Labour's Lost* is perhaps the most relentlessly Elizabethan of all Shakespeare's plays," claims *The Riverside Shakespeare*. "Filled with word games, elaborate conceits, parodies of spoken and written styles, and obscure topical allusions, it continually requires—and baffles—scholarly explanation. Nothing can ever make most of the puns and witticisms of *Love's Labour's Lost* seem contemporary again."[65]

The material represented such a challenge, in fact, that Shakespeare's play had not been adapted to the movie screen once in nearly a century of cinema. Yet Branagh developed an interesting thesis concerning the way he could make *Love's Labour's Lost* accessible again. It involved another genre also filled with word games and elaborate conceits: the movie musical.

"When I played *Love's Labour's Lost* in the theater, it always reminded me of the silly charming mood that you get with those old Hollywood musicals," he reported in an interview with Jay Rayner in the *Observer*, "And the text constantly refers to song and dance."[66]

"The fact is that, in a sense, Shakespearean comedies are Hollywood musicals," established Branagh. "Mistaken identity, songs, dances, slapstick, comedy wisecracks, they all exist in both."[67]

Furthermore, in the nineties, filmmakers around the world were coming back to the works of Shakespeare with new ideas. Reinvention was the name of the game, and Baz Luhrmann and Craig Pearce created a gangland, guns-and-cars remake of *Romeo and Juliet* in 1996. *Hamlet* (2000) moved into the world of modern corporations for Ethan Hawke's version of the tragedy, and Shakespeare's meditation on lust and jealousy, *Othello*, was reset in the world of competitive high school basketball in the sensual *O* (2001). Given such examples, Branagh's refashioning of Shakespeare as a musical comedy doesn't seem particularly outrageous.

"Now these stories are free for exploration in a way they weren't before. The canvas is blank again," Branagh reported. "There's a generation out there who have never seen one of Orson Welles's Shakespeare films or Zeffirelli's—or even one of ours. What we've done with *Love's Labour's Lost* might provoke hostile debate, but even that's a good thing."[68]

With his fusion of Shakespeare and musicals in mind, Branagh embarked on the first movie musical produced in the United Kingdom since *Absolute Beginners* in 1986.[69] The first order of business was trimming down Shakespeare's wordy comedy to accommodate musical numbers, and so the play was downsized to roughly 25 to 30 percent of its original length. Then came the real challenge: developing music and lyrics that could stand shoulder-to-shoulder with the immortal iambic pentameter of the Bard.

For a time, Branagh and composer Patrick Doyle toiled on new, original songs, but soon came to understand that anything they might concoct sounded woefully lame next to the timeless poetry of Shakespeare. They needed songs with a little heft, with a legacy and poetry all their own. Keeping this in mind, the filmmakers landed on the notion of peppering their film, now set in pre–World War II Europe, with authentic thirties movie show tunes. Among those drafted in this fashion were "The Way You Look Tonight" from *Swing Time*, "Cheek to Cheek" from *Top Hat*, "Let's Face the Music and Dance" from *Follow the Fleet*, "They Can't Take That Away from Me" from *Shall We Dance*, and "I Won't Dance" from *Roberta*. These tunes by Gershwin, Porter, and Berlin had the very quality of longevity—nay, immortality—that Branagh sought.

Adopting the same technique developed in Woody Allen's *Everyone Says I Love You*, Branagh cast actors not known for acumen with either song or dance. Alicia Silverstone, *Scream*'s (1996) Matthew Lillard, *Ronin*'s (1998) Natasha McElhone, and Adrian Lester from *Primary Colors* (1998) were among the talents who would costar with Branagh, who as Berowne had the meatiest role. Adding a little song-and-dance flair to the mix, scene-stealer Nathan Lane would also dance his way through the picture in a supporting role as the comic character, Costard. He even crooned a rather touching, half-time version of "There's No Business Like Show Business."

Preproduction on *Love's Labour's Lost* commenced in October 1998, and set construction started a month later at Shepperton Studios, where the film was shot. Among the few sets were a Park Quad and the King of Navarre's impressive library dome, where much of the action occurred. Aside from the film's climax, which referenced the romantic denouement of *Casablanca* (1942), and shot at an airfield in North Weald, Essex, the remainder of the film adopted the 1930s Hollywood approach and was sound stage bound.

Before filming, the cast attended Camp Branagh, a rigorous, intensive three-week acting program. "It was like Shakespeare meets *Fame* with all kinds of different classes, like dancing," Matthew Lillard described in an interview with *Cosmopolitan*.[70] The classes started at 8:00 a.m. sharp, included two hours of singing and dancing, and then the group moved to Shakespeare training.

There was little respite during production. No dance doubles were permitted on camera; no singing voices were dubbed or electronically altered, and often the musical numbers often had to be achieved in a single take. "We were punished a bit because it is physically quite hard to be doing a musical, a bit of a shock to the system," Branagh explained.[71] The shooting was made doubly difficult because, according to producer David Baron, none of the primary behind-the-scenes players on the film had any practical experience shooting musical numbers.[72]

Love's Labour's Lost opens in 1939, as the King of Navarre (Alessandro Nivola) and his three school chums (Branagh, Lillard, and Lester) swear an oath to beg off the luxuries of life—including women—for three years, while devoting themselves to study and the pleasures of the mind.

There is only one problem with this stoic contract: the beautiful princess of France (Silverstone) and three of her lovely cohorts (McElhone, Emily Mortimer, and Carmen Ejogo) are already en route to Navarre on a diplomatic mission, and in good conscience, the King cannot refuse them lodging. His reluctance dissolves all together when he falls head over heels in love with the princess.

Not surprisingly, love is in the air not only for the King, but for Berowne (Branagh) and Rosaline (McElhone), and the other couples too! However, the world is at war. While the couples dally in court, France falls to the Nazis, and there is a sad parting. The men of Navarre join the war effort as pilots. The long separation from their lady loves is difficult, but ends in a joyous reunion.

As the preceding synopsis makes clear, *Love's Labour's Lost* is a rather thin and airy story, but that's just perfect for a 1930s-style musical romp. Branagh understood he was facing a daunting challenge in making a movie so out of step with the times, and as the critics noted, *Love's Labour's Lost* represented his "riskiest Shakespeare adaptation yet."[73] But risk, of course, is the territory of all great art and all great artists.

"I don't mind in this case," Branagh stated, "if they laugh at us or with us."[74]

As it turned out, many critics didn't laugh at Branagh's efforts, and some actually applauded. "Branagh clearly knows his musicals and abides by the well-tested rules that made the classics classic. Sets are relatively few (a library courtyard, riverside, front garden) and evoke similar ones from past tunes; most dance numbers employ long takes with the full lengths of the dancer's body visible; and segues from dialogue into songs are musically seamless and psychologically apt," reported *Variety*'s Derek Elley.[75]

"The film's most impressive feature is the creative selection and placement of the songs," suggested film historian Patrick J. Cook. "The scoring of Branagh's veteran collaborator Patrick Doyle integrates the familiar melodies beautifully into the surrounding dramatic matrix, creating a fascinating sonic equivalent for the original play's verbal self-reference. They are often cued by an important Shakespearean word and develop some kind of implicit commentary on it."[76]

Those critics who didn't care for the film tended to find fault with Branagh's use of the Woody Allen approach, utilizing familiar, big-name stars to sing and dance, often beyond the range of their limited skills. "The singing is amateurish and the choreography, scaled down to the skills of people who aren't dancers, rather lame," complained John Simon in the *National Review*.[77]

Writing for the *Seattle Times*, Misha Berson noted that "Branagh isn't much of a tripper of the light fantastic and as a singer he ranks right up there with Woody Allen. Nor has he cast his gung-ho, but quasi-amateurish affair with true Broadway belters and twinkle-toes."[78]

Stanley Kauffmann opined in the *New Republic* that "most of the casting is dull or dreadful, most notably the two leads Alessandro Nivola as the King and Alicia Silverstone as the Princess. They are inadequate in every way."[79]

Love's Labour's Lost may not be a musical for the ages, but on a modest scale, it's a really fun movie. From the opening sequence, which begins with a lush overture, still images of our stars, and a background that appears to be a silk red pillow, this film strives to be exactly what its ad-line promised, "a new spin on the old song and dance." The attention to detail is marvelous, and the opening is evocative of the film musical's golden age.

On the positive side, Branagh is no slouch when it comes to understanding the tenets of 1930s era movie musicals, and he apes the style credibly. Taking a page from Fred Astaire's playbook, he employs long steady shots of his dancers in motion, rarely cutting away amid the moves. However, on the negative side of that equation, the actors just aren't fabulous dancers. Many are out of their depth, and the long shots tend to reveal this.

Like *Everyone Says I Love You*, *Love's Labour's Lost* radiates a genuine sense of joy about itself and the idea of romantic love, and in today's cynical climate, that's no small feat. In particular, "Cheek to Cheek" is staged with *joie de vivre*, as the love of the four smitten males catapults them right up into the air, to the apex of the King's dome. And Nathan Lane is terrific doing shtick with a rubber chicken in hand and later belting out "There's No Business Like Show Business." He starts slow and melancholic, and there's pathos and charm, and then the number builds to a full-on showstopper with the whole cast. Again, it may not be the best choreographed number in film musical history, but hey, it's certainly pleasant enough.

Other touches also evidence considerable charm. "Adrian Lester's graceful athleticism in 'I've Got a Crush on You' salutes Gene Kelly, there's a water ballet that positively drips Esther Williams, and Branagh has the cheek to swipe Astaire's 'Cheek to Cheek,'" writes Chris Hewitt.[80]

On closer inspection, creator Kenneth Branagh deserves hosannas for an audacious series of good decisions regarding *Love's Labour's Lost*. He edits Shakespeare, not a task one undertakes lightly, and comes out with a winning screenplay. He artfully couples the Bard's words with the classic tunes of Hollywood revealing a symmetry that's a bit uncanny. He also updates the story to the 1930s, thus allowing Movie-Tone reels to fill in story gaps in hiccuping-but-evocative black-and-white. With a war looming, the King's oath to give up the pleasures of the flesh takes on a new importance and meaning, seeming far less irrelevant than in the original play. He's devoting three years to his "study," and after a fashion, that sounds a bit like draft dodging, or at least a student deferment.

"Branagh's adaptation draws our attentions to the way in which the king has applied the code of the soldier to that of a scholar, and the suggestion is that the king has become a scholar partly so that he doesn't have to be a soldier. Like Zeffirelli's Romeo, Branagh's King has to consider what to do when he'd rather dance with his enemies than fight them," wrote Amy Scott-Douglas in the *Shakespeare Newsletter*.[81]

Another satisfying moment arrives in *Love's Labour's Lost* when Branagh, as Berowne, tap dances to the iambic pentameter beat of Shakespeare's words. It's not only a witty jest, it points out the explicitly musical quality of Shakespeare's words, and makes the point, quite legitimately, that Branagh's leap of faith is well placed, that music and the Bard fit together hand in glove.

The flaw inherent in *Love's Labour's Lost* is actually related to another one of Branagh's formative decisions. Editing the play was smart, given its density. Gershwin, Porter, and Berlin in tandem with Shakespeare is practically inspired. Updating the play to World War II works in the story's favor and makes the drama more comprehensible on some scale. However, what thematic purpose does the Woody Allen–*Everyone Says I Love You* model serve in this case? The script would only be enhanced by highlighting a cast *more* experienced with song and dance.

In Allen's film, the conceit was that the common man sings and dances too, and it doesn't matter if he sounds bad or fumbles about. *Love's Labour's Lost* doesn't concern the common man, nor his internal song. So this choice is actually the one that tends to undercut the film's success. One senses Branagh decided to go this route simply so he could appear in the picture himself, alongside the most high-profile actors. Frankly, the entire enterprise would have benefitted from better-trained crooners and hoofers.

It may also be something of a mistake to include a Fosse-inspired number (to the tune "Let's Face the Music and Dance"). Although it is splendidly shot and cut, with many close-up views of legs in fishnet stockings, bulging muscles, and the like, the style of cutting—though sexy—plays against the film's central metaphor, that this is, in fact, supposed to be a 1930s musical. Editors didn't cut musical film like that in those days, and so the Fosse number is out of step with the rest of the film. Again, the sequence almost seems self-indulgent, like Branagh wants to prove he has not only mastered the 1930s-style of musical, but *all* styles.

Still, give Branagh his props for endeavoring to broach something truly different, for coming up with an interesting metaphor that works, even if only for 65 percent of the time. With a better-trained cast and an abandonment of the Allen model, *Love's Labour's Lost* would have emerged a much stronger film. But I still come down on the positive side with this movie. There are many worse ways to spend an hour and a half than watching Kenneth Branagh deliver the words of the Bard and listening to the beautiful standards of Hollywood's old-time greats.

GOLDEN HEART

The late 1990s and early 2000s represent an epoch of real experimentation in the movie musical genre, not unlike the 1970s. After all, Woody Allen, Kenneth Branagh, Trey Parker, and Todd Haynes are not names one immediately associates with the format. In the year 2000, another unique talent also released a musical feature film, and like the efforts of the other inventive directors listed above, it was anything but what people had come to expect.

In 1995, Danish director Lars von Trier, working from his Zentropa Productions in the Copenhagen suburb of Hvidovre, signed on to the Dogma 95 artistic manifesto, in which a number of like-minded filmmakers pledged themselves to ten cinematic vows of chastity, thereby promising to eschew Hollywood excesses and use only handheld cameras and natural sound and lighting. Extravagant costumes and elaborate props were also strictly verboten.[82]

Von Trier, an artist with a communist background whose films have often been accused of being anti-American, set out in early 1999 to make a musical film built on the foundation of these tenets. The film, which he originally wanted to call *Taps*, eventually became *Dancer in the Dark* and was intended to be the third film of his informal Golden Heart trilogy. The first two ventures were the highly successful *Breaking the Waves* (1996), starring Emily Watson, and the infrequently seen *The Idiots* (1998).

The premise of all these von Trier pictures is that somewhere in the world there is a sweet, put-upon woman who plays by the rules, but is nonetheless destroyed by society. Or more specifically, "the little girl 'Goldenheart' is so good-hearted that she is prepared to sacrifice all she has to other people."[83]

Inspired by films like Douglas Sirk's *Magnificent Obsession* (1954), Lars decided to set his tale in 1960s in the U.S. state of Washington, a location and time where hanging was still the preferred method of capital punishment. Surprisingly, von Trier hoped to make his final Golden Heart movie in the musical format, because of his own admiration for the genre. "As a young man, I was very fond of musicals, and for me, musicals—especially film musicals—are connected with the United States. So it was a very important part of the story that Selma, a young woman who loved musicals so much, would come to the mother—or fatherland—of musicals."[84]

But here was the rub: von Trier also wanted his musical to adhere to those pesky Dogma 95 rules, and thus grant the musical genre the same sense of "freshness" he found exhilarating in films of that school.[85] "If I had made a musical in the beginning of my career, it would have been crane shots and tracking shots and people coming out of cakes and whatever, but those techniques are something that I've left behind me," von Trier told *Indie Wire*'s Anthony Kaufman. "The basic idea is that we wanted a feeling for the event."[86]

What von Trier devised was a film that would dramatically showcase the differences between "two levels of reality,"[87] one that was so-called normal life, one that was the musical-obsessed world of the protagonist, Selma. But first von Trier had to cast his Golden Heart, and at this point, one of the film's major contributors joined the production.

The singer Björk Gudmundstdottir, known popularly as Björk, released her first album when she was eleven years old and, by 1999, had become famous the world round for her unusual childlike persona, as well as her unique sound, which punctuated albums with titles like *Debut, Post,* and *Homogenic.*

At one point the lead singer of the Sugarcubes, this timid, fragile, innocent-seeming Icelander was, in one sense at least, the perfect collaborator for von Trier's project. Not only could Björk compose Selma's unique songs and sing them herself, she was also the perfect physical type for the leading role in his final Golden Heart film.

"I feel more comfortable inside a song than I do in real life," Björk reported in one interview. "And there's a great deal of escape from reality . . . in both me and Selma. I only feel safe and calm when I make music or sing. I understand the abstract in music, but people scare me."[88]

When Björk first met von Trier and read his *Dancer in the Dark* script, she fell in love with its lead character and began to cry. "I was sitting in this garden shed outside his house and just crying and ready to defend this girl in a quite material way," she told reporter Luaine Lee. "Then quite quickly I wrote most of the songs like in a month or two."[89]

Others in the cast of *Dancer in the Dark* included *Umbrellas of Cherbourg* (1964) beauty Catherine Deneuve, David Morse, Peter Stormare, and even the great Joel Grey had a (fantasy) tap-dancing cameo in the film. Principal photography began in April of 1999, and Trollhattan, Sweden, was utilized to double for Washington state.

Vincent Paterson, the choreographer who had worked on Sir Alan Parker's *Evita* and choreographed Madonna's Blond Ambition Tour, not only performed choreography duties on the project, but acted too, playing Selma's friend and drama teacher.

One of the most revolutionary aspects of *Dancer in the Dark* was von Trier's fashion of shooting the musical numbers. Immersed in his quest to capture the aura of a live event being transmitted, he filmed these fantasy sequences by deploying one hundred stationary Sony handheld cameras around his scenes.

Because Björk was singing all of her songs live, the musical numbers would only have to be filmed once and then subsequently cut using several of the one hundred options available. There were two considerable problems with this approach. The first was that it took a terribly long time to stage the shots, sometimes as long as two days to position the cameras (fifty cameras a day). Secondly, editing became a hugely laborious task. For instance, there were sixty-eight hours of material, and three thousand tapes utilized in just the first day of filming musical numbers, according to the DVD "making of" documentary. Thus it took the editing team six months to complete the musical numbers for the film. Ironically, given this herculean task, von Trier has gone on record since *Dancer in the Dark*'s release declaring the perfect way to shoot a musical number would have actually been with ten thousand cameras.

In contrast with the rigorously structured and observed musical sequences, *Dancer in the Dark*'s dramatic scenes were shot in von Trier's typical style, which meant no rehearsal, heavy improvisation, and a documentary-style feel courtesy of a herky-jerky handheld.[90] Almost immediately during production, reports began to circulate in the press that the director and his star weren't seeing eye-to-eye or getting along.

These confrontations soon became "the stuff of legend," and von Trier insisted it was because "Björk thought it was very difficult to get up and start at 8:00 a.m., because in the music business, you don't have to."[91]

Björk countered that she only walked off the set once—for two days—and that the incident occurred for "musical reasons."[92] Whatever the cause, it certainly appeared that the two didn't get along.

"Every morning, she said, 'I despise you, Mr. Trier,' and spit on the ground," von Trier told *Newsweek*. "That is unpleasant. She could have quit. I don't know why she didn't."[93]

Some reports indicate it took Björk as long as ten months to recover from shooting the film,[94] and others allege that the pop star suffered from physical and mental exhaustion as a result of the stress. Apparently, during that lengthy post-production span, Björk never spoke with her former collaborator, von Trier. However, sometimes out of great strife arises great art, and at the Cannes Film Festival where *Dancer in the Dark* premiered, the thirty-four-year-old actress took home Best Actress honors for her impressive performance as Selma. Even more significantly, the film won the coveted Palme d'Or.

The drama commences in *Dancer in the Dark* during the mid-1960s in Washington state as a kind-hearted Czech emigré named Selma (Björk) works long hours at a gloomy factory that mass-produces sink basins. When not toiling there with her friend Kathy (Deneuve), Selma lives in a trailer with her young son and saves all of her money in a secret hiding place.

Though Selma claims she is sending the money back to her father in Czechoslovakia, she is actually keeping the money safe for an operation. She fears her son will suffer from the same degenerative eye disease that is rapidly rendering her blind, and wants to pay for his much-needed surgery.

Even while Selma hides her condition from her friends and coworkers, and rehearses a local production of *The Sound of Music*, she learns from her landlord, policeman Bill (Morse), that he has badly mismanaged his own financial affairs. He is in a desperate spot and unwilling to tell his money-grubbing wife the truth about the trouble they are in. He asks Selma to borrow her money, but Selma refuses, because the money is for her son's operation.

Exploiting Selma's near-blindness, Bill discovers her hiding place and steals the money. When Selma learns it is missing, she confronts Bill and—because he is unstable and armed—precipitates a deadly shooting. Selma is imprisoned for Bill's murder and faces execution. After a devastating trial, her only solace—now, as in the factory before—is that she views the world as a Hollywood musical, where nothing terrible ever happens. As the day of Selma's execution arrives, she fears "the last number"—the final song that will signal the end of her story.

Moody and emotional, *Dancer in the Dark* opened the thirty-eighth New York Film Festival on September 22, 2000, and its distributor, Fine Line, aired spots for it on VHI, MTV and Comedy Central. The film opened in three theaters in New York on September 23, 2000, before going wider to a hundred theaters on October 6.[95]

Although the film had many supporters, the critical response to *Dancer in the Dark* was fiercely negative. Kenneth Turan dubbed it the "most morose of musicals,"[96] Stanley Kauffmann opined that Björk had a "feeble voice,"[97] and Jan Stuart of *Newsday* wrote that the film was "breast-beating melodrama of a level that would have been hooted off the desks of Lillian Gish and D. W. Griffith had it been sent to them eighty-five years ago."[98]

Others were even more harsh. "Its libretto might have been written by Karl Marx," concluded critic Carrie Rickey. "And its clunky dancers recall those Soviet musicals of the thirties, in which farm workers frolicked amid wheat threshers. The songs and dancers in *Dancer in the Dark* suck the available air out of an already oxygen-deprived affair."[99]

"Where other recent attempts to reinvent the Hollywood musical such as Kenneth Branagh's *Love's Labour's Lost* and Woody Allen's *Everyone Says I Love You* have been driven primarily by a love of the genre backed by solid knowledge of the rules (even while breaking them), *Dancer* seems determined to cannibalize the genre while constructing nothing fresh or substantial in its place," suggested *Variety*'s Derek Elley.[100]

There are all kinds of reasons why a viewer could dislike *Dancer in the Dark* should that be the path selected. It was set in America by a filmmaker who's never traveled to this country because of a fear of flying. It depicts a negative view of the American "free enterprise" system and seems to implicitly approve of communism, or perhaps merely socialism.

A reviewer predisposed not to like the film might even argue that *Dancer in the Dark* and its allegedly sadistic director takes inordinate pleasure heaping unfortunate events on its put-upon Golden Heart, Selma. She endures what no human being should ever endure, and sometimes the deck just seems stacked against her, no matter what decisions—wrong or right—she forges.

All these are surely reasons to resent the picture.

Still, this "melodramatic tragedy staged as a break-into-song musical"[101] is actually a truly amazing, heart-wrenching, and powerful example of the musical genre.

For one thing, it represents a dramatic bridge between the canon of Dennis Potter and Rob Marshall's *Chicago*, especially in how it utilizes music and dance in the narrative. Like Arthur in *Pennies from Heaven*, Selma dreams of the movie musical where "nothing dreadful" ever happens. And like *Chicago* (which would follow two years later), the numbers in *Dancer in the Dark* are all internal, and therefore character-based, occurring totally inside Selma's head, her daydreams.

"There's no denying the art of *Dancer in the Dark*," critic Manohla Dargis astutely wrote in *Harper's Bazaar*, "the conceptual reach and technological radicalism of von Trier's film are breathtaking . . . The numbers in *Dancer in the Dark* reflect Selma's hopes and desires in much the same way that Gene Kelly's in *An American in Paris* did, the difference being that von Trier has also stripped the musical of its romance and, more perversely, its optimism. The film glitters like a diamond, brilliant, and cold."[102]

This conceit of "elaborate interior monologues"[103] works as splendidly in *Dancer in the Dark* as it does in *Chicago*, but frankly the emotions are raw and exposed in von Trier's film. For all his ingenuity, *Pennies from Heaven* scribe Dennis Potter is first and foremost an intellectual, and satire purposefully creates a certain distance between viewer and film. *Chicago* is sexy, arousing and wholly entertaining, and it appeals to the senses, particularly the eyes. Its trial-of-the-century format reflects our times, and we enjoy the cynicism and sardonic wit. *Dancer in the Dark*, for all its so-called stacked deck against Selma, engages our hearts fully and forcefully in a way that few musicals ever have.

As viewers, we care about this woman as we witness her struggle to provide for her family; as we watch her toil at a thankless job. And we identify with her love of musicals and deep fantasy life, and wonder why life can't be like this oh-so-very-optimistic form of art and entertainment. The documentary, herky-jerky handheld filming style of the nonmusical scenes only lends these emotions more intensity. We feel as if we're right there with Selma in that tiny house, sharing that depressing kitchen table. There's an immediacy evident in *Dancer in the Dark* that's impossible to escape and that contrasts with the heightened colors and "drama" of the elaborately staged musical numbers. In mapping that gulf between reality and fantasy, that terrible contrast, *Dancer in the Dark* is nothing shy of a masterpiece.

"[W]hen the first musical interlude occurs forty minutes into the movie, the transition is exhilarating," wrote critic Brian D. Johnson, and he's absolutely right. Much as the number "Cell Block Tango" builds on the noises surrounding Roxie in prison in *Chicago* (a leaky faucet, etc.), *Dancer in the Dark* takes the noises of a "machine stamping out kitchen sinks" and corrals them as the foundation of the first musical fantasy.[104] Von Trier also captures the "atmosphere of a factory, truck, house, prison, and courtroom" to key us into the musical moments, then creates what the *Jakarta Post* termed a "fascinating composition, completely different from the conventional, glamorous Hollywood musical."[105]

And, it seems really weak to adjudicate the film "bad" because someone considers it (or von Trier) anti-American. It's actually more anticapitalism, but honestly, who cares if *Dancer in the Dark* is anti-U.S.? Has our country become so uptight about its values that it can't stand the slightest questioning of our system? Even in a fiction? If that's the case, art will never ring true, and all we'll be left with is propaganda.

The musical format is utilized adroitly within the structure of *Dancer in the Dark* to make a valid point about life in America, take it or leave it, accept it or reject it. Selma is a woman who works hard every day of her life, plays by rules, and cares only to provide for her son. But she can't make a living wage; she can't afford health care, and, basically, her quality of life is terrible. She escapes this depressing reality by connecting with art, with either a community theater production of *The Sound of Music* or by going to the movies with her friend Kathy and watching old-time musicals. The movie musicals cheer her, gird her, and bolster her to face everyday reality.

But in the end—as Selma's death scene makes plain—the movie musical is just a balm. Because Selma is not wealthy, she cannot afford a decent attorney and is sentenced to death. Because Selma is neither rich, powerful, nor important, it is permissible for her neighbor, Bill, to steal from her. This is a particularly flagrant abuse, considering that Bill is supposed to protect and serve the community. Instead, he abuses his power and position of authority as a police officer.

What *Dancer in the Dark* eloquently expresses is that good people, golden hearts, and middle-class families in America are not getting by, can't get by because of the system, and instead of trying to change that fact, they are retreating to utopian fantasy worlds, like the musical.

Some folks may not care for this message. Some people may argue with this thesis, but with forty-five million Americans doing without healthcare, with corporations and businesses like Wal-Mart reaping huge financial rewards on the backs of workers they underpay, with justice being—as the Kobe Bryant and O. J. Simpson cases have proven so dramatically—the best that money can buy, how can critics accuse *Dancer in the Dark* of being anything but honest? Selma may be facing a "stacked deck" in this film, but how many unfortunate Americans live that scenario every day?

"I thought *Dancer in the Dark* was the best movie released that year," says Todd Graff. "It was so emotional. It had the courage of its convictions. It set up a world where—even though the story itself is displaying an incredibly cynical, dark view of reality—her character was transparent. She was guileless. She was so innocent. They never shied away from that; they never tried to slick it up; they never tried to mitigate it. That's what this story was, and their commitment to telling that story was very brave."

"I'm a big fan of Lars von Trier's chutzpah," says *Hedwig* director John Cameron Mitchell. "He's amazingly innovative and cantankerous and fascinating, but I did find that one [*Dancer in the Dark*] difficult, because I didn't buy that everybody would have been so horrible to her. The stacked deck thing took me out of it. But I was amazed by his technique and touch with the actors. Everyone's so real. I'm always interested in what he wants to do, I just wasn't emotionally engaged. But then again, good friends of mine were devastated."

Emotionally intense, devastating, painful and pure, *Dancer in the Dark* remains an unforgettable film, and it is surely one of the most daring and finest musical movies created during the last quarter century.

—

The first year of the new millennium also brought a rollicking backstage rock musical to theaters, Cameron Crowe's autobiographical feature, *Almost Famous*. Set in the year 1973, the film (originally called *Untitled*) tells the tale of a precocious teenager named William Miller (Patrick Fugit) who gets a writing gig from *Rolling Stone* to tour with a rock band on the verge of becoming famous, called Still Water. On the lengthy road trip, William befriends the band's up-and-coming star, Russell (Billy Crudup), and falls in love with a "band aid" (read: groupie) named Penny Lane, played by Kate Hudson. While learning important life lessons, he must also contend with his worrying mother, played by Frances McDormand.

Still Water performs onstage throughout *Almost Famous*, and several concert performances are highlighted. The film boasts wall-to-wall tunes on the soundtrack, including "Sparks" by Peter Townsend, "America" by Paul Simon and Art Garfunkel, and even "The Chipmunk Song." One of the film's most charming moments occurs on the band's tour bus as the passengers spontaneously break into a performance of Elton John's "Tiny Dancer." Hudson and McDormand were nominated for Oscars for their performances.

A bit nuttier than *Almost Famous* was a quasi-musical extravaganza from the Coen Brothers, the fantasy-comedy *O Brother, Where Art Thou?* (2000). This quirky movie tells the unlikely and over-the-top tale of three convicts played by George Clooney, John Turturro, and Tim Blake Nelson, who escape from a chain gang during the Great Depression and undertake a journey to recover loot they hid before their incarceration. The film mimics the structure of Homer's *The Odyssey*, and includes encounters with 1930s-era equivalents of Sirens and the Cyclops. Appropriately, George Clooney's character is named Ulysses in this Deep South fantasy.

Shot in Mississippi, *O Brother, Where Art Thou?* also showcased a number of riveting old-fashioned country-bluegrass songs. Some of these ditties were ostensibly sung by the film's escapees, performing under the handle "The Soggy Bottom Boys." The big hit from the soundtrack was "I Am a Man of Constant Sorrow," and the *O Brother* album promptly become a double-platinum hit, selling eighty thousand units a week—and this was without even getting airplay on country radio![106]

Produced by T-Bone Burnett, the *O Brother* album featured tracks by Alison Krauss, Gillian Welch, Emmylou Harris, and Ralph Stanley, and nabbed a Grammy Award for Album of the Year. Even if the film wasn't really considered a musical first and foremost, the album's success proved that movies and music were still a profitable and potent combination.

SPARKLING DIAMONDS

The year depicted in Stanley Kubrick's *2001: A Space Odyssey* didn't see mankind reach Jupiter, but something else happened, something wonderful. The year 2001 actually proved to be the age of the movie musical's Hollywood comeback. In early summer of that year, a film titled *Moulin Rouge* played in theaters to packed auditoriums, and not only energized its audiences but the genre itself. Without *Moulin Rouge*, there could have been no *Chicago* in 2002.

Moulin Rouge dramatizes the story of a young bohemian poet named Christian (Ewan McGregor) who travels to Paris at the turn of the century. After moving into his garret, he becomes embroiled in a strange theatrical production called "Spectacular-Spectacular" with the diminutive Toulouse-Lautrec (John Leguizamo). Because the play requires investors, Christian visits the local dance club, the Moulin Rouge, to convince the owner, Zidler (Jim Broadbent), and his star, the beautiful courtesan Satine (Nicole Kidman), to be involved.

On the night Christian first visits the Moulin Rouge, Zidler and Satine are already pursuing their own investor, a villainous figure known enigmatically as the Duke (Richard Roxburgh). Satine sings a sensual version of "Diamonds Are a Girl's Best Friend," between cancans, but mistakes Christian for the Duke and takes the poet back to her boudoir instead. Zidler hastily corrects her error, but not before Christian has fallen head-over-heels in love with Satine. Working together, Satine, Christian, Toulouse-Lautrec, and Zidler convince the Duke to invest in "Spectacular-Spectacular," an investment which requires the total renovation of the Moulin Rouge into an upscale theater.

The Duke agrees to invest, but he is no easy customer. He demands that in exchange for his money, Satine marry him. Worse, he will hold the deed on the Moulin Rouge to assure that his new bride remains faithful. Zidler agrees to these terms, but all is endangered when Satine and Christian embark on a dangerous love affair.

As the rehearsals begin for "Spectacular-Spectacular," a series of near-disasters almost derail the show. The Duke grows increasingly jealous of Christian, and vice-versa, and worse, Satine learns that she is dying from consumption. On the night of the show, the love triangle is settled once and for all, and Christian and Satine declare their love for one another, "come what may . . ."

By the mid-1990s, Australian director Baz Lurhmann had already directed two international hits, the independently produced dance film *Strictly Ballroom* (1993) and the popular, modernist interpretation of William Shakespeare, the Leonardo DiCaprio and Claire Danes vehicle, *Romeo + Juliet* (1996). Luhrmann's next project, *Moulin Rouge* would prove his most popular and successful venture yet, and, at least in part, developed from his love of old-fashioned musicals, and one particular night at the movies.

Raised in Heron's Creek, New South Wales, Australia, Luhrmann developed at an early age a love for the magic of classic Hollywood movies, and especially, the big-hearted ones.

"I grew up in a place very isolated," he told reporter Luaine Lee in 2001. "We had a farm and a gas station and, for a while, we ran a small cinema. So we saw lots of old movies and I loved those artificial storytellings that made you *feel* the joy of *Top Hat* and *The Band Wagon* and the drama of *West Side Story*."[107]

Luhrmann's three films expanded on this classic Hollywood style, forming the Red Curtain trilogy that has energized movie fans the world over.

"The first movie, *Strictly Ballroom*, began with a red curtain opening, and it's a musical device," explains Craig Pearce, Luhrmann's cowriter and creative collaborator on all three enterprises. "It's a way of saying, 'We're going to tell you a story.' It's the same device as saying 'Once upon a time' or 'Far, far way in a land long, long ago.' Whatever the classic fairy-tale opening is. Opening the red curtain immediately tells the audience that this is a story, not naturalism, that we are very consciously telling you. That's the style of the piece."

Pearce and Luhrmann developed this grand, emotional style, which runs against the grain in the "gritty" and "realistic" Hollywood of the twenty-first century, because the two men share a vision of life.

"I'm drawn to this style because it has both a joy and, I guess, a fun about it, an irreverence that all of us should have in our lives. It also deals with things that I think are very important, and which I hold very dear," says Pearce.

"It's about expressing the really important things that have to do with the human experience that in one sense only happen to us a few times through life. We fall in love, we experience danger, we struggle against great adversity. We triumph, or we don't, and eventually, we die. We can really relate to those emotions, and in stories that deal with those big emotions, we're awakened from our everyday existence and reminded of the fundamental things of life."

Another influence on Luhrmann, leading up to *Moulin Rouge*, was the Indian cinema called Bollywood. In the mid-1990s, he and his wife, production designer Catherine Martin, visited a theater and watched one of these colorful spectacles, and came out of the experience wondering if they could create a cinematic form like that in the West, and whether a musical would work.[108]

"Baz and I have been fans of musicals for a long time," explains Pearce. "When I say 'fans,' I don't mean slavish fans. We really love musicals that work, and we were aware of the pitfalls of trying to do a modern musical and how often it doesn't work in a modern context. So Baz said to me, 'Let's do a third film that's really the ultimate expression of this style that we've developed.'"

And his pitch was an outrageous one.

"He came to me and said, 'I want to do a musical that's set in Paris of the 1890s, but it has modern music, and it's set in and around the Moulin Rouge, and it's based on the Orpheus myth, and Toulouse-Lautrec is in it as a character somewhere.'"

And Pearce's immediate response? "That should be easy! Let's knock it out before lunch, and retire to the club for dinner!" jokes the writer. "No, I said, 'That sounds fascinating, but how would you do it?' And indeed, that was the beginning of a very long journey trying to discover how indeed we would do that."

So commenced what Baz Luhrmann later described as "a five-year journey to reinvent the movie musical."[109] "Before we made the film, we did an archaeological dig through the history of the musical," Luhrmann told interviewer Graham Fuller. "What we found is that the stories don't change, but the way in which you tell them does. You have to find a code in any particular place and moment in time."[110]

The first order of business developing Moulin Rouge was finding Luhrmann's self-described "code," and that search involved the selection of a classic, universal, even mythic, structure on which to hang the specifics of the tale. In his pitch to his cocreator, Luhrmann had explicitly mentioned the Orpheus myth.

"Baz has always come to me with the genesis of the idea," Pearce describes, "but then we go and do a lot of research and really try to own the idea together. For a while, we said, 'Maybe that's not the right myth [Orpheus].' We looked at the quest myth, the Jason and the Argonauts/Odyssey kind of myth, but basically what we came down to is that in the style that we had evolved in those films [Strictly Ballroom, Romeo + Juliet], they're essentially love stories, and the Orpheus myth is a tragic love story.

"So we went back and looked at the myth of Orpheus," recounts Pearce. "Basically, the myth is about Orpheus, who is the most incredibly beautiful poet and singer. His songs and poetry are so beautiful that the rocks and the trees get up and follow him when he sings. He falls in love with Eurydice and marries her, but a snake bites her, and she dies. She goes down to the Underworld, but Orpheus cannot accept this, that he's lost her, and tries to get into the Underworld to get her back.

"Of course, the Ferryman won't take Orpheus across—because he's not dead—but Orpheus charms him with the power of his song. And when he gets to the Underworld, the gods ask Orpheus, 'What are you doing here? You're not dead!' But he makes them weep with the beauty of his music and they say, 'All right you can take Eurydice out of the Underworld.' But because they're gods— and tricky ones—there's a condition. The condition is that Orpheus cannot look back at Eurydice until they are out of the Underworld."

From there, as Pearce points out, there are many variations of the myth, but in all incarnations the end result is the same: Orpheus loses the love of his life. "In some versions, she says, 'Why won't you look at me? I don't know who you are! Maybe you're tricking me!' And when he gets out into the light, he looks back at her and she's still in the darkness of the Underworld. And of course she slips back, and he loses her forever. It's very much a tragic love story, so we committed to that myth."

In the end, that tale of intense love—and loss—was the film's theme. "Ultimately, *Moulin Rouge* is about going from being a hyper-idealistic young person to a more mature person who still has their ideals, but realizes that some things are bigger in life than all of us," says Pearce. "Like death."

The next important element of *Moulin Rouge* involved the titular establishment, the place (and metaphorical Underworld) where all the action would occur. "We spent a couple of months in Paris researching the original Moulin Rouge and what that was, and the Bohemian world," remembers Pearce. "And we realized that the original Moulin Rouge wasn't this chorus line with people doing high-kicks. It was the nightclub of your dreams. It was basically sex for sale. Montmartre, where the Moulin Rouge was built, was where all the artists hung out, and they did so because it was outside the walls of Paris, actually outside the city limits.

"It was 'anything goes' up in Montmartre. There were a lot of poor people there. Artists could get cheap accommodation; they could get girls to pose naked for them, because people were struggling," Pearce relates. "It became very fashionable for rich people to come in and get the excitement of being amongst the Bohemians and the poor people, so prostitution became huge there. [Then] this entrepreneur, Zidler, got the idea 'Wouldn't it be great to make this incredible night club?' and then the rich could come and feel comfortable. They'd have the excitement of being in a sleazy bohemian area, but the comfort of being in a really lovely nightclub."

For Pearce and Luhrmann, this was exciting information, because they understood that there were modern parallels; ones that today's movie audiences could relate to easily. "In a way, that's what Studio 54 was. 'Let's get all the stars to come, and we'll let all the young, good-looking artist people in for free, and the rich and powerful can mix with the young and beautiful,'" says Pearce.

Even better, the creators of *Moulin Rouge* understood that there was also a unique parallel regarding the "popular" music of the different centuries. "Musically, what you associate with the cancan, we see through our modern eyes as really tacky and hideous. But at that time, it was really like techno is today. 'Bang! Bang! Bang!' Really loud music. There was no amplification, there was no sound system, so it was basically the loudest noise that a bunch of live musicians could make onstage. It was wild and tribal, and the dancing didn't occur onstage, it would all happen in and among the crowd.

"It would be like hip-hop, and the dancers would battle each other on the dance floor to be the best dancer, and do outrageously dangerous things like kicks and splits, and what eventually happened was that the most glamorous, craziest dancers became the stars."

Understanding this dynamic, Pearce and Luhrmann realized that their Eurydice, their tragic heroine, should be a dancer. "Because [dancers] became stars, the rich men would take these women as their courtesans. Some of these women became very wealthy and very notorious, and a lot of the secondary characters in *Moulin Rouge* are based on real people," Pearce notes. "Nicole's character is also an amalgam of some of the real characters we discovered through our research.

"So then, we had this base with which to work. The girl character was a courtesan, and although some of these women were rich and famous, they were also really trapped by their circumstance and who they were, and the world they lived in. They could never really escape.

"Ewan's character is Orpheus. So who is Orpheus?" asks Pearce. "He's an incredible poet and musician, and he charms the gatekeepers of the Underworld through the power of his music and his song. So we spent a long, long time trying to work out what the dynamic of that was, and eventually we came up with the bohemians. They were the real people in that world. They weren't the tourists or the entrepreneurs. They were legitimately on the edge, expressing things they wanted to express, living fast and dying young. Through their art and poetry, they were expressing what they needed to express at that time, which was really the birth of modernism.

"So we said, 'Okay, our guy has to be *us*, really, taking the audience at large to the Underworld.' He's from the middle-class world and he wants to be an artist; he wants to be a bohemian. And the whole Moulin Rouge—the whole bohemian world—was the Underworld.

"Initially there were other locations in that bohemian underworld of Montmartre, but as we went on writing, we realized it was much more powerful if the Moulin Rouge was the whole world," Pearce describes. "You see Christian's garret, which was across the road from the Moulin Rouge, but the Moulin Rouge becomes a symbol for the Underworld at large. Satine getting out of the Moulin Rouge becomes symbolic for her getting out of the Underworld one day. And Christian, when he comes into the Underworld and they fall in love, he tries to help her achieve her dreams and get her out."

With a mythic structure and central location cemented, *Moulin Rouge* was well into its development, but that didn't necessarily mean that fashioning a final screenplay from these elements was going to be an easy task.

"Every day that we worked on it, we would just look at each other and shake our heads," reveals Craig Pearce. "The writing process was very long, and we went through a lot of really extreme options.

"At one point, the movie started in the First World War in the mud on the battlefields of Flanders, and Christian is dying, and he flashes back to this time—thirty years earlier—when he was a young man and he met this women, with whom he fell in love.

"There were lots of characters. There was one who was a bit like the character Maximillian in *Cabaret*. There was a whole scene where they [Christian and Satine] went ballooning with Toulouse-Lautrec and they went to this country estate that was owned by this Count von Groovy, this German aristocrat. There was a wild dinner party where Isadora Duncan and Sarah Bernhardt turned up and danced the fandango with Oscar Wilde on a table, and they were all fucked up on absinthe and opium. Basically, there was an orgy."

But Pearce and Luhrmann often found themselves pulling back from such wild, even trippy imagery. "Baz and I had this expression where we'd look at each other and say, 'Marge, get your handbag.' That was the comment of people as they saw that [orgy] scene, and told their wives they were going to leave the cinema. We used to say that to each other a lot. 'Marge, get your handbag.'

"There was a lot of stupid stuff in early drafts. We went down roads that just led nowhere; that were deadends. Writing the screenplay was a very torturous experience and took a long, long time. We were despairing a lot of the time, and we thought that it was never going to work, and it took a long time to really hit on the style. The style evolved slowly, and it became more and more coherent. Though some people would disagree with that."

From the very beginning, Baz Luhrmann and Craig Pearce intended to underscore their tragic love story with modern music, but what that intention actually meant, precisely, was not always so plain. The writers could have composed new songs, or used tunes already in existence. A choice had to be broached.

"Initially, we didn't know at all what the landscape was going to be, musically," Pearce acknowledges. "We thought maybe we would write the first draft of the screenplay, and then go to a composer to write a score. But at some point when we were writing it and were trying to figure out what form Christian's poetry would take, we hit upon this . . . *thing*.

"When Christian meets the bohemians, you must have a moment when they say, 'My God! You're an amazing poet!' So what do you do for that? Do you write new poetry? Well, we tried writing new poetry, and it was a disaster. We tried using poetry from the time, like Baudelaire or Rimbaud, and it seemed odd—you were suddenly in a totally different film."

What Pearce and Luhrmann required was something that didn't necessitate a judgment from the audience of "is it good or not," but rather something that would be instantaneously recognized as wonderful. In other words, only a song that was *already* considered a classic, a great song, could fit the bill. This approach not only was a shorthand for the audience to understand the nature of Christian's Orphean gift, but also a way to tell a joke. To squeeze out a laugh of recognition from the audience.

"We saw that it worked to have a comic device there," Pearce explains. "We decided not to deal with the fact that we do or don't like Christian's poetry, but deal with the fact instead that all of those characters, emotionally in the scene, think he's amazing.

"They're all searching for a line of poetry that fits the music, and Christian comes up with 'the hills are alive with the sound of music,' which when we hear it as an audience, we all laugh, because we know it really well. It's from the most well known musical ever. It has all that history and baggage, but for the bohemians, for the characters, they've never heard it before in Paris of the 1890s, and they say, 'Oh my God! That's so modern! That's incredible.' And we go, 'Okay, we're having a joke.' We're punning on this notion of bringing modern music into the past, and the past into the modern. He's a great poet! We get it! Now let's get on with it. Once we did that, we said, 'Well, what would be the sort of music Christian would write?'

"Seeing how we set up that convention, it made sense that the music he wrote would be familiar to us [as an audience.] So that was how it evolved. At certain points in the film, we knew we needed really specific storytelling lyrics here and there. One of those is when they're putting on the show 'Spectacular-Spectacular.' We wrote the lyrics to that. There was also a song [the Police's 'Roxanne'] where the Argentinian was telling the story of the tango, and he's reflecting what's happening upstairs with the Duke and Satine, and Christian has to sing about what's going on in his heart, his jealousy—'Why does my heart cry?'—so we wrote those lyrics because we had to be specific."

For many viewers, one of *Moulin Rouge*'s high points occurs atop a giant elephant sculpture when the love-struck Christian serenades a resistant Satine in machine-gun fashion with a variety of pop love songs. Their conversation becomes a battle of numbers, played out in the lyrics of famous pop tunes.

For this dramatic "Elephant Love Medley," the makers of *Moulin Rouge* deployed an arsenal of hits, including the Elton John–Bernie Taupin hit "Your Song"; "All You Need Is Love" by John Lennon and Paul McCartney; "I Was Made for Lovin' You" by Paul Stanley, Desmond Child, and Vini Poncia; "One More Night" by Phil Collins; "Pride (In the Name of Love)" by Bono and The Edge; "Don't Leave Me This Way" written by Kenneth Gamble, Leon Huff, and Cary Gilbert; "Silly Love Songs" by McCartney; "Up Where We Belong" by Jack Nitzsche, Buffy Sainte-Marie, and Will Jennings; "Heroes" by David Bowie and Brian Eno; and "I Will Always Love You" by Dolly Parton.

Featuring snippets of all these songs in a lover's duel was not merely showing off the creator's encyclopedic knowledge of contemporary love tunes, however. "It wasn't about 'wouldn't it be groovy or wouldn't it be fun,'" noted

Baz Luhrmann.[111] Instead, there remained a very specific purpose for all the musical choices within the narrative.

"Christian's got to do the ultimate thing," stresses Pearce. "It must be the ultimate expression of his Orphean gift so she will fall in love with him. It's obvious what it must be: a medley of the greatest love tunes of all time. On top of an elephant. In the Moulin Rouge. In the middle of the night. What else could it be?"

In other moments during *Moulin Rouge*, however, audience familiarity with pop tunes would have conspired against the sincerity of the love story, and Pearce and Luhrmann were aware of that factor too. "For Satine and Christian's secret song, which plays a big part at the end, we searched for a long time," Pearce describes. "But what we found is that having a known song for that [piece] didn't work at all. It had too much baggage, and we didn't want it to potentially be comic. We wanted it to be something fresh and new between them. And at that time, it [David Baerwald's 'Come What May'] was unpublished."

Old or new, the music in *Moulin Rouge* had to be entertaining, emotionally powerful, and most of all, relevant to the narrative. "That was the other thing that Baz and I were really conscious of, while we were writing *Moulin Rouge*," Pearce says. "We knew that every number had to advance the story. It had to get us to the next story point. Numbers like 'Like a Virgin' came out of the story, of Zidler needing to give the Duke wine all night long. And how big an idiot can the Duke be? So it has to be a pretty fantastic lie for him to believe Zidler one more time. It has to be a lie that goes to the Duke's deepest, darkest desire. When Zidler says, 'She [Satine] is like . . . like . . . like . . . a virgin,' you say, 'Okay, that's a valid point.' Let's see Zidler convince the Duke through song, through Madonna's 'Like a Virgin.' And of course, he hooks the Duke one more time."

Other songs would serve to define characters for the audience, like Satine's incredibly picturesque (and sexy) introduction to the film. In this case, the inventive writers blended two icons: Madonna and Marilyn Monroe. "We looked at Satine, and who she was as a character, and then we looked at how to express that character through modern music. What songs best express what she's about? Pretty quickly 'Diamonds are a Girl's Best Friend,' came to mind. The lyric itself—'Diamonds are a girl's best friend'—is very much about a 'material girl,' and then you very quickly think of Madonna. And indeed, in the clip [music video] of 'Material Girl,' Madonna quotes Marilyn Monroe. She's in a dress and men in top hats are around her. It's really quoting a Marilyn kind of thing, so there's a direct link there. By doing that, you say to the audience, 'This is set in 1899 at a weird nightclub, but do you get it? This is what this girl is about. This is her ethos and mantra in life.'"

The development of the music in *Moulin Rouge* occurred through a process of trial and error, hit or miss, as the right tunes and resonances were selected. "We do a lot of script readings when we write our scripts, especially with a musical, because you need to try out your material," Pearce explains. "You need to see how it works on the audience, and people had this comment that it [*Moulin Rouge*] was a musical for people who don't like musicals.

"I don't like musicals if the story isn't good, or the music isn't reinforcing something meaningful and adding to the storytelling. I don't like the musicals where you stop everything and have a three-minute film clip every five minutes," Pearce says. "It gets to be boring. I don't have any patience if the story isn't good. That's always what I care about most."

After honing and refining the script, it came time to cast *Moulin Rouge*. Like many enterprises of this new musical era, the point was not necessarily to cast accomplished singers and dancers. That was a more secondary concern.

"We erred on the side of good acting," Pearce explains. "When you're Rex Harrison in *My Fair Lady* or whatever, good acting always triumphs in film over someone who has a fantastic voice but can't act to save their life. We looked at options before we cast Nicole and Ewan. We were thinking, 'What are we going to do? Are we going to dub people?'"

Among those who auditioned for the starring roles of lovers Satine and Christian were future *Chicago* costars Renée Zellweger and Catherine Zeta-Jones and *A Knight's Tale* heartthrob Heath Ledger. But in the end, it was Nicole Kidman and Ewan McGregor (*Velvet Goldmine*) who made the cut. Jim Broadbent (*Topsy Turvy* [2000]) would play Zidler, and Richard Roxburgh, the despicable count. John Leguizamo was cast as the diminutive Toulouse-Lautrec.

"Fortunately, we found people in Ewan and Nicole who were brilliant actors, but also very musical, who had the capability," Pearce considers. "They committed to work really, really hard and to intensive singing training over a number of months—really a year—to get where they needed to get in this film. They worked so hard: the dancing training; the singing training; the workshops. We did a lot of workshops. There was so much rehearsing."

According to Luhrmann the stars took to the time-consuming, labor-intensive process like "ducks to water."[112] Luhrmann also described McGregor as an actor who "informs a love song" and as "the Frank Sinatra of this new period."[113] Kidman, who had prepared for the role of Satine by watching the films of Marilyn Monroe, Cyd Charisse, and Rita Hayworth, was complimentary of her director.[114] She noted that Luhrmann would push "early on in the piece," so that by the time filming began, the stars were comfortable with what they were required to do and willing to "try anything."[115]

Pearce remembers the rehearsal process as one of great intensity and creativity. "I was always around, through all the rehearsals, because that's the time when the script always develops a lot. As soon as you have an actor say a line or act in a scene, you see what's wrong with a scene. You see what doesn't work. Sometimes, you have three pages of dialogue, and an actor just needs to say one word and you get it."

Shooting the fifty-three million dollar film was a hectic time. Production on *Moulin Rouge* occurred at Fox Studios in Sydney, entirely on sound stages. Creating an even larger burden, the cast sang all their songs live rather than lip-synching to prerecorded performances, and Kidman reportedly fractured a rib on the set and injured her knee too.[116] Sadly, Baz Luhrmann's father passed away during shooting.[117] On top of all that, the production team was essentially crafting a hundred-million-dollar spectacle on half that amount.

"We only got the film made through a lot of people putting a lot of love into it," Pearce reflects, "working for less than they probably could have; working longer; working harder; working more cleverly. I really credit Catherine Martin [production designer] for her work. The way the sets were built, the way that world was constructed—there was a real appreciation that they had to be clever to get what everybody wanted for the money we had."

Pearce recalls the difficulties and triumphs of shooting, even though he wasn't a constant presence on the set. "During shooting, I don't hang around the set, because I think that's counterproductive," the writer explains. "The actors need to have license to make it their own, and I'm fortunate having Baz as the custodian of the script on the set. If something needs to be changed on the spot, he'll do it, or he might ring me up and ask me what I think. But I'm always close by.

"What happened with *Moulin Rouge* was that we did a lot of rewriting during shooting. Baz would come up to me and say, 'This scene isn't working,' or 'We need to cut this,' or 'We need to come up with a new idea here.' Often, I'd be working on that while they'd be shooting, and Baz and I would meet at the end of the day to go over it."

The issue was, as many scholars have noted concerning *Moulin Rouge*, the manner by which to revive the musical form, and also evolve it into something not just relevant, but experimental. "It's taking an old form—the musical—and turning it into a form you haven't quite seen before," Pearce considers. "It's a style that—while it has its roots going way, way back—is quite different than what came before it. You can't say it is like 'X.' It draws on 'X,' but it's really 'Y.' I do think it was risky. It certainly felt risky making it."

Sometimes, other folks didn't feel like participating in that risk. For instance, Fox refused to pay for the absinthe fairy optical effects that appeared early in *Moulin Rouge*, during Christian's celebration with the bohemians. Accordingly, thirty-eight-year-old Luhrmann ponied up three hundred thousand dollars of his own money to create the important illusion, and was eventually reimbursed by the studio.[118]

When it premiered in early June of 2001, *Moulin Rouge* took the world by storm. The film opened in the number one slot in France and the United Kingdom. It also did solid business in the United States, in part thanks to the release of a related video on MTV, "Lady Marmalade," featuring Christina Aguilera, Lil' Kim, and Pink. Word of mouth promptly began to grow about this unusual new musical, and before long, it was a full-fledged event.

Though opinions were divided, many in the critical community viewed the film as a trailblazer and a genre-reviver. Writing for *Variety*, Todd McCarthy noted that Luhrmann had outstripped "anything Hollywood has produced in years," and bore comparison to "the likes of Busby Berkeley in his ability to conceptualize and physically energize production numbers."[119]

Newsweek's David Ansen noted that in *Moulin Rouge*, Luhrmann had "raised the level of his game," deconstructing the musical and "reassembling it with a potency that hasn't been since *Cabaret*."[120]

Dubbed "The Rodgers and Hammerstein of the New Age,"[121] Lurhmann was also championed far and wide for the approach he and Pearce had developed so carefully in fashioning their tale and selecting its music. "It slashes through the distance that so many of us feel toward musicals, not just because the songs here are really our songs, but because the very incongruity evokes that casual, private dream world in which rock has become the daily libretto of our lives," wrote Owen Gleiberman in *Entertainment Weekly*.[122]

There were some reviewers who didn't like the film, and disapproved of its bold style. "*Moulin Rouge* is too hip to settle on one cohesive style, too *au courant* to involve the viewer in such quaint notions as story and character, too impressionistic to leave much of a lasting impression," suggested critic Glen Lovell.[123]

Writing for the *Seattle Times*, Mark Rahner complained that the film featured numbers that "would have given Busby Berkeley a meltdown": over-the-top characters, hyperactive editing and "camera work that'll make you ask, *voulez-vous a grand mal seizure avec moi?*"[124]

Pearce was prepared for these brickbats, and even sympathized with critics to an extent, some of whom might not quite understand what they were seeing. "This is a generalization, but I think the critics are always a little behind, because their job is to look at what's come before, and compare new things to what's come before. But if something that's never come before happens, you have to be a little confused at first.

"It comes down to personal taste," he suggests. "Some people don't like *Moulin Rouge*; some critics don't like *Moulin Rouge*, but it always elicits a really passionate response. You either really, really love it or you really, really hate it. Some critics really get it, and love it, and some don't get it—and hate it—because it offends their sensibilities; their notion of everything that's right about 'good' filmmaking. But *Moulin Rouge* is very consciously not 'good' filmmaking with good in quotes, because 'good' filmmaking can often just be *safe* filmmaking."

Pearce also has a notion as to why some critics easily discounted the film. "*Moulin Rouge* wears its heart on its sleeve, but hides its intellectual credentials. More thought went into *Moulin Rouge* than a lot of so-called European art-house films that critics might love. They [those films] wear intellectual and artistic credentials on their sleeves and bury their heart. I love both kinds of film, and there's a place for each, but that's their style. They're not overtly emotional. *Moulin Rouge* is overtly emotional, but the whole theory and philosophy as to why it is that way—there's a whole philosophy and intellectual thought process that has gone into evolving that style and designing that contract with the audience.

"I think the audience sometimes feels that they are being talked down to when they see *Moulin Rouge*," offers Pearce, "but I think it's the opposite. We, as filmmakers don't think there's any mystery. We know that as an audience, you are perfectly capable of seeing behind the veil. Either come along on the journey with us, or don't. Critics sometimes feel that their job is to look behind the veil and decide for the mere mortals in the audience what they think the message is. The mere mortals in the audience probably know more about media language than most critics."

Brash and impressive, bold and revolutionary, *Moulin Rouge* ultimately emerged as a sensation in the United States in the summer of 2001, despite critical and audience divisions. The film racked up a dynamite $340 million worldwide and even spawned a new cult.

As late as February 2003, a year and a half after its release, a "legion" of *Moulin Rouge* fans were still "clamoring" to see the movie in theaters, and 20TH Century Fox finally acquiesced to their demands, releasing the film for midnight showings at venues such as the Mann Festival Theater in Westwood.[125] This development is especially meaningful when one considers that the film had already been released on DVD and video for sometime beforehand, suggesting perhaps that the silver screen remains eternally the true home of the musical genre.

During the months following its initial release, *Moulin Rouge* received plenty of accolades. The "Lady Marmalade" video won MTV's Best Video of the Year Award, and *Moulin Rouge* picked up many more honors, including an Outstanding Achievement in Feature Films notice from the American Choreography Awards. The National Board of Review named it the best film of the year, and the effort won Best Picture, Best Actor, and Best Actress nods at the Hollywood Film Festival.

Perhaps the greatest honor was saved for last. *Moulin Rouge* was nominated for a slew of Oscars. In fact, it became the first musical since *All That Jazz* twenty-two years earlier to be nominated for Best Picture of the Year. Following in the tradition of Barbra Streisand and *The Prince of Tides* (1991), Baz Luhrmann was mysteriously slighted in the best director nominations, but Nicole Kidman was nominated for Best Actress.

"It was a great vindication, I suppose, of the journey that we had been on for so many years," states Pearce. "All those times when we said, 'Marge, get your handbag, this isn't going to work,' but we kept going. It was a symbol of it being worthwhile. I don't want to say that the Oscar nomination made it all worthwhile, because there are [also] many personal things that make it worthwhile. But an Oscar nomination is a symbolic way of saying that even though it is out there and experimental in many ways, it was embraced by the world at large. And that's a very nice feeling."

Miramax movie mogul Harvey Weinstein once stated that director Baz Luhrmann is an artist who has committed himself to "a mission to shake us from our sleep . . . so we can experience something new."[126] Nowhere on film or stage is that mission more plain than in Luhrmann's 2001 paean to tragic, passionate love, the dazzling *Moulin Rouge*.

Constructed upon a classical structure, namely the Orpheus myth, the film first radically deconstructs then inventively rejiggers the movie musical format, in the process presenting an emotional spectacle that works on the senses like a hallucinogenic assault—one moment, absurd; one moment, touching; the next, incredibly sexy.

Whereas the experience of watching many films produced today is decidedly passive, a surrendering acceptance of the given images as our eyes receive them, a viewing of *Moulin Rouge* engages every faculty it can sink its hooks into: the eye, the ears, the heart, and most importantly the brain.

This film is a movie musical on steroids, pumped up almost beyond recognition, and it transmits information to the viewer on an almost hyper-subconscious level at times. A complex thought process occurs while trying to discern the reasons a certain moment rings true, or feels familiar, or makes us laugh, or touches us the way it does. In other words, the film is unerringly smart, and built on carefully crafted foundations that don't become plain, let alone obvious, until the viewer starts digging into the vault of his or her own cinematic experiences.

For instance, this is a film that references every pop-culture touchstone from Gene Kelly's umbrella spin in *Singin' in the Rain* (in the "Elephant Love Medley"), to the 1997 James Cameron flick, *Titanic*. In the latter case, the Duke employs an armed henchman named Warner. Well, Warner just happens to be the name of the actor, David Warner, who played the armed henchman of Billy Zane—essentially the same role—in the Cameron film. In both cases, these soldier villains stand in the way of tragic love (and one lover dies), whether they be Leo and Kate in *Titanic* or Ewan and Nicole in *Moulin Rouge*. The Duke's Warner serves the same purpose as Billy Zane's Warner, and his name is thus more than a name, it's a coded signifier of a specific function and role within a tragic romance.

This meta-referencing of our pop-culture lexicon runs throughout the film, and evokes a feeling of both frenzy and passion through its re-rendering of past screen triumphs. One such amazing high point is the aforementioned

"Elephant Love Medley." In this staccato duel of would-be lovers, Christian attempts to win over Satine with his poetry, here in the form of popular love tunes, while her retorts are purposefully more rational and realistic. Christian's cogent argument is presented like a sampling of every philosophy about love to come down the pike in twenty years, as are his opponent's rejoinders.

However, the inclusion of these songs isn't simply a call for attention, not merely intellectual allusions for an audience weaned on radio hits to recognize and enjoy. Nor are the songs present in the scene merely because they grant the story a "timeless quality and a chance for stars Nicole Kidman and Ewan McGregor . . . to shine."[127]

They are present, on the first level, to capture a feeling of the moment: the enthusiasm of love. "By the end, she's a believer, and they're standing inches apart bellowing the lyrics from 'Heroes' at each other," wrote journalist Mary F. Pols. "You feel their spirits soaring, pushing them against each other and it is both inspirational and exciting."[128]

But again, there's something even more complex and profound at work, a second level. Watching this elephant medley, one feels an overpowering, unrestrained joy and happiness at the relationship we are seeing develop, but the sequence at the same instant also cannily positions viewers outside the narrative, in a position to reflect on what is being seen. As viewers, we are both deeply in the moment, falling in love with Kidman and McGregor, and far removed from it too, observing the careful construction of the moment's effect, recognizing each song as it comes up, and thus calling up past films, like *An Officer and a Gentleman* (1981), the origin of "Up Where We Belong." In moments like this, *Moulin Rouge* makes our brains tap dance.

"This is where you either get the film and say, 'Yes, I understand. I sign off on the contract the filmmakers are making with me,' or you say, 'This is really silly; they're poking fun at love. I don't understand,'" says Pearce.

"[But] what we're saying as filmmakers is that love is powerful; love is fundamental; love is really the thing that we're all searching for. Love is the thing that drives humanity, but it's also a very silly thing. It makes no sense. It's illogical. When we're in love, we do all these silly, damn stupid things. That's both its power and beauty, and its weakness. It depends what side of the fence you're on. If you're on the 'I'm in love' side of the fence, you're going to think this is incredible.

"We wanted to, I guess, have our cake and eat it too," Pearce suggests. "In a more naturalistic film, you wouldn't have done that. But in a really celebratory way, we're both laughing at the joke and also meaning what we say in a really heartfelt way."

"You have to accept the contract and be open to it," Luhrmann has stated. "In *Moulin Rouge*, when we say 'Truth, beauty, freedom, but above all love,' we mean every word of it. I believe in that absolutely."[129]

Moulin Rouge is a lunatic accomplishment. It crackles with intelligence, knowledge and passion, and runs on eight tracks at once—sly and fun, heartfelt and wicked. It represents a half-dozen things at any given moment, and yet operates most forcefully on a most primal level: a story of tragic love and innocence lost. Some people won't be willing to keep up with the breakneck pace or enjoy the filmmakers' caution-to-the-wind narrative approach, but if they try, the rewards are incredible.

"He [Luhrmann] doesn't make the kind of movies I'd make," says Joss Whedon, "but my love is large. I eat it [*Moulin Rouge*] with a spoon. I get cranky because it's all about cutting, but it's just so goddamned lush and beautiful and heartfelt and interesting that, at the end of the day, I don't give a rat's ass. I love it."

"Irwin Winkler loved that movie," says Jay Cocks. "With *Moulin Rouge* you admire what the guy was trying to do. You admire the concept of it, and the restlessness of it, and the drive of it . . . [but] because I can't adapt to the dramatic rhythm so easily of something like *Moulin Rouge*, it kind of leaves me behind."

"I think it's so awesome how well *Moulin Rouge* ultimately did," says *Velvet Goldmine* director Todd Haynes. "It proves that there's an audience that doesn't need to see the exact same shit all the time."

The musical genre is always—irritatingly—described as "moribund." But in the summer of 2001, thanks to *Moulin Rouge*, the format was popping out of its grave and doing a pirouette over the critics who proclaimed it dead. Thanks to a revolutionary new movie, the musical was back and more entertaining than before.

It had been a long climb back to the top of the box office, and the years from 1996 to 2001 reveal the disparity in approaches. Woody Allen, Kenneth Branagh, Christopher Guest and Trey Parker sought to use comedy as the avenue to make the format palatable again. Sir Alan Parker went for epic scope and spectacle with *Evita*; Todd Haynes gazed back at the glam rock age and the fantasy musical, and created a rock opera fantasy in *Velvet Goldmine*. Lars von Trier forged a social melodrama in *Dancer in the Dark*, giving us the most frankly painful and emotional musical in a generation.

But Baz Luhrmann adopted every one of these approaches and threw them into a blender to fashion his *Moulin Rouge*. General audiences were thrilled with the results, even if the old-schoolers objected to pop music in 1899 France, or the notion of untrained actors singing and dancing. For the first time since *Flashdance* in 1983, the movie musical held a new currency and immediacy with the popular masses, and more importantly, teenagers, again.

CHAPTER FOUR

From Hedwig and the Angry Inch to De-Lovely and Beyond

2001–2004

YOU KANT ALWAYS GET WHAT YOU WANTED

At a series of dramatic rock performances at the restaurant chain called Bilgewater's, a cross-dressing, "internationally ignored," would-be rock star named Hedwig recounts her life story in a quest to be accepted and loved.

Born to a single mother in East Germany in 1961—as a boy named Hansel—Hedwig spent the seventies listening to American and British rock music on the radio. Then, as a teenager, Hansel was romanced by an American soldier named Luthor. Luthor offered to marry Hansel and take him back to the U.S.—escaping the repression of East Germany. But to acquire a marriage license and emigrate to the West, Hansel had to leave something behind. He had to undergo a sex-change operation. Unfortunately, the surgery was botched, leaving Hansel with only an "angry inch," where once there had been six. Thus was born Hedwig.

Hedwig became Luthor's wife in the U.S., but once there, Luthor left him for another young man. Adding insult to injury, the Cold War ended and the Berlin Wall fell, rendering Hedwig's anatomical sacrifice unnecessary. Later, Hedwig formed a band to sing her original compositions and, before long, met an army brat named Tommy, who wanted to learn everything about rock'n'roll from Hedwig. When Hedwig fell in love with Tommy, he betrayed her and stole her songs, becoming the rock star Tommy Gnosis.

Now, as Hedwig and her band, the Angry Inch, shadow Tommy's big American tour, her husband Yitshak makes another betrayal by leaving Hedwig for a touring company of *Rent*. But Hedwig's topsy-turvy world is turned upside down during a chance encounter with Tommy Gnosis in a limousine, and the moment leads her down a new road of self-discovery.

This is the sad and strange tale of *Hedwig and the Angry Inch*, the 2001 film that followed *Moulin Rouge*, and kept the musical momentum going through the year. The film's director and creator, John Cameron Mitchell, is a true original, and along with composer Stephen Trask, the artist responsible for one of the truly great (and irreverent) rock-operas of our modern age. Like all the best works of art, Mitchell's stunning creation arises out of his sensibilities and context, his personal biography.

Mitchell was born in El Paso, Texas, and spent his youth as a army brat living on bases in Kansas and East Berlin. As a child, he watched many musical films, but doesn't consider himself a "huge musical film maven."

"In my childhood, the musical films that were most influential for me were *Oliver!* and *Mary Poppins*," Mitchell says. "My mom's British, so they have that 'British thing' about them. I really liked the ones that you would not think of as musicals, but which had a musical element, like *Willy Wonka & the Chocolate Factory* (1971) or *Bedknobs and Broomsticks* (1971) . . . I guess you could say *The Wizard of Oz* as well. So they tended to the more bizarre."

These film fantasies often featured characters breaking into song, but Mitchell didn't see that musical convention as an impediment to his interest. "I think that was really just something you grew up with. I didn't really question it."

As Mitchell grew older, he also went through a musical theater phase in high school and developed a love of Noël Coward. "I didn't really know the musicals, but I liked the songs. I was really into Noël Coward. I was really into Kander and Ebb. I was really into *Godspell* and *Pippin* and not so much *Hair*— that was later. I guess I really liked the jazz revues a lot."

When he was fourteen, Mitchell made the acquaintance of a figure who would also prove highly influential to his art. "A Marlene Dietrich–style figure with big hair," this woman was the babysitter of Mitchell's brother.[1]

"She was like a German version of America, sort of trailer trash with a German take," he describes her.[2] "My friend and I would go to her trailer and act out Barry Manilow's 'Copacabana' for her. She had lots of dates. They came in the front door and we went out the back."[3] With a penchant for "tube tops" and a taste for "cigarettes,"[4] this unique woman, part army wife and part prostitute, was an inspiration for the Hedwig character.

Mitchell's time in East Berlin, where his father, a military officer, served as a commander, also impacted the course of his career. He often frequented punk gay bars, and even crossed the line into the Communist East. On one such excursion, he saw *I Am My Own Woman* (1992), a film by Rosa von Prauheim. It concerned "this guy who lived as a woman through the Nazis and the communists," Mitchell describes. "That influenced me, being about this ultimate outsider."[5]

Back in the States, Mitchell began to consider how he might present his material in a provocative manner, and struck upon a performance of a play that was an unusual homage to German Expressionism.

"The thing that inspired me structurally—and just period—to make *Hedwig* was *The Black Rider*, which is playing in San Francisco right now," he says. "It's a revival of a Robert Wilson–directed piece; the music was by Tom Waits and the book was by William Burroughs. It was done by this famous Hamburg theater troupe called the Thalia.

"It was very Expressionist, and very Robert Wilson, but what was different was that there was a real story," Mitchell stresses. "Some of his other [works] are very nonnarrative and abstract. This one had a quite direct through-line. I thought, 'Okay, this reveals to me that musical theater can be anything that has songs and a story.' There are no tropes that you have to follow; there's no formula you have to follow. It really freed my mind to see this. And it's actually playing in San Francisco right now with Marianne Faithful and Matt McGrath, who played Hedwig [onstage] after I did.

"The other thing which was a good guide for us [Mitchell and composer Stephen Trask] was Sandra Bernhardt's show *Without You I'm Nothing*. Again, that one is not particularly narrative, but we liked the alternating monologue and song structure. And Stephen Trask and I really loved her sense of humor."

Plato's *Symposium* also provided fodder for Mitchell and Trask's creation, especially a speech by Aristophanes concerning the nature of men and women in prehistory, particularly the notion that "the sexes were three in number," and that each and every human was "in shape a round entity, with backsides forming a circle; he had four hands, an equal number of feet, one head with two faces exactly alike but each looking in opposite directions, set upon a circle neck."[6]

The myth continued to express how the pantheon of Greek gods grew angry after these lumbering hominid creatures launched an attack on them, and punished the mortals by using Zeus's lightning to cut them in two—into men and women. The result was that each of the newly created creatures "longed for his other half"[7]—thus forming the origin of love, and setting in motion Hedwig's quest to complete herself.

"That story comes directly from Plato's *Symposium*," Mitchell says. "It included the original story that [the song] 'Origin of Love' was adapted from."

Hedwig, the victim of a botched sex-change operation, was thus fully born. She has since developed into an amazing lead character, and one who incorporates all of these various and sundry influences. Perhaps she has been best described as a "walking, talking, gyrating spawn of opposites—male and female; Eastern bloc and glam rock"; and an "imperious, would-be star, and insecure needy child-(wo)man."[8]

John Cameron Mitchell and Stephen Trask's *Hedwig and the Angry Inch* began its "run" as a so-called drag show in New York City's gay rock club Squeezebox in 1994. The production was honed in a variety of modest venues, from birthday parties, clubs and theaters to a benefit held on someone's beach house deck,[9] but in the end, what emerged from this crucible was an innovative combination of raucous rock music, witty monologue, and pathos.

It was that commercial combination that brought *Hedwig and the Angry Inch* to the Off-Broadway Jane Street Theater in 1998 and kept it running for two years. It was the play's originality, daring, and laughs that inspired a gaggle of rabid fans called Hed-Heads, and eventually led to Hedwig merchandise like a designer fragrance from Demeter, inspired by the character and featuring the scent of "candy, cheap booze, stale cigarette smoke, hairspray, and a cheap hotel room . . . [and] rainy pavement."[10]

But just because there was already a cult around *Hedwig and the Angry Inch*, that didn't mean that making a movie from the play was going to be easy. In fact, the stage-to-screen process has been notoriously difficult, as big screen misfires like *A Chorus Line* and *The Fantasticks* prove dramatically. But John Cameron Mitchell, a veteran of Broadway (*Six Degrees of Separation*), television (*Law & Order*), and film (*Girl 6* [1996]), began developing a script and soon discovered that the secret to writing it was to remain flexible about, not necessarily faithful to, the versions that appeared on stage.

"A lot of stage-to-film adaptations fell into the pitfall of thinking that everything that they say is sacred," Mitchell suggests. "Because they're just not. I had been saying the words [in the play] for years, so I was bored with them and I was very excited to translate them into images. For example, we'd have a joke where Hedwig would wipe her face on a towel and say, 'Oh, it's the Shroud of Hedwig,' but in the film, you can tell the same joke without saying the words. You can just show the Shroud of Hedwig."

Film also provided the opportunity to utilize new formats, ones unavailable in small venues. "Onstage we had projections," he notes, describing "visual aids" used during certain monologues and songs, "so it just seemed natural to move it into animation since we were on film." In the movie, colorful cartoons by Emily Hubley brought life to Hedwig's diary and illustrated important musical sequences including "Origin of Love."

While thinking about all the new possibilities that film could open up for his rock opera, Mitchell also brought his protean *Hedwig and the Angry Inch* script to Sundance and continued developing the project there. Among those who stopped by to see the work in progress were superstar Robert Redford[11] and future *Camp* director, Todd Graff.

"He brought the script to the Sundance screenwriter's lab," Graff recalls. Graff worked with Mitchell at the lab there, and remains impressed with the script and its creator. "He's the real thing, Johnny," Graff notes. "He's a real artist and he has a real vision of the movies he wants to make, and he has the tenacity to make sure they get made that way."

Sponsored by New Line and Killer Films, John Cameron Mitchell shot the movie adaptation of *Hedwig and the Angry Inch* in Toronto and Ontario on a budget of approximately six million dollars. Adding another layer of difficulty, the film had to be shot in a mere twenty-eight days.

The project was Mitchell's directing debut, and he understood exactly what he wanted to see on film, and in particular, his vision involved a shooting style that fostered immediacy, right down to the use of handheld cameras.

"A pitfall I see in movie musicals is that the camera work and design can be so stylized that you can't really buy that these characters exist," Mitchell says of his approach. "You can imagine [they are real], but you know, even drag movies like *Priscilla, Queen of the Desert* (1994) are stylized. There are certain rules that people say you should do for comedy or for musicals, like 'the camera shouldn't move in a hand-held way.'

"To me that's very distancing, so I kept telling my designers and cinematographer that costumes, camera, design—everything—had to be believable in the real world, so that Hedwig is unusual and unique, but certainly, there *could* be a Hedwig," Mitchell considers. "For me, John Cassavettes is my real model of absolute reality."

Some of the changes between stage and film versions of Hedwig involved budget. "In the original script, Hedwig is performing in different venues, like an airport lounge or a bowling alley," Mitchell explains. "Budget required that we limit that, so we thought we would use one funny restaurant, and there happened to be a seafood place that was available and we just thought of all the jokes. But then we lost that place, and retro-fitted another place and kept the seafood theme. I think we even took the furnishings from the seafood place, and shot different corners of it to be different franchises. We just thought about the fun of it. It wasn't specifically a seafood metaphor, though it was kind of interesting when all the Jews are eating shrimp."

Directing the film's many songs—in various styles—also ran the gamut of experiences for Mitchell. "There was a whole year of stuff, so sometimes it was great and sometimes it wasn't," he explains. "During the shooting, it wasn't fun at all, because the pressure was too strong. I had too many hats to wear and too many wigs to wear.

"Probably the worst day was doing 'Sugar Daddy,' when we just had so little time. That was a single camera day, so it took longer, and I was sort of mad at some people for not doing their job, and feeling kind of despondent," Mitchell remembers. "But we got through it, and you know, each day was completely different. There was so little time to get the film made. If *Hedwig* had been done in the Hollywood system, it would take ninety days."

Another decision that complicated shooting involved the singing. Much of it had to be performed live to accommodate the more wild, rock and roll nature of the material, rather than via lip-synching. "For live singing, you have to use multiple cameras in order to edit correctly, because you have different performances every time," Mitchell explains.

"I did some story boarding and decided how to get into each song, but then, once the song started, often it was more like, 'Every cameraman for himself,' and the cinematographer would take over and decide who was where for the multiple cameras. Then we would do the key shots throughout the film to get in and out [of the numbers], and I would run over and check the monitor during rehearsal, and then do a few takes and look at it. It took up a lot of time, [and] there was a certain amount of stamina necessary to keep doing it over and over live."

Stamina is a term that often comes into play producing independent musicals. *Resourceful* is another. "When you have to make a 'musical'—in quotes, with the grand gestures and costumes—on an independent budget you have a really hard time being able to achieve the gestures Baz Lurhmann can achieve, because you just don't have the money," describes James Lyons, who is also thanked in *Hedwig*'s credits.

"John's film is an amazing testament to what you can do with very little money. Theresa Du Prez, who is the art director of that film, built that set where a trailer opens up, and it's incredible," Lyons describes. "They did it with nothing. I don't remember the exact budget, but I remember Theresa saying, 'My dad was a carpenter, I'll figure it out.' And in the past, that would have been the entire backlot of MGM working on that!

"It's fascinating how those gestures that we do get from older musicals are being transformed. We would do that if we could, [in independent film] but we don't have the bucks, so it looks like this now, rather than that."

One of the most unique aspects of *Hedwig and the Angry Inch* involves the way director Mitchell has seamlessly integrated the music video–style production number into the musical. In the final analysis, his fresh approach contributes much to the film's success. There are times during production numbers that Hedwig sings directly to the camera, and again, a feeling of immediacy (and compassion) is generated through this technique. Mitchell suggests that music videos were indeed part of his approach, which is interesting, since some directors try to avoid using music video–style techniques in musicals, usually to their detriment.

"Wig in a Box," in particular, could be carved right out of the film and aired on MTV as a video clip. "They [videos] were certainly around me," Mitchell notes of the format. "And there was certainly this question throughout [about] when Hedwig could look at the camera or—in other words—break the fourth wall. Was this [technique] going to ruin something emotional, or was it going to heighten something?"

However, "Wig in a Box," which in some fashion is Hedwig's soliloquy about her life, represented one of the few spots where the director and his crew deemed the video conceit helpful. "In other words, it would have been inappropriate in some songs, like 'Angry Inch,'" Mitchell says. "We had the convention that whenever Hedwig is performing in concert that she wouldn't [address the camera] because that would take you out of it a little bit, but for the ones that were a little more internal, it was possible.

"There were some [numbers] that were both internal and in concert like 'Midnight Radio' at the end. I suppose I could have looked at the camera, but it wasn't necessary," Mitchell says. "But that point of view [Hedwig's], was always important for us to think about."

After a hectic shooting schedule in which Mitchell served as both director and actor, he found that a whole new role awaited him after principal photography, that of film editor. The editing process was, much like shooting the film, one that he felt two ways about.

"I liked some of it," the director notes. "At the beginning, I really liked it, but then you realize that if you edit it the way you wrote it, very rarely does it work unless it's a very simple kind of film. So there's that moment of collapse where you kind of go, 'Oh, I don't know what to do,' and that's where your editor comes in to suggest things, cutting out everything unnecessary and then putting things back in."

In this case, Mitchell deleted some moments involving the band and Hedwig's manager, played by Andrea Martin, because they took away from Hedwig as the central and essential character of the film. It wasn't easy, since many of the cut sequences were comic gold and the direct result of Mitchell's improvisational style on the set.

"It's very important that an editor is a cowriter, really," Mitchell asserts. "So there were times when I just had to give everything up to him. And then, later on, your instincts come back and you start to be the director again. Again, that was many months, and some of it was great and some of it was nervewracking.

"The first screening of early cuts for colleagues were very nervewracking," Mitchell recalls. "That's where *All That Jazz* is a good model, because you realize you can do everything. Fosse uses every possible musical convention, so that felt very freeing. It was important to remind myself that this is all being told through Hedwig's eyes, so there was a license to be creative, because she's creative."

Mitchell also felt fortunate because he was allowed the opportunity to express his vision without interference. "I think we were really lucky in that New Line Cinema really got it. They never made me do anything I didn't want to do. The only limitations were those that everyone has to deal with—which is budget."

With his edited film in hand, Mitchell then presented *Hedwig and the Angry Inch* at a variety of festivals, and discovered that he'd shot and edited a winner. The film won the Best Feature award at the Austin Gay and Lesbian International Film Festival and Berlin International Film Festival. The movie nabbed the Audience Award at Sundance, and Mitchell picked up the director's award for drama. Revealing the mainstream acceptance of the film, Mitchell was also nominated for a Golden Globe after its theatrical release.

Critics agreed with the assessment of film festival judges and audiences, and *Hedwig and The Angry Inch* received a plethora of rave reviews when distributed beginning on July 20, 2001.

"Mitchell has done the damn difficult thing of giving a staged work a look that honors the original medium while recognizing that movies are a whole other shebang," noted *Entertainment Weekly*.[12] *Time* noted that the film, with its "glam-rock excess, catchy tunes and witty one-liners" could mean it was "this generation's *Tommy*. Only with better legs."[13]

Other reviewers championed the "unforgettable heroine" Hedwig in a "wonderfully odd, vivid and dynamic movie,"[14] and noted that when Mitchell struts, "he *struts*."[15]

Trask's magnificent score also won some much-deserved kudos when the *Orange County Register*'s Ben Wener remarked that "the music of *Hedwig* is a revelation, marking the first time since *Hair* that the dreaded concept 'rock musical' has succeed so well."[16]

Todd Graff—then enmeshed in the preparation of his own musical—remembers his impression of the film. "I think it was phenomenal. It's why I begged Stephen Trask to do *Camp*. It's revolutionary in some weird way. It takes a story that should be completely repugnant, or completely marginalized, but instead I laughed my butt off. And my heart breaks for this character."

Mitchell welcomes Graff's compliment, but doesn't necessarily believe that *Hedwig* is a revolutionary reinvention of the movie musical. "That's so nice. I don't really think of it that way," he reveals. "For me, anything I that I do is much more about whether it succeeds on its own terms. And I do think that it does. There are certain things that I think could have been better, partly due to the fact that I was directing and acting, so I couldn't concentrate as much on the acting as I wanted, or this or that. But—revolutionary or not—what gratifies me is that people say that it inspires them to do other things that are completely different.

"Ayn Rand—who I don't usually quote—says, 'Show me something marvelous, and it will allow me to do the same,' so that's the best compliment, if someone says, 'Oh, it me made me want to go write something.'"

For time immemorial, the musical film has risen or fallen not merely on the effectiveness of the individual song or dance, but on the human qualities of the film's characters. As much as any other genre, with the possible exception of the Western and its iconic cowboy "loners," the musical has always created memorable stars via this very factor. Just consider how often we equate musicals with characters or those performers who play them. Judy Garland in the *The Wizard of Oz*, Astaire and Rogers in their 1930s cycle, and of course Gene Kelly, and Julie Andrews. Even Elvis.

This explicit connection of the musical format to a specific character or star has no doubt accreted because the musical format boasts the singular capacity to function on a personal level. What could be more intimate than gazing into the eyes of another human being and watching him or her belt out fears, concerns, yearnings and sensitivities in song? Song lays bare for us the human soul, and that's why we remember with such affection Dorothy, Maria von Trapp, Sally Bowles, Evita, or even Björk's Selma in *Dancer in the Dark*.

Similarly, John Cameron Mitchell's *Hedwig and the Angry Inch* succeeds admirably as a filmed musical not merely because the score is remarkable (and the first original rock opera since *Velvet Goldmine*), but because it remembers the primacy of this human equation and acquaints audiences with a memorable and all-together unique character in the person of the incomparable Hedwig. This is a person who, in the sensitive hands of Mitchell, overcomes great and tragic adversity. Yes, she has suffered terrible betrayals in her life, but like the classic and mythic hero described by Joseph Campbell, she is always on an interesting journey.

What makes Hedwig a unique and approachable character is not necessarily her suffering (like Selma, for example, who appeals to us as one of von Trier's victimized Golden Hearts), but the fact that her quest is an intellectual and noble one at heart, one directed at discovering something extraordinarily valuable: her own true identity in the world.

On one hand, *Hedwig and the Angry Inch* asks the viewer to understand the story of Plato's *Symposium*, and therefore the longing within each human soul for another. This hunt is a kind of outward integration dependent on the perceptions and actions of another. On the other hand, the film's dialogue also explicitly (and humorously) contemplates philosopher Emmanuel Kant's (1724–1804) "Copernican Revolution," the theory that the human mind lacks the power to penetrate the veil of appearance and grasp the true nature of things.

Consider how Kant's critique of reason applies to Hedwig's dilemma. She is in search of her perfect other half, but really, what is Hedwig? A she or a he? Different individuals might have different answers to that question. There is no consensus, and so one must ask, is sexual identity the key to how we put ourselves together? If that is truly the case, then Hedwig is a doomed individual because she is neither sex and both sexes at the same time, always out of place because of the botched operation that created something new where her penis "used to be" and where her vagina "never was." Since society itself cannot agree on what she symbolizes, Hedwig cannot uncover that special person who will make her truly happy. With whom should she begin the search, a man or a woman?

The film also asks the viewer, through Plato's *Symposium* and Trask's composition "Origin of Love," to contemplate the notion that a union with another person completes us. But then the film soundly rejects that supposition, and spins the material in a new direction by relating that Hedwig can only find completeness and happiness when *she* perceives herself to be whole, a reflection of Kant's key principles. Instead of looking outward for validation, she must gaze within.

Visually, this theme is made evident when the tattoo branded on Hedwig's hip undergoes a radical transformation in the finale, following her epiphany, her self-discovery. The tattoo is no longer a half-moon seeking its opposite jigsaw puzzle piece on another leg, one theoretically belonging to a prospective mate, but rather a full circle representing wholeness, the accurate perception of one's self as total and integrated.

"I certainly think there's some self-integration that begins to happen at the end, and a realization that you probably need to be whole internally before you ask someone else," Mitchell says. "Self-unity is more important than having someone else complete you."

So Hedwig is a sympathetic and memorable character in the history of movie musicals because she wants and desires something crucial, an understanding of her identity. In musicals, it need not be so intellectual a quest. It could be simple, like Luisa's pining to see the larger world in *The Fantasticks*, yet that yearning must be present so that the characters and their songs engage us. It is to *Hedwig*'s credit that the "I want" crisis of its protagonist functions on a deep level, in the very realm of philosophy.

Mitchell makes Hedwig a compelling character not just because she reflects the universal human need to know how one "fits in," but through his startling visual touches. The handheld camera fosters a closeness with the character, and at times the audience literally seems to be present in the room with her.

Sometimes, this approach results in humor. In one number, Hedwig seduces Tommy, approaching the camera directly (representing his point of view). Her bedroom eyes seem to wink at us as she elegantly parts a sea of hanging laundry in her trailer, getting closer to her quarry. In a classic Hollywood, this moment may have occurred in a sheik's tent or behind lush silk curtains. Instead, the grand gesture is translated to the mundane world of middle America, and it's both funny and contextually appropriate.

More than that, a song that exposes Hedwig's feelings about herself is the jaunty "Wig in a Box." In this sequence, almost every shot reflects the director's attempt to pull us deeper into Hedwig's world and better understand her. As Hedwig sings directly to the camera, making eye contact with the lens in music video style, we are the recipients of her song and its message. At one point, the camera adopts the point of view of Hedwig herself as a blond wig is lowered dramatically toward the lens, towards our very eyes. Anyone can put on that wig, as Mitchell likes to say, and this image reinforces that notion.

At another point in "Wig in a Box," Hedwig addresses the camera again, and the lyrics invite us to sing along with her. A bouncing ball even shows up to facilitate the attempt, karaoke style. Finally, Mitchell literally smashes the fourth wall by having the trailer wall fall down and form a stage. All these dramatic visuals draw the audience deeper into the film, heightening sympathy, empathy, and understanding.

It's clear that Mitchell is a thoughtful artist, not just a hired hand interpreting the material, and *Hedwig and the Angry Inch* succeeds because he has incorporated all kinds of poignant symbols into his musical. For instance, throughout the film, Hedwig and the Berlin Wall are explicitly compared. Both were born in 1961, both were "destroyed" by being split (East vs. West, male vs. female), and each simultaneously represent two qualities. "There isn't much of a difference," the song "Tear Me Down" reminds us, between "a bridge and a wall."

The film even starts out with a blast of symbolism, as "America the Beautiful" plays on the soundtrack. "At the beginning of the play, Hedwig enters through the audience with her cape, which you can't see as well in the film, but it's a stars-and-stripes theme on the outside," Mitchell describes. "So it was America the Beautiful, Hedwig the Beautiful, and of course, inside is the wall. So it shows the double-sided coin that she is, so that was very interesting. Throughout, there's this dream of America that goes sour."

Indeed, but Hedwig is a character who triumphs, and that provides the film an enormous lift. At the end of *Moulin Rouge*, Satine is dead, even if bohemian ideals of truth, beauty, and love are reinforced. In *Dancer in the Dark*, Selma endures the number she hates, the one that ends a musical, and she dies. We identify with these characters, but there is a deep sadness to the proceedings (as there is in so many modern musicals, from *Cabaret* to *All That Jazz*). But in

Hedwig, there is a satisfying uplift, because as the film ends, Hedwig is finally on the road to self-discovery.

"Other people would call it very dark, because of the operation and this and that, and she's sort of raked over the coals by her lovers," Mitchell describes, "and it doesn't shy away from that, but I still think it's a fairy tale, you know."

Mitchell believes that some people even misinterpret the ending as dark or hopeless. "Some people saw it as a kind of bleak ending, but then the second time they saw it, they realized it was a very hopeful one. But hopeful *and earned*, I hope. Because certainly [there are] musicals and stories that tack on a happy ending that doesn't feel organic."

Hedwig is a film of "jaw-dropping originality," "humor and romance,"[17] but also one that remembers why in musicals audiences seek to connect to a person. It's to experience their deepest desires and needs. *Hedwig and the Angry Inch* remembers that truth, and gives the screen a memorable hero.

AND ALL THAT JAZZ . . .

A fable about "fame, notoriety and the press,"[18] *Chicago* took the long road to Hollywood success. The 2002 movie musical and Academy Award winner for Best Motion Picture of the Year, actually began its pop-culture lifespan eighty years ago in the early 1920s, when *Chicago Tribune* journalist Maurine Dallas Watkins (1896–1969), working the criminal courts beat, reported on the 1924 case of a woman who committed murder in the Windy City and blamed the act on a surfeit of jazz and liquor. The murderess was defended by a glitzy mob lawyer, and was acquitted, but her case proved something of a national sensation.

Watkins headed to Yale, leaving Illinois and journalism behind for a career in creative writing. She reframed the scandalous news story as an original play entitled *Chicago* and altered all the character names to protect the innocent or, in this case, the guilty. Her "merry murderess" became a lady with the handle Roxie Hart. The other *dramatis personae* included Roxie's hapless husband, Amos, a dead lover named Fred, and an unscrupulous lawyer, the redoubtable Billy Flynn.

Watkins's play premiered on Broadway in 1926 under the direction of George Abbott and soon made another leap, becoming a 1927 silent film called *Chicago* produced by Cecil B. DeMille. It starred Phyllis Haver as Roxie.

Over a decade later, Watkins's tale of immorality and celebrity was revived yet again in Hollywood, this time as a comedy, in the 1942 film named for its star *Roxie Hart*. Fred Astaire's beautiful dance partner, Ginger Rogers, essayed the role of a "gal who became a national pasttime," and William Wellman directed. After that high point, Watkins and her 1920s story slipped out of the spotlight for several decades.

By the mid-1970s, after directing *Cabaret* for the screen, dance legend Bob Fosse shepherded a new version of *Chicago* to the Broadway stage, with a book he cowrote with Fred Ebb and songs composed by the legendary Kander-and-Ebb team. Fosse's wife, Gwen Verdon, played the scheming Roxie Hart, and a pre–*Law & Order* Jerry Orbach was cast as the slick attorney, Billy Flynn, who—despite his protestations to the contrary—loved nothing but money. The new stage play also strongly enhanced another character, bringing her importance in *Chicago* lore to a new prominence: vixen Velma Kelly, played by Chita Rivera.

Achieving escape-velocity level frisson from the post-Watergate vibe of America in the mid-1970s, Fosse's *Chicago: A Musical Vaudeville* premiered in 1975 and satirized everything from the U.S. legal system to the concept of celebrity and the mass media. As was typical of Fosse, the show was highly sensual in presentation and sharper than the tip of a spear. But perhaps it was too sharp, for Fosse's *Chicago* achieved neither widespread popularity or acceptance with audiences seeking a night of escapism at the theater. The play ran almost a thousand performances in the age of innocence lost, but seemed too "on the nose" and angry for some fans.

Though nominated for nearly a dozen Tony Awards, Fosse's interpretation of *Chicago* lost every single honor it was up for on awards night, facing defeat at the hands of a much more palatable show that also premiered that year. Former film critic and author of *De-Lovely*, Jay Cocks, recalls the era. "One of the greatest musicals we [my wife and I] ever saw on stage was *Chicago*, which was directed by Bob Fosse. I saw *Chicago* a lot of times, took Marty Scorsese to see it, and I couldn't believe how dynamic the show was, how great it was.

"It opened the same year as *A Chorus Line*," Cocks continues. "*A Chorus Line* was the one that got all the notice. I thought *A Chorus Line* was lame . . . *Chicago* was the real deal."

In fact, at Stanley Donen's encouragement, Cocks sent Fosse a note on *Time* magazine stationery describing how fantastic he felt *Chicago* was. Fosse was notoriously injured by bad reviews, and Cocks was one of the few major critics who had not liked *Cabaret*, so this seemed like an appropriate gesture. Fosse sent back a thank-you note and made Cocks aware that his letter had been tacked up on a call board for *Chicago*'s cast and crew to read.

But even if *Chicago*'s fans were less numerous than those of *A Chorus Line*, Bob Fosse never stopped imagining ways to present the challenging material on film. This was a mighty hurdle, since the play was set in the 1920s and structured as a series of vaudeville acts which directly addressed audience members.

By 1984, four years after his last film, *Star 80*, Fosse was still contemplating the details of *Chicago* and reputedly even considering casting Madonna, a young up-and-comer in the pop-music scene, as Velma Kelly. When Fosse died in late September of 1987 at the age of sixty, *Chicago*'s development as a movie stopped cold.

Seven years later, producer Martin Richards, who owned the musical's rights, signed with movie mogul Harvey Weinstein and Miramax to produce *Chicago* as a film. A hot item because of his independently produced dance musical hit, *Strictly Ballroom* (1992), director Baz Luhrmann was offered the helm, but the Australian turned it down flat, unwilling to lay a hand on Fosse's material. Other directors who were also *not* interested in directing *Chicago* included Herbert Ross (*Pennies from Heaven*), Stanley Donen (*Singin' in the Rain*), and Milos Forman (*Hair*).

However, when a new Broadway version of *Chicago* was staged in 1996, the situation changed again. This stage production featured Ann Reinking—Fosse's former girlfriend—as Roxie, Bebe Neuwirth as Velma, James Naughton as Billy, and Joel Grey as Hart's hapless husband, Amos. Walter Bobbie directed this updated version, and felt that the new, post O. J. Simpson world of the 1990s actually made *Chicago* more relevant than ever. "In a way, the show is no longer a satire—it's a documentary," he told *Dance Magazine* in 1997.[19]

Healing old wounds, the new version of *Chicago* eventually won six prestigious Tony awards. To this day it's still playing at the Ambassador Theater. The show's good buzz jumpstarted the film project, and now the time seemed right for another go at *Chicago*, and a screenplay penned by Larry Gelbart seemed the perfect prescription to revive it. At this point, Goldie Hawn was attached to the project to star as Roxie, and Madonna was still on as Velma. But Goldie dropped out when Nicholas Hytner, director of 1996's *The Crucible*, came aboard.

At the behest of the powers-that-be, Gelbart rewrote the *Chicago* screen-play half a dozen times, and confided to the *Los Angeles Times* that it was one of "the most distasteful periods" in his professional life.[20] Hytner then recruited a second writer, Wendy Wasserstein, to take a stab at the script, while still desperately seeking his Roxie and hoping for Charlize Theron.[21]

Before long, Gelbart and the show's intended Velma Kelly—Madonna—were both off *Chicago* for good, and the period which followed amounted to a revolving door of casting suggestions based on whatever celebrity happened to be especially hot at the moment. This included everybody from John Travolta and Rupert Everett to Kevin Kline for the role of Billy. Nicole Kidman remained a top selection to play Velma, but by the time she expressed interest in the role, the actress had already signed on to make *Moulin Rouge* in Australia with Baz Luhrmann.

Sometimes, it seems like every director who ever made a musical in Hollywood was approached to revive *Chicago*, but rejected the offer, further hindering the film's production. However, one day in early 2000, a young talent named Rob Marshall, director of the TV movie *Annie* (1999) and a well-established choreographer in his own right, visited Miramax's offices. He had seen a production of *Chicago* on stage in Pittsburgh when he was fourteen years old, and always remembered it. But he wasn't even there to discuss *Chicago*, he hoped to be considered for another project.

"I went in," he told Daryn Kagan on CNN, "[and] they were looking for people to do the musical *Rent*, looking for a director. So I went to talk with them about that, and I basically said, 'Do you mind if I tell you what I'd do with the musical *Chicago* before we begin?' and I never spoke about *Rent*."[22]

Marshall had a clever notion about how to make *Chicago* feel contemporary, as well as avoid the old musical stereotype—so anathema to modern audiences—wherein people belt out songs in midsentence. In particular, Marshall envisioned the starstruck, celebrity-hungry Roxie Hart as "the prism through which to tell the story."[23]

In other words, all the production numbers would actually represent a sort of parallel reality (shades of *Dancer in the Dark*), a universe where Roxie dreamed of being onstage, performing numbers that related to her experiences in prison and on trial. For all intents and purposes, the music numbers thus became fantasy sequences that still permitted "the linear, realistic story that movie audiences expect, while retaining the showstoppers from Bob Fosse's 1975 stage production."[24]

Harvey Weinstein was impressed with Marshall's inventive pitch, and the rest is history. *Chicago* finally had a director. Quickly, Marshall supervised a rewrite of the script with *Gods and Monsters* (1998) author Bill Condon, a long-time fan of musicals, and than began an extensive period of casting. A veteran of musical theater who was still smarting over losing the role of Satine in *Moulin Rouge*, Catherine Zeta-Jones was the first actress to sign up, cast as Velma Kelly.

Finding a serviceable Roxie was much more time consuming. Gwyneth Paltrow was considered, but needed time off. Cameron Diaz was mentioned, but wasn't certain she had adequate singing and dancing skills.[25] *Velvet Goldmine*'s Mandy, Toni Collette, as well as *Resident Evil*'s Milla Jovovich, Mira Sorvino, and Marisa Tomei were among those performers who wanted the role and met with Marshall to discuss it. The actress he eventually selected came out of left field: Renée Zellweger. Zellweger was certainly athletic (a former gymnast), talented, and beautiful, but she had no practical musical experience.

Zellweger, who began her film career with a role in *The Texas Chainsaw Massacre: The Next Generation* (1994) alongside Matthew McConaughey, wasn't so certain she was the right choice for Roxie, at least initially. "I got this script, read it and I didn't understand it at all," she reported in an interview with Paul Fischer. "It just didn't translate at all. I don't know the musical. I hadn't seen it before, so I'd never seen any of the numbers performed, so I had no idea what any of the lyrics meant on the page."[26]

Still, Zellweger had Marshall at hello. Although she was reluctant to audition for him after a failed audition for *Moulin Rouge*, Zellweger did participate in an intense "work session" that finally led to her casting.[27] She also sang "Over the Rainbow" for Marshall during a dinner at Manhattan's Four Seasons restaurant.[28]

Hugh Jackman and Kevin Spacey were considered for the critical role of Billy Flynn, but Richard Gere, who had just finished shooting the Adrian Lyne film *Unfaithful*, won the part, even though he too lacked any considerable or recent musical experience. Back in the seventies, he had appeared in a stage production of *Grease*.

Although *Misery* (1990) star Kathy Bates had been widely discussed for the supporting role of Mama Morton (and had worked with Marshall on TV's *Annie* in 1999), it was *Bringing Down the House* (2003) star Queen Latifah who was cast in the role. Like many, Latifah appreciated the satirical elements of the material.

"I just thought it was really interesting; this idea of wanting to be famous and killing for it," she told Chris Hewitt. "It's really not so far-fetched, is it?"[29]

Also joining the cast was *Boogie Nights* (1997) and *Magnolia* (1999) star John C. Reilly as the hapless Amos Hart, a role he petitioned for via a dramatic and moving rendition of "Mr. Cellophane." Finally, one of *Charlie's Angels* (2000), Lucy Liu, was retained to play the small part of go-to-hell Kitty after a brief consideration of casting pop star Britney Spears in an effort to appeal to a younger crowd.

Six grueling weeks of rehearsal on *Chicago*, affectionately dubbed "boot camp," commenced in October 2001 following a lengthy and highly detailed cast reading, which included musical cues and underscoring. With Marshall's guidance, the *Chicago* cast rehearsed in four different studios simultaneously.[30]

"Richard tap danced for three months in one room and Renée practiced her singing in another rehearsal room, while Catherine worked out with dancers," Rob Marshall told interviewer Merle Ginsberg.[31]

"It was tough," reported Zeta-Jones. "I've never rehearsed so intensely for a movie in my life, and I probably won't ever again."[32]

While Marshall invented new choreography for the production numbers, eschewing some elements of Fosse's stylistics and dance vocabulary, others on the production team wove also their own brand of magic. Production designer John Myhre converted a warehouse in Toronto into a four-story vaudeville house—where all the numbers would be staged—and Colleen Atwood developed the film's period costumes, maintaining "a contrast between the real world Roxie lived in and the imagined world of the stage."[33]

Once filming began in Toronto, Marshall and his team, like so many musical filmmakers before them, faced a strenuous haul. They worked seven days a week, twenty hours a day for twelve weeks, in order to complete principal photography on *Chicago* on schedule. It was a hectic but smooth-running operation, and all the stars sung the praises of the first-time feature director Marshall, noting that despite the enormous pressures he must have felt, as well as the limitations of time and a forty-five million dollar budget, he never buckled.

Well, almost never.

Journalist Steve Wulf reported that at 2:00 a.m., while shooting a scene in the jail with his three leads, Marshall fell briefly into a kind of stupor.[34] He recovered from the momentary lapse, brought on by exhaustion, and it was a good thing too, since what the success of *Chicago* had at stake, noted executive producer Neil Meron, was nothing less than "the reclamation of the American musical film as a popular form of entertainment."[35]

No pressure there!

During shooting, by all accounts, Marshall always kept an open mind and was highly collaborative, taking time to assure that everything—every step—made sense within his view of *Chicago*'s particular world. For instance, Queen Latifah's big number, "When You're Good to Mama," was restaged to foster more interaction with the theater audience, thereby making it much more lively, and bawdier too.

In the editing room, Marshall worked with Martin Walsh to firm up the specifics of his vision, spending a great deal of time making the opening segment of his movie feel just right. "I just spent all day on five seconds of material," he told reporter Christopher Rawson. "I learned from Hal Prince that the first seven minutes of a movie or play set the rules."[36]

It was in this process of honing the material that the popular Broadway number "Class" was cut. Sung for the film by Zeta-Jones and Queen Latifah, the tune's placement near the film's climax had the effect of interrupting Roxie's trial and slowing the overall pace. Although the song asked pertinently about what has happened to fair dealing and pure ethics in today's world—and was actually utterly cynical—it just didn't fit the structure of the movie.

More interesting than the cuts made by Marshall, however, were the clips from *Chicago* that made it into the movie's trailer. When *Chicago* began to be advertised on TV, not a single clip indicated that the film was actually a musical. Not a snippet of dancing, not a note of a song. It was a musical stealth attack.

Not that the decision to shroud *Chicago*'s true nature seemed to bother critics in the slightest when the film was finally unveiled. Stephanie Zacharek of *Salon* judged the effort "devilishly grand" and noted that "Marshall orchestrates everything with near perfection."[37] The *New York Post*'s Jonathan Foreman raved that, without a doubt, *Chicago* was "the best movie musical since *Cabaret*,"[38] and the *Atlanta-Journal Constitution* called it a "helluva show" and gave it the grade of A+.[39]

The *Toronto Star* called *Chicago* "big, bright, brassy and almost dangerous to know,"[40] and Susan Stark of the *Detroit News* relished the fact that Marshall's freshman effort was "darkly glittering, determinedly jazzy and energetic almost to the point of frenzy."[41]

Rob Marshall's kinetic *Chicago* commences in the Windy City during Prohibition, with a young floozy named Roxie Hart who has big dreams. She wants to be a celebrity and star in her own show, just like jazzy entertainer

Velma Kelly. In fact, Roxie is so obsessed with stardom that she kills to make it happen, murdering her lover, Fred Casely (Dominic West), after learning he doesn't really have show business connections. Arrested for murder, over the protestations of her loyal but naïve husband, Amos, Roxie is hauled off to Cook County Prison, where she discovers that her own idol, Velma Kelly, is also incarcerated for the double-homicide of her sister and husband. Worse, Velma is getting all the attention in the press.

Mama Morton runs the prison and offers Roxie some advice. She sets Roxie up with a canny lawyer named Billy Flynn, who is equal parts publicist and attorney. He immediately makes Roxie a media sensation in Chicago, with the help of story-hungry reporters, transforming the murderer into a poor soul demented by "liquor and jazz."

Meanwhile, Roxie attempts to befriend Velma, but Kelly thinks she's too good for Roxie until their fortunes are reversed. As Roxie's day in court approaches, she resorts to ever more desperate moves to remain in the public eye, including faking a pregnancy. Behind bars, it's every girl for herself, but in the newspapers of the day, the world can't seem to get enough of Roxie Hart.

Billy manipulates evidence to make Roxie appear innocent and she finally wins her case, but finds that infamy is a fleeting source of stardom. She reluctantly joins forces with Velma for a new show and together these two "scintillating sinners" strut onstage.

In the history of musicals, *Chicago* may be a watershed more for what it achieves, rather than what it actually concerns. The film was the highest grossing out-and-out musical film in twenty-four years (since *Grease*), and that's nothing to sneeze at. It earned more than $340 million at the box office, and that tally meant, quite simply, that more movie musicals were inevitable.

Chicago builds on the good will afforded the format after the beloved *Moulin Rouge*, and develops the central conceit advanced by Lars von Trier's *Dancer in the Dark*, that musical numbers can be interior monologues and fantasies, and that cues in the real world (like the noises at a factory or the drip-drip-drip of a leaky faucet) can precipitate song and dance.

Beyond that, *Chicago* is the most breezily engaging and thoroughly entertaining musical to come around the bend in a long while. It doesn't require the complex mental acrobatics of the post-modern *Moulin Rouge*, but that established, it coheres brilliantly around a central, succinct thesis, that the legal system, the press, and celebrities are all intertwined as parts of a pop-culture hydra; one that feeds a gossip-hungry populace with a steady stream of scandal, scandal and more scandal.

Roxie's case is termed "the trial of the century," explicitly referencing the sensational O. J. Simpson murder trial from 1994, but the film's dialogue is really almost secondary. Paramount in *Chicago* is the music and imagery, because it is these elements that punctuate the film's satirical thesis.

In "We Both Reached for the Gun," Billy Flynn is depicted as a ventriloquist or puppet-master, putting words in his client's mouth. The press is characterized as marionettes on strings, dutifully reporting Flynn's every word as if the gospel, when his lies are actually made up from whole cloth. The press is supposed to be a bastion of responsible journalism, but not here. Instead, the quest for a wider readership leads to a reporting on only the most sensational aspects of Roxie's story. And every day, Billy dutifully feeds the press a new crumb, a new facet of the ongoing soap opera to keep the masses appeased. Not incidentally, these tidbits represent Billy's agenda.

"We Both Reached for the Gun" efficiently vets *Chicago*'s thesis because it reveals something new about the characters through visuals. For instance, the film's dialogue never meaningfully asserts such characterizations about Billy (that he manipulates the press and lies like a sonofabitch). Instead, the image of Billy with Roxie ensconced on his lap, mouthing his words, reveals everything the viewer needs to know. *Chicago*'s achievement is that form showcases content in a way mere words cannot, and in a fashion that is both recognizable and humorous. The story can move at such breakneck pace because so much critical information is conveyed through imagery, not dialogue.

"Razzle-Dazzle" is also staged with an abundance of style. This is the production number set at the trial, heretofore only metaphorically a three-ring circus. Not surprisingly, the courtroom is actually transformed into one, literally, in Marshall's hands, replete with glitter, feathers, trapeze acts, and juggling. The staging deliberately underscores Billy's point to Roxie before the trial, that the legal system is just another kind of show, one where the best and most flamboyant entertainer wins.

For my money, the most effective and interesting number in *Chicago* is "Cell Block Tango," in which the "six merry murderesses" describe why they are incarcerated. Like all the numbers, this one emerges from Roxie's fantasy world.

It begins with random sounds in the prison: footsteps, fingers tapping, and other noises. Then, as prison bars slide away like curtains, the sequence develops into a highly erotic dance about murder.

In fast succession, half-naked dancers emerges from their cells and recount their sad stories, all concerning the wrongs heaped upon them by men, via song and dance. Here Rob Marshall insightfully includes male dancers as both abusers and victims (a change from the stage version, in which the men don't appear) and features a crimson-red scarf to indicate how each man expires.

For the man who was poisoned, the scarf emerge from his throat. For the fella who ran into a knife—ten times—it emerges from his side, where his wounds originated. In Velma's vignette, the red scarf represents the blood on her hands after she murdered her husband and sister. Finally, when the lone innocent woman emerges from her cell to perform a ballet, the scarf is white, indicating innocence, and a kind of hush envelopes the number, an atmosphere of reverence. Unlike most characters in *Chicago*, this prisoner is not a liar.

Some folks may view the symbolism of the red and white scarf as obvious, but one should never forget that the musical is the genre of artistic expression, of representations and feelings, vetted through dance. The musical format approaches ideas and themes in a different fashion than a straightforward drama and therefore such symbolism, these coded representations of character and theme, are a critical element of its lexicon. At its core level, musicals are about expressing ideas in a pretty, artificial, and nonlinear way, and that's an art that has been lost as movies grow more realistic and technology-driven. *Chicago*, however, gets it right. It's an old-school, expressive musical. Besides being Fosse-esque, "Cell Block Tango" is also an explicit reminder that the best special effects are usually beautiful human bodies in motion, expressing a story or a feeling.

Chicago is also extremely inventive in the way that it leads viewers in and out of the production numbers, which are a fragment of Roxie's imagination. Marshall opens the film with a slow zoom into one of Roxie's eyes, letting us know that what we are about to witness is from her perspective, and that choice is a perfect opener that sets the tone for the two hours of kinetic, nonstop motion that follows.

In "Funny Honey," Roxie is questioned by the police for the murder of Fred Casely, and the harsh, interrogating illumination of the cop's flashlight becomes a spotlight that heralds her appearance on stage and the beginning of the song.

When Billy gets ready to present false evidence in court, Marshall has Gere tap dance, and again, the metaphor goes down smooth. We all know what it means to tap dance our way through a lie, and *Chicago* doesn't disappoint with Billy's moment.

Chicago is the very definition of razzle-dazzle. By turns sexy ("All That Jazz"), funny ("They Both Reached for the Gun"), and even just a little touching ("Mr. Cellophane"), it is perfectly, triumphantly, slickly entertaining. Like *The Sound of Music* or *Grease*, it is a machine that works.

The box office razzmatazz of *Chicago* is impressive too, and the film's sweep at the Oscars resulted in fevered speculation that the musical was back on top. The one-two punch of *Moulin Rouge* and *Chicago* certainly boded well for the genre.

"Steven Soderbergh said to me the other day, 'I want to make a musical, and they've got to sing and dance on the streets of New York,'" reported Miramax's Harvey Weinstein, a man who has stated on more than one occasion his desire and intention to be the new Arthur Freed. "So what it'll [*Chicago*] do is, it'll change what the formula of a blockbuster movie is. If you can get *Chicago* to gross $150 million, that means people don't have to make blockbusters that are idiotic. Instead of making the comic-book-hero blockbuster, they can [remake] *West Side Story*."[42]

Weinstein's vision of a post-*Chicago* world is optimistic, and it may still happen, but first the musical had to survive its first relapse. After two unqualified successes in *Moulin Rouge* and *Chicago*, the world of television was about to rain on the movie musical's parade. Again.

FROM THEATERS TO VIDEO

In 2002, the Fox Network had an unlikely ratings hit in a new program, an elaborate talent show called *American Idol*. This "reality" program about the search for a new pop star had already been a hit in Great Britain, where it is known as *Pop Idol*, and was an unholy combination of the *Star Search* and *The Gong Show* formats.

Unlike most conventional talent shows, however, the dramatic high point of this video enterprise came while watching three judges (all of 'em big wigs in the music industry) provide feedback to contestants during huge cattle-call auditions. Tempers might flare, or insults might fly. Another twist was that the judges had no real power to choose the contest winner. It was voters, using telephones or "text messages" who would select their favorite singer every week.

In America, the judges were kindly ex–pop star Paula Abdul, lukewarm exec Randy Jackson, and hard-hearted, tell-it-like-it-is rake Simon Cowell. The latter evidenced a breathtaking and awe-inspiring cruel streak and would often slam the less-talented participants with what essentially amounted to very harsh truths. He was particularly fun to watch.

American Idol was a locomotive in the ratings during its first (and succeeding) seasons, as during each contest the number of contestants dwindled from tens of thousands down to one over the span of ten weeks. It was a crucible of hard work, entertaining music, and often humiliating critical feedback. In the end, the final two contestants of the freshman season were two rather likable, if somewhat bland and callow youths: perky twenty-one-year-old Kelly Clarkson from Burleson, Texas, and wild-haired, twenty-four-year-old dynamo Justin Guarini from New York.

On the night of their big final showdown, Clarkson emerged victorious in the one-on-one musical combat, and was consequently crowned the first ever American Idol (to be followed in later seasons by Ruben Studdard and Fantasia Barrino).

During the summer, after the show was over, Fox kept *American Idol* momentum going, and Kelly and Justin embarked on a successful tour together. When Clarkson's debut album was released in April 2002, it rocketed to the number one slot on the Billboard charts and sold over eight hundred thousand copies.

Considering such dramatic *Idol* success, it was only a matter of time before someone planned to pair Kelly and Justin—who had always been plagued by questions about a romance—in a movie vehicle together. After all, in the past, the audiences had adored Astaire and Rogers, and Jeanette MacDonald and Nelson Eddy, right? Why not Clarkson and Guarini?

Accordingly, Kim Fuller, the screenwriter responsible for *Spice World* (1999), authored a screenplay that actually reflected the adventures of yet another beloved silver screen duo of yesteryear, Frankie Avalon and Annette Funicello.

In particular, the proposed film, *From Justin to Kelly* would be a "beach movie" about spring break, though, importantly, not the darker side of spring break. That taboo subject was reserved for another reality-based movie to be released the same summer, *The Real Cancun*, and *From Justin To Kelly* had to be a safe PG, so that all the twelve-year-old girls who loved *American Idol* on TV wouldn't feel disenfranchised.

"If people's expectations are going to be greater than it's-just-a-couple-of-kids-making-a-movie-and-having-fun, they'll be disappointed," noted Fuller, playing the low-expectations card. "It's not *One Flew Over the Cuckoo's Nest*."[43]

Former choreographer Robert Iscove, helmer of *Rodgers and Hammerstein's Cinderella* on TV in 1997, and the man who had missed directing *Chicago* by a hair, drew the assignment to direct the film. He established in the press that the film would be a "full-blown musical," but one that just happened to star Kelly and Justin. "People are expecting an *American Idol* movie, but it's not," he declared. "It's hip-hop musical theater meets pop rock."[44]

From Justin to Kelly is a fairy tale about a waitress and frustrated country singer named Kelly (Clarkson) who leaves her job in Texas to join two college friends, Kaya (the future Tony Award winner Anika Noni Rose) and Alexa (Katherine Bailess), on their spring break vacation in Miami. At the same time, Justin (Guarini), a well-known party boy from a Pennsylvania college, simultaneously makes plans for an unforgettable vacation, bringing along his own buddies, the always-scheming, smart-ass Brandon (Greg Siff) and the nerd, Eddie (Brian Dietzen).

Justin and Kelly fall in love at first sight on the beach, but must contend with jealous Alexa, a vixen who is unable to understand why Justin would prefer Kelly. Alexa inserts herself into the relationship and purposefully fails to relay text messages from one party to the other, leading to a comedy of errors and miscommunications. Meanwhile, Kaya falls hard for brawny Carlos (Jason Yribar), a local waiter who feels he isn't good enough for a college girl. Eddie also experiences difficulties hooking up with a blind date he chatted with on the Internet.

There's no lengths Justin won't go to win Kelly's heart, including a dangerous hovercraft race in the ocean, but just when skies look cloudiest for the young lovers, Alexa confesses her role in separating them. As spring break finally comes to an end, Kelly and Justin at last come together.

On a budget of twelve million dollars, *From Justin to Kelly* began filming on February 26, 2003. The cast and crew shot on location in Miami, Florida, where the temperature dipped precariously because of the winter season, sometimes as low as forty degrees. The cold put a damper on the "hot" romantic proceedings, and according to some reports (including one in *Film Threat*), Clarkson appeared miserable on the set.

The work days stretched sometimes to twenty hours, and the company had only thirty days to complete the picture. Novices Clarkson and Guarini worked with acting coaches, and rehearsed their dance moves for six hours a day. Travis Payne served as the film's choreographer, with assistant Stacy Walker, imbuing the dance moves with what Iscove called (in the DVD interviews of the film) "a contemporary feel." It was a rushed and difficult shoot, and on one occasion, Iscove (jokingly) told members of the press that his next project was "the sanitarium."[45]

To drum up enthusiasm for the movie's release, *American Idol* fans were allowed to vote at a *From Justin to Kelly* web site to decide which poster art they preferred to advertise the film,[46] thereby following up on the democratic principles of the show, which always allowed viewers to telephone in their votes for the singer they liked best.

The movie was originally scheduled for a release in the spring of 2003, on April 25, just as a new *American Idol* would be crowned on television, but the TV series was so successful that many thought the movie would be a surefire winner, and its premiere was rescheduled to a more hectic and competitive summer slot.

The first movie musical in general release since *Chicago*, *From Justin to Kelly* (or rather, *J2K*) opened in over two thousand theaters nationwide on June 20, 2003, and grossed a paltry $2.7 million. Adding insult to injury, box office receipts fell off a whopping 77 percent during its second weekend resulting in a gross that industry insiders described as a "jaw-dropping" $625,000.[47]

Perhaps not unexpectedly, given its origins as a TV program, movie reviewers let fly on *From Justin to Kelly*. "It's like *Grease: The Next Generation* acted out by the food-court staff at Sea World," opined Owen Gleiberman in *Entertainment Weekly*, after terming the film "Beach Blanket Stinko."[48]

Others lamented the fact that Guarini and Clarkson looked "like sixth graders in their school musical—uncomfortable and torturously rehearsed."[49]

Scott Foundas, writing for *Variety*, was more specific in his grievances. "The most resounding thuds in *From Justin to Kelly* . . . come from the musical numbers. Prior to moviemaking, Iscove cut his teeth on choreography, apprenticing under Michael Bennett; but the dancing here (choreographed by Travis Payne), while accomplished, consists of the same cookie cutter gyrations seen in countless contemporary music videos."[50]

Realizing they had a legitimate bomb on their hands, 20th Century Fox ripped *J2K* from theaters and planned a warp speed dump onto the DVD and video market. In fact, they planned the quickest such transition in history: a paltry twenty-nine days from theaters to video!

Still, the film didn't generate much heat in this secondary venue either, and *From Justin to Kelly* didn't look like it was ever going to gross much more than five million dollars, less than half the investment in the film.

As it turned out, *J2K* heralded a collapse of the Kelly and Justin mystique, at least temporarily. Justin's self-titled debut album sold a meager 135,000 copies on release[51] and dropped sixty slots on the Billboard chart from 20th to 80th place in just three weeks. His debut film with Clarkson, before year's end, racked up a startling number of Razzie Award nominations. It was nominated for Worst Film alongside *Cat in the Hat, Charlie's Angels: Full Throttle, Gigli,* and *The Real Cancun,* as well as Worst Actor (Guarini), Worst Actress (Clarkson), Worst Couple (Guarini and Clarkson), Worst Director (Iscove), Worst Excuse for an Actual Movie, Worst Remake or Sequel, and Worst Screenplay (Fuller).

But the real "worst" news for Guarini was that the next time an *American Idol* tour came up, the word came out that Kelly Clarkson would be sharing the stage with . . . *American Idol* runner-up Clay Aiken! She had gone from Justin to Clay in just a season.

Still, you can't keep an American Idol down. "I'm not a believer in doing things over," noted Guarini. "If we could go back and fix all our mistakes, we'd never learn anything."[52] True, if time travel were possible, audiences might have been spared eighty-one minutes of the misery that is *J2K.*

It would probably be stretching the matter to state that the oeuvre of Frankie Avalon and Annette Funicello represents a form of cinematic art. Nonetheless, those old beach films from the 1960s were fun and entertaining in their own fashion. Harmless time-wasters, they had a goofy good humor. If only *From Justin to Kelly,* a modern spin on this old-fashioned, teen-oriented material, had aimed so high. This is a truly unbearable film for many reasons, from the flat performances by the leads to the senseless plot, but mostly because it is a thoroughly jejune effort, designed from the beginning to serve as a commercial engine, an advertisement for a TV show.

Musicals, the format wherein hearts are laid bare in song and dance, always fall flat when no connection is forged between the performer and audience, and that's precisely what occurs here. Of course, all movies are about business and making money to varying degrees, but in *J2K* the quest for the all-mighty dollar just feels too close to the surface, perhaps because so many other elements, like story and characterization, seem empty.

From Justin to Kelly commences with a close-up of Kelly Clarkson onstage, belting out a country song, "I Won't Stand in Line," in a country-western bar, and she's actually pretty good. The camera pans around her in a semicircle as she gives it her all, and then comes a little joke: the camera's last revolution reveals she's singing to an empty venue. It's a good opening shot, and hopes are raised that there will be a modicum of cleverness in the film. One can also detect why Clarkson won the TV contest. She boasts a pleasant voice and a modest demeanor that isn't lacking charm. But then she opens her mouth to speak dialogue, attempts to emote, and, worst of all, adopts a Southern accent that sounds really, really fake. She's a Texan in real life, so there's no explanation for this, except her inexperience as a thespian.

The whole movie is that way. Elements that should be slam dunks are stumbling blocks instead. The movie feels as though it were conceived in the mind of an accountant, and tailor-made with the intent of appealing to a narrow segment of the audience, "the teen market." But those accountants apparently don't have children of their own, because the film is without any real sense, understanding, or appreciation of the demographic it seeks to attract.

By their very nature, adolescents are smart, sassy and clever—and don't appreciate being talked down to by old men in business suits. They question the status quo, and want to discover cinema that reflects their experience, or, perhaps, shapes it. This is why *Moulin Rouge* was such a hit with the under-twenty crowd. "This audience, unfamiliar with the movie musical," wrote Armond White in *Film Comment*, "is not looking for saviors, or just for entertainment, but for its voice."[53]

This generation won't discover that voice, or any reflection of itself anywhere near *From Justin to Kelly*. Instead of really concerning itself with the spring break experience, or even the realities of dating today, *From Justin to Kelly* occupies its scanty running time (eighty-one minutes) with the intricacies and fallacies of text-messaging minutiae, yet another unnecessary reference to the TV show and its voting. It is product placement as plot point.

The film also studiously avoids the real concerns of young people, like drinking, drugs and sex. It's *An American Idol* beach party, suitable for all family members! Accordingly, the characters are all one-note and designed to be just one thing: good-looking. Take the dork named Eddie, for instance. He boasts a buff, cut, well-muscled body that might be featured on the cover of a magazine. But we know that he's supposed to be a dork because he wears glasses and is played for comic relief.

The actor who portrays Brandon, Greg Siff, is given no real character to play, either, and balances this startling lack of personality by taking off his shirt and showing off his pecs. *Constantly.* Nothing wrong with a little nudity—male or female—on film, but the disrobing becomes a joke. In his first seven scenes,

Brandon is either seen with an open shirt or no shirt at all, and again, one senses the commercial viability of this novel approach. It's all image, baby! The movie can be described in one word: shallow.

And that's just *From Justin to Kelly* at its best. Even more insulting is the character of Alexa, the designated Iago of this romantic tragedy. She is a scheming bitch with a Deep South accent, because all audiences understand that women from the South are evil whores, right? Alexa has no motivation to get in the way of the inevitable (and somehow incestuous-seeming) Justin-to-Kelly hook-up, but the movie requires a conflict. In real life, people like Kelly and Alexa aren't friends. They move in different circles, and indeed, the movie has no explanation why these two stereotyped people, Ms. Nice and Ms. Evil, would hang out, let alone vacation together.

While *From Justin to Kelly* strains to keep its leads apart for as long as possible to provide a sappy happy ending, it takes time to genuflect to previous musical efforts. Remember how in *Grease* there was that dangerous drag race near the climax? Here we get the same thing, but transplanted to the beach. To win the hand of Lady Kelly, Sir Justin engages in a speed boat battle with Luke, his hapless nemesis for her affections. But the scene involving this vehicular joust evidences no tension, no suspense, nothing. It just happens and then ends, having no tangible or empirical relation to any other moment in the film.

From Justin to Kelly would just be another undistinguished, bad movie if it didn't feature several musical numbers. The presence of these production numbers however, elevate the film to the realm of full-blown disaster. A major problem in several numbers, particularly "The Luv" and "That's the Way I Like It," is overcrowding. There are too many players in most of the pieces, literally hundreds, and as a result Justin and Kelly are often lost in the shuffle, fronting an undulating mass of gyrating performers who are better dancers than either lead. Where's the clarity and precision of Busby Berkeley when you need it?

The first number after Kelly's turn at the bar is "The Luv," and it features wild pans across a meat market of young adults, all of whom could be super models. A crane shot reveals the whole sad affair as dancers use beach towels, skateboards, and gold-and-purple beach balls as props. Then, for some reason, in the middle of the song, the film cuts abruptly to views of the ocean, racing boats, and parasails. The camera even adopts an ominous *Jaws*-style angle coming up to the shore during the number, as if a great white is going to start hip-hopping with the teens. It's a grab bag of angles that don't cohere.

And just when you think a song can't get worse or more embarrassing, the whiter-than-lily-white Brandon starts to rap "Brandon's Rap."

For shame.

The numbers in *From Justin to Kelly* are never used in innovative or symbolic ways, and unlike *Chicago*, are staged awkwardly. Justin and Kelly's big love song, "Timeless," is lensed in a bizarre distancing fashion, as the two would-be lovers ride on a small boat cruising a picturesque canal. Justin is far behind Kelly, driving the boat, so he can't see her face. She is looking forward at the sea ahead, instead of back at the object of her desire. Worse, between Justin's multitasking and Kelly's glazed look, the sequence is cut to ribbons with reverse angles, over-the-shoulder shots and extreme long-distance views. The end result is that throughout "Timeless," our pining lovers rarely share the same frame. This is the song all about their love, their desire to be together and no emotional bond emerges at all. Endless, not "Timeless," is indeed how the number feels.

Other musical numbers are edited in baffling fashion. "It's Meant to Be" is the love song between Kaya and Carlos in a Latin bar, but the number is strangely abbreviated, cut off in the middle, as though audiences could not bear to spend one more moment outside the presence of the leads.

Alexa's song, "Wish upon a Star," is staged in another club, and Katherine Bailess, who plays Alexa, not only looks sexy in a revealing black dress, but seems a pretty good dancer. Her number promises to be sensual and a bit naughty as she struts across a bar surrounded by a circle of men who desire her. But at the very moment the choreography should reach a crescendo of sensuality, as Alexa straddles a male dancer on the floor, the moment is lost in a quick cut, as though it might just be too suggestive for a PG movie.

Even the final number, "That's the Way I Like It," fails badly to generate excitement. It features essentially the same staging as "The Luv," with hundreds of dancers in a beachlike setting, but with some strange herky-jerky robotic moves and an overdose of crane shots. It does nothing to wrap up the story, enlighten the viewer, or even leave the audience with a happy feeling. And this time, Brandon and Eddie *both* rap.

Coming out of *From Justin to Kelly*, one just can't help but think, reflecting on one's own life experiences, that young love never felt so . . . prepackaged.

HERE'S WHERE I STAND

The year 2003 ushered in a handful of interesting musical films, including Christopher Guest's latest documentary-style comedy, *A Mighty Wind*. With the same cast who populated his 1997 flick, *Waiting for Guffman*, Guest this time forged a comedy about three old-time folk music bands hoping to get one more shot at the limelight when they agree to appear on a public television concert, "Ode to Irving," a tribute to the late promoter who signed them up in the 1960s.

In this case, the musical acts were the Folksmen, the New Main Street Singers, and a lovely romantic duo called Mitch and Mickey. Guest's film opened in April 2003 and merited some splendid reviews for its affectionate touches and very authentic (if satirical) folk music ditties.

A Mighty Wind's most catchy and memorable song, the romantic ballad "A Kiss at the End of the Rainbow," was nominated for an Oscar for Best Original Song. Eugene Levy and Catherine O'Hara, who played Mitch and Mickey respectively, performed the number at the Oscar ceremony for an audience that included Christopher Guest and his wife and presenter, Jamie Lee Curtis.

A vastly different behind-the-scenes, backstage flick was *8 Mile*, the debut of rapper Marshall Mathers, or rather, Eminem. This film tells the story of a young rapper living in Detroit with his mom (Kim Basinger), and depicts his struggles in powerhouse nightly competitions to become a successful rapper/poet. Although arguably a drama rather than movie musical, the film pulsated with the wit and rhythm of rap music, making the case for this style as an art form.

"In *8 Mile*, Eminem raps, and might be in a car park about to get shot, but he'll use the power of words in a musical way to get out of a situation," stresses Craig Pearce, "which when you think about it—even though it's a gritty urban film—it's completely ridiculous, like all musical films are."

More overtly a traditional musical in style and intent was one of the many independently produced films of 2003, Todd Graff's *Camp*.

Todd Graff has appeared in films such as James Cameron's underwater epic, *The Abyss* (1989), and the Jay Cocks–penned future drama, *Strange Days* (1995), and also written screenplays for films as diverse as *Dangerous Minds* and *Coyote Ugly*, but early in Graff's life, this success in Hollywood did not seem a particularly likely outcome.

In 1974, at age fourteen, an adolescent Graff "stole his neighbor's car" and went "joy riding around Queens."[54] Graff's parents could have enacted any number of disciplines upon the troubled teen, imposed any sort of draconian punishment, but instead, they made a decision that changed the path of his life.

They enrolled the troubled lad at Stagedoor Manor in Loch Sheldrake, New York, a two-month intensive program for talented kids ages twelve to seventeen who had a bent for stage performance and musical theater. The camp boasts alumni as diverse as Mandy Moore, Jennifer Jason Leigh, and one future singing detective by the name Robert Downey Jr. Graff spent three joyous, engaging summers at Stagedoor as a camper and then returned for two more as a counselor, where the aforementioned Downey was one of his wards.[55]

Today, Graff is grateful for the choice his parents made in 1974, and isn't afraid to say so. "It absolutely saved my life, going to Stagedoor Manor," he acknowledges. "I was a kid who was not on a great road, and it took me about fifteen minutes of being there to have found a completely other way of looking at myself."[56]

Graff became aware of a valuable truth at Stagedoor Manor that he has never forgotten, and which even today drives his art and talent. "If you have a kid who does not necessarily fit into the box," he told this author, "then the answer is not to stuff him into the box. It's to make the box bigger."

This was a message that Graff desired to convey on film, and so he embarked in the mid-1990s on a five-year journey to create the film *Camp*, his directing debut. It was a project which would tell the story of those theatrical kids who were "different," and also document the joy of summers at Stagedoor, where young children would sometimes—and often amusingly—perform serious Tennessee Williams's monologues, or sing tunes meant to be warbled by middle-aged, world-weary thespians.

"I always knew that it would be a musical because—although they do stage plays there—what's fabulous about Stagedoor is the musicals," Graff says. "As soon as I was an adult and a screenwriter, it [Stagedoor] always stuck with me as an intriguing place to set a film, because beyond the craziness and the inappropriateness of the shows, and the chances to have these fabulous musical numbers, the heart of it always seemed to be the fact that these kids, myself included when I went there, felt like complete freaks for ten months of the year. Then when they would go to this place, miraculously everybody was just like them. That idea of finding a home somewhere was moving to me, and I thought it would give the movie a kind of bottom, a heart."

Graff also found inspiration for his project in film history, particularly in the latter-day, musical film canon. He remembered Sir Alan Parker's 1980 classic set at the New York School of the Performing Arts, *Fame*.

"*Fame* was a really obvious and genuine inspiration," relates Graff. But on even more basic terms, Graff understood that his movie would rest on the long-standing pillars of the format called the backstage musical, alternating numbers on stage with the trials and tribulations of the performers off stage.

"In many respects, that silhouette, the bones of *Camp*, are as old as the hills. It's *Babes in Arms*. It's 'We're gonna put on a show,'" says Graff, "but musicals are a genre like Westerns are a genre, or noir is a genre, and it's really about how you use and subvert the genre and exploit the fact that people come to the film with a certain set of expectations and rules in their head. As long as you're aware of them, you can use them or break them as you see fit."

At one point, Graff even planned an homage to *The Wizard of Oz*. "It is Oz," Graff stresses, referring to the welcoming and nurturing "over the rainbow"–quality environment of Stagedoor Manor. "I was originally going to shoot the beginning of the movie in black and white, and then when they [the kids] got off the bus [at the camp] I was going to make it in color. But that crossed the line from homage to direct rip-off."

When developing the story of *Camp*, Graff also looked to his own youthful experiences and even based the lead character, the straight kid Vlad (played memorably by Daniel Letterle in the film), on himself. "When I was that age, there was a lot of Vlad in me," Graff explains. "Which I'm not particularly proud of, but it's true. I was just kind of a jerky teenage boy. Probably manipulative like he is, though I was nowhere near as cute.

"You can fix things in movies that you couldn't fix in your real life," Graff reflects on his choice to revisit some aspects of his younger self. "I had that 'teenager testing limits and testing power' thing, and I was not as sensitive to other people's feelings as perhaps I should have been."

Also, the protagonist Vlad, being the so-called normal straight guy, provided Graff precisely the entrée he needed into the sometimes over-the-top, theatrical world of his summer camp, renamed Camp Ovation in the movie.

"I think I knew that it was such a hothouse atmosphere, such a strange and quirky place that I needed to have a character to follow through the movie who was like a stranger there, who didn't know all the rules. And so the audiences could get all kinds of information through him as he moved through the story," Graff considers. "Although I knew that I wanted the movie to be about the camp—and that it was going to be set there—I think probably the first character that came to me was him, because he was going to be my Virgil, leading us through."

Even at the earliest stages of planning *Camp*, Graff understood that the success or failure of the project would rest very heavily on the musical numbers he would be able to include. And so, as with many things in the world of moviemaking, it came down to matters of cost.

"I wrote in my wish list," Graff reports of the screenwriting process. "I got most of that wish list. 'The Ladies Who Lunch' in fact was a replacement, because I had written in a song from *Ballroom* entitled 'Fifty Percent.' That was the show that Michael Bennett did after *Dreamgirls* and was a flop. But the big, eleven o'clock number was a song called 'Fifty Percent' that was hilarious when a little girl sang it because she was playing a middle-aged woman deciding she was going to go ahead with her life as 'the other woman' to a married man because she would rather have 50 percent of him than all of anybody else. Only she's a little kid."

The problem was, the authors of the song wouldn't grant Graff the rights to use it. Fortunately, he found that *Camp* had a surprising supporter and sponsor who was more than willing to share his own remarkable and varied contributions to musical theater, Stephen Sondheim.

"We found out very early that he would give us songs, because there was no way to proceed with the movie if he didn't," Graff acknowledges. "He was really gracious and generous, and charged us virtually nothing. What he did charge us, he donated to charity. He said, 'I don't think this movie will ever get made, but if it does, yeah you can use my stuff.' Then, armed with that, we were able to go to other composers and say, 'Well, Stephen Sondheim gave us his stuff,' and everybody wants to be involved with something that he's given his blessing to. So that made it much easier to convince people that we were on the level because we were just a low-budget independent film."

Indeed, the cooperation of Sondheim assured that *Camp* was able to procure the rights to "Wild Horses" by the Rolling Stones, "Turkey Lurkey Time" from *Promises, Promises* by Burt Bacharach and Hal David, "Century Plant" by Victoria Williams, as well as "And I Am Telling You I'm Not Going" from *Dreamgirls* and Henry Krieger.

Sondheim's involvement greased the wheels for *Camp*, but that assistance behind-the-scenes didn't mean that the legend was necessarily willing to appear in the film, as Graff had originally petitioned. "He was adamant about not appearing in it," Graff reports.

"He said he's not an actor, and he hates his own acting and the way he looks on film, and he didn't want to do it," Graff recalls. "So I begged and begged and begged, and finally just before we started shooting, he agreed."

Sondheim's change of heart came about after Graff wrote him a letter explaining the situation. Graff noted that he had painted himself into a corner and could not have an actor playing Sondheim, and that, besides, it wouldn't have the same impact with another composer.

Cunningly, Graff also appealed to Sondheim's sense of the future. He told the legend, "'Surely your passion is musical theater, and part of that has to be passing it on to another generation, so that all musicals don't go the way of *Dracula* or *Jekyll and Hyde*.'"

At the bottom of the ninth, Sondheim acquiesced. "It was an unbelievable relief," Graff notes. And, to Graff's delight, Sondheim was also an absolute pleasure to direct. "He was a doll to work with. He was really easy, and he hung out with the kids," the director recalls. "He wouldn't even stay at a hotel. He slept at the camp in a bunk, just like everybody else."

Casting the remainder of *Camp* was even more arduous a task than persuading Sondheim to be in the flick, as Graff soon discovered. In fact, the film's preproduction phase lasted so long that *Camp* actually had to be cast twice in four years, because some original cast members were no longer young enough to pass as high schoolers when the film was finally ready to roll cameras.[57]

The veteran casting directors Victoria Pettibone and Bernie Telsey took tremendous pains to find the right group of youngsters for the project, pulling "diamonds in the rough"[58] from high school, local New York auditions (for Broadway musicals such as *Hairspray* and *Rent*), and elsewhere. Of paramount importance to Graff in assembling his cast was that a selected performer evidence real talent singing and acting, but not necessarily have a professional background in film or on stage. And, because of the short span of time in which to rehearse the film, Graff didn't want to waste time teaching his actors to unlearn bad habits.

"It was tough, because none of them were professional," Graff acknowledges. "A couple of them had done theater, but none of them had ever been in a movie or on television before. So it was grueling, because once we separated the wheat from the chaff, the individual audition sessions really dragged on . . .

sometimes five or six hours. And I would have ten or twelve kids [to see], and keep them in a waiting room, and then bring in three [at a time] to work on a scene. It wasn't just having them reading the scene and saying, 'Thank you very much,' because they weren't pros. You had to work with them to find out if you would be able to get it out of them when the time came.

"And then, I wanted to mix and match them with other kids; other choices that were up for the roles," Graff describes. "It just ended up being very time-consuming and rough on these kids, because they hadn't done a million auditions. It's not like they were seasoned, so for them it was tough."

Among those cast in the film were Robin De Jesus as Michael, a seventeen-year-old from Norwalk, Connecticut, who had never even auditioned before, Joanna Chilcoat as Ellen, a sixteen-year-old from Baltimore, and the aforementioned Daniel Letterle, a twenty-four-year-old actor from Cleveland, Ohio, seeking his big break in the Big Apple.

Others in the cast included the delightful Alana Allen as the villainous Jill and the truly remarkable Anna Kendrick as Fritzi, a talent who would go on to win an Independent Spirit Award nomination for her debut in the film.

Working with this group of talented kids was an energizing experience, but Graff found that during the intense rehearsal sessions, not all the teens were prepared for such hard, steady work. "The kids were great—they were always talented—but they weren't great until they got to the set," Graff explains.

"Their work ethic was not so good in rehearsal, because they weren't pros. Somehow it didn't sink in for them that they were actually making a movie that was going to be seen. They knew it intellectually, but they didn't connect with it, so they would not show up for rehearsal, or they would be late, or they would leave in the middle: crazy things that a professional actor would never do."

But Graff had a secret weapon to corral those wayward young talents. One of the film's producers happened to be a major movie star by the name of Danny DeVito. "A couple of weeks in, when I was just incredibly frustrated, I played one of my little aces in the hole," Graff reveals. The director asked DeVito to attend a rehearsal to see how things were going. The actor knew absolutely why he was invited, and made the most of his surprise visit.

"Suddenly there's a movie star walking in the door!" Graff exclaims. "From that day, they really worked hard."

Their efforts paid off in the end, because the cast came together on location, ready to work. "When they got to the set, this crazy alchemy happened, and they became pros," Graff remembers. "I don't know if it was seeing the crew. I don't know if was seeing dailies, so that they could see 'Oh God, that's me on the screen!' but for whatever reason, they really figured it out."

And it's a good thing too, because Graff faced his own set of challenges while shooting the low-budget film at Stagedoor Manor. For one thing, from his start date on August 26, 2002, he had less than one month to get the entire film in the can. For another, he had only $1.6 million with which to produce *Camp*.

"We just barely made it, by not going anywhere special," Graff explains, commencing an enunciation of all his hurdles when he began shooting the film in the summer 2002: "We couldn't afford to have a spike in the budget in any given area, and still be able to finance the film. The clearances were all on a favored-nation arrangement so the very cheap rate that Sondheim gave us, everyone else gave us too. We shot with kids who had never done anything, so they were nonunion actors, and we didn't have to pay Screen Actors Guild rates.

"We lived at the camp, we ate in the camp cafeteria, we shot on tape, because we didn't have the wherewithal to use multiple cameras and things that we really would have needed if we were going to shoot on film; We had twenty-two days to make the movie, and there are nine musicals numbers! I never had more than one day to shoot any musical number, and two numbers I had to shoot in one day!"

Graff also discovered that directing a film based on his own personal experiences, and filmed on his old stomping grounds was no picnic. "I was haunted, basically. It was like therapy. To be in a location where—sideways—a scene from my own life had happened, and now be directing two actors to reenact it, but make it turn out different because I wanted it to turn out different . . . it was crazy!"

And Graff also found out that the script needed to be reimagined in certain scenes to make the dialogue and characters harmonious with the reality of contemporary adolescence. "I was rewriting constantly. You know, I haven't been a kid in a long time," he explains. "The kids were consummate bullshit detectors. If something didn't feel right, they'd say [so]. They were talented, so if it wasn't working, it wasn't usually because they were wrong, it was because I was trying to make them do something that didn't feel natural to them.

"A lot of the rewriting that happened on the set was about realizing that I had let the side down a little in the writing, and trusting what they were bringing to it," Graff muses. "The whole reason that I cast them in the first place [was for] their reality and their naturalness." Graff says he had to let the script follow those qualities.

One problem scene involved the performance of "Century Plant," the critical number that is the turning point of the film and gets Bert Hanley into the kids' corner and jazzed to produce the big show. "I was stymied," Graff confesses. "I knew I wanted the number. I knew what I wanted to happen in it, but all through rehearsals it wasn't working, and it was really corny. It wasn't until we actually got to the location, which I saw for the first time the day we shot, that I knew we could throw out seven pages of dialogue, a scene leading into that number, and instead let the camera tell that story for the number without any dialogue and without any lyrics that are expressing anything overtly."

The primary difficulty filming *Camp* involved the brevity of the shoot. Filming sequentially was not an option. "We didn't have the luxury, schedule-wise," Graff explains. "For example we used several theaters, and all the numbers that were going to be in one theater we had to shoot in a row. Then, all the numbers that were going to be in another theater we had to shoot in a row, because we couldn't load everything in and everything out, back and forth, all the time. The original load-in for those things was so expensive."

A critical aspect of filming *Camp* involved capturing everything right during those important stage shows. Again, because of the abbreviated shooting schedule, there was no opportunity for the cast to sing live. The songs were prerecorded, and during shooting, the kids lip-synched to their own recordings, a process which presented its own set of challenges.

"It's the only way we could have done it, especially with kids," Graff acknowledges. "It's difficult to record sound live because you have to match from different camera angles or takes. It's just really hard. I would say that the biggest challenge for the kids is that they had to become great lip-synchers. I was constantly telling them to listen to what they had recorded in the studio before we got to the set, just play it in their ears on their iPods so that they could remember and replicate what they sang."

And there were other concerns. "It took a long time—always—to set up where the speakers were going to play the playback, because sound doesn't travel as fast as light. It was difficult to make it look like their mouths weren't always a hair ahead of the music. You had to then put the speakers further back so by the time the sound got to them, it matched. But they couldn't be too far back, because then you'd fall behind!"

Getting all the lights and camera moves right the first time was also a major headache. "It was tough. It took a lot of planning. We hired a really terrific stage-lighting designer. That's all he does, he lights shows. Then he worked with the cinematographer who was lighting for the camera. The two of them together were able to collaborate so that it would be able to look like something that was a real show, but the colors and lights made sense for the actual film."

The camera work was also a challenge. "What we did on the musical numbers—except 'Century Plant,' which takes place in the barn—was use multiple cameras. We had to, for a couple of reasons. One of them is that kids can't work full hours legally so you have fewer chances at coverage than you would with adult actors.

"When you're using three or four cameras, you can have your master wide shot. You can have one shot just roaming and picking up all kinds of things each take that you will be able to pick and choose from later. You can have one camera on a dolly, just going back and forth at the lip of the stage, so there is that sense of movement to some of the cuts. It was a process born out of necessity, but it actually helped, I think."

And Graff always had one ideal in mind when shooting his cast. "Any time you have kids, you need to exploit what is naturally their greatest gift, which is their passion, their energy and their stamina. When you're seeing kids perform, that's what you really want to see. So it was definitely important to encourage that, not that I had to encourage it too much. They were bouncing off the wall. *Camp*'s a musical, and musicals need a certain kind of energy level, I think."

But all the energy in the world can't make a difference when Mother Nature conspires to wreck a schedule. In particular, the film's opening number, an outdoor piece, was threatened when on the night of the shoot, a terrible storm and torrents of rain rolled in. Because the movie was almost finished, with just three days left to shoot, there was no time left in the schedule for second chances, and Graff knew it.

"I said, 'We're not going to get this number,'" Graff remembers. "I had a meeting with the other producers, and said, 'Listen, let's cut and run,' because although that number is great, I can tell the story without it. I can tell the story by cutting together a scene of Michael getting beaten up at the prom. As much as I wanted the number, I didn't have to have it, but the producers said, 'Are you insane?! You can't cut it!' And I said, 'But I don't see how I'm possibly going to shoot it!'"

Time was running out, so Graff gathered the cast and crew for a meeting, and gave them the skinny and a pep talk. "I said, 'The only way we're going to be able to shoot this number is if we do four days worth of shooting in three days.'" That left the *Camp* team one day at the end of the schedule to stage that number.

For the next two days, the cast and crew worked at a fever pitch, and things came together. "People were amazing! They were just nailing it! One take! One take!" Graff recalls. "They were just getting things incredibly well, and it allowed us to go back and steal that number on the very last day of shooting."

That last day came, and the number was shot successfully, into and through the night, right into dawn of the next morning, and the beginning of sunlight! But, to Graff's everlasting satisfaction, *Camp* had its opening number.

Working in the independent film milieu on a musical was something that Graff feels may have helped his management of the picture. There was no temptation, nor financial leeway, during shooting to go outside the strict parameters of the story he had invented. "I think that I trusted the story. I trusted that context was going to win the day," he notes. "The fact is, it's a movie about a camp that only has so many theaters. So if you started to mess with that too much, it would start to smell less real, less possible. If the sets were too grand, if the performances were too polished it, would stop feeling like real kids."

In other words, he understood the old maxim about low-budget films: Turn you limitations into advantages. "If you can't hide it, decorate it!" he jokes.

Camp continued through the rigorous process of editing, and as any director of a movie musical can testify, it's a difficult balance between songs and drama, and a delicate dance to move the narrative forward at a good pace. Graff had prepared well for editing too, which helped him get a leg up on the material. "After we wrapped the movie and before we went into the editing room, I took a hundred tapes of dailies—videotapes—and went through them, jotting down time codes so that I could say, 'Oh there's a great piece of Jenna turning upstage at 1.59.13 through 1.59.16,'" Graff explains. "Once that was done, rather than having to start from scratch while you're paying for an Avid rental, you can go straight to the pieces you already think might be worth putting in the film, and it gives you a lot of choices."

Graff also had another resource, his friendship with the director of *Boogie Nights* and *Magnolia*. "Paul Thomas Anderson is a close friend and was really a great help on *Camp*," Graff explains. "He came to the editing room and looked at early cuts of the movie. I've done the same thing for all of his movies. I'll go in and see early cuts and stuff, but he was really above and beyond the call."

The story of *Camp* commences as school lets out for the summer, and diverse teenagers gather at Camp Ovation, a musical theater camp for talented students dismissed as "misfits" by parents. But this summer is special at Camp Ovation. First, there's a straight boy there for a change, the charming Vlad (Letterle). Secondly, directing the summer's big show is Bert Hanley (Don Dixon), a washed-up Broadway songwriter, now an alcoholic. And thirdly, the camp has recruited a sports counselor, though he is bound to feel lonely in the world of musical theater!

Once at camp, Vlad rooms with Michael (De Jesus), a gay teen who loves Stephen Sondheim and who was beaten up at the school prom for arriving in drag. Estranged from his parents and peers, he's been sent to Ovation to make something of himself, but Michael is more interested in Vlad than in playing Romeo in *Romeo and Juliet*.

While Vlad and Michael develop a friendship, Vlad also romances Ellen (Chilcoat), an aspiring actress suffering diminished self-confidence because her father doesn't believe she can succeed in the business given her looks. Other Ovation-ers include Jenna (Tiffany Taylor), an overweight African American, whose jaw has been wired shut to prevent her from gaining weight, and dueling divas, Jill (Allen) and Fritzi (Hendrick).

As summer passes, rivalries intensify, stage numbers like "Turkey Lurkey Time" and "The Ladies Who Lunch" are performed, and Vlad encourages Hanley to resurrect a show that never saw the light of day. On the night of the big production, Jenna casts aside her metal jaw restrainer, Fritzi vanquishes the prissy Jill, and Vlad, Michael, and Ellen come to a reckoning about their unusual romantic triangle.

And, on the night of the show, Stephen Sondheim even shows up . . .

Armed with his final cut, Todd Graff began the journey to see *Camp* in theaters. The film played at the Sundance Film Festival in January 2003, went to Cannes in May, and closed the L.A. Film Festival in June. *Camp* then opened in theaters on July 25, where it grossed over $1.5 million during its run. It was the only IFC film in 2003 to cross the one-million-dollar barrier, and it did five times that much business when released on the video-DVD secondary market in February 2004.[59]

Camp's reviews were for the most part, quite positive. Peter Travers wrote in *Rolling Stone* that "Just when you thought that the numbing virus of *From*

Justin to Kelly had killed the goodwill towards the musical built up by *Chicago*, along comes *Camp* to get a new momentum rolling."[60]

The *Onion A. V. Club*'s Scott Tobias called the film "too high spirited and charming to resist,"[61] while *Newsweek*'s David Ansen noted it was a "hilarious rousing musical comedy."[62] Other critics reflected on the film's aura of "sheer joy"[63] and noted that "Todd Graff has created a tiny, unlikely gem"[64] with a "terrific sense of humor and captivating musical numbers that put to shame anything you'd see on *American Idol*."[65]

Among some film scholars and historians, *Camp* was viewed as the latest evidence of a resurgence in the movie-musical format, a discussion which Graff did not discourage. "I think if three or four films signify a resurgence, then yes," he said, acknowledging what he saw as a trend. "A lot of bad musicals got made a while back and people stopped going to them because they stunk. Sometimes they were made by geniuses—John Huston was a genius, but he should not have directed *Annie*. Richard Attenborough should not have made *A Chorus Line*. But then somebody somewhere along the line seemed to wise up."[66]

"It just has to be done really well," Graff continued his line of thought during our interview. "I think that if you're clever about it, like *Chicago* was, for example, you can find—as they found—a unifying device. Like when you're in Renée Zellweger's head, you're in a musical because she's so obsessed with musicals and stardom and being a performer, and that worked great. But it's not easy to come up with that device, I want to tell you."

Perhaps the greatest testament to *Camp*'s success came at the camp the film spotlighted, Stagedoor Manor. "The camp, which always did very well has exploded. You can't get near it," Graff notes. "They now have a waiting list of kids since the movie, who want to go there. I went up there a couple of times this summer to see them do a show and Dan Marino's son was there. It's really reached a whole new level."

Teenagers stand at the center of *Camp*, and nowadays, it sometimes feels like every teenager's grandmother absolutely loves movie musicals. While that's a nice thing, and a reflection of the genre's dominance several decades ago, it is not necessarily an encouraging sign regarding the survival of the genre in the twenty-first century. After all, grandmothers don't usually venture out to theaters for a big opening weekend, do they?

If the musical format is to rise once more in the modern multiplex, phoenixlike from the ashes of its own mid-1990s demise, it must appeal first and foremost not to the age-sixty-and-up demographic, but to younger audiences. It can accomplish this daunting task by reinventing its idioms for the twenty-first century, and unlocking new manners by which to relate to the experience of the twenty-first century.

Baz Luhrmann's *Moulin Rouge* navigated this tricky landscape perfectly and became a blockbuster in 2001. Popular and attractive stars Nicole Kidman and Ewan McGregor belted out modern pop tunes by the likes of Elton John, Sting, and Madonna, and the stylistic camera flourishes and dynamic editing choices resembled music videos on steroids. Christine Aguilera and other popular musicians even advertised the film after a fashion, with the popular (and sexy) video "Lady Marmalade" that appeared in heavy rotation on MTV.

Todd Graff's exuberant and low-budget *Camp* also makes a gung-ho effort to appeal to today's kids, though in decidedly less spectacular and aggressive fashion. Instead of (admittedly effective) pyrotechnics, Graff's film seeks to relate to today's youth, not so much through sound and fury, but through its understanding nature and temperate heart. This is a film that remembers—sometimes in excruciating detail—what it feels like to be a teenager, and hence a "misfit" or "outsider." And in general, that's quite important to a generation "unfamiliar with the movie musical" and looking not for "saviors" or "entertainment," but rather "its voice."[67]

Though Graff constructed *Camp*'s screenplay upon his own autobiographical experiences at Stagedoor Manor, recasting them into a contemporary drama, he also appropriated the age-old formula of the backstage musical, a formula wherein performances onstage make sense of emotional lives offscreen. But by bringing in a whole new subset of contemporary teen issues, Graff also infuses his musical with increased immediacy for its target audience.

"Movie musicals are frequently about what was," wrote critic Steve Ramos. "Graff strives for relevance by placing *Camp* around kids today. Just because the *Camp* kids weren't around during the heyday of movie musicals doesn't mean they don't know all the show tunes word-for-word."[68]

The film has considerable currency with young audiences because it doesn't shy away from the reality of today's world. In particular, *Camp* includes a nonjudgmental presentation of the homosexual's experience as a teenager in modern America. Gay bashing, feelings of isolation, estrangement from intolerant parents, and longing for sexual experience are all presented in *Camp* as part of Michael's natural and normal experience growing up, and it is important to note that this sort of material would not have been put to celluloid in a movie musical even a decade earlier.

Camp doesn't retreat from including homosexuality as a legitimate and acknowledged fact evident in the American mainstream and teenage scene, and therefore it reflects a truth in modern society that many films have not. Frankly, this is a new thing for the musical genre. The musical is not often a trailblazer, though some pictures in the 1970s, including *Cabaret, Jesus Christ Superstar, Tommy,* and *All That Jazz* certainly pushed the format ahead with their experimentation. But overall, movie musicals have often been interpreted as new renderings of so-called traditional values.

Richard Fehr and Frederick G. Vogel described the musical film's role of "conservative" place-holding in their text *Lullabies of Hollywood: Movie Music and the Movie Musical, 1915–1992*:

> Essentially a defense mechanism, the conventional musical permitted swarms of moviegoers to fend off the intrusion of a complex, unkind outside world. It never mattered to the refugees that their favorites of both sexes, easy on the eye and ear, were unrepresentative of the population, that their fairyland misadventures were insignificant, and that the entire cast functioned in an insular Anglo-Saxon society as devoid of racial diversity as it was of defeatism.[69]

Replace the phrase "racial diversity" with the words "sexual orientation" and one can detect the manner in which *Camp* has nudged the musical format into echoing today's zeitgeist. It has added the ingredient of realism to a genre renowned for artifice. Rather than fending off the complexities of real life, *Camp* acknowledges a love which, in old films, "dared not speak its name."

Camp's climax features one of the most daring scenes to appear in a movie musical, and probably to appear in any mainstream movie since 1999 (and David Fincher's incendiary *Fight Club*), a very conservative era in American cinema. In this surprising sequence, Vlad approaches Michael by the lake, and though he is the film's stereotypical "straight boy," offers himself sexually to gay Michael, stripping down nude before his friend.

Driven by his insecurity and need to be accepted, Vlad's action is inconsistent with his sexual identity, and Michael refuses his advances for that reason. The scene is important for a variety of reasons. Most importantly, it reveals

Michael to be a person of dignity who understands that Vlad's gesture comes not from physical attraction or love, but the desire to be liked.

Secondly, the underlying point of the scene with Vlad and Michael is that in a previous generation of "teen" film, this scene could never have played out with two men. But now, a potential homosexual encounter is depicted without criticism or judgment as merely another choice in a world of many choices. Being gay is right for some people like Michael, and wrong for others, like the rather manipulative Vlad. Like *Hedwig and the Angry Inch*, *Camp* says that knowing yourself is more important than which way you swing. This is perhaps the most progressive viewpoint about sexuality yet put forward in a "teenage" film because it neither demonizes nor sanctifies homosexuality or heterosexuality. The choices are depicted as equivalent, and today's youth—the generation that has grown up with *Will and Grace* (1998), *Boy Meets Boy* (2003), *Queer Eye for the Straight Guy* and other mainstream media enterprises concerning homosexuality—can relate.

For Todd Graff, making these points was a reason to create the film in the first place. "I always saw this movie as an independent film, and I brought it to Killer Films for a reason, and I wanted to be able to have it not be a typical studio teen movie," he says.

"And that scene [with Michael and Vlad by the lake] was really the heart of that desire I had. I wrote it so that they kissed. They really did kiss, and then Michael says, 'No! What are you doing? You don't want this!' But that got me an R rating, so in order for the movie to be able to be seen by the kids that the movie was about and made for, I had to trim it back. You should have seen it before I did [trim it back] because he [Letterle] shot it naked!

"It just seemed real to me," Graff continues. "It seemed honest to me that Vlad would go that far, and that Ellen would also still say, 'Yeah, okay, I'll date you.' And that Michael—bless his heart—would still end up left out in the cold. That just felt not movie-ish to me, but real, so it was there from the very first draft, even bolder."

By understanding the universality of teen angst (and worries about other matters including complexion, weight, desirability) and sexuality, director Todd Graff has assured that "the details all feel right in *Camp*."[70] Perhaps more to the point, Graff has made certain that the form of *Camp* echoes its content, by coloring the film with bouncy, upbeat and fluid camera moves that capture the energy, vitality and humor of the youthful performances.

From the first bravura production number to the closing credits and bright green title card blaring "C A M P" in big, capital letters, the film feels upbeat and true. An emotional highpoint of the film's is Jenna's rendition of "Here's Where I Stand," which takes place before the eyes of her critical parents and is transformed beyond its original context into a teen anthem about standing up for yourself when others, particularly parents, aren't supportive.

Camp works on two dramatic levels. On the first, it is a teen drama about universal adolescent issues, and on the second, it is an homage to popular culture, musical theater and show business. References to other movies abound in the picture, from *Boogie Nights* (1997) to *All About Eve* (1950) and beyond. Even the film's title, *Camp* is a double entendre, expressing the humor of seeing children perform way, way too adult material. One example of such "color-blind casting" sees young African American campers playing in a production of *Fiddler on the Roof*, and that's funny, as is the sight of teenage girls singing a tune about booze during "The Ladies Who Lunch."

"There's layered meaning to the title," says Lisa Schwarzbaum in *Entertainment Weekly*, "since the very nature of the place attracts troupers—many of them gay boys just getting the hang of their own sexuality,"[71] but one is grateful that the film never actually descends into camp. "I didn't mean it to be [campy]" says Graff. "The double entendre is certainly there and I was aware of it for a reason, but if it was just a campy movie, what's the point? It would become a one-joke movie."

Instead, Graff's is a sincere film, and one that also makes a point about show business and the difficulty of sustaining a career there. In one caustic sequence, Bert Hanley lays out all the problems for the kids (whom he considers "freaks") and declares, "Bob Fosse is dead" and "Times Square is an amusement park."

"The movie needed to have some voice of reality," Graff notes of the Hanley monologue. "Because [the camp] is a crazy place on some levels. Kids come to this place and pour so much into it. They're so desperate to belong, and it [the movie] needed to have somebody there to articulate the opposing point of view. I tried to set up from the beginning that the film is going to go to some darker places than *Meatballs* (1980) or *Without a Paddle* (2004), or whatever camp movies you have in cinema vocabulary when you sit down to watch the movie. [For example], you're in the first two minutes of the movie and you're seeing a drag queen get queer-bashed."

Evita (1996)

TOP She loves you and hopes that you love her too. Eva (Madonna) sings "Don't Cry for Me Argentina" on the balcony at Casa Rosada during *Evita*.

BOTTOM He must love her. A man of the people, Che (Antonio Banderas) waltzes with Argentina's first lady, Eva Perón (Madonna), in Sir Alan Parker's spectacular *Evita*.

TOP Argentina's power couple: Juan (Jonathan Pryce) and Eva Perón (Madonna), from *Evita*.

BOTTOM They're not through with love. Manhattan liberal Bob Dandridge (Alan Alda) dips his wife, Steffi (Goldie Hawn), in Woody Allen's paean to old-fashioned musicals, *Everyone Says I Love You.*

OPPOSITE PAGE

He's just (Jerry) Devine! Eddie Izzard takes a phone call on behalf of his rock star client, Brian Slade, in Todd Haynes's outrageous *Velvet Goldmine.*

Evita

Everyone Says I Love You (1996)

Velvet Goldmine (1998)

Velvet Goldmine

ABOVE Perfect and poisonous: Enigmatic glam-rock star Brian Slade (Jonathan Rhys-Meyers) and American rocker Curt Wild (Ewan McGregor) get together (or do they?) in *Velvet Goldmine*.

TOP Satan is from Venus and Saddam is from Mars. The Devil and the former dictator of Iraq share a bed together (in hell) during the animated musical *South Park: Bigger, Longer & Uncut.*

BOTTOM The S word? From left to right, Eric Cartman, Mrs. Broflovski, Kyle, Mrs. Marsh, and Stan listen while counselor Mr. Mackie (not pictured) recites the boys' vulgarities, in *South Park: Bigger, Longer & Uncut.*

South Park: Bigger, Longer & Uncut (1999)

Love's Labour's Lost (2000)

ABOVE Cheek to cheek:
Rosaline (Natasha McElhone)
and Berowne (Kenneth Branagh)
fall in love in the Shakespearean
musical *Love's Labour's Lost*.

OPPOSITE PAGE

TOP Clueless? The Princess
(Alicia Silverstone, front) sits with
her entourage (receding: Natasha
McElhone, Carmen Ejogo,
Emily Mortimer) while waiting for
the men of the King's court in
Love's Labour's Lost.

BOTTOM They've sworn off love:
The men of the king's court in
Love's Labour's Lost: Berowne
(Branagh), Longaville
(Matthew Lillard), the king
(Allesandro Nivola), and Dumaine
(Adrian Lester).

Dancer in the Dark (2000)

TOP Golden Heart: Selma (Björk)
faces the music (for murder) in an
American courtroom in Lars von
Trier's tragic *Dancer in the Dark*.

BOTTOM Breaking into song: Selma
escapes her dreary existence (and
the courtroom) by seeing life as a
musical, in *Dancer in the Dark*.

Pretty peasant: The great Catherine Deneuve, who once starred in romantic musicals such as *The Umbrellas of Cherbourg* (1964), is a factory worker in *Dancer in the Dark*.

OPPOSITE PAGE

TOP The cast of Spectacular-Spectacular, an Indian, bohemian musical about Truth, Love and Beauty. It's a dry run for the show within a show in the dazzling *Moulin Rouge*.

BOTTOM The doomed (and gorgeous...) lovers of *Moulin Rouge*, Satine (Nicole Kidman) and Christian (Ewan McGregor).

Moulin Rouge (2001)

ABOVE An amazing and colorful look at the passionate, dynamic, and frenetic world of Baz Luhrmann's watershed *Moulin Rouge*: This scene takes place inside a courtesan's boudoir, inside an elephant, at the Moulin Rouge. That's Christian (McGregor) embracing a "sparkling diamond" named Satine (Kidman).

Hedwig and the Angry Inch (2001)

The beautiful (but confused) Hedwig (John Cameron Mitchell) takes the stage at Bilgewater's in *Hedwig and the Angry Inch*.

TOP Tommy Gnosis (Michael Pitt) and Hedwig (Mitchell) share a microphone in *Hedwig and the Angry Inch*.

BOTTOM Wig in a box. Surrounded by his band (the Angry Inch), Hedwig (Mitchell) adorns another wig in one of *Hedwig*'s catchiest and best-orchestrated numbers.

TOP Mr. Cellophane: Amos Hart (John C. Reilly) waits for a verdict in his wife's murder trial while a dancer hangs on. From Rob Marshall's Academy award–winning *Chicago*.

BOTTOM They both reached for the gun: Murderesses Roxie Hart (Renée Zellweger) and Velma Kelly (Catherine Zeta-Jones) strut in the finale of *Chicago*.

OPPOSITE PAGE

If you're good to mama: Queen Latifah—as Mama Morton—works up a crowd in *Chicago*.

Chicago (2002)

From Justin to Kelly (2003)

OPPOSITE PAGE

Americans idle: Kelly (Kelly
Clarkson) and Justin (Justin
Guarini) grind hips (and audience
nerves) between text messages in
From Justin to Kelly.

BELOW Hot rod: Dan Dark's 1950s
fantasy musical takes explicit form
in Keith Gordon's psychological
The Singing Detective.

The Singing Detective (2003)

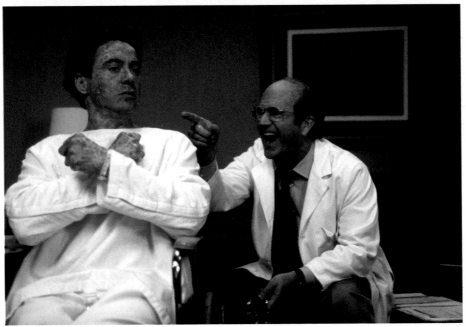

The Singing Detective

Camp (2003)

OPPOSITE PAGE

TOP Invading the frame: Dan Dark's fantasy detective (Robert Downey Jr.) is accompanied by a phalanx of imaginary dancers as they enter Dark's hospital, in a crucial (and brilliantly composed) sequence from *The Singing Detective*.

BOTTOM The passion of the psychologist: Dan Dark (Downey) is tended by Dr. Gibbon (Mel Gibson in heavy make-up) during a session in *The Singing Detective*.

ABOVE He's melting hearts (straight and gay): Daniel Letterle is the guitar-strumming Vlad in *Camp*.

LEFT Michael (Robin de Jesus) and Ellen (Joanna Chilcoat) have a crush on the same guy in *Camp*.

OPPOSITE PAGE

TOP True love: Linda (Ashley Judd) and Cole Porter (Kevin Kline) enjoy one of Cole's shows in the Irwin Winkler biopic *De-Lovely*.

BOTTOM Let's misbehave. Robbie Williams croons in *De-Lovely*.

Camp

De-Lovely (2004)

De-Lovely

Andrew Lloyd Webber's The Phantom of the Opera (2004)

ABOVE Man or monster? The Phantom (Butler) plays his music of the night in *The Phantom of the Opera*.

RIGHT She's having a big hair day. Minnie Driver plays the comic relief, Carlotta, in *The Phantom of the Opera*.

Andrew Lloyd Webber's The Phantom of the Opera

Camp is a film with abundant energy, and its heart is in absolutely the right place. At times, some scenes feel almost cliché or silly, such as when—darn it—those rascally campers teach the old alcoholic a lesson about life. But such sappy or corny moments are also an authentic part of the musical's artificial, expressive nature. First and foremost, this is a film for teenagers, and perhaps the more maudlin moments won't seem old or trite to them, but rather like accurate reflections of their youthful experience.

MUSICAL NOIR

Director Keith Gordon has fashioned a successful directing career by selecting challenging material and then forging artistic, meaningful films, whether it be *Mother Night* (1996), *Waking the Dead* (2000), or his 2003 quasi-musical feature, *The Singing Detective*. Although a whole generation of horror movie fans remember Gordon from his youthful performances in chillers like Brian De Palma's *Dressed to Kill* (1980), and John Carpenter's *Christine* (1983), this talent has also earned a devoted fan base and critical acclaim through his bold, often avant-garde, behind-the-scenes efforts.

Gordon portrayed a young (and much put upon) Joe Gideon in Bob Fosse's autobiographical film, *All That Jazz*, but even that credit in an acknowledged movie musical classic doesn't mean that this director necessarily prefers musicals to other film genres. Still, Gordon recalls that musicals are one piece of the puzzle informing his art—and his choices in art—over the years.

"As a kid growing up, I saw all of the great musicals that everybody saw, like *Singing' in the Rain*—and I loved them as much as everybody did. Those are great, wonderful, fun movies, and they still hold up," he considers. "But I was certainly drawn to things that were a little experimental, a little different. Look at *All That Jazz*—that's much more my taste."

Like many, Gordon wasn't always exactly comfortable with the long-standing musical conceit of the drama stopping short and the characters spontaneously breaking into song and dance. "What's funny is that it never bothered me in old movies, because the old movies didn't feel very realistic to begin with," the director considers. "It always seemed like the whole thing was a conceit. You look at the old films, and the acting is very unnatural for the most part. Everything is clearly a set. So within that artifice, I don't think it bothered me."

But by the era of Vietnam, Richard Nixon, and the "new freedoms" of a more personal cinema, all that changed. "There were some people later on, trying to do more traditional musicals in the 1960s and 1970s that looked dopey to me because the acting was naturalistic and the sets were natural, and suddenly everybody was singing," confesses Gordon.

Still, the traditional musical format of the 1950s felt "odd" to Gordon in a way that the new, revolutionary efforts of the late 1970s did not. "Some of the more experimental musicals that embraced the artificiality in a new way, whether it was *All That Jazz* or the miniseries *The Singing Detective*—where the idea was that it was happening in somebody's brain—allowed it [the musical] to not seem so dopey. There were new rules of order."

In particular, Gordon remembers attending a play in New York in the 1970s, and a life-changing experience at the theater. "There was this musical done by children. It was poems written and performed by ghetto kids who were not really actors. It was almost an opera. I remember seeing that when I was a kid, and thinking that it was amazing because it so transcended the cliché of what a musical was in terms of tone and subject matter.

"Here you had twelve-year-old kids singing about the first time they did heroin, and I remember just being blown away," Gordon describes. "This was a whole different use of the style to say different kind of things and to evoke very different emotions. So that was something I remember really loving. Even *Hair* was big when I was a kid—and that was breaking so many rules. There was also *Jesus Christ Superstar* and the rise of the rock opera when I was growing up."

And then came another indelible influence in Gordon's life, the English screenwriter and playwright Dennis Potter (1935–1994). A man who suffered from terrible psoriasis and arthritis, Potter was a writer beloved in his native United Kingdom for his subversive, witty, revolutionary reworking of genres on TV. He has been called "quirky" and "cranky,"[72] but also widely acknowledged as the engineer of "intellectual slapstick of the highest order."[73]

In and out of the hospital throughout the 1970s because of his condition, Potter contributed a number of groundbreaking works to the medium of television, including a BBC miniseries, *Pennies from Heaven* (1978), starring Bob Hoskins, which was later remade in the United States as the impressive Herbert Ross feature with Steve Martin. Though quite well-received by critics, the film was a bomb in the U.S., earning back less than four million dollars on a budget of twenty-two million. Still, the film garnered several Oscar nominations, including one for Potter in the category of Best Screenplay adapted from another work.

Keith Gordon's first exposure to Potter's work was *Brimstone and Treacle* (1982), and he later became a fan of Potter's "antimusical" trilogy, which included not only *Pennies from Heaven*, but *The Singing Detective* (1984) and *Lipstick on Your Collar* (1993).

The Singing Detective probably remains the most appreciated of these fine works. A 415-minute miniseries consisting of six parts, the BBC production was directed by John Amiel. It aired in the United States on PBS in 1986 after some eight million viewers caught it on the BBC, and was hailed as the best film of the year by *New York Times* critic Vincent Canby.

The Singing Detective starred Michael Gambon as a hospital patient named Philip E. Marlow who—because of his painful psoriatic condition—retreated into fantasies involving film noir and elaborate 1940s-style musical numbers. Bouncing with tunes like Bing Crosby's "Accentuate the Positive" and the Andrew Sisters' "Bei Mir Bist Du Schön," the miniseries was caustic, brave, controversial, political, touching, and, make no mistake, autobiographical.

"Potter as a writer always had the strength of honesty, even in his nonmusical stuff, as well as his musical stuff," Gordon considers. "He's a man who was never politically correct, never afraid to address difficult stuff head on, and from what I can gather, [he] was a pretty angry guy. It's scary to think, but everybody I talked to who knew him said that this [character in *The Singing Detective*] was him. That he was deeply sarcastic. That he did not suffer fools gladly and could be quite vicious. And yet at the same time, he had another side that could be quite loving and quite brilliant—also not unlike the character.

"He went to an extreme, as I think Brecht did in theater, of using the very conventions [of a genre] to comment on themselves and then comment on the larger world. This was really interesting to me," Gordon reflects. "I was a huge fan. Potter was taking musicals and reinventing them . . . and he was using the idea of music to comment on society, and even on how musicals themselves shape our view of the world."

It was an example the director always admired, and would some day have the opportunity to emulate.

By the nineties, the financial failure of the American remake of *Pennies from Heaven* was far in the past, and Dennis Potter was renowned for writing the screenplays of a variety of critically acclaimed films, from the murder-mystery *Gorky Park* (1983) to the fantastic *Dreamchild* (1985). Yet as the artist grew increasingly ill, Potter harbored hopes that someone in America would produce a feature-length version of his popular miniseries, *The Singing Detective.*

To facilitate that eventuality, Potter actually penned a new screenplay himself in 1992, updating the material dramatically and including a more upbeat ending for his film's protagonist, here renamed Dan Dark.

But in Hollywood, things often progress slowly, and Potter did not live to witness his new script produced. In fact, more than eight years after his demise due to cancer of the pancreas, his *Singing Detective* script was still making the rounds, still circulating through Tinsel Town.

"I was a big Potter fan, and in 1992, when Potter first wrote the script for the film, it was going around Hollywood," Gordon recollects. "My agent sent it to me, but said, 'We're probably not going to be able to get you in the door on this, but I know you're a big Dennis Potter fan and would like to read it.' Well, I read it, and I loved it and, of course, I couldn't get in the door on it.

"At that point, everybody was talking about doing it as a huge seventy million-dollar musical. And it was going to star Jack Nicholson at one point, or it was going to star Dustin Hoffman, or Anthony Hopkins, and it was going to be Barry Levinson directing," Gordon notes. "I don't know how true any of those things were, because in Hollywood every day there's a new rumor of who is doing what project. But it was always being approached by a studio with that overblown production approach, so I couldn't get in the door."

Still, every six months or so, Gordon's agent would check on the project to see if a director had been assigned. "As the years went by, I even got a meeting on it once or twice," says Gordon, "but I could tell they weren't taking me that seriously because they wanted an Oscar-winning director who'd made films that grossed a hundred million dollars—because they saw this as some huge investment. But in the end, the piece was so weird that it was never going to be made that way. Especially after *Pennies from Heaven* failed commercially, and lost a lot of money."

But then arrived another player in the game: a pre–*Passion of the Christ* (2004) superstar named Mel Gibson. With his partner Bruce Davey, Gibson and his production company, Icon, acquired the rights to the screenplay from Potter's family (Sarah, Jane, and Robert Potter). The two producers described the project as a shared "passion" and one they had lived with for "ten years."[74]

"Really it was Mel in 2001, I guess, who got the rights because he really loved the original. He had the idea to do *The Singing Detective* as an independent film, or as a smaller film, a film for certainly under ten million dollars," Gordon explains.

"He held onto it for a while, and I think the thing that pushed him over the edge to actually try and make it was when he got the brainstorm of doing it with [Robert] Downey [Jr.]. He and Downey are good friends. I think they've been close ever since *Air America* (1990), and he just loved the idea of giving this film as a gift to Robert, because Robert was getting out of jail and everything."

In fact, according to reports, Gibson visited Downey in his "court-ordered treatment house" and lobbied the troubled thirty-seven-year-old actor to take the part.[75] Though Downey was significantly younger than Michael Gambon had been when he essayed the part for the BBC, there seemed to be an odd synchronicity between the life experience of the film's protagonist, Dan Dark, and Downey, who had battled a much-publicized drug addiction for years.

"I was revealing myself, essentially," Downey reported to the press of the character. "And believe me, it's a lot weirder for me than it would be for anyone who watches it."[76]

In particular, Downey, a recent Golden Globe and SAG Award winner for his work on the TV series *Ally McBeal*, found some common ground with the impulses of angry, sarcastic Dan Dark. "There's that whole idea of being able to use an affliction as a weapon," he said, "and there's nothing better for someone who's abused drugs as frequently as I. The best defense is a good offense."[77]

"I think it was a genius insight on Mel's part to realize that where Robert was in his life would be a perfect mesh for this character," Gordon reflects. "Both in the sense of 'Here's a character who is a lost, angry person finding his way towards the light,' but also in the sense that Robert, for the first time in his life, was trying to stay really grounded in what was present, and I think this character needed that."

With Downey set to star in the remake, the hunt began in earnest for a director. Robert Downey Jr. and Keith Gordon had worked together on the Rodney Dangerfield comedy vehicle, *Back to School* (1986), and gotten on very well during the shoot. Over the years, Downey also had made a special effort to keep in touch with Gordon, and expressed enthusiasm about the idea of appearing in one of his features.

"Suddenly they were calling me in to meet them, and talk with them about this," Gordon remembers his arrival on the project. "But then nothing happened for months and months, and I said, 'Oh, I guess I blew it. I guess they don't want me.'"

But all that soon changed. "I got this phone call saying, 'We start in ten weeks, do you want to do it?'" Gordon remembers. "Which was great and kind of awful [at the same time], because it meant I had much less preparation time than I'd ever had on a film before, on what was arguably the most complicated film I'd ever done! On the upside, it just made me dive in without worrying too much, or thinking too much, or second-guessing myself too much. I just had to go and start getting ready to make the film."

But in accepting the assignment to direct, Gordon immediately understood that some people would not care for his or—for that matter—*any* reinterpretation of the material. For in the years since the 1980s, *The Singing Detective* had transcended its original context and become a sort of "national treasure" in the United Kingdom, "one of the best regarded miniseries in the history of world TV."[78]

"I knew that many people would compare it negatively to the original," admits Gordon. "But this was one of the last things Potter wrote—literally on his deathbed. It was his idea and his desire, and I thought, 'I don't care why people think I'm doing it,' because I loved this guy's work, and it means a lot to me."

But even getting it straight in his own head didn't help Gordon with some of the more vocal naysayers. "I was getting hostile, hostile, hostile letters finding their way to me before we started production. I was in preproduction and I would be getting letters from people in England saying, 'You fucker! How dare you do this?! I hope you fail! You're digging up a great man's grave!'"

How did the director handle the brickbats? With a little help from a friend. "What was pointed out to me by Potter's longtime agent is that when the original series aired on BBC, it got very mixed reviews," Gordon notes. "People were of two minds about it. It did not win most of the TV awards that are the equivalent of our Emmy Awards. It was *not* seen as the greatest thing ever done. It was only over time that it came to be regarded as this untouchable piece of perfection. But she [the agent] said that everybody was really disappointed that they didn't get more support from the critics at the time. The irony now is that it *has* become this untouchable piece of perfection, and the agent said, 'Dennis never thought it was.' There were plenty of things he thought could have been done better."

Interestingly, Potter's redone screenplay addressed those very weaknesses he perceived in the popular BBC miniseries. Specifically, his new script reformulated a number of important elements. The detective angle of the story was no longer set in the 1940s, but rather the 1950s. The action also moved across the pond, from England's Forest of Dean to America's West. And, in something of a shocker, the new Potter-written *Singing Detective* even featured a considerably more upbeat ending.

For Gordon, it was critical to stay true to this vision, spelled out on the page, and not rehash to what had already been accomplished in the miniseries. "If you look at the interviews that Potter did, there's a really amazing one right near the end of his life, for example, called *The Last Interview*. It's available on tape, and it was done for the BBC. He knows he's dying at that point, and he's taking morphine and smoking cigarettes through the whole interview—it's kind of amazing," Gordon describes.

"But one of the things that's clear is that as he approached the end of his life, his world view was changing. Basically the attitude late in his life was 'Yes, my life has been horrible and miserable, and I've been screwed over, and I've had this horrible disease, but you know what? I'm still glad I'm here.' That's something I don't know he felt ten years earlier.

"Just like the character of Joe Gideon is Bob Fosse, Philip Marlow/Dan Dark is Dennis Potter," Gordon says. "I think he wanted the chance before his death to revisit essentially himself, but in a slightly more optimistic way, because I think he did come to feel like some kind of redemption is possible. That it [life] isn't all just shit and then you die. That there is the chance that one can transcend; that the world is worth being a part of. I think that was part of his motivation to revisit the character."

And what of Potter's choice to change the era from the 1940s to the 1950s, and switch locales to America? "There were real reasons Potter did it," Gordon says. "People can like it or not like it, but there are clearly reasons he made those choices. First of all, Potter was always—among other things—a social satirist. He was always interested in skewering and examining the culture of the society he was writing about. England in the 1940s was a very specific moment. The end of the war was also the end of England as a global power, and there was certainly a loss of identity that came with that. This was a nation losing its power, and his character was a man who had lost his power in life. These were the things he was doing by examining that era [in the miniseries.]

"I don't know that America in the 1940s has the same resonance. Whereas America in the 1950s had something else that he [Potter] was examining, that weird schizophrenia of what he calls in the script 'the sexuality of proto–rock and roll'—this kind of outwardly free and wild thing. Yet at the same time, it was still a very repressive society where women were either whores or virgins.

There was the blacklist going on and McCarthyism. It was a very different time, but it was a much richer time with which to deal with the irony of the themes he was interested in.

"Some people complained that the noir stuff [we did] didn't look as rich as the stuff in the original series," Gordon continues, "and that's because 1950s noir is different from 1940s noir. When it was Bacall and Bogart, they were A-list films, and yes, they were rich films. But by the fifties it was all Sam Fuller, and noir had been relegated to B-movies that were being made for nothing. Which is why the style of those films is so interesting and so cheesy at the same time. That's what we were dealing with."

Even the change in the character's name from Philip Marlow to Dan Dark is evidence of Potter's switch on his own material, a substituting of one decade's popular culture for another. "Dan Dark is such a Mickey Spillane, cheesy kind of a detective name," Gordon notes. "It's a very different kind of feel, but I think he was doing that to explore his theme in a new way."

With a cast of A-list actors that included Robin Wright Penn, Oscar-winner Adrien Brody, Jeremy Northam, and Katie Holmes, Keith Gordon commenced shooting his seven-million-dollar production of *The Singing Detective* in Los Angeles on April 23, 2002.[79]

The film was lensed sequentially,[80] and producer Mel Gibson assumed a critical role in the film, portraying Dark's oddball psychologist, Dr. Gibbon, a role he played under heavy makeup. Downey also spent a great deal of time under makeup to re-create Potter's disfiguring psoriasis (a makeup job that Gambon had once claimed was the most painful of his career[81]), and the design for Dark's damaged visage came from the crew's intensive research of the actual disease and textbook photographs of its horrible effect.[82]

While directing the film, Gordon kept in mind a strong fidelity to Potter's 1992 script. He was guided by Potter's notes, in particular, about the manner that the musical numbers should be staged and what songs should be used to bring his vision to life.

"He left a wonderful legacy of thousands of pages of interviews," Gordon reiterates. This bank of knowledge meant that Gordon was often able to determine Potter's intent. Besides, the script itself afforded a high degree of specificity, down to choice of song titles. But acquiring them wasn't always easy.

"We made this film for about seven million dollars, and that meant that we couldn't do what Hollywood normally does, which is throw hundreds of thousands of dollars per song at publishers and musicians," Gordon explains. "Our whole music budget was a couple of hundred thousand dollars, so we had to go out and make remarkable deals. We had a wonderful guy who did get the rights for us, [music supervisor] Ken Weiss. He had to go out and do all the negotiating. It wasn't hard for me, but I'm sure he had a lot of moments where it was a nightmare.

"The one song that Potter had in his script that we couldn't get was Fats Domino's 'Blueberry Hill.' That was the one song where the estate, or the publishers . . . they just weren't interested in cutting a deal," Gordon remembers. "They still wanted whatever it was, $180,000. So we replaced it with the Conway Twitty song 'It's Only Make Believe.'" I felt it had a similar emotional vibe. Both songs came from the same era, and there was something about the feel of it that felt right to me."

Also, it was Potter's decision that all the songs in the film be lip-synched to original artist renditions, a decision that goes against the contemporary trend of nonmusical actors singing their own songs in films as diverse as *Everyone Says I Love You, Love's Labour's Lost, Dancer in the Dark,* and *Moulin Rouge*. Instead, it harkens back to the tradition Potter established in *Pennies from Heaven*.

"There was a little talk about that in the beginning, because Robert wanted to do his own singing," Gordon explains. "But Potter . . . was very explicit about why he would never want his pieces done otherwise [than lip-synching]. His whole concept was that these songs are not the character's feelings, but society forcing itself out of the character's mouth. If you have the character singing in his own voice, then you're making a very different comment. Then you're saying, 'Oh, this is the feeling of the character,' not 'Oh this is the culture coming out of the human being, whether he wants it to or not.' It was integral to Potter's concept.

"The one thing we did do was have Robert sing the song under the end credits: 'In My Dreams,'" Gordon explains. "When there's that reprise, it's Robert. I liked that, because to me there was a little sense of 'Okay, for one brief moment, this character has found his own voice.'"

Overall, however, Gordon concurred with Potter's edict that the music should be lip-synched. "For a film like *Everyone Says I Love You,* which is a film I really like a lot, it's a much sweeter thing," Gordon stresses. "It's a movie about people trying to deal with their feelings. So if those actors had been lip-synching, it would have been distancing. It would have felt artificial in a bad way.

There's something very endearing about an actor who can't sing well, trying to sing. Because it is so human, and most of us feel that we can't sing. That can be a wonderful thing, but it does evoke a very specific kind of emotion, and you have to want that tone.

"With Potter, it's so Brechtian. It's a comment on a comment on a comment. You don't want anything that's going to undermine the distancing effect of the approach. Again Potter even said, 'I don't care if the lip-synching isn't perfect. I don't care if you're aware of lip-synching.' It should be kind of messy. It's a very kind of specific style that doesn't really apply to much of anything else, and yet affected a whole generation.

"Potter was the first to say that a lot of songs he used in his pieces were awful songs, which is really interesting," Gordon reflects. "He said, 'I'm not picking things because they're great art, but because these are the songs that when I was a kid got branded into my brain by being on the radio every five minutes.' So they became part of how he saw the world, whether or not it was a good thing.

"You can find different quotes from Potter where on one hand he says, 'These songs are the hymns of our time,' and he'd be clearly loving his memories, and then other times he was sarcastic and dark about it: 'This shows how shallow we've gotten, and it paints a very shallow view of ourselves in the world.'"

Once the songs were selected and rights acquired, Gordon had the assistance of choreographers Bill and Jacqui Landrum (*O Brother, Where Art Thou?*, *The Big Lebowski* [1996], *The Doors* [1991]), to bring the numbers to life onset.

"They had done a lot of odd, playful, strange stuff—instead of things that were more standard," Gordon explains. "Basically, they were very good at taking my thematic ideas and finding equivalents in the dance. They had a group of dancers they liked to work with, and they showed me pictures of [the dancers] faces, and I'd say, 'Yeah, this kind of face works for the scene,' and then they'd basically start rehearsing on their own. I'd come in, and they'd show me what they were doing, and I'd say in a very naïve way, 'This part is really working for me; this part isn't working for me. Can this be sexier? Can this be sadder?' And they would do it.

"It was really a fun experience for me to sit there and get to oversee it, and be the general of the army, but not be the one having to actually plan out the move-by-move thing," Gordon explains. "It was wonderful, because for everything I expected of the dancers, they would find a way to get to it. The dancers were amazing. I've always respected dancers in a kind of generic way, but now I was blown away, because they would just change everything in front of me and come up with a whole new approach to something.

"I loved these people. They were great. The process was definitely one of a lot of talking and a lot of rehearsing, but it was really a matter of translation too," Gordon reflects on directing the musical segments.

In *The Singing Detective*, Dan Dark lives up to his name. He isn't necessarily a pleasant or attractive character. He seems to hate women, and he is very angry. And yet, as the protagonist of the film, it is necessary that Dark be identifiable, even likeable to audiences.

"What I think is important when you do something like that is to have an actor like Robert Downey who has—on some level—an inherent empathetic quality," Gordon considers. "There's something about Robert that is so sad and so lost as an actor and as a human being, that I think you'll stay with somebody like that, even though they are so difficult and horrible. I can think of other actors—even wonderful actors—who you wouldn't be able to put up with because you wouldn't have seen that there was something more human underneath.

"Gambon did it brilliantly in his way, but it takes a very special kind of actor, and a very careful arcing of the character to be able to go to such dark places and still, somewhere, an audience feels 'I like this guy in spite of himself.' That really speaks to the genius of an actor and a certain kind of talent that certain actors have. As a director, your job is to help modulate that as carefully as you can, and get different kinds of takes. Somewhere the anger is more, [and] takes where the anger is less."

Gordon remembers reviewing all of Downey's film work prior to shooting and understanding that there would have to be a considerable change in the actor's *modus operandi*. "One of the things I said to Robert at the very beginning was, 'You love to use your body; you love to move; you love to use your hands; you're very physically expressive. That's great, but now you're playing a guy who can't [be that way].'

"I said, 'You need to start dealing with the fact that it hurts every time he [Dan] moves anything. That's going to drive you crazy as an actor.' I said, 'You can do two things with this. You can either rebel against it, and be really cranky towards me and everybody else, or you can find the anger in the man and the focus of the man,'" Gordon remembers. "And he got it immediately, and really worked hard with that.

"Even in rehearsals, he would do things like bind his hands together, so he couldn't use them," Gordon describes. "And it would drive him nuts! But it was very important because that's where a lot of the anger came from. Because Robert is not by nature an angry human being. He's a guy who's done himself a lot of violence in his life, but he's not done that to the people around him. That's where he's very different from this character. Dan Dark really takes his anger out on the people around him, and I think Robert's anger was always pushed inward . . . and so I think the very physical frustration of not being able to us his body helped him to find that really angry, nasty place . . . which did not come easy for him. He was very nervous going into the role that he would not be able to be that dark."

So much so that, on certain occasions during shooting, Downey would ask for the set to be cleared. "For some of the most emotional scenes we cleared everybody out. Even some of the actors weren't there," Gordon reports. "The scene in the hospital bed when he [Dan] breaks down early in the film—when we actually shot the scene, Robert said—and he was very nice to the other actors—'I know this sounds crazy, but I kind of need you guys to leave because I'll be too embarrassed to really go there with everybody here.'"

With the set cleared, only the director and cinematographer remained with Downey, leaving the director to accomplish some fancy footwork during Downey's intense moments.

"Basically, I did the off-camera [reactions] with him for his closeup take where he's breaking down, because we had developed that trust," says Gordon. "I wish somebody had photographed it, because I was running around the room to where the different eye lines of the characters he was theoretically talking to, and at the same time really staying focused on him emotionally, so that he could make contact with me. He was crying and I was crying, so it was an interesting challenge, but I think he needed that level of security to go to those places."

Another hurdle that Downey had to surmount involved his predilection to improvise. "We talked early on about the fact that improvising Potter is like improvising Shakespeare," says Gordon. "There's a very specific rhythm and a very specific voice, because you have to be careful if you start improvising too much. At first, Downey was very resentful—'That's what I do'—but before too long, he started to enjoy the precision of the language.

"There are a few improvised moments in the movie, but he got so good, so familiar with Potter's voice that I couldn't tell you off the top of my head where things were improvised. It was never the obvious things. It was never the cultural references or things like that. But Downey really subsumed that for this. He really understood after a while that if you start improvising Dennis Potter, you're going to sound like somebody badly improvising Dennis Potter."

After shooting *The Singing Detective*, Gordon was confronted with the task of editing the film, and finding the right music to complement the scenes. This was not easy, considering how vastly the mood of the film changed as it straddled noir, musical and hospital psycho-drama.

"When you go into editing, you start playing with a scratch score. You put music on the movie to see what kind of music works," Gordon sets the scene. "I had the feeling—and I was right—that whatever style score music we put on the movie, it sucked. Because if you put really good score music on it, it turned the musical numbers into just camp. It made them too jokey. It was like, 'Here's the good music; here's the silly music.' And when you put fifties jokey music on the rest of the movie, it made it all seem like a sophomoric joke."

Gordon's solution was unique. "The only thing that made sense to me was to try and find 1950s music like 'Harlem Nocturne,' which would be 'of a piece' with the [musical] songs, and use that for whatever score we had."

This solution helped make the film coalesce, and after *The Singing Detective* premiered at the Sundance Film Festival on January 17, 2003, it wasn't long before Paramount Classics agreed to distribute the movie. It opened in limited release on October 24, 2003, and stayed in theaters until early January 2004. However, the number of theaters showing the film never went beyond a meager forty-five—making it difficult to find, even if audiences were seeking it out.

The Singing Detective's critical response was decidedly mixed. Many critics appreciated certain facets of Gordon's work, but apparently were reluctant to praise a remake of such a beloved piece. Many critics drew invidious comparisons with the Michael Gambon original. Roger Ebert was among the few who accepted the movie on its own terms. He liked the film and gave it three stars upon a second viewing. After an initial screening at Sundance he wasn't sure about the picture, but he "found it a more moving experience" the second time around.[83]

Other critics didn't seem to want to give the film the benefit of the doubt. Writing for *The Spectator*, Mark Steyen noted that the compression of Potter's original story made the film appear like "a brisk travelogue round the original."[84] Martin Hoyle of the *Financial Times* called *The Singing Detective* "an honorable, interesting failure,"[85] while others labeled it a "caustic, messy, fascinating whole,"[86] and assessed it "too fragmentary and weird for the multiplex masses."[87] Rex Roberts, writing for *Film Journal International*, lamented that the film hit "sour notes," was "static" and "burdened with shtick."[88]

Despite these critiques, virtually all reviewers found a great deal to praise in Downey's lead performance. "He touches so many emotional bases, one gets dizzy watching him," enthused *People*'s Leah Rozen.[89] The film landed on the home video/DVD secondary market in early 2004, allowing a whole new audience to see Gordon and Potter's radical reinterpretation of the material.

The Singing Detective opens in the hospital. Suffering from disfiguring psoriatic arthritis, pulp novelist Dan Dark (Downey) spends day after agonizing day convalescing in a bright ward. Resentful and feeling alone, Dark often retreats to an alternate and much more palatable reality, namely that of his first novel's lead character, a singing gumshoe working the case of a murdered woman. Dark fantasizes himself (and his nurses) performing 1950s numbers like "At the Hop" and "Mr. Sandman," but also imagines that his loving and concerned wife (Wright Penn) is disloyal and embroiled in a torrid affair with an agent named Mark Binney (Northam), who—in Dark's fevered imagination—is trying to steal a valued screenplay of his novel, *The Singing Detective*.

Dark's strange fantasies take an even darker turn when memories of his deceased mother flood in around him. He remembers seeing her engaged in a tryst years earlier, at his father's gas station in the desert. He also remembers a desperate trip to Los Angeles, and his mother being forced to prostitute herself. Two men he met on a bus in childhood also appear as gangsters in his fantasies.

As a quirky therapist, Dr. Gibbon (Gibson), helps Dark sort out his issues and family history, Dark begins to unravel his memories and fantasies and return to reality as it is, not as he fears it. But even as his skin condition gradually improves, Dark finds his fantasies unwilling to let go. They crowd in on his reality in one last surge. Gangsters from one world, vicious movie agents from another, and even the singing detective himself invade the hospital and force Dark to confront himself and the darkness inside.

There seems to be little doubt that the new musicals of the era covered in this book (1996–2004) have reparsed the underlying tenets of the genre to represent new symbols and ideas. In particular, *Dancer in the Dark* and *Chicago* constructed their musical numbers as the daydreams of their leading ladies, creating alternate realities with an all-singing, all-dancing nature. Keith Gordon's *The Singing Detective* has much in common with this approach, as the director has strived to create competing realities around his protagonist, Dan Dark, a man who is just as likely to fall into a crime story or a big production number as find himself back in his unpleasant and overlit hospital room.

But unlike *Dancer in the Dark*, which uses the alternate reality to reveal the gentle side of its Golden Heart, Selma, or *Chicago*, which uses the musical numbers to skewer celebrity, the press, the justice system and more, *The Singing Detective* utilizes its alternative reality for another purpose: to delve deep into psychology.

What is revealed in *The Singing Detective* is the layered, multiplaned imagination of a man who is suffering. At one level is "reality," the world of psoriasis and hospitals. At another is Dark's dimension of escape, his daydreams and fantasies—and that's where the music and the noir portions of the film reside. Interestingly, Dan Dark uses this layer of reality (the musical layer), almost precisely as American moviegoers once utilized the film musical in their lives, particularly in the Great Depression.

"In America," wrote Rick Altman in his landmark text, *The American Film Musical*, "the movie theater constitutes a refuge from the high seriousness of art . . . the American movie theater is a haven from culture, a darkened dreamworld in which spectators can finally release their repressed desires, fears, angers, and frustrations."[90]

In this case, Dan is not escaping economic woes or a deeply frightening world, or even the rise of fascism, but his own personal conflicts. He is angry about his disease and frustrated about his immobility, but his real fears emerge from the film's third dimension: Dark's personal memories of his mother and his childhood, which are buried one step beyond the imaginary and musical world of the singing detective. Thus, Dark uses his own internal "mental movie," the world of the singing detective, to escape from bleaker places.

Accordingly, the artistic success of the film is very much dependent on how clearly this theme of Dan Dark's competing realities plays out. What many critics missed, or ignored, is that Gordon's mise-en-scène played brilliantly with this notion, fostering through visuals and production design an understanding and visual reflection of Dark's splintered, multilayered psyche.

"As a filmmaker, for me there's nothing better than if you have form and content working together feeding each other. Those are my favorite films as a film viewer, so certainly as a filmmaker, I'd want to have my films have that same quality," Gordon explains. "The piece does exist in these different worlds, and I thought it was very crucial that each world have its own identity. I did things with every element when I could.

"The hospital was very overlit," he elucidates. "It was almost too bright, because I thought, 'Here's a man who is ashamed of who he is and ashamed of how he looks.' So what's worse for somebody like that than fluorescent lights? First of all, they make everybody look ugly. Secondly, he's like a bug under a microscope—he can't escape. He's surrounded by light: everything's bright; everything's shiny and reflective . . . there's even a mirror on the wall. The bug under a microscope analogy was something we talked about a lot while we were making it."

Even the blocking of the actors reflected the grimness of the hospital reality. "I wanted him to be trapped in that world, so we tended to frame him in the middle of the frame," Gordon reveals, "to force him into the center of things in a very square composition, so he really was a prisoner in that world."

The positioning of Downey's character in the center of many shots not only framed him as a prisoner, but also had a secondary effect that is rather interesting. It is clear by his placement within shots that he is physically and metaphorically a "man alone," another crucial aspect of the tale.

"Among the things that Potter was interested in and you see it in little ways throughout the film is that very American idea of the man alone,' Gordon explains. "That's not such an English thing. It's a very American idea: one man against the world. Isolating him [Dark] in a room, Potter was just underlining that thing. In England, society is much more a society. In America, there is the mythology of the lone man. All those things were just changes Potter was trying to play with so he wasn't repeating himself."

The noir world (which was also the musical world), was depicted in a different palate than Dark's life in the hospital to differentiate the layers of reality. "The noir world was his escape, so we went to a very dark place, where there are shadows that somebody who feels ugly can hide in, even though it's also a dangerous place because you can't see it," Gordon reflects. "But beyond that, the noir world was an unfinished world because he's writing it as he goes along; he's coming up with it. So it was very important to me that the sets appear unfinished; that the walls weren't there; that there's a dreamlike sense of 'I know there's a bar and a girl, but I don't know what else is there.'"

This concept worked remarkably well, and some critics took note. "Some of the visuals are striking," wrote Chris Vognar. "Dan's apartment, at least as it appears in his fantasies, has the depth and shadow of an Edward Hopper painting, and some of the Art Deco touches create the illusion of a nightmare Hollywood gone to seed."[91]

By differentiating the contrasting compartments of Dark's mind and memory, Gordon provides audiences nice visual clues about how all the material is tied together as a whole, with one arena of Dark's mind often flooding the other. This plan for the film succeeded in making what could have been a remote and incomprehensible film something much more touching and emotional.

Given this plan, it is not surprising that certain symbols from Dark's real life also found representation in his escape world and personal memories. "There's a scene where he sees his mother being seduced by Binney, and there's a painting of a pink Cadillac on the wall," Keith Gordon notes. As audiences who have seen the film will recall, that pink Cadillac is also the centerpiece for Dark's sexual fantasy with Nurse Mills, set to the tune of "At the Hop."

Thus, the symbol of Cadillac connects Dark's subconscious mind to his escape world in a tangible way. Delightfully the film is packed with similar symbols which hint at the strange interconnections and byways of the complex human mind. These clues are not immediately recognizable, but certainly make *The Singing Detective* an even richer film on a second viewing.

The musical numbers in Dan Dark's head represent his escape from an unpleasant world, and one of the most interesting aspects of the film involves the climax, wherein that musical fantasy world marches right into the "real" world of the hospital, an assault from the fantasy realm. Eagle-eyed viewers will note that the vanguard from the dreams, led by the Singing Detective himself, forms a symmetrical triangle, an arrowheadlike phalanx advancing into the ward. That the assault should be overtly symmetrical, with Downey in the lead, and three singing floozies balanced on either side of him, is perhaps a genuflection to the classic musicals of Hollywood, like those of Busby Berkeley, where dancers would form geometric shapes (often seen from above) to entertain stunned audiences. Here, the effect is reflective, but also serving a quite different purpose, dramatizing an almost military-style advance.

"Sometimes it was conscious, looking at musicals and saying, 'Oh,'" Gordon notes of his visual flourishes. "Other times it is just subconscious. I see the shots in my head. I do remember that shot, I remember walking down the hall and having the image of this V of people behind him. It relates to things in old movies, and it's kind of ironic, this very formal shape."

Writing about Keith Gordon's mise-en-scène for *Senses of Cinema*, film scholar Peter Tonguette insightfully observed that it "reflects the traps in which his characters are caught; influenced by Stanley Kubrick, he prefers symmetrical compositions and slow formal zooms which emphasize characters existing within—rather than controlling—a given space."[92]

Gordon considers the analysis and agrees with it. "I'm very drawn to symmetrical images. Kubrick certainly was my favorite director when I was a kid. I love his movies. Even when I was in junior high school doing still photography, my photographs tended to be very symmetrical, very balanced. It seems to be part of my aesthetic."

Here, the director's propensity for symmetrical images meshes perfectly with movie musical tradition, and visually demonstrates a collision of worlds: Dark's impression of the musical in his escape world, with the harsh, over-lit reality of life in a hospital ward. Other touches in the film reveal his bursts of anger and lack of mental discipline, as in the sequence inside the hospital with gyrating dancers and spinning gurneys, shot from that Busby Berkeley–style overhead angle.

The Singing Detective succeeds as a "uniquely dark and bizarre fantasy-reality," not just because of its wild eruptions "into musical numbers,"[93] but because the film's director understands how to marshal the essence of the musical format to vet his story. The musical elements comment on a character's need for his escape, counterbalance his feelings of entrapment, and also, in typical Potteresque style, reveal the influences of pop culture on a particular soul. As an unconventional musical experiment, and one in which form determinedly reflects content, the film represents an unqualified success, even if director Gordon remains a bit reluctant to reduce his complex work of art to the simplistic genre stereotype of "musical."

"I had a running joke whenever I introduced the movie, because when you do these movies you take them to film festivals," Gordon describes. "I would start my little introduction by saying, 'This film is just your average, everyday musical, comedy, drama, surrealist character study, Brechtian look at society of a man in a hospital bed, in a detective story murder mystery.' The whole thing is that it takes on all these genres and puts them together. Certainly, a musical is a big part of what it is. The wonder of Potter's stuff is that it is as crazy to call it a musical as it is to call it a film noir, as it is to call it a character study. There's no easy word for this, or any of Potter's most interesting work."

WHAT IS THIS THING CALLED LOVE?

The 2004 musical biography *De-Lovely* opens at a moment of sadness. At the moment of his death, elderly songwriter Cole Porter is visited in his home by a sympathetic angel named Gabe (Jonathan Pryce), who escorts the cantankerous composer on a tour of his life that resembles one of Porter's many elaborate stage productions.

The elderly Porter (Kevin Kline) watches from his perch in a theater seat as the events from his early life unfold before him. In particular, he is struck by the beauty and elegance of his beloved wife, Linda Lee Thomas (Ashley Judd), as a young woman. Porter recalls how the couple fell in love so many years earlier, flirting in 1920s Paris to "Well Did You Evah!," and how, later, they married despite certain personal difficulties. Foremost among these were Porter's sexual appetite and desire for other men.

However, even through the difficult times, Linda supported Cole on his amazing odyssey, one that took him from the celebrated stages of Broadway and his first hit song, "Let's Do It, Let's Fall in Love," to the movie studios of Hollywood, and even, once, to a movie auditorium, where Linda and Cole saw their own (highly fictionalized) life unfold in the 1946 film *Night and Day*, starring Cary Grant and Alexis Smith.

While preparing for his final reckoning with Gabe, Cole recalls the terrible riding accident that cost him his legs, and also Linda's terminal fight with cancer, which eventually took her away from him. Through it all, Cole's personality, temperament, and talent shone in a series of beloved compositions.

The life story of legendary composer Cole Porter (1891–1964), first recounted on celluloid in *Night and Day*, was a whitewash of Porter's real biography, one that included love and talent, but also pain and the taboo of promiscuous homosexuality. The artists behind *Night and Day* had no other choice in their style of presentation because the Motion Picture Production Code of the day did not permit any indication, let alone dramatization, of homosexuality.

By the time Irwin Winkler, producer of such films as *Rocky*; *New York, New York*; *Raging Bull*; *The Right Stuff*; and *Good Fellas*, approached screenwriter and former movie critic Jay Cocks about *De-Lovely*, movie mores had changed dramatically in America. In particular, homosexuality had come out of the Hollywood closet, meaning that Porter's story could be told without "covering up" certain aspects.

Jay Cocks first became involved with the new effort, *De-Lovely*, while writing a screenplay about the musical collaborations of Duke Ellington and Billy Straithorn. At his home in Maine, he answered a phone call from his friend, Winkler.

"Without preamble, he said, 'What do you think about a movie about Cole Porter?' And without preamble or due consideration, I said, 'Great, I'm in,'" Cocks remembers.

As it turns out, a new Cole Porter film became possible because of an encounter between Winkler and someone from the Cole Porter Trust, which manages his estate.

"Irwin had conversations with a wonderful man named Bob Montgomery, though he is not related to the great star of the thirties and forties," Cocks explains. "Bob was a lawyer who was the head of the Cole Porter Trust and knew Porter for the last fifteen years of Porter's life."

The appeal of a new Porter biography came from the fact that the Cole Porter Trust intended to grant the filmmakers free use of the composer's catalog, and was making no restrictions on the dramatization of his personal life. "The wheels starting turning in Irwin's head, and he called me," Cocks says.

"Because Irwin had worked from the get-go with the Cole Porter Trust and Bob Montgomery, we were given virtually unlimited access. We could use any song we wanted, and there was some sort of number with it, but it was very, very high. If we had used all the songs we were allowed, we would have had a three-and-a-half-hour movie! They said something like 'Use any three dozen songs that you want!' Wow! That was like discovering Long John Silver's treasure."

With the assistance of the Cole Porter Trust, Cocks began delving into the details of Cole Porter's life and fashioning the script, a process that eventually took more than three years. "I became fascinated with the relationship between Porter and his wife, Linda, and Irwin and I agreed that it should really be the bedrock of our story," Cocks notes.

One of the most interesting aspects of their relationship was how each participant saw it, and what each gave to the other. "It was her belief—her unswerving belief—in his potential, in his gift, that became his bulwark," Cocks says. "She wasn't patronizing him, in the literal sense. She wasn't setting him up in the life so he could compose. He had plenty of money. What she gave him was something he couldn't find anywhere: belief, acceptance, and true love. And it kind of went beyond the biology."

But that didn't mean that Linda couldn't feel pain, either, when her husband sought out (male) lovers for companionship. In fact, it was this pain that represented the other side of their love story. "She made a bargain that she thought she could fulfill, but she couldn't," Cocks explains. "Part of the reason she couldn't was that he became so flagrant in a way that endangered not only their relationship, but his talent, I mean his success. In that time, I think that if he had ever been outed, it would have been all over for him, even though by then he was considered one of the greatest American songwriters. The scandal would have ruined his career."

On the other hand, Cole Porter was always totally up front with Linda about his desire to be with male sexual partners. He didn't hide anything from her. "He saw no reason to apologize for who he was, what he needed, or what he wanted," notes Cocks.

The screenplay for *De-Lovely* would gaze at all these aspects of the unusual Porter marriage in a way more complex, real, and human than *Night and Day* was allowed. And in fact, it would delve even further, into new territory. For example, Cocks discovered something that gave *De-Lovely* an even deeper breadth.

"There's a point of biographical information that's never been seen anywhere before this movie. It came from Bob Montgomery at the Cole Porter Trust. When Irwin and I were preparing the movie, we had lunch one day with Bob, and he said, 'I think that Cole and Linda tried to have a baby.' This was coming from someone who knew Cole Porter and knew Linda for the last couple of years of her life, but had access to aspects of Porter's life that most people, even good friends didn't know.

"So we were really struck by this, when he told us that," Cocks explains. "Because it seemed to speak a lot to the depth of their relationship. Irwin wanted to use this, but my journalistic caution intervened, and I said, 'I'd like to get this substantiated from someone else,' and Irwin said, 'Oh God, how are we going to do that?'"

Cocks found a way. He made a call to a professor at Yale who had helped on the music in the film, and who teaches the Great American Songbook. He contacted a friend of Porter's named Jean Howard, once a reigning socialite of Beverly Hills society, who, in turn, confirmed the details.

"Unfortunately, she died before we could talk with her, but Bob [Montgomery] talked to her about this, and she said, 'Yes, they did try to have a baby and Linda had a miscarriage,'" Cocks reports. "I took this as a very good second source, because Porter had proposed to Jean Howard two years after Linda died. She turned him down and he never mentioned it again.

"I reasoned it out with Irwin this way," Cocks explains. "I said, 'This is really a revelation.' This is a couple who lived in a cocoon of wealth and Bohemian celebrity. They didn't have to fool anybody into thinking they were just plain folks by having a baby. They must have wanted to have a baby. I just got the impression they had to be doing it for themselves, so we used it."

So with these new biographical details to support *De-Lovely*'s love story, all that remained was for a studio to green light the project and finance it. No easy task, but to Cocks's surprise, everything came together rapidly.

"Just a few weeks after [Winkler called], I came down to New York, and we had a meeting with a fellow from MGM named Michael Nathanson. We told him a little about what we wanted to do, about which we knew very little at that point, and he said, 'I'll do it.'"

Cocks contrasts this relatively easy effort with the normal process of getting a studio's backing. "Usually, it's a process of cajoling, pleading, threatening, begging, getting mad . . . all that stuff. But in this particular case, Michael took a big leap. He went for it right way, and it was because we talked about what we envisioned as the love story between Cole and his wife, Linda . . . this deeply conflicted love story that they both shared. I think that [the love story] combined with Michael's knowledge of music is what sparked him, so that's how it got set up. That, and the tremendous quality of the music."

But exactly what kind of movie was *De-Lovely* going to be? A biography? A musical? Both? "I never thought of this as a musical," Cocks admits. "I thought of it as a dramatic story with music. I'm not just splitting hairs here. There's a world of difference. I think if I thought of this as a musical, I would have been hamstrung, hog-tied and otherwise incapable of proceeding, because I don't think that I would have had the first idea how to do that. It might be fun to try now, but I never thought of it as anything but a dramatic story with music, and I actually wrote the lyrics of the songs into the script as I went along.

"I knew the songs so well—of course, I had my lyric book—so whenever I got to a point [in the script] where Cole Porter seemed to be able to write things better than I, I would immediately put one of his songs in. That's one explanation for why there's so much music in the movie, because he can always write better than me, and he can always write more deeply and more intimately about himself than me.

"It was a process of osmosis," Cocks describes. "I never really made a list of songs and said, 'Okay, we have to do these.' The use of the songs depended very much on the lyric content and the way the lyrics seemed to refract the dramatic biography I was dealing with. So by the time I started writing, which was after maybe six months of research, I already knew a lot of these songs in my head. I knew the trajectory of his life, and as I got to an episode, a thought would occur to me—or not.

"There were a couple of set pieces I had in mind," Cocks acknowledges, noting "Love for Sale" as one he had designs on for a specific scene. "'Be a Clown' was also conceived as a set piece."

Interestingly, while immersed in the writing process Cocks discovered that including the lyrics of Porter's songs in the text/screenplay also helped readers to better understand the material and its thematic import. "When they're down there [in the script], it lets the reader get some sense of the emotional impact of the song in the scene much more effectively than if you just write, 'They sing "So in Love."'"

Another element of the script involved the bookend structure that saw Cole Porter reviewing his life as a stage production. "We saw his life as something of a big musical in an era where people dressed up and wore fancy clothes," Irwin Winkler reported. "We thought it would be interesting if we looked back as if it were a theatrical production and through that format, we found a way to show what happened."[94]

"It seemed to evolve from the choice of doing this thing as the story of a man going over his own life," Cocks agrees. "He was a musical guy, and I thought it was more than likely that he would see his life as a musical. That's the most logical thing, and it serves my purpose very well in terms of vocabulary, it all came from that. Cole Porter was a very, very theatrical guy. He lived that way, he spoke that way—with a kind of theatrical flamboyance and Ivy League inflections. That was him. That's the way he was, at least in my imagining."

When the film was reviewed, some critics hinted that *De-Lovely* aped Bob Fosse's structure in *All That Jazz*, but Cocks says that's not really the case. "I saw the guy in *Variety* comparing this to *All That Jazz*, which I kind of understood, because it's impossible to make a movie with music and not deal with Bob Fosse, not to have him looking over your shoulder going 'uh, uh, uh!'

"*All That Jazz* comes from *8½*, and *8½* is a true masterpiece. So we worked off *All That Jazz* maybe the way Fosse worked off *8½*, generation to generation. I was more influenced, actually, by a piece of Bob Fosse's that was not a movie, but the last theater piece he did called *Big Deal*. It was fantastic! It was a musical version of *Big Deal on Madonna Street* (1958), an Italian comedy made in the late 1950s. It was a satire of all the caper movies that were done at the time, so Fosse took this movie and reset it in 1930s Depression Chicago, used all stage music—meaning there was no original music in it. It was all Tin Pan Alley songs of the period. And the motif he used—the way we used 'In the Still of the Night' [in *De-Lovely*]—was 'Bye Bye Blackbird.'

"It ended on a melancholy note," Cocks describes. "It contradicts Jonathan Pryce's advice in *De-Lovely* and ends in a ballad version of this song, 'Bye Bye Blackbird,' in a very melancholy way. It was so beautiful. I told this to Ann Reinking when she came to a screening of *De-Lovely*, but I don't think she believed me. I think she thought we were poaching on *All That Jazz*. In fact, it was much more in my mind about his musical *Big Deal*, and two movies that were very, very important to me in one way or another. One was *A Matter of Life and Death* (1946), and the other was Lindsay Anderson's *O Lucky Man!*, which is still the greatest dramatic musical ever made, I think."

With Cocks's carefully crafted screenplay in hand, two-time Tony winner and *In and Out* (1997) star Kevin Kline was cast as Porter, Ashley Judd joined the production as his long-suffering wife, Linda, and Jonathan Pryce, *Evita*'s Juan Perón, essayed the role of the mysterious, ethereal Gabe.

Kline conducted extensive research for his star turn, reading five biographies of Porter and speaking with several people who knew him, or knew stories about him. "I was surprised by his voracious appetite for pleasures of the flesh," Kline reported, "the way he was curious about things aesthetic, gastronomic, smoking, drinking, ballet, music, art, beautiful men, beautiful women, passion for music . . ."[95]

Behind the scenes, Irwin Winkler, a director who Judd described as possessing "the poise and equanimity of a real old school gentleman,"[96] also lobbied Jay Cocks for the inclusion of certain Porter songs he favored.

"Irwin said to me, we have to put in 'True Love,' and I said, 'Well, Irwin, most our drama has already taken place by the time Porter wrote that, and he [Porter] said he didn't like that anyway. He thought it was a bad song. And Irwin said, 'I love that song,' and I've been around at least long enough to know that it doesn't do much good to argue when the director has his heels dug in that way.

"You just find another way to do it, and do it that way," suggests Cocks. "So, we were over at Kevin's house one day rehearsing, and he was at the piano, and his son came home from school and sat down next to him. I said, 'Why not have this song as a duet with a kid instead of Bing Crosby and Grace Kelly in *High Society* (1956)? Porter really did write it for *High Society* in the early 1950s and always thought poorly of it, but I didn't think it was so much of a stretch to say 'All right, well maybe he could have written it in the thirties and stuffed it in a trunk and pulled it out for emergencies,' so that's where we did it.

"And then, at a later date, we thought it might be fun for Ashley to sing it, but when you see the movie, you hear Cole say to Sara Murphy, 'It's not me. Linda thinks it is.' It's a very, very sweet, classy, simple, sentimental song which nevertheless gets a toehold in your subconscious, which is probably one reason why it was such a hit."

Production on *De-Lovely* commenced on May 5, 2003, and continued through July at international locations, including London. Producer Charles Winkler, Irwin's son, shot second unit on the project, including material of Porter on horseback during his riding accident, and Stephen Endelman served as the film's musical supervisor. Kevin Kline, a performer with an outstanding singing voice, sang a whopping fourteen numbers for the film (including "Be a Clown" and "In the Still of the Night"), and 95 percent of his work was performed live, rather than lip-synched.[97]

Costume designer Janty Yates, who had won an Academy Award for her efforts on Ridley Scott's *Gladiator* (2000), designed many of the film's extraordinary costumes, noting that "Cole Porter and his gang were the role models for [F. Scott] Fitzgerald's *Tender is the Night*. They were the most happening gang in Europe at the time."[98]

In conjunction with Yates's exemplary work, fashion icon Giorgio Armani contributed components of Kline and Judd's wardrobe to the film for nothing, frequently spending seven hours fitting Kline in costume.[99] Kline had thirty-eight costume changes in *De-Lovely*, Judd, an amazing forty-eight, and overall, more than a thousand extras needed to appear just right so as to vividly re-create Cole Porter's elegant world from the 1930s right up to the 1960s.

As one might guess, it wasn't merely the look of Cole Porter that needed to be accurate, but the sound too. On this front, Irwin Winkler made the controversial decision that in addition to his stars Kline and Judd, the bulk of Porter's tunes would be performed by contemporary, twenty-first-century artists. Kline himself believed it was a miscalculation to feature modern singers belting out Porter's classic tunes,[100] but others, including MGM's vice chairman and chief operations officer, Chris McGurk, saw bringing in contemporary performers as a "big factor in broadening support"[101] for the film with the under-twenty-five demographic.

The roster of stars proved impressive, with Sheryl Crow singing "Begin the Beguine," Alanis Morrisette belting out "Let's Do It, Let's Fall in Love," Elvis Costello performing "Let's Misbehave," Robbie Williams and the incomparable Natalie Cole doing "Ev'ry Time We Say Goodbye."

Balancing these stars—and their schedules—wasn't necessarily a walk in the park. "You know, Stephen Endelman did such a beautiful job with the music in the whole movie, arranging it, conducting it, casting all the voices, dealing with the various musicians as they showed up, and according to their very busy schedules [and] recorded the songs," Ashley Judd noted.[102]

And, as the final cut proved rather dramatically, the conceit worked. "If it had not been a good move for the music, Irwin wouldn't have done it," Cocks considers. "The first decision was: who can do this in a valid way that's also interesting and new and fresh? So we thought of these people. I thought they were fantastic. I thought Alanis was a huge surprise. I thought Sheryl Crow— who has taken a couple of lumps, partly because she sings a very unorthodox arrangement of 'Begin the Beguine'—gave a fantastic performance. We arranged it that way because we needed it that way dramatically and emotionally.

"The thing that we hadn't thought about too much, and I'm glad we didn't is that people who love . . . The Great American Song book tend to be as proprietary as classical music lovers. As proprietary and as conservative. So they don't like it when new people come moving in. They don't mind it when someone like Diana Krall does it, because she's got jazz creds, but when you've got someone coming in who's a rock singer, it doesn't matter that they're delivering a fantastic version of the song, like Sheryl Crow or Alanis Morrisette. These people bristle."

Though there were indeed some negative responses to the inclusion of folks like Costello, Crow, and Morrissette, other critics credited the gamble as a "successful risk," rather than a tactic that seemed like "a transparent" commercial ploy.[103]

When *De-Lovely* premiered at the Cannes Film Festival on May 22, 2004, the new musical was seen not just as a new chapter in the understanding of Porter the man and composer but as a tribute to MGM itself, which was celebrating its eightieth anniversary. Opening in early July 2004, the film, like virtually every musical to come along since 2002's *Chicago* (including *The Singing Detective* and *Camp*), received mixed reviews. *Entertainment Weekly* noted that it created a "genuine alchemy" and allowed audiences to accept the story of Porter's life because "the songs so fully express his spirit."[104]

Film Journal described *De-Lovely* as a "poignant, elegant film,"[105] and the *Seattle Times* called it a "a sleek elegy for a time long gone,"[106] but others were less impressed. Writing for *Time*, Richard Schickel noted that after a showing, viewers would "straggle out . . . lost in a fog of gloom."[107]

Variety's Todd McCarthy appreciated Kline's performance yet made invidious comparisons with *Chicago*, noting that *De-Lovely* was "indebted" to that film "for its strategy of layering levels of reality in a musical context."[108]

For his part, Cocks felt such criticism was off the mark, though it surely revealed how Rob Marshall's award winner was still on the minds of the critical community.

"This guy said it takes a lot from *Chicago*, and I said, 'What is he talking about?' What does this have to do with *Chicago*? Yes, they sing and they dance, but there's nothing in common with it!"

Cocks is right, the layering of realities in a musical wasn't an initiative begun with *Chicago*, but rather a long-standing facet of films as diverse as *Dancer in the Dark*, and going back further, *All That Jazz*, and especially the works of Dennis Potter. *Chicago* worked exceptionally well with the conceit of multiple realities, but *De-Lovely* had its own unique vibe, to be certain.

As we have witnessed elsewhere in this book, the musical films that are most appreciated by audiences, and which survive from one generation to the next, are those that understand how best to deploy song and dance to express a mood, a yearning or a particular thesis. A good production number at just the right moment should forward the plot, reveal character, or comment on the action in some illuminating fashion.

De-Lovely is a film that remembers that lesson, but also boasts a strong leg up on some of its modern competition, because its songs are all written by a giant in the field. Porter's lyrics are so strong, so laced with double meanings, humor and wit, that this foundation grants writer Cocks and director Winkler plenty of opportunities to forge a multilayered, self-reflexive film of tremendous value.

Throughout *De-Lovely*, we hear Cole Porter's incomparable lyrics, as though some kind of Greek chorus, commenting on pertinent moments in his personal life. It is a testament to Cocks's writing skill and Winkler's visual acumen that their film runs the gamut, marshaling songs for ironic, funny, and even sympathetic purposes. The result is a movie that, unlike many screen biographies, feels layered and deep rather than shallow and clichéd.

Or to put it more plainly, Porter's songs are the perfect soundtrack against which to play Porter's life, and *De-Lovely* makes the most of that simple fact.

Night and Day could not achieve this symbiosis because of the limitations placed on that film that was made in the 1940s. There were aspects of Porter's life that had to be ignored back then, swept under the carpet or sugarcoated for mass consumption, so the result was an imperfect creation.

Benefitting from the relaxed morals of the twenty-first century, *De-Lovely* doesn't hold back. "Anything goes," to quote Porter, and so the film is full of surprises, laughs, and genuine emotions when it could have seemed remote, overly reverent or staid.

On its most basic level, *De-Lovely* is a showcase for Porter's work, and as such, it introduces his oeuvre to a new generation. On this level alone, the film works splendidly.

"If they were just breezy, frivolous songs, if they were simply witty, the guy would have been Noël Coward," Cocks reflects. "Now, Noël Coward was a good songwriter who occasionally achieved some depth, but nothing like Porter's. Noël Coward was multifaceted, so he did a lot of other things as well, and maybe spared himself going into some depth. Porter, on the other hand, was only a songwriter and could concentrate on that, and could fulfill himself emotionally with that—and through that—in a way that probably Noël Coward didn't need to. But what gives Cole Porter's music that enduring power are these fundamental qualities—Olympian qualities—of beauty, passion, sensitivity, and honesty. I mean, extraordinary honesty like in 'Experiment,' and ravishing melodies. What happened to these guys who could write these melodies?

"I saw a quote of Alan Jay Lerner's recently where he said, 'Of all of us, Cole Porter was the only one who could write a truly passionate love song,'"

Cocks says. "That was the other kind of organizing principle for me. 'In the Still of the Night' has to be one of the greatest songs ever written. That song has haunted me since I first heard it, since I first recognized it as a kid, and I knew that I somehow wanted that to be the dramatic spine of the movie. That's why he's writing it through the entire movie, and I knew it had to be the last song in the film."

But other songs are utilized with equivalent skill. Consider, for instance, "Night and Day." In *De-Lovely*, this song is rehearsed on stage by an uncertain young actor, and Porter joins him, teaching him how to perform it. On one level, this song and scene itself reveal the complexity and artistry of Porter's composing, but on another, deeper level all together, the tune represents the music of arousal, as the two men sing a duet.

Standing face-to-face, if not cheek-to-cheek, in close quarters, their eyes meet. As the song becomes increasingly intense, so does their glare. Behind their eyes is the joy arisen from a successful performance, but also the thrill of competition, the uncertainty of trying to keep up, and a powerful feeling of give and take. It isn't just a song, it's foreplay. As Porter and the actor (John Barrowman) continue singing and "Night and Day" becomes more forceful, more embroiled in the obsessive vocabulary of the song's language, the audience literally feels the heat of Porter's stimulation. The staging of the number has revealed something powerful and stirring about the song—and about Porter the man—and colored it in a new way.

"That was Fred Astaire's song," Cocks reminds us. "He sang that song. Irwin had a great idea. He said, 'I think there should be a song about music, about song,' and there happened to be a chapter in one of these excellent biographies of Cole Porter . . . there was a description of writing 'Night and Day' and how difficult it was structurally. So I just paraphrased that description, and made it into a dramatic scene between Cole and this guy. But the sexual underpinnings do work very well there. The song kind of scandalized people.

"The sexual element of those songs doesn't really get played up that much, nor the passionate nature of his music, and this was the thing that always fascinated me from the very beginning about Porter," Cocks considers. "We celebrate him for being so urbane and amusing; so blithe and sophisticated: like Oscar Wilde with a piano, but in fact, he had another side to him. Porter would write these amazingly, fearless, openhearted love songs—passionate love songs. Like 'So in Love' and 'In the Still of the Night,' which were two of the most important songs of his entire life for me, and that's why they were made so prominent in the movie."

The performance of "Night and Day" precedes a liaison between Porter and the actor in a park, so what it heralds is not just metaphorical, but literal foreplay. As audience members, we know by listening to the lyrics and watching the interaction of the two men that they are aroused.

Another song, "Love for Sale," is played over a brilliantly shot, extended sequence in a gay nightclub in Hollywood. By this point in the film, Porter and Linda have become estranged over his liaisons, and the impression is that Hollywood has pushed them even further apart with its more "permissive" nature. Cole now has dozens of men to choose from—literally—and his encounters with them take on a distinctly less romantic, more businesslike feel.

Whereas earlier we saw Cole's tenderness with a male Russian dancer he was in bed with in Venice, in Hollywood it's almost like a revolving door for targets of opportunity. Winkler shoots this sequence in one lengthy, unbroken shot that lasts for several minutes. As the camera prowls the nightclub, we are privy to Cole's assignations and meetings, going upstairs and downstairs, meeting men in booths and at the bar, etcetera. Noticeably Cole's clothes change—as do his conquests—in this lengthy uncut shot, thereby indicating visually that Porter's search for physical satisfaction had become endless, an ongoing, unending blur, a parallel to the idea of "love for sale."

"I always wanted to do 'Love for Sale' that way, though I never conceived of it as a single shot," reports Cocks. "Most people don't realize it is a single shot. It's quite amazing. I don't know how long it takes. It's a very long—six or seven minutes—steadicam shot panning and panning around that room. It's really a very subtle virtuosity that I didn't realize. Irwin had to tell me, but it was really brilliantly done."

Other songs in *De-Lovely* reveal the same flair. "Anything Goes" becomes a mantra for Cole's increasingly outrageous personal behavior, to Linda's chagrin. "Be a Clown" plays ironically as Cole's "sellout" song to Louis Mayer after agreeing to work in Hollywood and write songs that he feels dumbdown his clever style. "True Love," as Cocks has described, reaches for a different meaning in a duet between Linda and a child, a forecast of the Porters' desire to have a baby. "Blow, Gabriel, Blow" plays perfectly into the metaphor of the archangel and his trumpet, as Cole is about to head to the afterlife. Even the cabaret hit "Experiment" was reformulated by Cocks and Winkler in brilliant fashion as a kind of manifesto for Porter, sung at a Hollywood wrap party. In this setting, after a discussion with Linda about his sexual encounters, there is little doubt about what this song really means.

"When you see a song that actually is a big cabaret favorite, but that a lot of people don't know, like 'Experiment' which he sings at the party—wow!" Cocks says. "That's really like waving the red flag, which he almost literally did. He'd have all male parties at his house and have this flag up."

Sometimes in *De-Lovely*, the songs work simply as the punctuation on very emotional sequences, having no need to play on multiple layers. Take for example, "Ev'ry Time We Say Goodbye." This haunting song plays at Linda's bedside at the time of her death, the ultimate goodbye. One need not interpret its placement on any level other than face value. "She's dying in his arms. What's he going to do?" says Cocks. "I fell back on my ever-reliable, failsafe method: bring on a song. He had a song for that, so I put in 'Ev'ry Time We Say Goodbye.'"

Cocks has said that he didn't write a movie musical, but in point of fact, his work in *De-Lovely* proves that he understands precisely the very complex nature of the format, and the ways in which music can spotlight a film's theme, or shade characters in different ways. He has used the music of the artist to give audiences new insights about the man, and that is why *De-Lovely* is so lovely. Sumptuously filmed with beautiful period details, great performances, and featuring the work of an American genius, *De-Lovely* in many ways feels like an MGM musical from the 1950s—only with modern sensibilities.

De-Lovely also fits in with this author's theory about successful musicals. The ones that tend to succeed are those that somehow relate to show business. *Singin' in the Rain* concerned the movie era when silents became talkies, *All That Jazz* focused on a man working in theatre who saw his life as an ongoing production number, even down to his death. "Putting on a show" has been the bedrock of musicals from *Babes in Arms* to *Fame*, to *Waiting for Guffman*, to *Moulin Rouge* and *Camp*. Even *Dancer in the Dark*, featuring a heroine obsessed with Hollywood musicals (particularly *The Sound of Music*) reflected back on the world of show business as a counterpoint.

De-Lovely is no exception. The setup is a musical revue of Cole Porter's life, and more specifically, much of the language in the film is explicitly theatrical. Gabe warns Porter not to begin or end his musical with a ballad, for instance. In another sequence, Porter, acting as a director, instructs his younger self to fully pronounce all his consonants. Even the tender and loving scene of Cole and Linda in their bedroom, preparing to make love, evokes the theater. Porter enters the bedroom and asks Linda how he should "play the scene," indicating not just a show-business allusion, but the fact that in being with a woman, even one he loves, there is a degree of "acting."

"That was a very difficult scene to write," Cocks describes. Or at least it was until he settled on following through with the show-business allusions. "That was exactly my solution. His dialogue was really the writer talking. 'How are we going to play this?' 'What are we going to do?' And when she said, 'Why don't we just play?' it really set the tone for the scene, and it came out great.

"But boy, that was one of the last things I wrote in the script!" Cocks acknowledges. "Irwin kept urging me, 'We've gotta have this scene! We've gotta have this scene!' I kept resisting it, not because it wasn't a good idea, but because I thought I couldn't do it."

In *De-Lovely*, Cocks and Winkler have actually given the world the equivalent of a new book musical featuring Cole Porter as the composer. Still, Cocks resists interpreting his film as a musical.

"A book writer for a musical has a real challenge, where you have to mesh smoothly with the composer," he suggests. "And the composer really has primacy here over the book writer don't you think? Certainly the book writer's contribution might be more subtle, and might be like the string on which a strand of pearls is hung, but the songs are the pearls. You [a book writer] might be a little more of a mechanic than you might be under other circumstances, when you're just dealing with something that's great drama, or when you're bringing music into a drama, as I did here."

If 2003 proved to be the year of the backstage musical with *A Mighty Wind*, *Camp,* and even the razzle-dazzle of *8 Mile*, then 2004 appeared to be the year of the musical biopic.

In addition to *De-Lovely*, the biography of Cole Porter, 2004 would also include *Ray*, the biography of the late, great pianist and blues singer Ray Charles. Directed by Taylor Hackford (*White Nights*), the movie was filmed in New Orleans (doubling as Atlanta) and made under the title *Unchain My Heart: The Ray Charles Story*. It starred Jamie Foxx as the legendary Ray, an assignment the actor earned only after meeting Ray and his family and establishing his chops at the piano alongside the blind artist.[109]

Once shooting had begun, Foxx endured twelve to fourteen hours a day in special contact lenses to mimic Ray's handicap,[110] but his amazing performance went far beyond physical mimicry. "I wanted to touch some part of his spirit. That's all," the actor described. "There were a lot of little touches which I tried to layer—his musicality, his warmth, his sense of balance, his posture."[111]

The result of Foxx's efforts was a heartfelt performance that earned Foxx an Oscar for Best Actor in early 2005. Although the film itself received mixed reviews, mostly for seeming like such a familiar and traditional biopic, critics singled out Foxx's contribution. "His portrayal is an exalting tribute to a flawed, fascinating musical icon," wrote Philip Wuntch for the *Dallas Morning News*.[112] Audiences agreed, and the film earned a staggering $20.1 million on its opening weekend, Halloween 2004.[113] Filmed on a budget of $40 million, the film reached hit status by early 2005, grossing more than $71 million and still going strong.

Anticipated at the end of 2004 was the year's third musical biopic. This time, the story of 1950s crooner, Bobby "Mack the Knife" Darin was the subject matter of a twenty-four-million-dollar film directed by actor Kevin Spacey, who also played the charismatic Darin. Spacey's costar was Kate Bosworth as Sandra Dee and the film opened in just one theater in New York on December 17 with the ad-line "In the era of cool, he was the soundtrack." The film went to limited release on the last weekend of the year, December 29, 2004, and showed at 383 theaters.

MUSIC OF THE NIGHT

A student of history might argue cogently that the period between 1996 and 2004, the era surveyed most closely in this text begins and ends with Andrew Lloyd Webber. The artist's *Evita* revived the movie musical format in 1996, and his *Phantom of the Opera* was the last major musical debut of 2004, bowing on December 22 in limited release.

And like Sir Alan Parker's *Evita* nearly ten years earlier, there was a great deal riding on the success or failure of *Phantom of the Opera*. There were high expectations all around for this epic, a property based on the fantastically popular stage musical that first bowed in London in 1986 and came to American shores in 1988. Not only were the "phans" of this production absolutely rabid about it, but they number in the tens of millions.

In fact, *Phantom of the Opera* could arguably stake ground as the best known and most popular stage musical of all time. It is certainly the most profitable stage production in history, having grossed more than $3.3 billion as of 2004. The show has also been honored with four dozen notable awards (including multiple Tony and Olivier Awards), and even has the distinction of having sold forty million copies of its cast album, another record breaker. The stage show also made household names of its West End and Broadway stars, Michael Crawford and Sarah Brightman (Mrs. Llyod Webber), and radically reinvented Gaston Leroux's 1911 horror story (filmed memorably with Lon Chaney in 1925 and Claude Rains in 1943) as a "Beauty and the Beast"–style tragic romance.

But like *Evita*, *The Phantom of the Opera* has faced more than its fair share of tumult on the way to the silver screen. It once looked destined for the screen as early as 1990, on the heels of the popular stage production, but matters both commercial and personal scuttled the project. Specifically, Lloyd Webber was divorced from singer Brightman during this time.[114]

Then came the debacle of *I'll Do Anything* in 1994, and Hollywood suddenly didn't want to do musicals anymore. After waiting for years for Hollywood to green light his film, Lloyd Webber took matters into his own hands and bought back the rights to the property from Warner Bros. Still, no one was exactly eager to mount a production that would surely be expensive, not to mention technically complex.

But all that changed after *Moulin Rouge* and *Chicago*. The success of these efforts enabled Lloyd Webber and his fifteen-year collaborator on the project, director Joel Schumacher, the opportunity to resurrect the tragic phantom for the screen just when musicals were again becoming acceptable. Lloyd Webber had first contacted Schumacher about directing the film after seeing Schumacher's *The Lost Boys* (1987), and he had been impressed by the artist's "incredible visual sense."[115]

Interestingly, the long distance from the theatrical presentation, forged more than fifteen years earlier, also granted Schumacher the chance to put his individual stamp on the project, without so much concern about a slavish devotion to the source material (featuring music by Lloyd Webber and lyrics by Charles Hart and Richard Stilgoe.) "I think we were . . . more removed from the success of the show than we would have been if we made it in 1990," he admitted. "That would have been looming over us a lot more."[116]

In particular, the dozen intervening years gave Schumacher an opportunity to be inventive with casting choices. In his sixties, Michael Crawford was now deemed too old to play the titular part without it seeming unintentionally creepy, and so Schumacher could make changes without risk of overtly offending the Phan-faithful. He returned Christine to the character's original conception, as a naïve eighteen-year-old, not a thirty-year-old singer. Likewise, the Phantom could be a much younger man. Suddenly, the musical was, not unlike *Moulin Rouge*, concerned with first love and tragic love, thus more accessible to audiences still harboring reservations about the format.

In casting Christine, Joel Schumacher discovered an exciting and promising leading lady in eighteen-year-old Emmy Rossum, an actress who had heretofore not revealed her range in small parts in such films as Clint Eastwood's *Mystic River* (2003) and the global-warming blockbuster, *The Day After Tomorrow* (2004). But Rossum, who had never seen the Lloyd Webber show prior to casting, had begun singing for the New York Metropolitan Opera at age seven, and knew her way quite expertly around a song.[117] She also had a quality of naïve charm that made Christine's belief in an "Angel of Music"—really the Phantom—seem believable rather than contrived.

For the role of the iconic Phantom, Schumacher selected (with Lloyd Webber's approval), a Scottish heartthrob who had played another horror movie legend in Wes Craven's *Dracula 2000*, the smoldering Gerard Butler. The thirty-five-year-old actor, who had been chosen over such luminaries as John Travolta and Antonio Banderas, had been the lead singer in a rock band during his college days, but he studied with a voice coach for the challenging role of the Phantom[118] and described the act of singing the tragic part as a "wondrous and thoroughly inspiring experience."[119]

Schumacher and Lloyd Webber also strived to make the property feel more overtly cinematic (and thus less stagey). In this spirit, Schumacher took Lloyd Webber's chandelier crash, a highlight of the opera's first act, and moved it to the climax for effect. He also created a violent duel in the cemetery sequence between Christine's suitor Raoul (Patrick Wilson) and the Phantom, and focused more attention on the underworld of the Opera Populaire, the universe of actors, makeup people, costumers, light technicians and the like. On top of all this, Schumacher and Lloyd Webber even came up with an "origin" for the Phantom, explaining how he came to be at the opera in the first place.

This not only makes the Phantom even more heroic in a Byronic sense (i.e., sympathetic), but deepens the character of Madame Giry, played by Miranda Richardson.

Budgeted at sixty million dollars, principal photography on *The Phantom of the Opera* commenced in late 2002 and spread across eight sound stages at Pinewood Studios in the UK. Unlike most musicals, where actors lip-synch to prerecorded tracks, Schumacher attempted something different. The actors sung to temporary tracks so that they had "total freedom to act the music," and then, after shooting, returned to a recording studio to hone their performances.[120]

After several months of editing by renowned cutter Terry Rawlings, it came time to promote the film. Unlike *Chicago*, which cloaked its nature as an all-singing, all-dancing musical in its prerelease advertisements and trailers, *The Phantom of the Opera* was billed openly and proudly as "the world's biggest musical."

Andrew Lloyd Webber's The Phantom of the Opera opened on 622 screens in the United States on December 22, 2004, and grossed an impressive four million dollars, catapulting it into the tenth slot for the weekend box office. Impressively, its numbers grew during the second weekend, by nearly five million dollars. General release began on January 22, and the movie had grossed a respectable seventy million dollars worldwide at the time of this book's publication. Perhaps not a blockbuster, but a hit nonetheless.

Alas, this doesn't mean critics actually liked it. In fact, the reviewing community was fiercely divided over the film's merits. CNN's Christy Lemire called it a "bombastic monstrosity,"[121] while Daniel Neman of the *Richmond-Times Dispatch* wrote that "director Joel Schumacher heads first into a world of visual excess, doing nothing to refute his reputation as the worst director in America."[122]

Others, like Roger Ebert, made efforts to praise the film but go after the source material. "I do not think Lloyd Webber wrote a very good musical," Ebert suggested. "The story is thin beer for the time it takes to tell it, and the music is maddeningly repetitious."[123]

Others rather appreciated *The Phantom of the Opera*. "On its own, the film is just about perfect," raved Colin Covert for the *Minneapolis Star Tribune*. "Viewers who accept it on those terms will be swept away."[124]

That seemed to be the trick—an acceptance of the conventions of musical theater heralded a good review; while dislike of musical theater seemed to portend a negative one. Perhaps one reason the film has drawn such varying reactions is that it makes no apologies for what it is. It is audacious spectacle, overblown musical theater all the way through. There is no special contract (like the interior monologues of Selma in *Dancer in the Dark* or Roxie Hart in *Chicago*) to make it palatable or easier to relate to. There is little psychological, political, or social depth (like *Camp, Evita,* or *The Singing Detective*), and it clearly lacks the humor of *South Park: Bigger, Longer & Uncut* or *Everyone Says I Love You*. Nor does *The Phantom of the Opera* depict an actual real-life person or true events, like the well-received biopics *De-Lovely* and *Ray*.

Instead, *The Phantom of the Opera* is unabashed musical theater. By turns pompous, big, emotional, and grand, it will strike many viewers as camp, others as a faithful re-creation (with a few tweaks) of a popular property.

Joel Schumacher, never the most restrained of directors, delves whole hog into epic storytelling here, marshaling every tool in his director's quiver, from computer generated imagery to colorization, to make this film a sumptuous visual feast. Some may think it overdone, but really, that's kind of the point, isn't it?

Certainly, it is difficult to take seriously a moment such as Christine's snow-laden stroll through an overcrowded cemetery teeming with gothic statuary, but the image is so lovely and baroque that one gasps at the audacity on display. Reality is taken up a notch to the grand style of Lloyd Webber's overblown music. And this, lest we forget, is what the traditional movie musical form is *supposed* to be about. Not championing naturalism, but artifice. Old-fashioned musicals featured worlds where the locations and settings represented the inner minds and drives of the characters, and this *Phantom of the Opera* lives up to that tradition.

It is also true that Christine's first visit to the Phantom's underground lair lacks menace and mystery, and feels oddly Disneyesque with its automated, rising and lowering, fully lit candelabra, but even this touch seems forgivable. The passion and enthusiasm of the young cast make up for most questions of logic and these lapses into camp, at least for this viewer. By the time the film has reached the Phantom's opera, a fiery, hellish staging of *Don Juan*, it had me in its grip. I enjoyed the seduction, wondered what course Christine would choose, and felt blown away by the pure grandeur of the whole enterprise. Call me a romantic, but for me, it worked.

Butler is a fine actor anyway, but he brings considerable presence to this role, making the Phantom a genuine Byronic hero: doomed, self-loathing, but not without moments of glory and genius. Yet it is Emmy Rossum who emerges as the real treat, and, one suspects, Schumacher knows it.

He "understands what he has in Rossum and often frames her with the sort of closeup that evokes a Golden Age movie star in her budding glory,"[125] suggested Lisa Kennedy in the *Denver Post*. "She's a heart-stopping presence,"[126] *Newsweek*'s David Ansen agreed, and indeed, she holds the attention of the audience through all the camera acrobatics, special effects, and musical crescendoes like a seasoned pro. This is a star-making performance, pure and simple. Rossum is dazzling to gaze upon, guileless in her innocence, and an accomplished singer with an astonishing voice.

Though it may be dismissed as silly, overserious kitsch, *The Phantom of the Opera* is actually sort of refreshing. For once, a musical doesn't feel the need to explain itself, to rationalize the qualities of its genre. It makes no apologies for what it is, and evidences great joy in the artifice of a form Americans once adored. Realism is shunned in this *Phantom of the Opera*, and that will trouble the literal minded but thrill the romantics.

The period between 2001 and 2004 truly represents a high time for movie musicals. *Chicago* was the great crowd-pleaser to be sure, but fare like *A Mighty Wind, Camp, The Singing Detective,* and *De-Lovely* also proved that musical films could once again speak meaningfully to contemporary audiences. *The Phantom of the Opera* itself is something that would have been impossible to sell in 1994: an old-fashioned musical.

And damned proud of it.

CHAPTER FIVE
Cathode Razzle-Dazzle

The Musical on Television

FAIRY-TALE TELEVISION

In the good old days, when musicals were big business at the box office, television was often dismissed as a dirty cousin to cinema, a black sheep. Sure the boob-tube was siphoning off cinemagoers, and therefore a threat, but scholars didn't view TV as anything approaching an art form.

Much has changed since those days, and few people today see television placing second in any contest. TV programs become movies; movies become TV shows; and actors leap from one venue to the other without repercussions or discussions of "slumming." Everything's intermingled now, and it's one big, happy entertainment world.

The fortunes of television art were bolstered considerably in the 1990s, the period of this book's focus, when a bevy of innovative series creators from David Lynch, Steve Bochco, David E. Kelly, and Aaron Sorkin to Chris Carter and Joss Whedon led the hourly drama format into new territory, and subsequently a new apex, with deeper characters, continuing storylines and story arcs, and more witty dialogue. Stronger, more overtly cinematic visuals also accompanied many of these programs, particularly *Buffy the Vampire Slayer* (1997–2003), *The X-Files* (1993–2002), and *NYPD Blue* (1993–2005), thereby making the argument for TV as art, a media designed for vetting long-form stories across many chapters.

The musical format has succeeded on TV before in small doses as special one-night events, especially in the 1950s and 1960s, but in the 1990s television again welcomed the musical with open arms, and proved a rather nice shelter for the genre as its fortunes in movie houses rose and fell and rose again.

Two men have been especially crucial in bringing the musical to TV: Storyline Entertainment producers Craig Zadan and Neil Meron, who also produced the film, *Chicago*. In 1993, after deciding that they would only work in television if capable of bringing "something different to it,"[1] they embarked on a project that would have a decade's worth of repercussions.

On December 12, 1993, Zadan and Meron presented Bette Midler as Mama Rose, a role Ethel Merman had memorably played on stage in the 1950s, for a three-hour adaptation of the Broadway show *Gypsy*. Featuring familiar songs from the Jule Styne–Stephen Sondheim score, including "Let Me Entertain You," "Everything's Coming up Roses," and "Small World," the musical comedy about an aggressive backstage mother boasted sterling production values. Critics liked it too, and the movie performed surprisingly well in the ratings. Completing the circle, it was eventually nominated for twelve Emmy Awards.

Gypsy was such a watershed, in fact, that musical pop star Whitney Houston soon communicated with Storyline Entertainment and informed the producers she wanted to do a musical on TV too. The result of this telephone call was the development of a new version of *Cinderella*. This proved a daunting task, however, as the story had already been adapted successfully to television twice before, once headlining Julie Andrews in 1957 and then again starring Lesley Ann Warren in 1965. The Julie Andrews production reeled in a whopping one hundred million viewers.[2]

Instead of fearing invidious comparisons to past glories, Meron and Zadan went for broke. The new version of *Cinderella* retained Whitney Houston as an executive producer, but because of the singer's recent pregnancy, Houston opted not to take the titular role, instead playing the Fairy Godmother. In her stead, the eighteen-year-old star of UPN's *Moesha* (1996–2001), a charmer named Brandy, was cast. Brandy's album had already sold four million copies,[3] so her casting was a move that made sense, especially as the new version of *Cinderella* was being eyed as a multicultural take on the material.

The twelve-million-dollar production, entitled *Rodgers and Hammerstein's Cinderella*, was directed by Robert Iscove (*From Justin to Kelly*), choreographed by Rob Marshall (*Chicago*), and also came to star Bernadette Peters (*Pennies from Heaven*), Whoopi Goldberg, and Jason Alexander. "This was an extremely ambitious production in terms of doing a musical and spending the amount of money we did and attracting the cast we did," noted Charles Hirschhorn, the president of Walt Disney TV.[4]

The new *Cinderella* aired November 2, 1997, and drew positive notices. "It's a whirlwind of images and activity and sounds, a cartoon come to life. And that's probably pretty much what it should be," wrote Ray Richmond in *Variety*.[5]

More importantly, the color-blind reimagination of *Cinderella* racked up ABC's highest rating in that time slot in years, by some accounts, garnering sixty million viewers.[6] Other reports indicate the viewership was actually nearer thirty-four million, but even that figure was an amazing coup in an age when network ratings were slipping.[7] The TV movie won an Emmy for Best Art Design (for Randy Ser), and Marshall and Iscove were each nominated too, for Best Choreography and Direction, respectively.

The unexpected success of *Cinderella* led to a full production slate of musicals for television, not just on ABC, but across the board. ABC and Storyline Entertainment immediately reteamed in 1999 for a new adaptation of the Broadway smash, *Annie*. Rob Marshall directed an all-star cast that included Kathy Bates, Alan Cumming, and *Alias*'s Victor Garber as Daddy Warbucks. Alicia Morton played Annie. The TV-movie shot in the summer of 1999 for air during November sweeps, and again, Emmy nominations rolled in. This time, Marshall picked up a win for Best Choreography.

Next up from the prolific Storyline assembly line was a new version of another Rodgers and Hammerstein epic, *South Pacific*. Heralded as "the most expensive TV production in network history,"[8] the production filmed on location in Australia, and starred Glenn Close, Harry Connick Jr., and Rade Sherbedgia. Winning two Emmy nominations, the lush Rodgers and Hammerstein remake also broke into the Top Ten weekly rankings in the Nielsens rating.

Who said audience didn't like musicals anymore?

A remake of *The Music Man* starring Matthew Broderick and Victor Garber arrived in 2003 and, like its predecessors, picked up a handful of Emmy nominations. It was a pale reflection of the original 1962 film starring Robert Preston, and by now, the Storyline TV movies were becoming part of the expected landscape, and thus less gloriously received. The formula had been set: a popular property (i.e., brand name), a big star, and presto, good ratings. The problem was that nobody seemed to be investing the time to make *original* musical films for television.

Outside of ABC, MTV itself also got into the musical business in the 1990s, presenting *Carmen: A Hip Hopera* starring Beyoncé Knowles, Mekhi Phifer, Mos Def, Wyclef Jean, and Lil' Bow Wow in May 2001. The music network followed *Carmen* with a musical version of the classic novel *Wuthering Heights* in 2003. Erika Christensen, Mike Vogel, Christopher Kennedy Masterson, and

Katherine M. Heigl starred in the $3.5 million production, which shot in Puerto Rico. Stephen Trask, the composer of *Hedwig and the Angry Inch* and *Camp*, contributed the music.

Already announced for future consumption were several additional ABC–Storyline Entertainment musicals, including *1776*, *Once Upon a Mattress*, *The Wiz*, *Mame*, *Fiddler on the Roof*, and *The Hunchback of Notre Dame*. MTV was reportedly preparing a musical version of *Faust* and a new interpretation of *The Phantom of the Opera* called simply, *Phantom*.

On television in the mid-to-late-nineties, the musical was anything but dead, and the venue proved a fertile training ground for artists of the twenty-first-century musical cinema like Marshall, Iscove, Zadan, and Meron.

COP ROCK . . .

One-off television adaptations, special event programming featuring popular and well-known shows, such as *Annie* or *South Pacific*, are one thing, but what about all-singing, all-dancing musical presentations during hour-long TV episodes? That's an entirely different story. Still, several artists have tried it over the years, often at their own peril.

Once upon a time, there was a sung-through musical television program that became the stuff of legend, and its very name is today an easy shorthand for high-concept entertainment gone horribly awry. Of course, I write of the infamous *Cop Rock* (1990). This was a program that ran on ABC for eleven episodes, from September 26 to December 26, 1990. Created by Steve Bochco, the series was, as the title indicates, an unlikely fusion of gritty cop TV paradigms with the artificial format of the movie musical. The series not only frightened away viewers (and frequently ranked in the Nielsen cellar at eightieth place[9]), but scared critics too. *People Weekly*'s David Hiltbrand got cold sweats, dreading "to think how bad" *Cop Rock* could possibly get after the show settled in "for a few weeks" and was "struggling for viable melodies."[10]

Still, there exists a small devoted following that fervently believes *Cop Rock* was not the pop-culture disaster the brand name portends. "I think the show will be held up in years to come as brilliant, although maybe ahead of its time," ABC president Bob Iger boldly predicted at the time of the show's debut.[11]

Maybe he had a point. The TV series did win two Emmys, for editing and Randy Newman's music and lyrics in the pilot.

Other authorities stake out a different claim for *Cop Rock*, considering it the revolutionary harbinger of 1990s efforts by creators like David E. Kelly.

"In television, Bochco's series served as a stepping stone or hinge between Potter's *The Singing Detective* and comedies and musical dramedies, particularly *Ally McBeal* and other musical episodes of series including *The Drew Carey Show, Chicago Hope,* and *Buffy the Vampire Slayer*," suggests scholar George Plasketes in his article "*Cop Rock* revisited: unsung series and musical hinge in cross-genre evolution," which appeared in the *Journal of Popular Film and Television*.[12]

No doubt he's right. But that doesn't mean *Cop Rock* was any good. And it only got worse as it went along, depending sometimes on crossovers with more popular Bochco shows, such as *L.A. Law* (1986–1994) and even *Hill Street Blues* (1981–1987).

"*Cop Rock* was very bad," states *Buffy the Vampire Slayer* creator Joss Whedon. "I have very specific reasons why I think it was bad, and they have to do with how hard it is to make a good musical. It was an ill-conceived idea in the first place, but poorly executed by very talented people."

An important missing link or not, *Cop Rock* initially had the effect of scaring everybody in the TV industry away from musicals, not encouraging more of 'em.

Still, that didn't mean that musicals weren't sneaking back into episodic television in other, less extreme ways. In 1991, an animated series called *The Simpsons* premiered on Fox, and after a few seasons, began to occasionally lampoon the musical format in a number of episodes. In the series's fourth season, an episode titled "A Streetcar Named Marge" reimagined the work of Tennessee Williams as a musical. Another show, "Marge vs. the Monorail" was a spoof of *The Music Man*.[13] There was even an episode that depicted little Lisa Simpson as an Evita Perón figure in her public elementary school when she ascended to the class presidency.

"You only have to look at *The Simpsons*," Craig Pearce suggests. "That's a very specific contract with the audience that they really love and get. Within *The Simpsons*, you can have someone breaking into song and you do, quite a bit. It's Any Town, but an extraordinary version of Any Town. Homer is everyman, but a rather extreme version of everyman. So within that contract that is made, it's very easy for characters to break into song and dance."

Song and dance didn't just happen on *The Simpsons* either. The ABC sitcom *The Drew Carey Show* (1995–2004)—another series about the everyman—also began to develop "quirky musical numbers" to spice up its sitcom half-hours.[14] These musical episodes featured songs like The Vogues' "Five O'Clock World" and Tower of Power's "What Is Hip." The show was a hit in the Nielsen ratings too, and again, the music-oriented episodes proved among the most beloved.

"You see a lot of TV shows doing what I refer to as variety shows and calling them musicals, and I would say this about *Everyone Says I Love You* and *Cop Rock*, where they do a scene and then have a song," reports Joss Whedon. "If the song isn't the scene, then there's no point in having the song. If the song isn't the dramatic climax and culmination and very meat of the scene, then it really is a variety show. You did a skit, then you did a song."

In the late 1990s, elements of the musical format began to become even more an integral part of the pop culture fabric. David E. Kelly's *Ally McBeal* (1997–2002), often staged zany musical numbers in office bathrooms, set musical sequences in a nightclub, and even had singer Vonda Shepherd among its regular cast to belt out a variety of nostalgic golden oldies about love and romance.

Ally McBeal, along with David Kelly shows like *The Practice* (1997–2004), also pioneered a cliché called "the sad walk home," a musical sequence that seemed to end every dramatic hour in the late 1990s. Here, a dejected character has learned a valuable life lesson and walks home alone on the street, brooding, as a great old song on the soundtrack accompanies this solitary march.

This sequence wasn't really a musical number per se, but each production seemed to understand that artists could say things better and more powerfully with music; that emotions are suddenly more touching if accompanied by a beloved nostalgic tune.

"The musical montage has become such a staple of film and TV that scripts must be thirty pages long by now: 'He walks down the street. Cue oldie,'" says Joss Whedon. "Whether it's modern pop or a bunch of standards . . . it's just a really boring video. If they would just dance to pass the time while they're walking sadly down the street, they would do us all a favor."

ONCE MORE WITH FEELING

When I interviewed Joss Whedon for this book, he opened the interview by telling me that he "was ready to give" me what he believes will be "the most in-depth analysis of Drew Carey's *Geppetto*" yet published.

That didn't happen, but what I did learn is something that might surprise the casual *Buffy the Vampire Slayer* fan. In addition to his incredible talents in writing and directing movies and television, Whedon also happens to be an unrepentant aficionado of classic movie musicals. More than that, it is a subject about which he is incredibly passionate, and committed.

"Dancing is my favorite thing to watch," he says. "Everything that's great about cinema can be pretty much expressed by Fred Astaire's feet. Every guy who ever jumped through a plate-glass window in the eighties was doing that because he couldn't dance. Action replaced the musical in a way, as this exultant expression of human endeavor . . . people doing what you can't believe they can do. The closest thing we had to great dancer movies in that decade was Jackie Chan."

Considering his sensibilities, it shouldn't come as a surprise then, to learn that when Joss Whedon needs to relax, he heads for his laser disc collection, grabs the remote control, and slips right into to the equivalent of musical nirvana.

"My favorite musical number is Fred Astaire and Joan Leslie in *The Sky's the Limit* (1943)," he describes. "It [the movie] came and went, and nobody cared. It happened to be put out on laserdisc, as so many great old movies were that nobody cared about. It's not a great movie; its most famous number is 'My Shining Hour.' It also has Fred Astaire introducing the song 'One for My Baby,' where he does a huge, drunk, kick-a-lot-of-glasses dance, which is great fun. I happen to be a huge Joan Leslie fan. I adore her. She plays a USO show girl, and he's a fighter pilot pretending to be a draft dodger who's following her around. He gets up on stage with her, and she says, 'Go away, I'm doing my number' and of course, they starting dancing. It is absolutely like therapy for me. When I freak out—which is more often than I care to say—I can put this on. Chapter five on my laser disc."

Given Whedon's familiarity and love of movie musicals, perhaps it is no shock that his series, the much beloved *Buffy the Vampire Slayer*, featured a full-blown, book-style musical during its early sixth season, in 2001. It was an idea, according to Whedon, whose time had finally come.

During the fourth year working on *Buffy*, Whedon directed a brilliant and frightening silent episode called "Hush" in which Buffy Summers and her Scooby Gang lose the ability to speak because of the supernatural intervention of ghoulish villains known as the Gentlemen. The experience of crafting that unique tale led to ideas that would eventually inform the musical episode, "Once More with Feeling."

"With 'Hush,' and this goes for the musical too, I never made episodes that were stunts for the sake of stunts. I wouldn't do a black-and-white episode, because that's not the experience of the people within the episode. If I can't make it about them, then there's no excuse for doing it," Whedon describes.

"The fact is, the silent episode made sense in that world, as horror. To be unable to scream is a terrifying thing, and it made sense in *Buffy*. What was interesting about it was that when I started to write it at first, I was just terrified. I thought, 'At least I know Buffy is going to have sex with her boyfriend. That's two minutes I know they don't have to talk, and we'll watch.' Then as we went through the season, I realized it was too early for them to have sex, and was like, 'Oh, I lost my crutch, I'm a dead man, I'll never be able to do this!' But what was interesting was that I came to the realization that the show was really about communication, about the fact that when we stop talking, we start communicating. The idea of language getting in the way of real communication. When I realized that, everything became very interesting. The reason I'm going on and on in a really boring fashion about this, is that 'Once More with Feeling' was kind of the sequel to that.

"The thing about musicals is you sing what you can't say. In the same way as shutting up [in 'Hush'] caused everybody to open up in ways they hadn't before, singing did the same thing. So the episodes were really a pair, because they said, 'People can't really talk to each other, but when they're in a situation that transcends language, they will find out the truth about themselves.' Ultimately, that's the most important thing in writing a musical, and the reason why a lot of things that call themselves musicals in the modern era have not been. The heart of the matter—what the person is feeling, what the person needs to communicate, the great revelation, the denouement, whatever it is— all of this should be expressed through song, or there is no reason to have a song. Unless someone's a really good dancer. Or you're bored."

Joss Whedon's "Once More with Feeling" opens with the familiar denizens of Sunnydale going about their normal lives. But when Buffy, the Chosen One and slayer of demons, patrols the local cemetery, she unexpectedly finds herself singing a yearning ballad, "Going Through the Motions."

The next morning, her friends, the Scooby Gang, confirm that they too have been inexplicably bursting into song. This precipitates a round of research, and before long, Buffy and her friends are exploring the notion that a demon has come to town, one who can make people act as though they are performing a "wacky Broadway nightmare."

In the course of their songs, Buffy and her friends begin to reveal hidden facets of themselves. For instance, Spike, a platinum-headed vampire in love with the Slayer, reveals his amorous feelings in the rock and roll tune, "Rest in Peace." Buffy's buddies Anya and Xander sing of their fear of marriage and commitment in a 1930s-style pastiche called "I'll Never Tell." Giles, Buffy's mentor, sings a sad song about his fear that his presence in town is actually holding the Slayer back, keeping her from growing up.

Finally, when Buffy's little sister Dawn is captured by the demon, Sweet, Buffy must put on a show-stopping number to rescue her. Unfortunately, in the process, Buffy reveals more of her own dilemmas and yearning to her friends than she might have wished.

"Musicals on TV can be self-indulgent; they can be pointless," Whedon considers. "*Xena* did it. It worked for *Xena*. It's that kind of universe too. It worked in a different way than it worked for *Buffy*, but it certainly wasn't out of the blue for them."

Another reason to craft a musical episode on *Buffy* involved the nature of the show's talent. Many of the actors on the series had it in them to, quite frankly, sing their hearts out. "I had a few cast members who were singers, particularly Tony [Anthony Stewart Head], who had done singing on stage, and *Rocky Horror*, and we used to talk about it all the time, because we were both aficionados. And I was like, 'I could never write a musical episode of *Buffy* because it would take six months,' but then after five years [with the show on the air], I actually took time off, so I had six months to write the episode. So I used it; about four months to write it and two months to prep it before we actually shot for eight days. It might have been a little more than eight days."

One of the complexities of creating a musical within the narrative structure of a dramatic TV series with continuing plot lines involved scheduling. "We were always behind in breaking stories," Whedon describes. "It was hard to keep the show afloat, and by that time *Angel* (1999–2004) was on the air. But at the end of that season [five], we pile-drove story breaking."

At that point, with seven episodes of the sixth season mapped out, it was possible for Whedon to determine precisely how his musical story would fit in, and where in their continuing story arcs the characters would be during his hour. Planning in advance also gave the cast opportunity for input about the singing and dancing.

"And what everybody got was the chance to say, 'I like this, I like that,'" Whedon reveals. "Ally [Alyson Hannigan] was like, 'I have no voice. I'm game, but you don't want to feature me.' I knew that Amber [Benson] had a great voice and loved to sing, and so I made their scene together her ballad to Ally.

"I knew Tony was my ballad guy. I knew James [Marsters] was my rock-'n'roll singer, and Michelle [Trachtenberg] wanted to dance a little. I knew what everybody's strength was. What I didn't know was how good Emma [Caulfield] was going to be. That was a revelation, but I knew she was my musical comedy girl . . . so everybody got to do what they were comfortable with. I built the thing around what I knew they could do, or what I believed they could do."

But that doesn't mean that cast and crew members weren't frightened by the prospect of creating a musical, a far cry from horror and fantasy. "There were not no tears," Whedon says. "There were *some* tears. Some of them were fake; some were real. There was some joy. What there wasn't was anybody saying, 'Well, it won't really happen.' Because I think they'd figured out by that time that no matter how insane it sounded, if I said I was going to do something, I tended to do it. So there was resignation."

Whedon, who comes from a background in musical theater, not only crafted the episode's narrative to fit the tenor of the series and the specific story arc, but then composed music and wrote lyrics for a whopping eleven songs. He was already a triple threat (writer-director-producer), but now his repertoire had doubled!

"I had some lessons on the piano before I started *Buffy*, but then *Buffy* took over my life and I stopped doing everything," Whedon explains. "Basically, I could bang out a few chords, and I was spending more and more time doing that. What I did do was teach myself guitar. There were some songs [for the episode] that were going to need to be written on a guitar, like Spike's song and 'Where Do We Go From Here?' There were a few songs where you wanted a different vernacular. But I did write all that stuff . . . and I cannot play it."

While directing "Once More with Feeling," there was a ghost haunting the set, according to Whedon, and it was one even Buffy couldn't slay. "*Cop Rock* came up plenty of times, mostly from me, who watched almost every episode," jokes Whedon.

Actually, shooting the musical (on basically four locations) went smoothly and Whedon kept his eye on the bigger picture, even if grandeur was difficult to achieve on a tight budget and within the constraints of a TV schedule. "Did

I yearn for a vista?" he asks. "I wouldn't have hated one, but I thought that we managed to create something that felt bigger than normal life, more transcendent and more beautiful."

To facilitate that look, Whedon brought in classic old cranes for certain shots, and did as much cutting in-camera as was possible. "I was able to do everything I wanted," he says. In particular, Whedon was happy with the sweep and epic quality of the episode's first big number, "Going Through the Motions," which depicts Buffy singing about her personal issues and ennui while also combating vampires and demons in a graveyard. Set at night, this number sets the tone for the delightful hour to come.

"That number was very specifically the Disney number, what Jeffrey Katzenberg used to refer to as the 'I Want,' the yearning ballad. Stylistically, it's very much of that idiom too," Whedon relates. "I really wanted that very Disney, perfect yearning moment, and to have Buffy come out of a big note from behind a dusting vampire—which couldn't have been more perfect. And then there's this dust circling lazily out of the corner of the frame as the song ends. That to me . . . I was just in Heaven."

When "Once More with Feeling" aired on November 6, 2001, it was actually an extended hour of *Buffy the Vampire Slayer*, clocking in at forty-eight minutes instead of the routine forty-two. The positive response was instantaneous and overwhelming. Everybody, including *TV Guide*, adored the show and the magic spell it had cast. Television critic David Klein called the musical "absolutely captivating," and "like nothing I've seen on regular series television, and I've watched and written professionally about TV for more than twenty years."[15]

Viewer response even more over positive, if that was possible. Fans loved the show and were quick to rate "Once More with Feeling" as one of the best (if not the very best) hour of *Buffy*'s impressive multiyear run. Some viewers who had never been fans of *Buffy* watched the episode and became fascinated with it.

"It's got, in a weird way, its own cult, separate from the show," Whedon admits. "People love music, and this is the thing that people forget, and it's easy to forget, because if you do it wrong—hello *Newsies*! Which, by the way, I own, so I shouldn't be dissing it.

"It's such an alchemy," Whedon says of the musical form. "It's so hard to get it right, but if a musical really does hit people, they'll love it more than any damn thing in this world. Because music speaks to people more than anything else. It just does. It's the most ephemeral—and without being too specific—the most meaningful art that there could possibly be. When you put in exciting lyrics, characters you love, and all that good stuff, everything heightens. It takes you to another level of existence.

"I'm glad I pulled it off. There were times when I was terrified. James Marsters said while we were shooting that episode that 'if we don't have the shit scared out of us at least once a year, we're not doing our jobs.'"

Mission accomplished.

Despite the success of "Once More with Feeling," Whedon has been in no hurry to pepper his other series with musical episodes, despite his love of the genre.

"I was asked, 'Do you want to do a musical episode of *Angel* or *Firefly*?'" Whedon reveals. "And I said, 'Not in a million years.' Those shows don't lend themselves to it. The thing about *Buffy* is that you do the musical episode without violating the reality of *Buffy*. That's the most important thing to me. What's hilarious about working in fantasy is that you can say, 'The evil twin thing? That's not reality, that's bullshit! Who buys that?! But the dwarf growing out of someone's head is fine . . . ' You have this seemingly arbitrary, but in fact, very strict sense of what can go on in this world.

"And Buffy is so sophomoric, romantic, colorful, tense, sexual . . . I think half the episodes feel like they're about to burst into song anyway. There's so much to say about every relationship in it. To me, my favorite moment in the musical is Giles and Tara singing together, their duet to Buffy and Willow. Those are two totally different relationships. Neither one is the central love relationship on the show, but they carry as much weight as anything. And that's the kind of show *Buffy* is. And it's also a comedy. So to say a demon has come in who causes musicals makes perfect sense in that world. It doesn't make sense in the *Angel* world to me. It definitely makes no sense in the *Firefly* world. It's a different kind of choice."

Between *Moulin Rouge* in theaters in June, and *Buffy*'s "Once More with Feeling" on TV in November, the year 2001 proved to be a time when the musical form received heightened visibility, not just in the press, but among an almost virgin audience: the fan boy (and I count myself in that demographic). Between *Stars Wars* lead McGregor (and a raft of amazing visual effects) in *Moulin Rouge* and a droll musical hour on a favorite television production, a certain slice of the populace who previously bore precious little interest in musicals were suddenly dealing with the form, and appreciating its glories for perhaps the first time since they were dragged to *Grease* in the 1970s, or to *Flashdance* by their girlfriends in the eighties.

Phantom of the Genre

As we dance into the twenty-first century, the movie musical survives. The format is off life-support and in recovery. Now the doctors (i.e., movie critics) just need to confirm the diagnosis.

The continuing debate about whether or not musicals are really "dead" is, in some senses, an artificial one. When the majority of critics were blindsided by *Moulin Rouge* and *Chicago* in 2001 and 2002, and enjoyed these efforts, the genre was suddenly "back" with a big fat exclamation point.

Yet in the years since 2002 and *Chicago*'s impressive Oscar performance, critics have been just as quick to pounce on the fact that the anticipated musical comeback never arrived. This assessment comes despite the debut of unique and worthwhile musicals like *Camp, The Singing Detective,* and *De-Lovely,* in less than two years. Perhaps this focus on bad news results from the reviewer's obsession with the horse race—whether or not a musical grosses a ton of money—rather than the artistic success of individual films.

Frankly, not every musical is going to generate the same business *Chicago* did, just as not every animated film is a *Shrek 2*, or every action-adventure film, *Spider-Man 2*. However, when a *Hulk, Van Helsing,* or *The Chronicles of Riddick* fails at the box office, critics do not immediately jump to the conclusion that action-adventure is dead as a viable genre. And the same is undeniably true of musicals.

"If they make four of them, and they all lose money, and they're not popular," musical historian Thomas Hischack lamented after *Chicago*, "we'll be right back where we were."[1]

"They're like Westerns," suggests Joss Whedon. "They just don't make that many of them, so every musical has to have at least nine articles asking 'Will this revive the musical?' And westerns have to have 'Will this revive the western?' You don't see 'Will this revive the women's picture?' 'Will this revive the Miami drug lord movie?' It's part of the curse. The term [musical] itself connotes something archaic. If you could think of a new name for it, then it might not be such a problem."

Even with critics second-guessing its condition, the genre will nonetheless survive, even if not every single new musical emerges as a blockbuster for the ages. *Camp, The Singing Detective,* and *De-Lovely* were all produced on smaller budgets and have staked out interesting territory. They've handed off the baton and audiences are waiting for the next generation to grab it.

"I'd like to see more of the experimentation," relates director Todd Haynes, "because I think it's a delirious genre. It's crazy and it should stay radical and unexpected, and connected to innovation and experimentation, and not some kind of mainstream mindlessness. There's something that's too weird about it."

In the end, experimentation and innovation may not prove as impressive to studios as the box office haul of *Moulin Rouge* or *Chicago*, but these elements are surely signs that the genre is getting back on its feet.

Looking to the future, one can already detect this is true. In contrast to the mid-1990s, when musicals were so despised that they were unable to garner release (*The Fantasticks*), or were forced to undergo musical-extraction surgery (*I'll Do Anything*), musical films dot a number of production slates as this book goes to press.

Mel Brooks's *The Producers*, which was once a nonmusical film, back in 1968, then a hit musical stage show on Broadway, is soon to complete the circle. It will soon premiere as a full blown movie musical with Nathan Lane and Matthew Broderick re-creating their popular Broadway performances.

A remake of *Bye-Bye Birdie* is due from Columbia pictures in the next year too, and those prolific *Chicago* producers Meron and Zadan have been toiling on another musical remake, this time of that eighties kitsch classic, *Footloose*—where the characters actually sing.[2]

Before long, audiences can also anticipate Universal's new version of *Jesus Christ Superstar* for *The Passion of the Christ* age, and an updated rendering of *Carmen*—possibly to star Jennifer Lopez.[3]

After the success of *Chicago*, Harvey Weinstein claimed he wanted to be the next Arthur Freed, and so Miramax has *Pippin* already in development. Director John Turturro's original vision, *Romance and Cigarettes* stars Susan Sarandon and James Gandolfini, and looks perched to take *The Singing Detective* approach to the next level. Even the long-awaited and much delayed *Rent* has now been greenlit, and begins shooting in 2005 in San Francisco.[4]

"Can musicals survive on screen?" asks Jay Cocks, on the subject this book has examined. "Well look, nobody would have thought that you could get away with a ballet ending in a movie until *The Red Shoes*. And that's why, when *The Red Shoes* became a hit, there had to be a big ballet number at the end of *Singin' in the Rain*. So they did the 'Broadway Melody' number. Again, Stanley Donen told me this. Could you do it again? Yes!

"You can do *anything*," Cocks stresses. "Anything is a tool, you just have to fit it into the proper context."

And that's the hard part. Critics may complain about either the dearth or the death of musicals, but the fact is, they aren't easy films to make, and that's a fact that's not likely to change.

"I think what people come to realize when they study musicals is that the musical is really the hardest thing to do," suggests Craig Pearce. "There are all these elements. There's the music, there's the singing, there's the dance. These are all things that you don't normally do in a film, and just from a physical standpoint, they're difficult."

Despite challenges, there's every reason to believe that, given current trends, behind the red curtain awaits another *Moulin Rouge*, another *Chicago*, another *De-Lovely*, *Velvet Goldmine*, or *Hedwig*, each ready to put its stamp on the genre.

Todd Haynes presents our closing thought: "It's easy for people to dismiss the musical, and say, 'Oh, it's just so unreal! People break into song!' But movies are unreal! The whole nature of that medium is about taking us somewhere else, so in that spirit, the musical is one of the strongest examples of what film can be."

If that's the case, and inventive filmmakers keep that in mind, then musicals will keep razzle-dazzling us for decades to come, in shapes and fashions even the MTV generation can't begin to imagine. The fact of the matter is, thanks to the artists who keep the format humming, something great may be coming. Who knows? It's only just out of reach—down the block, on a beach . . .

Maybe tonight . . .

APPENDIX A
Conventions of the Movie Musical

1996–2004

Musicals during the modern era of "rebirth" circa 1996–2004 built on the rich and varied history of the musical format over the decades of the twentieth century. The filmmakers behind these often extraordinary films are quite inventive, but they also construct their new entertainments on past triumphs, adapting old conceits and expressing them in a fresh vernacular, or if you prefer, within a new "contract." Below is a list of common movie musical conventions that were in use during this period and the films wherein they appear. (For a notion to become one of the modern musical's conventions, it must reappear in the era at least three times.)

Willkommen: The Narrator/Master of Ceremonies

In Bob Fosse's *Cabaret*, Joel Grey portrayed the (possibly) sinister Master of Ceremonies at Berlin's Kat-Kat Club. His character reappeared throughout the film in new, relevant musical numbers that revealed different shades of the story. Many movie musicals of the modern age have found it convenient to include an analogous character, one who offers a unique perspective on the drama unfolding, and sometimes even serves as the story's narrator, either musical (the band leader in *Chicago*), dramatic (D. J. in *Everyone Says I Love You*), or, as in the case of *Evita*'s Che, both.

1. Che (Antonio Banderas), *Evita* (1996)
2. D. J. (Natasha Lyonne), *Everyone Says I Love You* (1997)
3. Female voiceover narrator, *Velvet Goldmine* (1998)
4. Christian (Ewan McGregor), *Moulin Rouge* (2001)
5. The bandleader (Taye Diggs), *Chicago* (2002)

Pennies from Heaven: The Hangman's Noose

(aka, "Hang the Bastard/Hang Him High")

During the climax of Herbert Ross's movie adaptation of Dennis Potter's *Pennies from Heaven* (1981), our protagonist, Arthur Parker (Steve Martin), is arrested for a crime he didn't commit, and the innocent man is led to the gallows, where he is eventually executed. For some reason, the hangman's noose has become a recurring image in this new age of movie musicals, as has the scenario of an innocent citizen arrested and eventually executed, or rescued at the last minute.

1. *Cannibal: The Musical* (1999)
2. *Dancer in the Dark* (2000)
3. *Chicago* (2002)

The Hills Are Alive With . . .

Considering the fact that Robert Wise's *The Sound of Music* (1965) is one of the top-grossing musicals of all time, perhaps it is no surprise that a variety of musicals from the new era explicitly reference the film in dialogue and song. The hills are alive with homage in:

1. *Everyone Says I Love You* (1997): After the "Hooray for Captain Spalding" number, Woody Allen's character, Joe Berlin, makes explicit mention of *The Sound of Music* song "Climb Ev'ry Mountain."
2. *Dancer in the Dark* (2000): When Bjork's Golden Heart, Selma, is having a bad day, facing incarceration and eventually execution, all she can do to stop the madness is sing from that classic *Sound of Music* composition "My Favorite Things." Also, throughout the film, Selma is working on a community theater production of *The Sound of Music*.
3. *Moulin Rouge* (2002): In attempting to express the new bohemian modernism, Christian the poet, played by Ewan McGregor, belts out the opening refrain from the Wise film's song "The Sound of Music."

I Won't Dance, Don't Ask Me/(Woody Allen Method)

Although it would have surely been unheard of in the aeon of vaudeville, or Hollywood's golden age of musicals, in the age between 1996 and 2004, directors have selected casts with no prior history, training, or experience as singers and dancers. Although these actors often undergo strenuous work camps, like *Love's Labour's Lost*'s so-called Camp Branagh, it's still a new tune for the movie musical.

1. *Everyone Says I Love You* (1997)
2. *Love's Labour's Lost* (2000)
3. *Moulin Rouge* (2001)
4. *Chicago* (2002)

Make 'Em Laugh/Be a Clown

The age of the movie musical rebirth has also been one in which filmmakers understood succinctly the link between comedy and music. Indeed, humor has been a primary conduit through which the musical has returned to prominence, especially circa 1997–2000.

1. *Everyone Says I Love You* (1997)
2. *Waiting for Guffman* (1997)
3. *South Park: Bigger, Longer & Uncut* (1999)
4. *Cannibal: The Musical* (1999)
5. *Love's Labour's Lost* (2000)
6. *A Mighty Wind* (2003)
7. *Camp* (2003)

Babes in Arms: The Backstage Musical

Another handy and reliable movie musical conceit resurrected from the dawn of the format is the backstage musical. In this style of film, offstage personal dramas balance onstage musical performances. Essentially, the backstage musical is a handy way of featuring musical performance and dance without featuring the dreaded taboo of "bursting into song," opera-style. Interestingly, some of these films, such as *Velvet Goldmine* and John Cameron Mitchell's *Hedwig and the Angry Inch*, merge formats.

1. *Waiting for Guffman* (1997)
2. *Velvet Goldmine* (1998)
3. *Hedwig and the Angry Inch* (2001)
4. *Camp* (2003)
5. *A Mighty Wind* (2003)
6. *Andrew Lloyd Webber's Phantom of the Opera* (2004)

Well Versed in the Classics

A number of fascinating contemporary musicals fashion their screenplays not just on musicals of ages past, but on classic literature and myth:

1. *Love's Labour's Lost* (2000): William Shakespeare's *Love's Labour's Lost*
2. *O Brother, Where Art Thou?* (2001): Homer's *The Odyssey*
3. *Moulin Rouge* (2001): The Orpheus Myth
4. *Hedwig and the Angry Inch* (2001): Plato's *Symposium*
5. *Andrew Lloyd Webber's Phantom of the Opera* (2004): Gaston Leroux's *Phantom of the Opera*

From Stage to Screen

Movie musicals have an easier time getting backing and financial support if they are based on a brand name, a popular show. This has been true of movie musicals for generations, and the Rodgers and Hammerstein movies of the 1950s, like *Oklahoma!* (1955) and *The King and I* (1955) are perfect examples. Even in this new age, stage-to-screen adaptations are plentiful:

1. *Evita* (1996)
2. *Hedwig and the Angry Inch* (2001)
3. *Chicago* (2002)
4. *Andrew Lloyd Webber's Phantom of the Opera* (2004)

Note: An ancillary to this law might be called "From TV to Silver Screen," and would feature such spin-offs from television as *From Justin to Kelly* (2002) and the adaptation of Dennis Potter's BBC miniseries, *The Singing Detective* (2003).

It's All in Your Head

Since movie audiences of the new age apparently have difficulty accepting the tradition of folks bursting into song outright, many musicals have sought another outlet for this tradition. In particular, these films have included musical production numbers (singing and dancing), but writers and directors vetted them as being simply "internal fantasies." They are daydreams, fantasies, or even hallucinations, and therefore breaking into song and dance is acceptable. This tradition actually goes back to Hollywood musical films like Vincente Minnelli's *An American in Paris*.

1. *Dancer in the Dark* (2000)
2. *Chicago* (2002)
3. *The Singing Detective* (2003)

The Yearning Ballad

In this age or any other, movie musicals must feature a yearning ballad, a tune in which the audience gets to hear the main character's "I Want," their burning desire and longing. Virtually every movie musical has one of these. Below are just a few notable examples:

1. *Evita* (1996): "Don't Cry for Me Argentina" (Evita just wants to be loved); "You Must Love Me" (Evita just wants to be loved)
2. *Everyone Says I Love You* (1997): "All My Life" (Julia Roberts wants love); "I'm a Dreamer (Aren't We All)" (Drew Barrymore wants romance)
3. *South Park: Bigger, Longer & Uncut* (1999): "Up There" (Satan wants to leave hell and live on earth)
4. *Moulin Rouge* (2001): "One Day I'll Fly Away" (Satine wishes she could escape the underworld of the Moulin Rouge)
5. *Hedwig and the Angry Inch* (2001): "Wig in a Box" (Hedwig wants be herself)
6: *From Justin to Kelly* (2002): "Anytime" (Kelly wishes Justin would love her); "Timeless" (Justin wants to love Kelly)
7. *The Phantom of the Opera* (2005): "Music of the Night" (The Phantom wants to seduce Christine into his world with his music)

Note: This particular conceit also works for TV musicals. In *Buffy the Vampire Slayer*'s "Once More with Feeling," Buffy sings of her desire to be a normal girl and, more to the point, to just feel human again in "Going Through the Motions."

Mistaken Identities

For some reasons, movie musicals seem obsessed with the device of mistaken identities. One character is mistook for another, and a wacky comedy of errors ensues.

1. *Waiting for Guffman* (1997): Paul Benedict's character (Not Guffman) is mistaken for the theater agent, Mort Guffman, during the film's conclusion, resulting in disappointment for the cast of *Red, White and Blaine*.
2. *South Park: Bigger, Longer & Uncut* (1999): Brian Dennehy mistakes himself for the boys' hero. They're really singing about Brian Boitano.
3. *Love's Labour's Lost* (2000): Costard mistakes the letters of Berowne and Don Armado, causing a case of mistaken identities with their individual love objects, particularly Rosaline.
4. *Moulin Rouge* (2001): Satine inadvertently takes Christian to be the Duke and invites him back to her boudoir.

Happy Endings

Named in honor of Liza Minnelli's number in Martin Scorsese's *New York, New York* (1977), this convention requires, sadly, some element of an unhappy ending. Often, this results from a death. This cliché proves that musicals aren't always happy and cheery.

1. *Evita* (1996): Eva Perón dies
2. *South Park: Bigger, Longer & Uncut* (1999): Kenny dies
3. *Dancer in the Dark* (2000): Selma dies
4. *Moulin Rouge* (2001): Satine dies
5. *De-Lovely* (2004): Cole Porter dies; Linda Porter dies

Independent's Day

A great way of making low-risk, high-experimentation movie musicals in the 1990s and 2000s has been through the auspices of the independent film movement. Some indie musicals are:

1. *Velvet Goldmine* (1998)
2. *Dancer in the Dark* (2000)
3. *Hedwig and the Angry Inch* (2001)
4. *Camp* (2003)
5. *The Singing Detective* (2003)

APPENDIX B
Musical Credits

1996–2004

Evita (1996)

THE MOST ANTICIPATED MOTION PICTURE EVENT OF THE YEAR

Andrew G. Vajna presents, a Cinergi–Robert Stigwood–Dirty Hands Production of an Alan Parker Film, *Evita*. Based on the play *Evita* by Tim Rice with music by Andrew Lloyd Webber. Produced on Broadway by Robert Stigwood in association with David Land.

Credits

Director:	Alan Parker
Casting:	John and Ros Hubbard
Choreographer:	Vincent Paterson
Costume Designer:	Penny Rose
Music Supervisor:	David Caddick
Music Producer:	Nigel Wright
Film Editor:	Gerry Hambling
Production Designer:	Brian Morris
Director of Photography:	Darius Khondji
Associate Producer:	Lisa Moran
Line Producer:	David Wimbury
Producers:	Robert Stigwood, Alan Parker, Andrew G. Vajna
Screenplay:	Alan Parker, Oliver Stone
Music:	Andrew Lloyd Webber
Lyrics:	Tim Rice

Starring

Madonna:	Eva Perón
Antonio Banderas:	Ché
Jonathan Pryce:	Juan Perón
Jimmy Nail:	Agustín Magaldi
Victoria Sus:	Dona Juana
Julian Littman:	Brother Juan
Olga Merediz:	Blanca
Laura Pallas:	Elisa
Julia Worsley:	Erminda
Maria Luján Hidalgo:	Young Eva Perón
Servando Villamil:	Cipriano Reyes
Andrea Corr:	Perón's Mistress
Peter Polycarpou:	Domingo Mercante

Everyone Says I Love You (1997)

Sweetland Films Presents a Jean Doumanian Production, *Everyone Says I Love You.*

Credits

Director:	Woody Allen
Casting:	Juliet Taylor
Choreographer:	Graciela Daniele
Music Arranger/Conductor:	Dick Hyman
Director of Photography:	Carlo DiPalma
Production Designer:	Santo Loquasto
Film Editor:	Susan E. Morse
Costume Designer:	Jeffrey Kurland
Producer:	Robert Greenhut
Executive Producers:	Jean Doumanian, J. E. Beaucaire
Co-executive Producers:	Charles H. Joffe, Jack Rollins, Letty Aronson
Co-producer:	Helen Robin
Writer:	Woody Allen

Starring

Edward Norton:	Holden Spence
Drew Barrymore:	Skylar
Natasha Lyonne:	D. J.
Alan Alda:	Bob
Gaby Hoffman:	Lane
Natalie Portman:	Laura
Lukas Haas:	Scott
Goldie Hawn:	Steffi
Julia Roberts:	Von
Patrick Cranshaw:	Grandpa
Woody Allen:	Joe Berlin
Tim Roth:	Charles Ferry
David Ogden Stiers:	Mr. Spence

Velvet Goldmine (1998)

A MAN'S LIFE IS HIS IMAGE.

THE RISE OF A STAR . . . THE FALL OF A LEGEND

Newmarket Capital Group, Goldwyn Films International, Miramax Film Film Four and Zenith Present a Zenith Productions–Killer Films Production in Association with Single Cell Pictures a Film by Todd Haynes, *Velvet Goldmine*.

Credits

Director:	Todd Haynes
Casting:	Susie Figgis
U.S. Casting:	Laura Rosenthal
Original Score:	Carter Burwell
Music Supervisor:	Randall Poster
Choreographer:	Lea Anderson
Production Designer:	Christopher Hobbs
Executive Producers:	Sandy Stern, Scott M. Meek, Michael Stipe
Co-producer:	Olivia Stewart
Producer:	Christine Vachon
Film Editor:	James Lyons
Director of Photography:	Maryse Alberti
Writer:	Todd Haynes

Starring

Ewan McGregor:	Curt Wild
Jonathan Rhys-Meyers:	Brian Slade
Toni Collette:	Mandy Slade
Christian Bale:	Arthur Stuart
Eddie Izzard:	Jerry Devine
Emily Woof:	Shannon
Michael Feast:	Cecil

South Park: Bigger, Longer & Uncut (1999)

UH OH!

ALL HELL BREAKS LOOSE!

A Scott Rudin and Trey Parker–Matt Stone Production, in Association with Comedy Central, Paramount Pictures and Warner Brothers, *South Park: Bigger, Longer & Uncut*.

Credits

Director:	Trey Parker
Director of Animation:	Eric Stough
Music and Lyrics:	Trey Parker
Additional Music, Lyrics, and Score:	Marc Shaiman
Line Producer:	Gina Shay
Film Editor:	John Venzon
Producers:	Trey Parker, Matt Stone
Executive Producers:	Scott Rudin, Adam Schroeder
Coproducers:	Anne Garefino, Deborah Liebling
Animation Producer:	Frank C. Agnone II
Writers:	Trey Parker, Matt Stone, Pam Brady

Starring

Trey Parker:	Stan Marsh, Eric Cartman, Satan, and others
Matt Stone:	Kyle Broslofski, Kenny McCormick, Saddam Hussein, and others
Mary Kay Bergman:	Liane Cartman, Sheila Broslofski, Sharon Marsh, Wendy Testeberger, and others
Isaac Hayes:	Chef
Bruce Howell:	Man in Theatre
Deb Adair:	Woman in Theatre
Jennifer Howell:	Bebe
George Clooney:	Doctor
Brent Spiner:	Conan O'Brien
Minnie Driver:	Brooke Shields
Dave Foley:	The Baldwin Brothers
Saddam Hussein:	Himself
Eric Idle:	Dr. Vosknocker
Mike Judge:	Kenny's Goodbye

Love's Labour's Lost (2000)

A NEW SPIN ON THE OLD SONG AND DANCE

A Miramax Films Release of an Intermedia Films and Pathe Pictures Presentation in Association with the Arts Council of England, Le Studio Canal+, and Miramax Films of a Shakespeare Film Production, *Love's Labour's Lost.* Based on the play by William Shakespeare.

Credits

Director:	Kenneth Branagh
Casting:	Randi Hiller and Nina Gold
Executive Producers:	Guy East, Nigel Sinclair, Harvey Weinstein, Bob Weinstein, Alexis Lloyd
Producers:	David Barron, Kenneth Branagh
Choreographer:	Stuart Hopps
Music Editor:	Gerard McCann
Music:	Patrick Doyle
Production Designer:	Tim Harvey
Film Editor:	Neil Farrell, Dan Farrell
Director of Photography:	Alex Thomson

Starring

Kenneth Branagh:	Berowne
Richard Briers:	Nathaniel
Richard Clifford:	Boyet
Carmen Ejogo:	Maria
Daniel Hill:	Mercade
Nathan Lane:	Costard
Adrian Lester:	Dumaine
Matthew Lillard:	Longaville
Natascha McElhone:	Rosaline
Geraldine McEwan:	Holofernia
Emily Mortimer:	Katherine
Alessandro Nivola:	King
Anthony O'Donnell:	Moth
Stefania Rocca:	Jacquenetta
Alicia Silverstone:	Princess
Timothy Spall:	Don Armado
Jimmy Yuill:	Dull
Alfred Bell:	Gaston
Daisy Gough:	Isabelle
Graham Hubbard:	Eugene

(CONTINUED ON NEXT PAGE)

(CONTINUED FROM PREVIOUS PAGE)

Paul Moody:	Jacques
Yvonne Reilly:	Beatrice
Ian Stuart Robertson:	Hippolyte
Emma Scott:	Celimene
Amy Tez:	Sophie

Dancer in the Dark (2000)

IN A WORLD OF SHADOWS, SHE FOUND THE LIGHT OF LIFE.

A Fine Line Release of a Zentropa Entertainment, *Dancer in the Dark*

Credits

Director:	Lars von Trier
Casting:	Avy Kaufman, Joyce Nettles
Music:	Björk
Lyrics:	Lars von Trier, Sjón Sigurdsson
Choreographer:	Vincent Paterson
Producers:	Anja Grafers, Els Vandevorst, Fridrik Thor Fridriksson, Finn Gjerdrum, Torleif Hauge, Tero Kaukomaa, Mogens Glad, Poul Eric Lindeborg
Production Designer:	Karl Juliusson
Director of Photography:	Robby Müller
Film Editors:	Molly Malene Stensgaard, François Gédigier
Writer:	Lars von Trier

Starring

Björk:	Selma
Catherine Deneuve:	Kathy
David Morse:	Bill
Peter Stormare:	Jeff
Joel Grey:	Oldrich Novy
Vincent Paterson:	Director
Cara Seymour:	Linda
Jean-Marc Barr:	Foreman
Vladica Kostic:	Gene
Udo Kier:	Doctor
Zeljko Ivanek:	D. A.

Moulin Rouge (2001)

THIS STORY IS ABOUT TRUTH, BEAUTY, FREEDOM, BUT ABOVE ALL, LOVE

NO LAWS. NO LIMITS. ONE RULE. NEVER FALL IN LOVE

A 20th Century Fox release of a Bazmark Production, *Moulin Rouge*

Credits

Director:	Baz Luhrmann
Casting:	Ronna Kress
Australian Casting:	Chris King
Producers:	Martin Brown, Baz Lurhmann, Fred Baron
Co-producer:	Catherine Knapman
Associate Producer:	Steve E. Andrews
Original Music:	Craig Armstrong
Music Director:	Marius DeVries
Choreographer:	John O'Connell
Production Designer:	Catherine Martin
Director of Photography:	Donald M. McAlpine
Film Editor:	Jill Bilcock
Writers:	Baz Luhrmann, Craig Pearce

Starring

Nicole Kidman:	Satine
Ewan McGregor:	Christian
John Leguizamo:	Toulouse-Lautrec
Richard Roxburgh:	The Duke
Jim Broadbent:	Zidler
Garry McDonald:	The Doctor
Jacek Koman:	The Unconscious Argentinian
Matthew Wittet:	Satie
Kerry Walker:	Marie
Caroline O'Connor:	Nini Legs in the Air
David Wenham:	Audrey
Christine Anu:	Arabia
Natalie Mendoza:	China Doll
Lara Mulcahy:	Mome Fromage
Kylie Minogue:	Green Fairy

Hedwig and the Angry Inch (2001)

AN ANATOMICALLY INCORRECT ROCK ODYSSEY

New Line Cinema presents a Killer Films Production, *Hedwig and the Angry Inch*. Adapted from a work for the stage by John Cameron Mitchell (text) and Stephen Trask (music and lyrics).

Credits

Director:	John Cameron Mitchell
Casting:	Susan Shopmaker
Music and Lyrics:	Stephen Trask
Line Producer:	Colin Brunton
Producers:	Christine Vachon, Katie Roumel, Pamela Koffler
Executive Producers:	Michael De Luca, Amy Henkels, Mark Tusk
Executive Music Producer:	Alex Steyermark
Animation Sequence and Art Work:	Emily Hubley
Hedwig's Hair and Make-Up:	Mike Potter
Production Design:	Thérèse DePrez
Film Editor:	Andrew Marcus
Director of Photography:	Frank G. DeMarco
Screenplay:	John Cameron Mitchell

Starring

John Cameron Mitchell:	Hedwig/Hansel
Andrea Martin:	Phyllis Stein
Michael Pitt:	Tommy Gnosis
Alberta Watson:	Hansel's Mom
Stephen Trask:	Skszp
Rob Campbell:	Krzysztof
Theodore Liscinski:	Jacek
Michael Aronov:	Schlatko
Miriam Shor:	Yitzhak

Chicago (2002)

IF YOU CAN'T BE FAMOUS . . . BE INFAMOUS.

A Producer Circle Company Production, a Zadan–Meron Production, a Miramax Films Presentation, *Chicago*. Based on the musical play *Chicago*. Direction and choreography for the stage by Bob Fosse. Based on the play by Maurine Dallas Watkins. Book of the musical play by Bob Fosse and Fred Ebb

Credits

Director:	Rob Marshall
Casting:	Laura Rosenthal, Ali Farrell, Tina Gerussi
Producer:	Martin Richards
Executive Producers:	Craig Zadan, Neil Meron Sam Crothers, Bob Weinstein, Harvey Weinstein, Meryl Poster, Julie Goldstein, Jennifer Berman
Production Design:	John Myhre
Director of Photography:	Dion Beebe
Choreographer:	Rob Marshall
Musical Supervisor:	Maureen Crowe
Screenplay:	Bill Condon
Music:	John Kander
Lyrics:	Fred Ebb

Starring:

Renée Zelwegger:	Roxie Hart
Catherine Zeta-Jones:	Velma Kelly
Richard Gere:	Billy Flynn
John C. Reilly:	Amos Hart
Queen Latifah:	Mama Morton
Taye Diggs:	Bandleader
Lucy Liu:	Kitty Baxter
Christine Baranski:	Mary Sunshine
Dominic West:	Fred Casely
Colm Feore:	Martin Harrison
Chita Rivera:	Nickie
Mýa Harrison:	Mona
Susan Misner:	Liz

From Justin to Kelly (2003)

THE TALE OF TWO AMERICAN IDOLS

20th Century Fox presents a 19 Entertainment Production, *From Justin to Kelly*

Credits

Director:	Robert Iscove
Casting:	Roger Mussenden
Musical Supervisor:	Michael Fey
Original Score:	Michael Wandmacher
Choreographer:	Travis Payne
Film Editors:	Casey Rohrs, Tirsa Hackshaw
Production Designer:	Charles Rosen
Director of Photography:	Francis Kenny
Executive Producers:	Gayla Aspinall, Simon Fuller
Producer:	John Steven Agoglia
Co-producers:	Bob Engelman, Nikki Boella
Writer:	Kim Fuller

Starring

Kelly Clarkson:	Kelly
Justin Guarini:	Justin
Katherine Bailess:	Alexa
Anika Noni Rose:	Kaya
Greg Siff:	Brandon
Brian Dietzen:	Eddie
Jason Yribar:	Carlos
Theresa San-Nicholas:	Officer Cutler
Justin Gorence:	Greg
Christopher Bryan:	Luke
Yamil Piedra:	Darren
Marc Macaulay:	Mr. O'Mara
Toi Svane Stepp:	Lizzie
Louis Smith:	Vee Jay

Camp (2003)

A COMEDY ABOUT DRAMA

YOU CAN'T FIT IN WHEN YOU STAND OUT.

IFC Productions present a Jersey Films, Killer Films, Laughlin Park Production, *Camp*

Credits

Director:	Todd Graff
Casting:	Bernard Telsey, Victoria Pettibone, Will Cantler, David Vaccari
Choreographers:	Michelle Lynch, Jerry Mitchell
Musical Director:	Tim Weil
Music Supervisor:	Linda Cohen
Producers:	Katie Roumel, Christine Vachon, Pamela Koffler, Danny DeVito, Michael Shamberg, Stacey Sher, Jonathan Weisgal
Executive Producers:	John Wells, Richard Klubeck, Jonathan Sehring, Caroline Kaplan, Holly Becker, Daniel S. Levine
Co-producers:	Allen Bain, Dan Levine
Production Design:	Dina Goldman
Director of Photography:	Kip Bogdahn
Film Editor:	Myron Kerstein
Writer:	Todd Graff

Starring

Daniel Letterle:	Vlad
Joanna Chilcoat:	Ellen
Robin de Jesus:	Michael
Steven Cutts:	Shaun
Tiffany Taylor:	Jenna
Sasha Allen:	Dee
Alana Allen:	Jill
Anna Kendrick:	Fritzi
Don Dixon:	Bert
Stephen Sondheim:	Himself

The Singing Detective (2003)

ALL CLUES, NO SOLUTIONS

WHEN IT COMES TO MURDER, SEDUCTION AND BETRAYAL, HE WROTE THE BOOK. NOW HE'S LIVING IT.

Paramount Classics–Icon Productions present *The Singing Detective*. Based on a TV series by Dennis Potter

Credits

Director:	Keith Gordon
Casting:	Denise Chamian
Choreographers:	Jacqui and Bill Landrum
Producers:	Mel Gibson, Steven Haft, Bruce Davey
Executive Producer:	Stan Wlodkowski
Co-Producers:	Jane, Sarah and Robert Potter
Director of Photography:	Tom Richmond
Film Editor:	Jeff Wishengrad
Screenplay:	Dennis Potter

Starring

Robert Downey Jr:	Dan Dark
Robin Wright Penn:	Nicola/Nina/Blonde
Mel Gibson:	Dr. Gibbon
Jeremy Northam:	Mark Binney
Katie Holmes:	Nurse Mills
Adrien Brody:	First Hood
Jon Polito:	Second Hood
Carla Gugino:	Betty Dark/Hooker
Saul Rubinek:	Skin Specialist
Alfre Woodard:	Chief of Staff
Amy Aquino:	Nurse Nozhki
David Dorfman:	Young Dan Dark

De-Lovely (2004)

A LOVE THAT WOULD NEVER DIE AND MUSIC THAT WOULD LIVE FOREVER

An MGM Release, *De-Lovely*

Credits

Director:	Irwin Winkler
Casting:	Nina Gold
Music Director:	Stephen Endelman
Music and Lyrics:	Cole Porter
Choreographer:	Francesca Jaynes
Executive Producers:	Simon Channing-Williams, Gail Egan
Production Designer:	Eve Stewart
Producers:	Rob Cowan, Georgina Lowe, Charles Winkler, Irwin Winkler
Director of Photography:	Tony Pierce-Roberts
Film Editor:	Julie Monroe
Writer:	Jay Cocks

Starring

Kevin Kline:	Cole Porter
Ashley Judd:	Linda Porter
Jonathan Pryce:	Gabe
Kevin McNally:	Gerald Murphy
Allan Corduner:	Monty Woolley
Sandra Nelson:	Sara Murphy
Keith Allen:	Irving Berlin
James Wilby:	Edward Thomas
Kevin McKidd:	Bobby Reed
Peter Polycarpou:	Louis B. Mayer
Richard Dillane:	Billy Wrather
Edward Baker-Duly:	Boris Kochno

Musical Performers

Robbie Williams, Lemar, Elvis Costello, Alanis Morissette, John Barrowman, Caroline O'Connor, Sheryl Crow, Mick Hucknall, Diana Krall, Vivian Green, Lara Fabian, Mario Frangoulis, Natalie Cole

Andrew Lloyd Webber's
The Phantom of the Opera (2004)

THE WORLD'S BIGGEST MUSICAL!

A Warner Bros. presentation of a Really Useful/Scion Films production, *Andrew Lloyd Webber's The Phantom of the Opera*. Based on the novel by Gaston Leroux

Credits

Director:	Joel Schumacher
Casting:	David Grindrod
Music Director:	Nigel Wright
Music and Lyrics:	Andrew Lloyd Webber
Choreographer:	Peter Darling
Executive Producers:	Jeff Abberley, Julia Blackman, Keith Cousins, Louise Goodsill, Paul Hitchcock, Ralph Kamp, Austin Shaw
Production Designer:	Anthony Pratt
Producer:	Andrew Lloyd Webber
Director of Photography:	John Mathieson
Film Editor:	Terry Rawlings
Writers:	Andrew Lloyd Webber and Joel Schumacher

Starring

Gerard Butler:	The Phantom
Emmy Rossum:	Christine
Patrick Wilson:	Raoul
Miranda Richardson:	Madame Giry
Minnie Driver:	Carlotta
Ciarán Hinds:	Firmin
Simon Callow:	Andre
Jennifer Ellison:	Meg Giry
Murray Melvin:	Reyer
Kevin McNally:	Buquet

Notes

Introduction

1. Kenneth Turan, *The Los Angeles Times*, December 6, 1996, 1.
2. Richard Barrios, *A Song in the Dark: The Birth of the Musical Film*, Oxford University Press, New York, 1995, 3.
3. Todd Berliner, "The Sounds of Silence: Songs in Hollywood Films Since the 1960s—Critical Essay," *Style*, Spring 2002, 1–11.
4. Moira McDonald, "Songs Are Given Center Stage in Cole Porter Biopic *De-Lovely*," *Knight Ridder/Tribune News Service*, July 3, 2004, K6571.
5. David Thomson, "Sweet Unison," *Sight and Sound*, April 1997, 20.
6. Christopher Sharrett, "Consolations of the Musical," *USA Today*, January 2001, 59.
7. Jose Arroyo, *Sight and Sound*, February 1997, 20.
8. Ron Weiskind, "Are Musicals Hollywood's Comeback Kids?" *Post-Gazette*, April 21, 2002.
9. Bob Graham, "Genres Never Really Die: Musicals and Westerns may seem to fade away, but they always come back," *The San Francisco Chronicle*, June 17, 2001, 35.
10. John Burlingame, "Mining Gold from Cole: *De-Lovely* is MGM's attempt to extend its musical heritage," *Variety*, April 19, 2004, S18–S19.
11. "Movie Musicals Are Back with a Bang," *Associated Press*, December 25, 2002.
12. Doug Nye, "Musicals Are Back and Cyd Charisse Is Dancing," *The State*, May 1, 2003, 1-3.
13. Todd Leopold, "Sing a Song of Movie Musicals: Is the venerable genre going to make a comeback?" *CNN.com*, May 27, 2003, 2 of 3 http://www.cnn.com/2003/SHOW-BIZ/MOVIES/03/26/movie.musicals
14. Paul Karon, "Genre Transfusion: *Rouge, Park, Lantana* helmers reinvent classic forms," *Daily Variety*, January 15 2003, A1–A3.
15. Heather Wisner, "Moviemakers Put Motion Back in Pictures," *Dance Magazine*, December 2000, 60.

Chapter One: The Old Razzle-Dazzle

1. Donald Crafton, *Talkies: American Cinema's Transition to Sound, 1926–1931 (History of American Cinema 4)*, University of California Press, 1999, 23.
2. William K. Everson, *American Silent Film*, DaCapo Press, 1998, 3.
3. Richard A. Blake, "Certainly *Chicago*," *America*, March 31, 2003, 23.
4. Stanley Green, *Hollywood Musicals Year By Year, 2nd Edition*, Hal Leonard, 1998, 5.
5. Aljean Harmetz, *The Making of the Wizard of Oz: Movie Magic and Studio Power in the Prime of MGM, 16th Edition*, Hyperion, 1998, 3.

6. Danny Peary, *Cult Movies: The Classics, the Sleepers, the Weird and the Wonderful*, Delacorte Press, 1981, 287.
7. John Kobal, *Gotta Sing Gotta Dance: A History of Movie Musicals*, Exeter Books, New York, 1983, 197.
8. Clive Hirschhorn, *The Hollywood Musical*, Crown Publishing Inc, New York, 1981, 15.
9. Richard Fehr and Frederick G. Vogel, *Lullabies of Hollywood: Movie Music and the Movie Musical, 1915–1992*, 1993, 223.
10. Stanley Green, *Hollywood Musicals Year by Year*, Second Edition, Hal Leonard, 1998, 166.
11 "American Masters Online presents and extended interview with *Gene Kelly* filmmaker Robert Trachtenberg," http://www.prbs.org/wnet/americanmasters/database/kelly_g_interview.html
12 Andrew J. Rausch, "Sure I'll Do It: An Interview with Robert Wise," *Bright Lights Film Journal*, http://www.brightlightsfilm.com/35/robertwise1.html
13. Harry Kreisler, "The Wise Touch: Conversation with Robert Wise," Conversations with History: Institute for International Studies, UC Berkeley, February 28, 1998, 9 of 10.
14. "Movers and Shakers of Movie Musicals" (The Oscars/Where Are They Now?) *People Weekly*, April 8, 2002, 130+.
15. "Movers and Shakers of Movie Musicals" (The Oscars/Where Are They Now?) *People Weekly*, April 8, 2002, 130+.
16. Ephraim Katz, *The Film Encyclopedia: the Most Comprehensive Encyclopedia of World Cinema in a Single Volume,* Harper and Row, 1979, 812.
17. Harry Medved with Randy Dreyfuss, *The Fifty Worst Films of All Time*, Warner Books, 1978, 148.
18 Harry and Michael Medved, *The Golden Turkey Awards,* Perigee Books, 1980, 87.
19. Scott Simon, *Weekend Edition Saturday*, National Public Radio, January 4, 2003, 2 of 5.
20. David Zinman, *Fifty Grand Movies of the 1960s and the 1970s*, Crown Publishers, Inc., 1986, 96.
21. Jay Cocks, "Lindsay Anderson: 1923–1994; in celebration," *Film Comment,* Nov-Dec 1994, 7–10.
22. Paul Byrnes, "The Singing Detective," SMH.com.au, July 10, 2004, 1 of 2. http://www.smh.com.au/cgi-bin/common/popupPrintArticle.pl?path=articles/2004/07/09
23. Alan Jones, "Little Shop of Horrors," *Cinefantastique*, January 1987, 18.

Chapter Two: Razzle-Dazzle Fizzles

1. "War Stories: Bette's Big Gamble," *Entertainment Weekly,* December 20, 1991, http://www.ew.com/ew/report/0,6115,316534-2-2-7//260502/1_00.html
2. James Greenberg, "The Sound of Money," *Connoisseur,* February 1992, 22.
3. John Calhoun, "Newsies: Hollywood returns to the big budget musical," *Theatre Crafts,* April 1992, 30.
4. "Faces to Watch: Christian Bale, All the News That's Fit, He'll Sing," *Entertainment Weekly,* January 31, 1992, http://www.ew.com/ew/report/0,6115,309414_7_0_,00.html
5. "Newsies," *Teen Magazine*, June 1992, 56.
6. Thomas R. King, "Disney Gambles on Risky Musical Format," *The Wall Street Journal*, April 7, 1992, B1 and B10.
7. Ralph Novak, "Newsies," *People Weekly,* April 27, 1992, 17–18.
8. Owen Gleiberman, "Newsies," *Entertainment Weekly*, April 17, 1992, 40.
9. Nisid Hajari, "The Reich Stuff," *Entertainment Weekly,* March 12, 1993, 42.
10. Leah Rozen, "Swing Kids," *People Weekly,* March 15, 1993, 17.
11. Owen Gleiberman, "Swing Kids," *Entertainment Weekly,* March 12, 1993, 42.
12. Jamie Diamond, "Bringing You a Hollywood Musical...Without Music," *The New York Times*, January 30, 1994 H13, H23.
13. Pat H. Broeske, "Anything Goes?" *Entertainment Weekly,* September 24, 1993, 8–9.

14. Richard Corliss, "Still Lucky Jim? Comedy Czar James L. Brooks tries to fix the movie that used to be a musical (*I'll Do Anything*)," *Time*, January 13, 1994, 102–104.
15. Anthony Lane, "Anything Goes," *The New Yorker*, February 7, 1994, 10.
16. Benjamin Svetskey, "Clown Jewel," *Entertainment Weekly*, May 30, 2003, http://www.ew.com/ew/report/0,6115,454075-2-2-1//233612/1_00.html
17. Richard Corliss, "Still Lucky Jim? Comedy Czar James L. Brooks tries to fix the movie that used to be a musical (*I'll Do Anything*)," *Time,* January 13, 1994, 102–104.
18. Pat H. Broeske, "Anything Goes?" *Entertainment Weekly*, September 24, 8–9.
19. Marc Peyser with Mark Miller, "A Musical Loses Its Voice," *Newsweek*, February 7, 1994, 61.
20. Stanley Kauffmann, "*I'll Do Anything*," *The New Republic,* March 7, 1994, 30–31.
21. Ty Burr, "*I'll Do Anything*," *Entertainment Weekly*, August 12, 1994, 66.
22. Ellen O'Brien, "Joey's 'Fantastick' Voyage," *The Boston Globe,* March 23, 1995, 63.
23. Scott Foundas, "*The Fantasticks*," *Variety*, September 18, 2000, 30.
24. David Mermelstein, "Unabashedly Old Fashioned *Fantasticks* Hits Screen," *Variety*, September 18, 2000, 64.
25. Jason Cochran, "*Fantasticks* Voyage," *Entertainment Weekly*, May 2, 1997, 72.
26. Andy Dursin, "The Real Gladiator," *Film Score Monthly*, February 26, 2001, http://www.filmscore-monthly.com
27. Abbie Bernstein, *Back Stage West*, "*Fantastick* Journey," September 28, 2000, 6.
28. Chris Willman, "The Plight *Fantasticks*," *Entertainment Weekly*, June 2, 2000, 70.

Chapter 3: 1996 – 2001, From Evita to Moulin Rouge

1. Nigel Andrews, "The Final Curtain or a Fresh Start for the Movie Musical?" *The Financial Times*, December 14, 1996, WFT1.
2. Kenneth Turan, *The Los Angeles Times*, December 25, 1996, 1.
3. "Pfieffer Turns Down Roles for Kids," WENN, October 2, 2002, 2 of 2, http://www.imdb.com
4. Mitchell Fink, "Don't Cry For Her," *People Weekly*, April 25, 1994, 37.
5. Richard Zoglin, "Mad for Evita," *Time Magazine*, December 30, 1996, 134–138.
6. Gregory Cerio, "Don't Yell at Me, Argentina," *People Weekly*, February 26, 1996, 48–50.
7. Lisa Leigh Parney, "Is that Madonna Really Singing?" *Christian Science Monitor*, December 6, 1996, 15.
8. Sir Alan Parker, *The Making of Evita*, September, 1996, 8.
9. Michael Medved, *New York Post*, December 24, 1996, 33.
10. Sir Alan Parker, *The Making of Evita*, September, 1996, 18.
11. Larry King, "Interview: Madrona Reviews Life on Larry King Live," *CNN*, Tuesday January 19, 1999, http://www.cnn.com/SHOWBIZ/Music/9901/19/madonna.llkl/#thcater
12. Stuart Miller, "Selling *Evita* to the Masses: Retailers around the country are betting Madonna's upcoming star turn will spark a style revolution," *Newsweek*, November 11, 1996, 92.
13. Vivian Infantino, "Don't Cry for Her," *Footwear News*, January 27, 1997, S10.
14. Larry Flick. "Radio Embraces *Evita*." *Billboard*, October 26, 1996, 1.
15. Mitchell Fink, "The buzz on Madonna's Movie" *People Weekly*, December 23, 1996, 37.
16. "Que Fiesta: Madonna and pals pop up at the premiere of her new movie *Evita*," *People Weekly*, January 13, 1997, 100–101.
17. Richard Corliss, "*Evita*," *Time Magazine*, December 16, 1996, 72.
18. David Ansen, "*Evita*," *Newsweek*, December 16, 1996, 63.
19. Brian D. Johnson, "*Evita*," *Maclean's*, December 3, 1996, 103.
20. John Simon, "*Evita*," *National Review*, January 27, 1997, 57.
21. David Denby, *New York*, December 9, 1996, 72.
22. Gary Susman, "Plain Song and Dance," *The Boston Phoenix*, January 16–23, 1997, 1 of 1, http://www.bostonphoen.com/alt1/archive.movies/reviews/01-16-97/EVERYONE_BAR.html

23. Richard Zoglin, "All Singing All Woody," *Time Magazine,* December 9, 1996 81–82.
24. Gary Arnold, *"Everyone Says I Love You,"* *Insight on the News,* January 20, 1997, 38–39.
25. Jonathan Coe, *"Everyone Says I Love You,"* *New Statesman,* April 18, 1997, 40–42.
26. "Drew Barrymore: The Well-Rounded Interview," *Well Rounded.com,* March 1997, 1 of 1. http://www.well-rounded.com/reviews/drewbarrymore_intv.html
27. "Kenneth Branagh: CrankyCritic Star Talk," *The Cranky Critic,* 3 of 6, http://www.crankycritic.com/qa/kennethbranagh.html
28. "Interview: *Everyone Says I Love You,*" *Edward Norton Information Page,* 1 of 1, http://www.edward-norton.org/audio/esilyclips.html
29. Ruthe Stein, "Film Review—Everyone Won't Say They Love Allen Film But Woody's Musical has Clunky Charm," *The San Francisco Chronicle,* January 17 1997, 2 of 3, http://www.sfgate.com/cgi-bin/article.cgi?file=/c/a/1997/01/17/DD947.DTL&type=printable
30. www.natalieportman.com
31. Mitchell Fink, "Woody Allen Tells Us He Had to Cut Five Musical Numbers," *People Weekly,* February 3, 1997, 39.
32. Joseph Cuneen, *"Everyone Says I Love You,"* *National Catholic Reporter,* February 7, 1997, 10.
33. Jack Mathews, *Newsday,* December 24, 1996, 83.
34. Stanley Kauffmann, *"Everyone Says I Love You,"* *The New Republic,* November 11, 40–41.
35. Richard Schickel, *Time,* December 9, 1996, 81.
36. David Denby, *New York,* December 9, 1996, 72.
37. Brian D. Johnson, *"Everyone Says I Love You,"* *Maclean's,* February 3, 1996, 66.
38. John Kenneth Muir, *Best in Show: The Films of Christopher Guest and Company,* Applause Theatre and Cinema Books, 2004, 111.
39. Dafna Lernish, *"Spice World*: Constructing femininity in the popular way," *Popular Music and Society,* February 2003, 17.
40. George Meyer, "Getting Ziggy Wid'It *Velvet Goldmine* is the History of Glam Rock in the Gloaming, with a Personal Twist," *Sarasota Herald Tribune,* November 27, 1998, 18.
41. Bob Ivry, *"Velvet Goldmine* is a Stunning Look at Glam Rock Era," *Knight Ridder/Tribune News Service,* November 4, 1998, K7716.
42. Graham Fuller, *"The Empire Strikes Back,"* *Interview,* November 1998, 98–106.
43. Graham Fuller, *"Oh! You Pretty Things,"* *Interview,* December 1998, 10s.
44. Chris Petrikin, "Some Like It Hot: Weinstein in drag to glamorize *Velvet* preem, *Daily Variety,* May 11, 1998, 184.
45. Todd McCarthy, *"Velvet Goldmine,"* *Daily Variety,* May 25, 1998, 56–57.
46. David Ansen, "A Sprinkling of *Ziggy Stardust,*" *Newsweek,* November 9, 1998, 70.
47. Jan Stuart, *"Golden Eye,"* *The Advocate,* November 10, 1998, 71.
48. Stuart Klawans, *"Velvet Goldmine & American History X,"* *The Nation,* November 30, 1998, 32.
49. Jonathan Romney, *"Velvet Goldmine,"* *New Statesman,* October 23, 1998, 35–36.
50. Piper Weiss, *"Cannibal the Musical,"* *Back Stage,* April 20, 2001, 44.
51. Lisa Nesselson, *"Cannibal! The Musical,"* *Variety,* May 24, 1999 72.
52. "*South Park: Bigger, Longer & Uncut* Opening June 30 in Theaters Met Deadlines Using Database," *PR Newswire,* June 17, 1999 0698.
53. Karen Moltenbrey, "Highs and Lows," *Computer Graphics World,* September 1999, 48.
54. "Reel World: This week in Hollywood (*South Park* movie fights ratings board; other movie news)," *Entertainment Weekly,* May 28, 1999, 117.
55. Peter Bart, "Do Censors Need Censoring?" *Daily Variety,* July 12, 1999, 4.
56. Kevin Maynard, *"South Park: Bigger Longer & Uncut,"* *The Advocate,* May 23, 2000, 91.
57. Leslie Felperin, *Sight and Sound,* September 1999, 55.
58. Stuart Klawans, "Bewitched," *The Nation,* September 6, 1999, 34.
59. "The Best Cinema of 1999," *Time,* December 20, 1999, 99.

60. Chris Willman, "Anything Goes: It Ain't Cole Porter, but scores for *South Park* and *Runaway Bride* may be the next best thing to the fast-fading film musical," *Entertainment Weekly*, August 13, 1999, 73+.

61. Richard Corliss, "Sick and Inspired: The *South Park* movie has a mean streak – and a song in its heart," *Time Magazine*, July 5, 1999, 75.

62. David Ansen, *Newseek,* July 5, 1999, 58.

63. David E. Thigpen, "The Sweet Sound of *Magnolia:* Aimee Mann's tales of romantic distress find emotionally satisfying release on a vibrant new soundtrack," *Time,* December 19, 1999, 108.

64. Charles Taylor, "*The Player,*" *Salon.com*, June 9, 2000, 1 of 1, http://www.salon.com

65. *The Riverside Shakespeare*, Houghton Mifflin, Boston, 1972, 174.

66. Jay Rayner, *The Observer*, "What a song and dance," Sunday, March 26, 2000, http://film.guardian.co.uk/Feature_Story/feature-story/0,4120152666,00.html

67. Neil McDonald, "Branagh's *Labour's Lost,*" *Quadrant*, April 2002, 56–63.

68. Sarah Gristwood, "What Is This Thing Called *Love's Labour's Lost?*" *The Guardian*, Monday, March 27, 2000, http://film.guardian.co.uk/feature_story/0,412015256,00.html

69. David Lister, "Shakespeare Meets Busby Berkeley," *The Independent* April 17 1999, 11.

70. Dennis Hensley, *Cosmopolitan*, June 2000, 182.

71. "On the arts: Kenneth Branagh Goes Musical in *Love's Labour's Lost,*" *CBC Radio*, June 2000, 1 of 1, http://www.branaghcompendium.com/artic.cbc.00.html

72. Kenneth Turan, *Los Angeles Times*, June 9, 2000, 6.

73. Graham Fuller, "Love's Labour's Lost," *Interview*, June 2000, 60.

74. "Stratford Shaw and Branagh," *Maclean's*, June 19, 2000, 53.

75. Derek Elley, "*Love's Labour's Lost,*" *Variety,* February 21, 2000, 36.

76. Patrick J. Cook, "*Love's Labour's Lost,*" George Washington University, USA, January 11, 2000, http://www.nottingham.ac.uk/film/journal/filmrev/love's-labour's-lost.htm

77. John Simon, "A Will But No Way," *National Review*, June 19, 2000.

78. Mirsha Berson, "*Love's Labour's Lost,*" *Knight Ridder/Tribune News* Service, June 19, 2000, K1633.

79. Stanley Kauffmann, "On Films—Well, Not Completely Lost," *The New Republic*, July 10, 2000, 32.

80. Chris Hewitt, "*Love's Labour's Lost,*" *Knight Ridder/Tribune News Service*, June 15, 2000, K687.

81. Amy Scott-Douglass, "Woman and Alternatives to Warfare in Some Films by Zeffirelli, Branagh and Luhrmann," *Shakespeare Newsletter*, Winter 2002, 109–110.

82. Rand Richards Cooper, "Dark and Darker: *Dancer in the Dark* and *Get Carter,*" *Commonweal*, November 3, 2000, 20.

83. Bern Rheinhardt, "*Dancer in the Dark*, Written and Directed by Lars von Trier," *World Socialist Web Site*, October 31, 2000, 1 of 3, http://www.wsws.org/articles/2000/oct2000/danc-031prn.shtml

84. Guy Flatley, "Film's Most Daring Director Delivers Again," *Interview*, October 2000, 1 of 2.

85. "Lars von Trier speaks about *Dancer in the Dark,*" http://home.swipnet.se/~w-10797/bjork/dancer.htm

86. Anthony Kaufman, "Interview: Lars von Trier Comes Out of the Dark," *Indie Wire*, September 22, 2000, 1 of 1, http://www.indiewire.com/peopleint_vonTrie_Lars0922.html

87. Gavin Smith, "*Dancer in the Dark*: Lars von Trier, filmmaker—Interview," *Film Comment*, September 2000, 4 of 5.

88. Mats Brastedt and Robert Borjesson, "The World's Most Charming Voice: soon on the big screen," *Expressen Noje*, June 11–12, 1999, 1 of 1, http://unit.bjork.com/specials/ui/DITD/articles/expressen.com

89. Luaine Lee, "*Dancer in the Dark* Star Says Reports of Strife Were Exaggerated," *Knight Ridder/Tribune News Service*, October 16, 2000 K4447.

90. Jamie Painter Young, "Embracing the Dark," *Back Stage West*, October 12, 2000, 8.

91. Damon Wise, "No Dane, No Gain," *The Guardian*, Sunday, October 12, 2003 1–6, http://film.guardian.co.uk/print/0385847725262-101730,00.html

92. David Ansen, "Light and Dark: Bjork's acting debut is one of the falls most controversial movies," *Newsweek*, September 25, 2000, 66.

93. "*Newsweek* Interview: Lars von Trier," *Newsweek*, March 28, 2004, 1 of 1, http://www.Newsweek.MSNBC.com

94. Jane Cornwell, "Bjork Goes Berserk," *The Bulletin with Newsweek*, December 12, 2000, 90–91.

95. Charles Lyons, "Publicists Tap *Dancer* Auds for von Trier Pic," *Daily Variety*, October 9 2000, 6.

96. Kenneth Turan, *The Los Angeles Times*, October 6, 2000, 2.

97. Stanley Kauffmann, "On Films: True and Utterly False," *The New Republic*, October 16, 2000 40.

98. Jan Stuart, *Newsday*, September 22 2000, B2.

99. Carrie Rickey, "*Dancer in the Dark*," *Knight Ridder/Tribune News Service*, October 5, 2000, K294.

100. Derek Elley, "*Dancer in the Dark,*" *Daily Variety*, May 22, 2000, 22.

101. Bill Kelley, "*Dancer in the Dark,*" *Knight Ridder/Tribune News Service*, October 4, 200, K7810.

102. Manohla Dargis, "Singin' and the Dane," *Harper's Bazaar*, September 2004, 40.

103. Glenn Lovell, "*Dancer in the Dark,*" *Knight Ridder/Tribune News Service*, October 5, 2000 K294.

104. Brian D. Johnson, "Singin' on the Brain: Bjork hits an ethereal note as a day-dreaming martyr," *Maclean's*, October 16, 2000, 74.

105. "*Dancer in the Dark* Offers Beauty Despite Tragedy," *Jakarta Post*, October 1, 2001, JAP)190069759.

106. Steven Gaydos, "Brother'-ly love goes global," *Daily Variety*, June 25, 2001, 8.

107. Luaine Lee, "Baz Luhrmann's love of movie musicals spurred *Moulin Rouge*," *Knight Ridder/Tribune News Service,* May 21, 2001, K4649.

108. Rebecca Murray, "Baz Luhrmann Talks Awards and *Moulin Rouge*," *About.com,* March 9, 2002 1 of 1, http://romanticmovies.about.com/library/weekly/aa030902.html

109. Gregg Kilday, "Luhrmann left Out of Big Dance," *Hollywood Reporter*, February 13, 2001, 1 of 1.

110. Graham Fuller, "*Moulin Rouge* Gives the Screen a Musical Make Over," *Knight Ridder/Tribune News Service*, May 11, 2001, K1022.

111. Paul Fischer, "Strictly Baz," *The Movie Insider*, December 4, 2001, 1 of 1, http://www.themovie-insider.com/interviews/interview.php?cid=33.

112. Alexandra Fawcett, "Baz Luhrmann," *Total DVD*, March, 2002, http://www.totaldvd.net/features/interviews/200203BazLuhrmann.php

113. "Ewan McGregor Should Be a Rock Star," *WENN*, November 27, 2000, http://www.imdb.com

114. "No Longer on Cruise Control," *Tiscali*, Summer 2001, 1 and 2, http://www.tiscali.co.uk

115. Scott B, "A Trip to *Moulin Rouge* with Nicole Kidman," *Film Force*, May 18, 2001, 1 of 1, http://www.filmforce.ign.com/articles/200/200220p1.html

116. Ellen A. Kim, "Nicole Kidman Can-Cans On," *Hollywood.com*, May 13, 2001 1 of 1, http://www.hollywood.com

117. Bruce Newman, "*Moulin Rouge* Director Reaches Right for the Heart," *Knight Ridder/Tribune News Service*, May 30, 2001 K0135.

118. John Horn, "The Land of Baz: From filling gas tanks to making *Moulin Rouge*, Aussie showman Baz Luhrmann has always been over the top," *Newsweek*, May 28, 2001 58.

119. Todd McCarthy, "*Moulin Rouge*," *Variety*, May 14, 2001, 21.

120. David Ansen, "Yes, Rouge Can, Can, Can: Not since *Cabaret* has a musical had such a kick," *Newsweek*, May 28, 2001, 61.

121. Paula Moore, "'*Moulin Rouge*' Full of Excesses," *Denver Business Journal*, June 1, 2001, 27A.

122. Owen Gleiberman, "Ballroom Blitz: In the frenetic musical *Moulin Rouge*, Nicole Kidman and Ewan McGregor look for love in a Paris gone pop," *Entertainment Weekly*, May 25, 2001, 48.

123. Glen Lovell, "*Moulin Rouge* Takes Cues from Better Musicals," *Knight Ridder/Tribune News Service,* June 14, 2001 K6090.

124. Mark Rahner, "*Moulin Rouge* Can-Can Overdo It," *Knight Ridder/Tribune News Service,* December 24 2001, K1366.
125. "Fox Gives *Moulin Rouge* Back to Fans for Midnight Shows...Because They 'Can't-Can't Can't Get Enough!" *Business Wire,* February 28, 2003, 5425.
126. Samantha Miller, Mark Dagostino, "All That Baz: Moving on from *Moulin Rouge,* Baz Luhrmann turns a century-old soap opera into Broadway's new hot ticket," *People Weekly,* January 13, 2003, 93.
127. Vern Perry, "*Moulin Rouge* is a Dazzling Trip," *Knight-Ridder/Tribune News Service,* December 24, 2001 K1326.
128. Mary F. Pols, "*Moulin Rouge,*" *Knight Ridder/Tribune News Service,* May 30, 2001, PK0136, 2 of 3.
129. Dave White, "Moulin rumba: Baz Lurhman creator of the fantasy musicals *Moulin Rouge* and *Strictly Ballroom,* redefines 'gay sensibility by including straight folks too: The Hollywood Issue — Brief Article—Interview," *The Advocate,* April 2, 2002 1 of 1.

Chapter 4: *From Hedwig and the Angry Inch to De-Lovely and Beyond*

1. Jane Crowther, "John Cameron Mitchell: "*Hedwig and the Angry Inch,*" *BBC* Film, August 23, 2001, http://www.bbc.co.uk/print/films/2001/08/23/hedwig_and_the_angry_inch_interview.shtml
2. Chris Vognar, "Bringing Hedwig to the Screen was a Rouge Awakening," *Dallas Morning News,* July 27, 2001.
3. Christopher Ciccone, "John Cameron Mitchell: Interview with male impersonator and film director —Interview," *Interview,* February 1999, 1 of 4, http://www.findarticles/com/p./articles/mi_M1285/is_2_29/ai_53747398/print
4. Chris Vognar, "Bringing Hedwig to the Screen was a Rouge Awakening," *Dallas Morning News,* July 27, 2001.
5. Cynthia Fuchs, "Interview with John Cameron Mitchell, Writer/Director/Star of *Hedwig and the Angry Inch,*" *PopMatters,* Summer 2001, http://www.popmatters.com/film/interviews/mitchell-john-cameron.html
6. Mark P.O. Morford and Robert J. Lenardon, *Classical Mythology,* Longman, 1991, 157.
7. Mark P.O. Morford and Robert J. Lenardon, *Classical Mythology,* Longman, 1991, 158.
8. Steven Rea, "*Hedwig and the Angry Inch,*" *Knight Ridder/Tribune News* Service, August 2, 2001, K0921.
9. David Noh, "Inches from Stardom: John Cameron Mitchell," *Film Journal International,* August 2001, 16.
10. Kerry Diamond, "*Hedwig*: Demeter's cinematic scent," *WWD,* June 22, 2001, 7.
11. B. Alan Intercourse, "Interview: Agent Orange: John Cameron Mitchell on *Hedwig and the Angry Inch,*" *Movie* Web, July 16, 2001, http://www.movieweb.com/news/news.php?id=2394.
12. Lisa Schwarzbaum, "Slice of Life: *Hedwig and the Angry Inch* is a wonderfully kitschy rock opera," *Entertainment Weekly,* July 27, 2001, 45.
13. Jumana Farouky, "*Hedwig and the Angry Inch*: Directed by John Cameron Mitchell," *Time International,* September 17, 2001, 73.
14. Rene Rodriguez, "*Hedwig and the Angry Inch,*" *Knight Ridder/Tribune News Service,* August 2, 2001, K0936.
15. Henry Sheehan, "A Stirring *Hedwig* Goes Far Beyond Camp," *Orange County Register,* July 23, 2001.
16. Ben Wener. "Rock Musicals Don't Get Much Better than *Hedwig.*" *Orange Country Register,* January 8, 2002.
17. David Noh. "Inches from Stardom: John Cameron Mitchell." *Film Journal International,* August 2001, 16.

18. "*Chicago* Razzle-Dazzles Over $100 Million in Domestic Box Office on Same Night That Director Rob Marshall Honored as DGA's Best Director; First Musical Since *Grease* to pass $100 million." *PR Newswire*, March 2, 2003 NYSU02002032003.

19. Hilary Osterle. *Dance Magazine*, February 1997. http://www.findarticles.com/p/articles/mi_m1003//is_n2v71/ai_1907975

20. Michele Willens. "A Razzle-Dazzle Pitchman." *The Los Angeles Times*, November 3, 2002. http://www.losangelestimes.com

21. Steve Daly. "*Chicago's* Hope: All That Glitz. All That Glam. All That Jazz: After many frustrating tryouts Broadway's '*Chicago*' has danced its way into movie theaters. And Oscar is sure to be watching." *Entertainment Weekly*, January 17, 2003, 20+.

22. "Interview with Director of *Chicago*." *CNN.com*. March 6, 2003. http://www.cnnstudentnews.cnn.com/transcripts/0303/06/lt.03.html

23. Steve Wulf. "Rob Marshall: *Chicago*." *Entertainment Weekly*, February 21, 2003 101.

24. Mark Miller. "His Kind of Town: *Chicago* has put first-time director Rob Marshall in the loop. Now Hollywood is dancing to his tune." *Newsweek*, January 27, 2003, 67.

25. Steve Daly. "*Chicago's Hope:* All That Glitz. All That Glam. All That Jazz: After many frustrating tryouts Broadway's Chicago has danced its way into movie theaters. And Oscar is sure to be watching." *Entertainment Weekly*, January 17, 2003 20+.

26. Paul Fischer. "Renee Sizzles on Screen in Old *Chicago*." *Girl.com*. 2003. http://www.girl.com.au/reneezelwegerchicago.htm

27. Phyllis Goldman. "*Chicago* a Hit—He Had it Comin': A one on one with Rob Marshall." *Back Stage*, July 4, 2003, 24.

28. Steve Daly. "*Chicago's* Hope: All That Glitz. All That Glam. All That Jazz: After many frustrating tryouts Broadway's *Chicago* has danced its way into movie theaters. And Oscar is sure to be watching." *Entertainment Weekly*, January 17, 2003, 20+.

29. Chris Hewitt, "Queen Latifah Says Movie Musical *Chicago* Is Dressed to Kill." *Knight Ridder/Tribune News Service,* January 2, 2003 K2219, 2 of 2.

30. Phyllis Goodman. "Making '*Chicago*' a Hit—He Had it Comin': A one on one with Rob Marshall." Back Stage, July 4, 2003, 24.

31. Merle Ginsberg. "Marshall Law," *WWD*, December 2002, 12.

32. "*Chicago* Cast Put Through Musical 'Boot-Camp' to Reach Oscar Glory," *Europe Intelligence Wire*, February 11, 2003.

33. Keith Bush. "Dressed to Kill: From *Sleepy Hollow* to *Chicago,* Colleen Atwood creates beautiful costumes for beastly characters." *KeithBush.com*, 2003. http://www.keithbush.com/article_atwood.htm

34. Steve Wulf. "Rob Marshall: *Chicago*," *Entertainment Weekly,* February 21, 2003, 101.

35. Steve Daly. "*Chicago's* Hope: All that glitz. All that glam. All that jazz: After many frustrating tryouts Broadway's *Chicago* has danced its way into movie theaters. And Oscar is sure to be watching." *Entertainment Weekly*, January 17 2003 20+.

36. Christopher Rawson. "The Starry Cast of *Chicago* Follows Rob Marshall's Lead in his Big-Screen Directing Debut." *The Post-Gazette*, April 21, 2003. http://post-gazette.com/ae/20020421chicago0421fnp1.asp

37. Stephanie Zacharek, "*Chicago,"* *Salon.com,* December 27, 2002. http://www.salon.com/ent/movies/review/2002/12/27/chicago/index_np.html

38 Jonathan Foreman, "First City," *The New York Post*, December 27, 2002. http://www.nypost.com/movies/65597.htm

39. Eleanor Dingle Gillespie, "*Chicago,"* *Atlanta-Constitution Journal.* http:///www.accessatlanta.com/ovies/content/shared/movies/C/chicago.html

40. Peter Howell, "*Chicago,"* *The Toronto Star,* December 26, 2002. http:/www.thestar.com

41. Susan Stark, "*Chicago* Puts on Quite a Show," *The Detroit News*. December 27, 2002. http://www.detnews.com/2002/entertainment/0212/27/ea-45306.htm

42. Josh Young, "If You're Good to Harvey, Harvey's Good to You," *Entertainment Weekly*, March 7, 2003, 32.

43. Nancy Miller, "Summer Lovin': American Idol Kelly Clarkson hits the big screen with *From Justin to Kelly*. But are audiences ready for a moment like this?," Entertainment Weekly, June 13, 2004, 60+.

44. Tom Gliatto, "Big Screen Idols: Sure, they can sing. But will Justin and Kelly make it as movie sweethearts?" *People Weekly*, June 16, 2003 148.

45. Nancy Miller, "Summer Lovin': American Idol Kelly Clarkson hits the big screen with *From Justin to Kelly*." But are audiences ready for a moment like this?," *Entertainment Weekly*, June 13, 2004, 60+.

46. "Fans to Vote on New Poster for America's Newest Movie Idols' Debut Film: *From Justin to Kelly.*" *Business Wire*, February 26, 2003, 5665.

47. Scott Hettrick, "The Life Preserver: Not since the Vanilla Ice movie *Cool as Ice* in 1991 has the industry seen such a rush to home video." *Video Business*, July 7, 2003 31.

48. Owen Gleiberman. "*From Justin To Kelly*: a.k.a. Beach Blanket Stinko—two former Idols fall flat in a tone-deaf teen musical." July 11, 2003, 61.

49. Kelly Mullen. "Film Review: From bad to worse in *Justin to Kelly*." *The America's Intelligence Wire*, June 26, 2003.

50. Scott Foundas "*From Justin to Kelly*." *Variety*, June 30, 2003, 24.

51. Greg Adkins, "Justin Guarini: Fallen American Idol?" *People Weekly*, December 22, 2003, 21.

52. Greg Adkins, "Justin Guarini: Fallen American Idol?" *People Weekly*, December 22, 2003, 21.

53. Armond White, "That Thing They Don't (three recent movie musicals)" *Film Comment*, March–April 1997, 45.

54. Mary F. Pols, "Stagedoor to Screen: Todd Graff bases first movie on theater camp." *Knight-Ridder/Tribune News Service*, August 15, 2003.

55. Mary F. Pols, "Stagedoor to Screen: Todd Graff bases first movie on theater camp." *Knight-Ridder/Tribune News Service*, August 15, 2003.

56. Lauric Hibbard, "Todd Graff's *Camp* Experience." *CBS News*, August 14, 2003, 1 of 2. http://www.cbsnews.com/stories/2003/08/13/earlyshow/leisure/celebsport//printable568089.

57. Jamie Painter Young, "Setting Up *Camp*: When you can't cast a project through traditional routes, you have to get creative." *Back Stage West*, July 17, 2003, 1–3.

58. Jamie Painter Young, "Setting Up *Camp*: When you can't cast a project through traditional routes, you have to get creative." *Back Stage West*, July 17, 2003, 1–3.

59. "IFC Goes '*Camp*': Marks a transitional year," *Hollywood Reporter*, January 7, 2004, 67.

60. Peter Travers, *Rolling Stone*, July 17, 2003. http://www.rollingstone.com

61. Steve Tobias, *The Onion a.v. Club*. Summer 2003. http://www.theonionavclub.com/review.php?review-id=6650

62. David Ansen, "Snap Judgement," *Newsweek*, August 4, 2003, 57.

63. Amanda Schurr. "With Pluck and Moxie, Kids at *Camp* will win your heart." *Sarasota Herald Tribune*, August 29, 2003, 13.

64. "Energetic Cast Saves '*Camp*' film." *Asia Africa Intelligence Wire*, June 10, 2004.

65. Connie Ogle, "*Camp*." *Knight Ridder/Tribune News Service*, August 7, 2003, K4901.

66. Jay Richardson, "Director Todd Graff: Interview with Director of *Camp*." *FutureMovies.co.uk*. 1 of 4. http://www.futuremovies.co.uk/friendly_filmmaking.asp?article=46

67. Armond White, "That Thing They Don't (three recent musicals)." *Film Comment*, March–April, 1997, 45.

68. Steve Ramos, "Stage Struck: Filmmaker Todd Graff relives his teenage years with his musical *Camp*." *Cincinnati City Beat*, Volume 9, Issue 41; August 20–August 26, 2003, 1 of 3. http://www.citybeat.com/2003-08/20/printable/film2.html

69. Richard Fehr and Frederick G. Vogel, *Lullabies of Hollywood: Movie Music and The Movie Musical, 1915–1992*, McFarland and Company Inc., Publishers, 1992, 244.

70. Chris Hewitt, *"Camp," Knight-Ridder/Tribune News Service*, August 17, 2003.

71. Lisa Schwarzbaum. "*Camp:* Extravagance rules in an endearing but underdone drama." *Entertainment Weekly*, August 1, 2003, 62.

72. Rex Roberts, *"The Singing Detective." Film Journal International,* November, 2003, 56–57.

73. Kirk Honeycutt, *"The Singing Detective." Hollywood Reporter,* January 21, 2003, 89–90.

74. Chris Gardner, "Par Classics Books Rights to *Detective*," *Hollywood Reporter*, February 7, 2003, 1–2.

75. Mark Caro, "A Sobering Journey," *The Chicago Tribune*, November 2003, 3 of 5. http://www.rdjfan.com/articles/chicago-tribune-03.asp

76. Ed Grant, "Singin' the Clues," *Video Business,* April 7, 2003, 14.

77. Michael Fleming, "Gumshoe Thriller at Icon," *Daily Variety*, February 26, 2002, 1–2.

78. Mark Caro, "A Sobering Journey," *The Chicago Tribune,* November 2003, 3 of 5. http://www.rdjfan.com/articles/chicago-tribune-03.asp

79. Vicky Hallett, "Singing for his story," *U.S. News and World Report*, April 28, 2003, 10.

80. *Associated Press*, "Singing to Sundance," January 21, 2003. http://entertinment/msn.com/news/article.aspx?news-112776

81. Thomas Chau, "On the Phone: Keith Gordon of *The Singing Detective*," *Cinema Confidential* October 23, 2003. http://www.cinemaconfidential.com

82. Molly Marshall, Nicola Ries, Bill Taggart, "*The Singing Detective*: Interview with Director Keith Gordon" March 18, 2003. http://www.psoriasis.org/resources/publications/singingdetectiveinterview.php

83. Roger Ebert, *"The Singing Detective." Chicago Sun-Times.* November 7, 2003. http://www.suntimes.com/ebert/ebert_reviews/2003/11/110706.html

84. Mark Steyn, "Potter Mismatch," *Spectator*, November 15, 2003, 66–67.

85. Martin Hoyle, "Downey Gets Under the Skin of his Role: CINEMA: Martin Hoyle wonders if Keith Gordon's version of *The Singing Detective* is up to scratch." *The Financial Times.* November 13, 2003, 19.

86. Chris Hewitt, "*The Singing Detective*," *Knight Ridder/Tribune News Service,* November 6, 2003, K4150.

87. "The Big Picture—*The Singing Detective*." *Europe Intelligence Wire,* November 13, 2003.

88. Rex Roberts, "*The Singing Detective*." *Film Journal International*, November 2003, 56–57.

89. Leah Rozen., "*The Singing Detective*: Robert Downey Jr., Mel Gibson, Robin Wright Penn, Katie Holmes." *People Weekly,* November 3, 2003, 36.

90. Rick Altman, *The American Film Musical*, Indiana University Press, 1987, 59–60.

91. Chris Vognar, "*The Singing Detective*," *Knight Ridder/Tribune News Service*, November 6, 2003, K3494.

92. Peter Tonguette, "Off-Key: What the critics missed in *The Singing Detective*," *Senses of Cinema*, April 30, 2004. http://www.sensesofcinema.com/contents/04/30/singing_detective.html

93. Joel Isaac Frady. "North Carolina State U: Film Review: *The Singing Detective* a topsy-turvy turn of psyche." *The America's Intelligence Wire*, November 25, 2003.

94. Dan Bennett, "Director uses Music As Key to Unlock Porter's life." *NC Times*, July 7, 2004, 1 of 2. http://www.nctimes.com/articles/2004/07/13/04/entertainment/movies/7_7_0413_24_19.prt

95. Mike Szymanski, "*De-Lovely* Experience. Ashley Judd and Kevin Kline bring Cole Porter's life to the big screen." *Zap2It.com*, July 2004. http://www.entertainment.msn/com/celebs/article/aspx?news=162717

96. Neil Minow, "Writer Neil Minow sat down with *De-Lovely* star Ashley Judd to talk about the film." *Yahoo Movies*, July 2004. http://www.movies.yahoo.com/movies/feature/delovely.html

97. Rebecca Winters, "Making over the Porters," Time, June 7, 2004, 139.

98. Samantha Critchell, "Period Costumes are Delightful, Delicious in *De-Lovely.*" *The America's Intelligence Wire*, July 2, 2004.

99. Diana Saenger., "Irwin Winkler's *De-Lovely* Embraces a Lost Hollywood Glamour." *About.com,* June 28, 2004, 1 of 1.
http://www.romanticmovies.about.com/od/delovely/a/delovely062804_P.htm

100. David Germain, "Kline Talks About *De-Lovely* as Composer Cole Porter," *Reno-Gazette-Journal*, July 21, 2004, 2 of 2. http://www.rgi.com/news/printstory.php?id=76094.

101. John Burlingame, "Mining Gold from Cole. *De-Lovely* is MGM's attempt to extend its musical heritage." *Variety*, April 19, 2004 S18,

102. Jeff Otto, "Interview: Ashley Judd and Kevin Kline. They're *De-Lovely.*" *Film Force*, July 1, 2004, 1 of 1. http://filmforce.ign.com/articles/527/527723p1.html?fromint=1

103. Christy Lemire, "At the movies: *De-Lovely.*" *The America's Intelligence Wire,* July 2, 2004.

104. Owen Gleiberman, "*De-Lovely:* A melodious biopic takes a de-charming look at Cole Porter." *Entertainment Weekly,*, July 9, 2004, 63.

105. Wendy R. Weinstein, "*De-Lovely,*" *Film Journal International*, July, 2004, 71.

106. Moira McDonald, *The Seattle Times*, July 3, 2004.

107. Richard Schickel, "It's De-Pressing! A new Cole Porter biopic plays the great songwriter's life in a minor key." *Time*, July 5, 2004, 90.

108. McCarthy, Todd. "*De-Lovely.*" *Daily Variety*, May 24, 2004, 2.

109. Carla Hay, "Director Hackford on the Genius of *Ray.*" *Billboard*, November 20, 2004, 18.

110. Ann Marie Cruz, "Plight Unseen." *People Weekly*, May 31, 2004, 122.

111. Aldore D. Collier, "Jamie Foxx Gives Awesome Performance in Acclaimed Movie *Ray.*" *Jet*, November 1, 2004, 52.

112. Philip Wuntch, "*Ray,*" *Knight Ridder/Tribune News Service*, October 29, 2004, K3371.

113. "Movie *Ray* Hauls in $20.1 Million Over Premiere Weekend." *Jet*, November 15, 2004, 10.

114. Steve Pratt, "Phan...tastic." *Europe Intelligence Wire*, December 9, 2004.

115. Faridul Anwar Farinordin, "The Great Phantom Alliance." *Asia-Africa Intelligence Wire*, December 11, 2004.

116. "Film *Phantom* Worth the Wait," *Sci-Fi Wire*, December 21 2004. http://www.scifi.com

117. "Emmy Rossum Hits a High Note," *Star*, December 20, 2004, 7.

118. Louis B. Hobson, "*Phantom* Pain," *Calgary Sun*, December 19, 2004. http://www.calgarysun.com

119. Stephen Schaefer, "Lead Role in *Opera* is a High Note for Butler," *The Boston Herald,* December 21 2004. http://www.theedge.bostonherald.com/movieNews

120. Steve Pratt, "Phan...tastic," *Europe Intelligence Wire*, December 9, 2004.

121. Christy Lemire, "*Phantom* a Bloated Nightmare. Big Images, little charm in movie adaptation of musical," *CNN*, December 22, 2004. http://www.cnn.entertainment.com

122. Daniel Neman. *The Richmond-Times Dispatch*, January 1, 2005, G58.

123. Roger Ebert, "*Phantom* Merits a Look, But Don't Bother Listening," *Roger Ebert.com*, December 22, 2004. www.rogerebert.com

124. Colin Covert, "Movie Review: *Phantom of the Opera* offers a touch of class," *Star Tribune,* December 22, 2004. http://www.startribune.com

125. Lisa Kennedy, "*Phantom* unveils a new beauty, but it doesn't do beast any good," *The Denver Post*, December 22, 2004. http://www.denverpost.com

126. David Ansen, "*The Phantom of the Opera*: Into the Night," *Newsweek*, December 20, 2004, 58.

Chapter Five: Cathode Razzle-Dazzle: The Musical on TV

1. Betsy Sharkey, "If the Slipper Fits...two producers with a track record in musicals for TV take on a classic, with a slight twist," *Mediaweek*, August 18, 1997, 17–18.
2. Terry Kelleher. "*Rodgers and Hammerstein's Cinderella*," *People Weekly*, November 3, 1997, 17.
3. "Spotlight," *Time for Kids,* October 31, 1997, 7.
4. Lynette Rice, "ABC tries on *Cinderella*," *Broadcasting & Cable*, October 27, 1997, 30–31.
5. Ray Richmond, "*Rodgers and Hammerstein's Cinderella*," *Variety*, October 27, 1997, 32.
6. "*Cinderella* TV Movie Special Produces Spectacular Rating for ABC," *Jet*, November 24, 1997, 63.
7. Denise Lanctot, "*Rodgers and Hammerstein's Cinderella*." *Entertainment Weekly*, February 13, 1998, 74.
8. "TV Reviews: *South Pacific*." *WENN*, March 26, 2001, 1 of 1. http://www.imdb.com
9. Dick Adler, "Will advertisers cop a plea for *Cop Rock?*" *Adweek, Eastern edition*, November 12, 1990, 50.
10. David Hiltbrand, "*Cop Rock*," *People Weekly*, October 1, 1990, 10.
11. Steve Coe, "Thumbs Up, Thumbs Down for Network Musicals: ABC confident of *Cop Rock*"; NBC cancels *Hull High*."
12. George Plasketes, "*Cop Rock* Revisited: Unsung series and musical hinge in cross-genre evolution." *Journal of Popular Film and Television*, Summer 2004, 64–75.
13. Chris Vognar, "*Simpsons*' Musical Spoofs Worthy of an Encore." *Knight Ridder/Tribune News Service*, June 16, 2004 K3653.
14. David Poland, "Hit Parade." *Entertainment Weekly*, March 28, 1997, 14.
15. David Klein, "Emmy-worthy *Buffy* Musical Slays This Critic," *Electronic Media*, July 9, 2002, 6.

Conclusion: Phantom of the Genre

1. George M. Thomas, "Success of Two Movies Has Studios Tuning Up More," *Akron Beacon Journal*, March 6, 2003, 1 of 1.
2. Rebecca Traister, "Waiting for the Razzle-Dazzle. *Chicago* Was Supposed to Usher in a New Age of Movie Musicals. So Where Are They?" *The New York Times*, February 29 2004, AR 19.
3. Andy Seiler, "Future Looks *De-Lovely* for Movie Musicals." *USA Today*, August 21, 2003, 2 of 2.
4. Rebecca Traister, "Waiting for the Razzle-Dazzle. *Chicago* Was Supposed to Usher in a New Age of Movie Musicals. So Where Are They?" *The New York Times*, February 29 2004, AR 19.

Selected Bibliography

Books and Essays

Altman, Rick. *The American Film Musical*. Indiana University Press, 1987.

Astaire, Fred. *Steps in Time*. Cooper Square Publishing, First Cooper Square Press Edition, June 2000.

Cardullo, Bert, ed. *The Film Criticsm of Vernon Young*. University Press of America, 1990.

Crafton Donald. *Talkies: American Cinema's Transition to Sound, 1926–1931 (History of the American Cinema 4)*. University of California Press, 1999.

Everson, William K. *American Silent Film*. DaCapo Press, 1998.

Fehr, Richard and Vogel, Frederick G. *Lullabies of Hollywood: Movie Music and the Movie Musical 1915–1992*. McFarland and Company Inc., Publishers, 1992.

Giannetti, Louis. *Understanding Movies, Fifth Edition*. Prentice Hall, 1990.

Green, Stanley. *Hollywood Musicals: Year By Year, 2nd Edition*. Hal Leonard, 2000.

Harmetz Aljean. *The Making of The Wizard of Oz: Movie Magic and Studio Power in the Prime of MGM, 16th Edition*. Hyperion, 1998.

Katz, Ephraim. *The Film Encyclopedia: The Most Comprehensive Encyclopedia of World Cinema in a Single Volume*. Harper and Row Publishers, 1979.

Mailer, Norman. *Marilyn*. Grosset & Dunlap, Inc., 1973.

McCabe, John. *Cagney*. Carroll and Graff Publishers, 1999.

Medved, Harry, with Dreyfuss, Randy. *The Fifty Worst Films of All Time*. Warner Books, 1978.

Medved, Harry and Medved, Michael. *The Golden Turkey Awards*. Perigee Books, 1980.

Morford, Mark P.O and Lenardon, Robert J. *Classical Mythology*, Fourth Edition. Longman, New York and London, 1991.

Muir, John Kenneth. *Best in Show: The Films of Christopher Guest and Company*. Applause Theatre and Cinema Books, 2004.

Parker, Sir Alan. *The Making of Evita*. September, 1996.

Peary, Danny. *Cult Movies: The Classics, the Sleepers, the Weird, and the Wonderful*. Delacorte Press, New York, 1981.

Rubin, Martin. *Showstoppers: Busby Berkeley and the Tradition of Spectacle*. Columbia University Press, 1993.

Springer, John. *A Pictorial History of the Movie Musical*. Castle Books, 1966

Taylor, John Russell. *Great Movie Moments*. Crescent Books, New York, 1987.

The Movie Book. Phaidon Press Limited, 2002.

The Riverside Shakespeare. Houghton Mifflin Company, Boston, 1974.

Wlaschin, Ken. *The Illustrated Encyclopedia of the World's Greatest Movie Stars and Their Films from 1900 to the Present Day*. Harmony Books, 1979.

Yudkoff, Alvin. *Gene Kelly: A Life of Dance and Dreams*. Backstage Books, 1999.

Zinman, David. *Fifty Grand Movies of the 1960s & 1970s*. Crown Publishers, Inc., New York, 1986.

Periodicals

Adams, Noah. "Review: Movie *Hedwig and the Angry Inch*." *All Things Considered* (NPR), July 20, 2001.

Adkins, Greg. "Justin Guarini: Fallen American Idol?" *People Weekly*, December 22, 2003, 21.

Adler, Dick. "Will advertisers cop a plea for *Cop Rock*? *Adweek*, Eastern Edition, November 12, 1990, 50.

Ansen, David. "*Evita*." *Newsweek*, December 16, 1996, 63.

Ansen, David. "A Sprinkling of Ziggy Stardust." *Newsweek*, November 9, 1998, 70.

Ansen, David. "*Light & Dark*: Bjork's acting debut is one of the fall's most controversial movies." Newsweek September 25, 2000, 66.

Ansen, David. "Snap Judgement." *Newsweek*, August 4, 2003, 57.

Ansen, David. "The Phantom of the Opera: Into the Night." *Newsweek*, December 20, 2004, 58.

Arnold, Gary. "Everyone Says I Love You." *Insight on the News*, January 20, 1997, 38–39.

Arroyo Jose. *Sight and Sound*. February, 1997, 40.

Bart, Peter. "Do Censors Need Censoring?" *Daily Variety*, July 12, 1999, 4.

Bennett, Dan. "Director Uses Music as Key to Unlock Porter's Life." *NC Times*, July 7, 2004, 1 of 2. http://www.nctimes.com/articles/2004/07/13/entertainment/movies/7_7_0413_24_19.prt

Berliner, Todd. "The Sounds of Silence: Songs in Hollywood Films Since the 1960s—Critical Essay." *Style*, Spring 2002, 1–11.

Bernard, Jami. "*The Singing Detective*." *Knight Ridder/Tribune News Service*, November 3, 2003, K2566.

Bernstein, Abbie. "*Fantastick* Journey." *Back Stage West*, September 28, 2000, 6.

Berson, Misha. "*Love's Labour's Lost.*" *Knight Ridder/Tribune News Service*, June 19, 2000, K1633.

Blake, Richard. "Certainly *Chicago*." *America*, March 31, 2003 23.

Broesky, Pat H. "Anything Goes?" *Entertainment Weekly*, September 24, 1993, 8–9.

Brown, Scott and Downey, Robert Jr. "Downey Fresh: Watching the Detective." November 7, 2003, 53.

Bullock, Marcus. "Treasures of the Earth and Screen: Todd Hayne's film, *Velvet Goldmine*." Discourse, Fall 2002 3–27.

Burr, Ty. "I'll Do Anything." *Entertainment Weekly*, August 12, 1994, 66.

Cerio, Gregory. "Don't yell at me, Argentina." *People Weekly*, February 26, 1996, 48–50.

Cochran, Jay. "*Fantasticks* Voyage." *Entertainment Weekly*, May 2, 1997, 72.

Cocks, Jay. "Lindsay Anderson: 1923–1994; In celebration." *Film Comment*, Nov–Dec 1994, 7–10.

Coe, Jonathan. "*Everyone Says I Love You*." *New Statesman*, April 18, 1997, 40–42.

Coe, Steve. "Thumbs Up, Thumbs Down for Network Musicals; ABC Confident of Cop Rock; NBC Cancels Hull High." *Broadcasting*, October 29, 1990, 32.

Collier, Aldore D. "Jamie Foxx gives awesome performance in acclaimed movie 'Ray.'" *Jet*, November 1, 2004, 52.

Cooper, Rand Richards. "Dark and Darker: *Dancer in the Dark* & *Get Carter*." *Commonweal*, November 3, 2000, 20.

Corliss, Richard. "Still Lucky Jim? Comedy czar James L. Brooks tries to fix the movie that used to be a musical." *Time*, January 31, 1994, 102–105.

Corliss, Richard. "Evita." *Time*, December 16, 1996, 72.

Corliss, Richard. "Sick and Inspired: The South Park movie has a mean streak—and a song in its heart." *Time*, July 5, 1999, 75.

Corliss, Richard. "Branagh Faces the Music: His bad-singing, bad-dancing *Love's Labour's Lost* suggest the end of the rein of King Ken." *Time*, June 12, 2000, 82.

Cornwell, Jane. "Bjork Goes Berserk." *The Bulletin with Newsweek*, December 12, 2000 90–91.

Critchell, Samantha. "Period costumes are Delightful, Delicious in *De-Lovely*." *The America's Intelligence Wire*, July 2, 2004.

Cuneen, Joseph. "*Everyone Says I Love You*." *National Catholic Reporter*, February 7, 1997, 10.

Cuneen, Joseph. "Dancing Fools." *National Catholic Reporter*, June 30, 2000, 18.

Dale, Grover. "Choreographer Bitten by Acting Bug!" *Dance Magazine*, September 2000, 68.

Daley, Steve. "Chicago's Hope: All that glitz. All that glam. All that jazz: After many frustrating tryouts Broadway's *Chicago* has danced its way into movie theaters. And Oscar is sure to be watching." *Entertainment Weekly*, January 17, 2003, 20+.

Dargis, Manohla. "Singing and the Dane." *Harper's Bazaar*, September 2000, 400.

David Denby. *New York*, December 9, 1996, 72.

Diamond, Jamie. "Bringing You a Hollywood Musical...With No Music." *The New York Times*, January 30, 1994, H13 and H23.

Diamond, Kerry. "*Hedwig*: Demeter's Cinematic Scent." *WWD*, June 22, 2001, 7.

DoCarmo, Stephen N. "Beyond good and evil: Mass culture theorized in Todd Haynes' *Velvet Goldmine*." *Journal of American and Comparative Cultures*, Fall-Winter 2002, 395–398.

Eisner, Ken. "Seattle embraces new *Love's*." *Daily Variety*, May 15, 2000, 72.

Elley, Derek. "*Love's Labour's Lost*." *Daily Variety*, February 21, 2000, 36.

Farinordin, Faridul Anwar. "The Great Phantom Alliance." *Asia-Africa Intelligence Wire*, December 11, 2004.

Farouky, Jumana. "*Hedwig and the Angry Inch*: Directed by John Cameron Mitchell." Time International, September 17, 2001, 73.

Flick, Larry. "Radio Embraces Evita." *Billboard*, October 26, 1996, 1–2.

Fink, Mitchell. "Don't Cry for Her." *People Weekly*, April 25, 1994, 37.

Fink, Mitchell. "The Buzz on Madonna's." *People Weekly*, December 23, 1996, 37.

Fleming, Michael. "Gumshoe Thriller at Icon." *Daily Variety*, February 26, 2002, 1–2.

Fleming, Michael. "Detective Gets its Girl." *Daily Variety*, April 4, 2002, 1–2.

Foundas, Scott. "*The Fantasticks*." *Variety*, September 18, 2000, 30.

Foundas, Scott. "*From Justin to Kelly*." *Variety*, June 30, 2003, 24.

Frady, Joel Isaac. "*The Singing Detective*—A topsy turvy turn of psyche." The America's Intelligence Wire, November 25, 2003.

Fuller, Graham. "*The Empire Strikes Back*." *Interview*, November 1998, 98–107.

Fuller, Graham. "Oh! You Pretty Things." *Interview*, December, 1998 102.

Fuller, Graham. "*Love's Labour's Lost*." *Interview*, June 2000, 60.

Fuller, Graham. "*Moulin Rouge* gives the screen musical a make over." *Knight Ridder/Tribune News Service*, May 11, 2001 K1022.

Gardner, Chris. "Par Classics Books Rights to *Detective*." *Hollywood Reporter*, February 7, 2003, 1–2.

Gardner, Chris. "Buyers spark '*Camp*' fire: 3 distribs tune up for Graff musical." *Hollywood Reporter*, February 25, 2003, 78–79.

Gaydos, Steven. "*Brother*'-ly love goes global." *Daily Variety*, June 25, 2001, 8.

Germain, David. "Kline Finds *De-Lovely* Role as Composer Cole Porter." *The America's Intelligence Wire*, July 2 2004.

Ginsberg, Merle. "Marshall Law." *WWD*, December 20, 2002, 12.

Gliatto, Tom. "Big Screen Idols: Sure, they can sing. But will Justin and Kelly make it as movie sweethearts?" *People Weekly*, June 16, 2003 148+.

Gleiberman, Owen. "Swing Kids." *Entertainment Weekly*, March 12, 1993, 42.

Gleiberman, Owen. "Ballroom Blitz: In the frenetic musical *Moulin Rouge*, Nicole Kidman and Ewan McGregor look for love in a Paris gone pop." *Entertainment Weekly*, May 25, 2001, 48.

Gleiberman, Owen. "*From Justin to Kelly*: a.k.a. Beach Blanket Stinko—two former Idols fall flat in a tone-deaf teen musical." *Entertainment Weekly*, July 11, 2003, 61.

Gleiberman, Owen. "*De-Lovely*: A Melodious biopic takes a de-charming look at Cole Porter." *Entertainment Weekly*, July 9, 2004, 63.

Goldblatt, Henry. "*From Justin to Kelly*." *Entertainment Weekly*, August 22 2003, 119.

Goldman, Phyllis. "Making *Chicago* a Hit—He Had It Comin': A one on one with Rob Marshall." *Back Stage*, July 4, 2003, 24.

Goondale, Gloria. "Movie Musicals are Back, but Think MTV." *Christian Science Monitor*, March 21, 2002, 1 of 2.

Graham, Bob. "Genres Never Really Die. Musicals and Westerns may seem to fade away, but they always come back." *The San Francisco Chronicle*, June 17, 2001, 35.

Grant, Ed. "Singin' the clues." *Video Business*, April 17, 2003, 14.

Groves, Don. "*Dancer* Kicks Up Heels in O'seas Tour." *Daily Variety*, January 29, 2001, 12.

Gutman, Barry. "*Hedwig and the Angry Inch*." *Video Business*, October 29, 2001, 17.

Gwin, Peter. "*Dancer in the Dark*." *Europe*, December 2000, 46.

Haagensen, Erik. "Turning night into day in *De-Lovely*." *Back Stage*, June 25, 2004, 23.

Hallett Vicky. "Singing for his story." *U.S. News and World Report*, April 28, 2003, 10.

Harris, Dana. "*De-Lovely* closes Cannes." *Daily Variety*, March 9, 2004, 5.

Harvey Dennis. "*Hedwig and the Angry Inch*." *Variety*, January 29, 2001 48.

Hay, Carla. "Film Success Paves Way for Slate of TV Musicals." *Billboard*, August 30, 2003 9–10.

Hensley, Dennis. "Cosmo Q & A (actor Matthew Lillard). *Cosmopolitan*, June 2000, 182.

Hettrick, Scott. "The life preserver: not since the Vanilla Ice movie *Cool as Ice* in 1991 has the industry seen such a rush to home video." *Video Business*, July 7, 2003, 31.

Hewitt, Chris. "*Love's Labour's Lost*." *Knight Ridder/Tribune News Service*, June 15, 200, K687,

Hewitt, Chris. "*Camp*." *Knight Ridder/Tribune News Service*, August 17, 2003.

Hewitt, Chris. "*The Singing Detective*." *Knight Ridder/Tribune News Service*, November 6, 2003, K4150.

Hiltbrand, David. "*Cop Rock*." *People Weekly*, October 1, 1990, 10.

Hobson, Louis B. "*Phantom* Pain." *Calgary Sun*, December 20, 2004. http://www.calgarysun.com

Holste, Gayle. "Branagh's *Labour's Lost*: Too much, too little, too late." *Literature-Film Quarterly*, July 2002, 228–230.

Honeycutt, Kirk. "*The Singing Detective*." *Hollywood Reporter*, January 21, 2003, 89–90.

Horn, John. "The Land of Baz: From filling gas tanks to making *Moulin Rouge*, Aussie showman Baz Luhrmann has always been over the top." *Newsweek*, May 28, 2001, 58.

Hoyle, Martin. "Downey Gets Under the Skin of His Role: Cinema: Martin Hoyle wonders if Keith Gordon's version of *The Singing Detective* is up to scratch." *The Financial Times*, November 13, 2003, 19.

Infantino, Vivian. "Don't Cry for Her." *Footwear News*, January 27, 1997, S10.

Isherwood, Charles. "Baz on Broadway: the *Moulin Rouge* filmmaker applies his brand of avant garde populism to Puccini." *Daily Variety*, October 21, 2003, A26.

James, Alison. '*Dark*' victory at Euro Film Awards." *Daily Variety*, December 11, 2000, 62.

Johnson, Brian D. "*Evita*." *Maclean's*, December 30, 1996, 102–103.

Johnson, Brian D. "*Everyone Says I Love You*." *Maclean's*, February 3, 1997, 66.

Johnson, Brian D. "Singin' in the Brain: Bjork hits an ethereal note as a day-dreaming martyr." *Maclean's*, October 16, 2000, 74.

Jones, Alan. "*Little Shop of Horrors*." *Cinefantastique*, January 1987, 17–21.

Karon, Paul. "Genre Transfusion: *Rouge, Park, Lantana* helmers reinvent classic forms." *Daily Variety*, January 15, 2002, A1–A3.

Kauffmann, Stanley. "*I'll Do Anything*." *The New Republic*, March 7, 1994, 30–31.

Kauffmann, Stanley. "*Everyone Says I Love You*." *The New Republic*, November 11, 1996, 40–41.

Kauffmann, Stanley. "On Films—Well, Not Completely Lost." *The New Republic*, July 10, 2000, 32.

Kauffmann, Stanley. "On Films—True and Utterly False." *The New Republic,* October 16, 2000, 40.

Kelleher, Terry. "*Rodgers and Hammerstein's Cinderella.*" *People Weekly,* November 3, 1997, 17.

Kelly, Bill. *Dancer in the Dark* Works on its Own Terms." *Sarasota Herald Tribune,* October 6, 2000, 13.

Kemp, Stuart. "Fortissimo Film Packs Up Rights to Graff's *Camp. Hollywood Reporter,* November 5, 2002, 12–13.

Kilday Gregg. "Luhrmann Left Out of Big Dance." *Hollywood Reporter,* February 12, 2002, 1 of 1.

Kinder, Marsha. "*Moulin Rouge.*" *Film Quarterly,* Spring 2002, 52–60.

Kit, Zorianna. "Music of night calls Rossum to '*Phantom.*'" *Hollywood Reporter,* May 27, 2003, 4–5.

Klawans, Stuart. "*Velvet Goldmine* & *American History X.*" *The Nation,* November 30, 1998, 32.

Klawans, Stuart. "*Bewitched.*" *The Nation,* September 6, 1999, 34.

Klein, David. "Emmy-Worthy *Buffy* Musical Slays This Critic." *Electronic Media,* July 8, 2002, 6.

Krauz, Enrique and Heifetz, Hank. "*Evita.*" *The New Republic,* February 10, 1997, 31–37.

Kung, Michelle. "*The Singing Detective.*" *Entertainment Weekly,* March 26, 2004, 79.

Lanctot, Denise. "*Rodgers and Hammerstein's Cinderella.*" *Entertainment Weekly,* February 13, 1998, 74.

Lee, Elyssa. "All That Baz: *Moulin Rouge* Director Luhrmann's Big Night." *In Style,* June 1, 2003, 200.

Lee, Luaine. "*Dancer in the Dark* Star Says Reports of Strife Were Exaggerated." *Knight Ridder/Tribune News Service,* October 16, 2000, K4447.

Lee, Luaine. "Baz Luhrmann's Love of Movie Musicals Spurred *Moulin Rouge.*" *Knight Ridder/Tribune News Service,* May 21, 2001, K4649.

Lemire, Christy. "At the Movies: *De-Lovely.*" *The America's Intelligence Wire,* July 2, 2004.

Lister, David. "Shakespeare Meets Busby Berkeley." *The Independent,* April 17, 1999, 11.

Lovell, Glenn. "*Dancer in the Dark.*" *Knight Ridder/Tribune News Service,* October 4, 2000, K7810.

Lyons, Charles. "Publicists Tap *Dancer* Auds for von Trier Pic." *Daily Variety,* October 9, 2000, 6.

Maynard, Kevin. "*South Park: Bigger, Longer & Uncut.*" *The Advocate,* May 23, 2000, 91.

McCarthy, Todd. "*Velvet Goldmine.*" *Daily Variety,* May 25, 1998, 56–67.

McCarthy, Todd. "*Moulin Rouge.*" *Daily Variety,* May 15, 2001, 21.

McCarthy, Todd. "*De-Lovely.*" *Daily Variety,* May 24, 2004, 2.

McClintock, Pamela. "*Detective* directive." *Daily Variety,* October 14, 2003, 19.

McDonald, Moira. "Songs are given center stage in Cole Porter biopic *De-Lovely.*" *Knight Ridder/Tribune News Service,* July 3, 2004, K6571.

McDonald, Neil. "Branagh's *Labour's Lost.*" *Quadrant,* April 2002, 56–63.

Meyer, George. "Getting Ziggy Wid'It: *Velvet Goldmine* is the history of Glam Rock in the gloaming— with a personal twist." Sarasota Herald Tribune, November 27, 1998, 18.

Miller, Mark. "His Kind of Town: *Chicago* has put first-time director Rob Marshall in the loop. Now Hollywood is dancing to his tune." *Newsweek,* January 27, 2003, 67.

Miller, Nancy. "Summer Lovin': American Idol Kelly Clarkson hits the big screen with *From Justin to Kelly.* But are audiences ready for a moment like this?" *Entertainment Weekly,* June 13, 2003, 60+.

Miller, Samantha. "All That Baz: Moving on from *Moulin Rouge,* Baz Lurhmann turns a century-old opera into Broadway's new hot ticket." *People Weekly,* January 13, 2003, 93+.

Miller, Stuart. "Selling *Evita* to the Masses: Retailers around the country are betting Madonna's upcoming star turn will spark a style revolution." *Newsweek,* November 11, 1996, 92.

Moltenbrey, Karen. "Highs and Lows." *Computer Graphics World,* September 1999, 48.

Morgan, Laura. "South vs. North." *Entertainment Weekly,* March 10, 2000, 10.

Morris, Wesley. "*Hedwig and the Angry Inch.*" *Film Comment,* July–August 2001, 76–77.

Mullen, Kelly. "Film Review: From bad to worse in *Justin to Kelly.*" *The America's Intelligence Wire,* June 26, 2003.

Mussolini, Romano. "*Swing Kids.*" *Entertainment Weekly,* August 13, 1993, 78.

Neman, Daniel. *The Richmond-Times Dispatch,* January 1, 2005, G58.

Nesselson, Lisa. "*Cannibal! The Musical*" *Daily Variety,* May 24, 1999, 72.

Newman, Bruce. "*Moulin Rouge* director reaches right for the heart." *Knight Ridder/Tribune News Service*, May 30, 2001, K0135.

Nguyen, Hanh. "Armani designs Judd's *De-Lovely* duds." *Knight Ridder/Tribune News*, July 3, 2004, K7004.

Noh, David. "Inches from Stardom, John Cameron Mitchell." *Film Journal International*, August 2001, 16.

Noh, David. "*Camp*." *Film Journal International*, June 2003, 50.

Nye, Doug. "Musicals are Back, and Cyd Charisse is Dancing." *The State*, May 1, 2003, 1–3.

O'Brien, Ellen. "Joey's '*Fantastick*' Voyage." *The Boston Globe*, March 23, 1995, 63.

Oei, Lily. "*Camp* Sings Out at Gotham Bow." *Daily Variety*, July 24, 2003, 15.

Ogle Connie. "*Camp*." *Knight Ridder/Tribune News Service*, August 7, 2003, K4901.

Parney, Lisa Leigh. "Is That Really Madonna Singing?" *Christian Science Monitor*, December 6, 1996, 15.

Perry Vern. "*Moulin Rouge* is a Dazzling Trip." *Knight Ridder/Tribune News Service*, December 24, 2001, K1326.

Petrikin, Chris. "Some Like It Hot: Weinstein in drag to glamorize *Velvet* preem." *Daily Variety*, May 11, 1998 184.

Peyser, Marc and Miller, Mark. "A Musical Loses its Voice." *Newsweek*, February 7, 1994, 61.

Plasketes, George. "*Cop Rock* Revisited: Unsung series and musical hinge in cross-genre evolution." *Journal of Popular Film and Television*, Summer 2004, 64–73.

Poland, David. "Hit Parade." *Entertainment Weekly*, March 28, 1997, 14.

Pols, Mary F. "*Moulin Rouge*." *Knight Ridder/Tribune News Service*, May 30, 2001, K0136.

Pols, Mary F. "Stagedoor to screen: Todd Graff bases first movie on theater camp." *Knight-Ridder/Tribune News Service*, August 15, 2003.

Pols, Mary F. "Kline makes *De-Lovely* Hum Right Along." *Knight Ridder/Tribune News Service*, July 2, 2004, K5768.

Pratt, Steve. "Phan...tastic." *Europe Intelligence Wire*, December 9, 2004.

Rahner, Mark. "*Moulin Rouge* Can-Can Overdo It." *Knight Ridder/Tribune News Service*, December 24, 2001, L1366.

Rea, Steven. "*Hedwig and the Angry Inch*." *Knight Ridder/Tribune News Service*, August 2001, K0921.

Rechtshaffen, Michael. "*Camp*," *Hollywood Reporter*, July 8, 2003, 18–19.

Rice, Lynette. "ABC tries on *Cinderella*." *Broadcasting and Cable*, October 27, 1997 30–31.

Richmond, Ray. "*Rodgers and Hammerstein's Cinderella*." *Variety*, October 27, 1997, 32.

Rickey, Carrie. "*Dancer in the Dark*." *Knight Ridder/Tribune News Service*, October 5, 2000, K294.

Roberts, Rex. "*The Singing Detective*." *Film Journal International*, November 2003, 56–57.

Rodriguez, Rene. "*Hedwig and the Angry Inch*." *Knight Ridder/Tribune News Service*, August 2, 2001, K0936.

Romney, Jonathan. "*Velvet Goldmine*." *New Statesman*, October 23 1998, 35–36.

Romney, Jonathan. "Falling Flat." *New Statesman*, September 18, 2000, 44.

Rotello Gabriel. "Musicals and the Gay Gene: Last word." *The Advocate*, March 18, 2003, 1 of 2.

Rozen, Leah. "*Swing Kids*." *People Weekly*, March 15, 1993, 17.

Rozen, Leah. "*The Singing Detective*: Robert Downey Jr., Mel Gibson, Robin Wright Penn, Katie Holmes." *People Weekly*, November 3, 2003, 36.

Rozen, Leah. "*De-Lovely*: Kevin Kline, Ashley Judd." *People Weekly*, July 12, 2004, 30.

Sandla Robert. "Everything's Coming Up Bette." *Dance Magazine*, December 1993, 84–85.

Schaefer, Stephen. "Lead Role in *Opera* is a High Note for Butler." *The Boston Herald*, December 21, 2004. http://www.theedge.bostonherald.com/movieNews

Schickel, Richard. "*Tone Deaf*: For once, a movie that was better on television." *Time*, November 3, 2002, 77.

Schickel, Richard. "It's De-Pressing! A new Cole Porter biopic plays the great songwriter's life in a minor key." *Time*, July 5, 2004, 90.

Schilling, Mary Kaye. "Vamping it Up: *Buffy* finds a song in its heart with a showstopping musical episode." *Entertainment Weekly*, November 9, 2001, 18+.

Schurr Amanda. "With pluck and moxie, kids at *Camp* will win your heart." *Sarasota Herald Tribune*, August 29, 2003, 13.

Schwarzbaum, Lisa. "Lower the Bard: Kenneth Branagh sets Shakespeare to music (and dance) in the heavy-handed trifle, *Love's Labour's Lost*." *Entertainment Weeky*, July 9, 2000, 50.

Schwarzbaum, Lisa. "Slice of Life: *Hedwig and the Angry Inch* is a wonderfully kitschy rock opera." *Entertainment Weekly*, July 27, 2001, 45.

Schwarzbaum, Lisa. "*The Singing Detective*: A ditty-delivering Downey Jr. dazzles as a delusional detainee." Entertainment Weekly, October 31, 2003, 55.

Schwarzbaum, Lisa. "Camp: Extravagance rules in an endearing but underdone drama." *Entertainment Weekly*, August 1, 2003, 62.

Scott-Douglass, Amy. "Women and alternatives to warfare in some films by Zeffirelli, Branagh, and Luhrmann." *Shakespeare Newsletter*, Winter 2001, 109–110.

Seligman, Craig. "*Velvet Goldmine*." *Artforum International*, October 1998, 102–105.

Seller, Andy. "Future looks *De-Lovely* for movie musicals." *USA Today*, August 21, 2003.

Sharkey, Betsy. "If the slipper fits...two producers with a track record in musicals for TV take on a classic, with a slight twist." *Mediaweek*, August 18, 1997, 17–18.

Sharrett, Christopher. "Consolations of the Musical." *USA Today*, January 2001, 59.

Sheehan, Henry. "A stirring *Hedwig* goes far beyond camp." *Orange County Register*, July 23, 2001.

Simon, John. "*I'll Do Anything*." *National Review*, March 21, 1994, 71–72.

Simon, John. "*Evita*." *National Review*, January 27, 1997, 57.

Simon, John. "A Will But No Way." *National Review*, June 19, 2000.

Simon, Scott. *Weekend Edition Saturday, National Public Radio*. January 4, 2003, 2 of 5.

Smith, Gavin. "*Dancer in the Dark:* Lars von Trier, filmmaker—Interview." *Film Comment*, September 2000, 1–5. http://www.findarticles.com/p/articles/mi_m1069/is_5_36/ai_65643699/print.

Steyn, Mark. "Potter Mismatch." *Spectator*, November 15, 2003, 66–67.

Stroupe, Katherine. "Newsmakers." *Newsweek*, November 19, 2001, 82.

Stuart, Jan. "*Goldeneye*." *The Advocate*, November 10, 1998, 71.

Svetkey, Benjamin. "The Post Production; forget the vision thing—can he cut it; a director gets the edit sweats." *Entertainment Weekly*, November–December 1997, 24.

Thigpen, David E. "The Sweet Sound of *Magnolia*: Aimee Mann's tales of romantic distress find emotionally satisfying release in a vibrant new sound track." *Time*, December 13, 1999, 108.

Thomas, George M. "Success of Two Movies Has Studios Tuning Up More." *Akron Beacon Journal*, March 6, 2003, 1 of 1.

Thomson, David. "Sweet Unison." *Sight and Sound*, April 1997, 20.

Torre Nestor U. "Success of *Moulin Rouge* results in musical films revival." *Phillippine Daily Inquirer*, March 18, 2002, 1 of 2.

Traister, Rebecca. "Waiting for the Razzle-Dazzle, *Chicago* Was Supposed to Usher in a New Age of Movie Musicals. So Where Are They?" *The New York Times*, February 29, 2004 AR 11, AR19.

Tucker, Ken. "Gypsy." *Entertainment Weekly*, December 10, 1993, 60–61.

Vognar Chris. "Bringing *Hedwig* to the Screen Was a Rouge Awakening.' *Dallas Morning News*, July 27 2001.

Vognar, Chris. "*The Singing Detective*." *Knight Ridder/Tribune News Service*, November 6, 2003, K3494.

Vognar, Chris. "*Simpsons* musical spoofs worthy of an encore." *Knight Ridder/Tribune News Service*, June 16, 2004, K3653.

Weinstein, Wendy R. "*De-Lovely*." *Film Journal International*, July 2004.

Weiss, Piper. "*Cannibal the Musical*." *Back Stage*, April 20, 2001, 44.

Wener, Ben. "A Measure of Credit of *Hedwig* Trask." *Orange County Register*, July 31, 2001.

Wener, Ben. "Rock Musicals Don't Get Much Better Than *Hedwig*." *Orange County Register*, January 8 2003.

White, Armond. "That Thing They Don't (three recent movie musicals)." *Film Comment*, March–April 1997, 45.

Wickstrom, Andy. "*I'll Do Anything*." *Video Business*, July 8, 1994.

Willman Chris. "Anything Goes: It ain't Cole Porter, but scores for *South Park* and *Runaway Bride* may be the next best thing for the fast-fading film musical." *Entertainment Weekly*, August 13 1999, 73+.

Winters, Rebecca. "Making Over the Porters," *Time*, June 7, 2004.

Wisner, Heather. "Moviemakers Put Motion Back in Pictures." *Dance Magazine*, December 2000, 60.

Wulf, Steve. "Rob Marshall: *Chicago*." *Entertainment Weekly*, February 21, 2003, 101.

Wuntch, Philip. "Ray." *Knight Ridder/Tribune News Service*, October 29, 2004, K3371.

Young, Jamie Painter. "Embracing the Dark." *Back Stage West*, October 12, 2000, 8.

Young, Jamie Painter. "Setting up *Camp*: When you can't cast a project through traditional routes, you have to get creative," *Back Stage West*, July 17, 2003.

Zoglin, Richard. "All singing All Woody." *Time*, December 9, 1996, 81–82.

Zoglin, Richard. "Mad for *Evita*." *Time*, December 30, 1996, 134–137.

"The Big Picture—*The Singing Detective*." *Europe Intelligence Wire*, November 13, 2003

"Cannes Gets *De-Lovely*; Cannes to Celebrate *De-Lovely* and MGM's 80th Anniversary with Screening and Concert." *PR Newswire*, March 10, 2004.

"*Chicago* Cast Put Through Musical 'Boot-Camp' to Reach Oscar Glory." *Europe Intelligence Wire*, February 11, 2003.

"*Chicago* Razzle-Dazzles Over $100 Million In Domestic Box Office On Same Night That Director Rob Marshall Honored as DGA's Best Director; First Musical since *Grease* to pass $100 million." *PR Newswire*, March 2, 2003, NYSU02002032003.

Cinderella TV movie special produces spectacular rating for ABC." *Jet*, November 24, 1997, 63.

"*Dancer* Debate: Is the latest from Lars von Trier, *Dancer in the Dark*, a classic or a rock? Two views." *Entertainment Weekly*, September 22, 2000, 44.

"Emmy Rossum Hits a High Note." *Star*, December 20, 2004, 7.

"Energetic Cast saves *Camp* film." *Asia Africa Intelligence Wire*, June 10, 2004.

"Fans to Vote on New Poster for America's Newest Movie Idols' Debut Film: *From Justin to Kelly*." *Business Wire*, February 26, 2003, 5665.

"Fox Gives *Moulin Rouge* back to Fans for Midnight Shows...Because They 'Can't, Can't Can't Get Enough!" *Business Wire*, February 28, 2003, 5425.

"Gaul Graces *Hedwig*." *Variety*, September 2001, 2.

"Heat Index: Weekly Rating (0–10) of Sizzle and Fizzle." *Advertising Age*, June 20, 2003, 23.

"Idol Chatter." *Video Business*, September 1, 2003, 16.

"IFC goes *Camp*: marks a transitional year." *Hollywood Reporter*, January 7, 2004.

"Killer Films." *Marketing*, August 30, 2001, 7.

"*Love's Labour's Lost*." *The Advocate*, June 6, 2000, 55.

"More Music Stars *Get De-Lovely*: Natalie Cole and Others Added to Stellar Cast of MGM Cole Porter Musical." *PR Newswire*, July 18, 2003.

"*Moulin Rouge* Goes to Hell and Back to Put the Camp in a Hallucinatory Musical Hall Bohemian Fantasy." *Bangkok Post*, August 1 2001, BKPO18111938.

"Movers and Shakers of Movie Musicals" (The Oscars/Where Are They Now?) *People Weekly*, April 8, 2002, 130+.

"Movie *Ray* Hauls in 20.1 Million over Premiere Weekend." *Jet*, November 15, 2004, 10.

"Phantom heads for fall launch with Schumacher." *Hollywood Reporter*, February 18, 2003, 93.

"Que Fiesta: Madonna and pals pop up at the premiere of her new movie, *Evita*." *People Weekly*, January 13, 1997, 100–101.

"Reel World: This week in Hollywood." *Entertainment Weekly*, May 28, 1999, 117.

"Roundtable: The Cast of *Camp*." *Entertainment Weekly*, February 27, 2004.

"*South Park: Bigger, Longer & Uncut* Opening June 30 in Theaters Met Deadlines Using Database." *PR Newswire*, June 17, 1999, 698.

"*South Park: Bigger, Longer & Uncut*, Slated for Nationwide Release on June 30th." *Business Wire*, June 29, 199, 173.

"Stratford, Shaw and Branagh?" *Maclean's*, June 19, 2000, 53.

"*The Best Cinema of 1999*." *Time*, December 20, 1999, 99.

"Whitney Houston and Brandy Star in TV Movie *Cinderella*." *Jet*, November 3, 1997, 44–47.

Internet

Anderson, Jeffrey M. "*Love's Labour's Lost* An Interview." *Combustible Celluoid*, May 24, 2000, 1 of 1. http://www.combustiblecelluloid.com/intken.shtml

B., Scott. "A Trip to *Moulin Rouge* with Nicole Kidman." *Film Force*, May 18, 2001, 1 of 1. http://www.filmforce.ign.com/articles/2002/200220p1.html

Blackwelder, Rob. "Director Keith Gordon is a passionate movie buff who shuns the limelight to work on projects that enthrall him." *Spliced Wire*, October 4, 2003. http://www.splicedonline.com/03/features/kgordon03.html

Brastedt, Mat and Robert Borjesson. "The World's Most Charming Voice—soon on the big screen." *Expressen Noje*, June 11 and 12, 1999. http://unit.bjork.com/specials/ui/DITD/articles/expressen.html

Brown, Laurie. "Kenneth Branagh Goes Musical in *Love's Labour's Lost*." *CBC Radio*, June 2000, 1 of 1. http://www.branaghcompendium.com/artic-cbc00.html

Bush, Keith. "Dressed to Kill: From *Sleepy Hollow* to *Chicago*, Coleen Atwood creates beautiful costumes for beastly characters." *Keith Bush.com*. http:/www.keithbush.com/article_atwood.htm

Byrnes, Paul. "*The Singing Detective*." *SMH.com.au*, July 10, 2004, 1 of 2. http://www.smh.com.au/cgi-bin/common/popupPrintArticle.pl?path=articles/2004/07/09

Caro, Mark. "A Sobering Journey." *Chicago Tribune*, November 16, 2003. http://www.rdjfan.com/articles/chicago-tribune-03.asp

Chau, Thomas. "On the Phone: Keith Gordon of *The Singing Detective*." *Cinema Confidential*, October 23 2003. http://www.cinemaconfidential.com

Ciccone, Christopher. "John Cameron Mitchell: Interview with male impersonator and film director." *Interview*, February 1999, 1 to 4. http://www.findarticles.com/p/articles/mi_m1285/is_2_29/ai_53747398/print

Cook, Patrick J. "*Love's Labour's Lost*." Institute of Film Studies, University of Nottingham, January 1, 2000, 1 of 1. http://www.notingham.ac.uk/film/journal/filmrev/love's-labour's-lost.htm

Covert, Colin. "Movie Review: *Phantom of the Opera* offers a touch of class." *Minneapolis Star Tribune*, December 22, 2004. http://www.startribune.com

Crowther, Jane. "John Cameron Mitchell—*Hedwig and the Angry Inch*." *BBC Films*, August 23, 2001. 1 of 1. http://www.bbc.co.uk/print/films/2001/08/23/hedwig_and_the_angry_inch_interview.shtml

Dexter Steve. "A Song and Dance about *Chicago*." *Film Stew.com*, January 17, 2003. http://www.filmstew.com/Content/DetailsPrinter.asp?ContentID=5001

Dursin, Andy. "The Real *Gladiator*." *Film Score Monthly*, February 26, 2001. www.filmscoremonthly.com

Ebert, Roger. "*The Singing Detective*." *Chicago Sun-Times*, November 7, 2003. http://www.suntimes.com/cgi-bin/print.cgi

Ebert, Roger. "*Phantom* Merits a Look, But Don't Bother Listening." *Roger Ebert.com*, December 22, 2004. http://www.rogerebert.com

Fawcett, Alexandra. "Baz Luhrmann." *Total DVD*, March 2002, 1 of 1. http://totaldvd.net/features/interviews/2000203BazLuhrmann.php

"Film *Phantom* Worth the Wait." *Sci-Fi Wire*, December 21, 2004, http://www.scifi.com

Fischer, Paul. "Strictly Baz." *The Movie Insider*, December 4, 2001, 1 of 1. http://www.themovieinsider.com/interviews/interviw.php?cid=33.

Fisher, Paul. "Renee Sizzles on Screen in Old *Chicago*." *Girl.com*. http://www.girl.com/au/reneezell-wegerchicago.htm

Flatley, Guy. "Lars von Trier—Interview, Film's Most Daring Director Delivers Again." *Interview*, October 2000, 1 of 1. http://www.findarticles.com/articles/mi_m1285/is_10_30/ai_66675869/pg_2.

Fuchs, Cynthia. "Interview with John Cameron Mitchell, writer/director/star of *Hedwig and the Angry Inch*." *Pop Matters*, Summer 2001. http://www.popmatters.com/film/interviews/mitchell-john-cameron.html

Fuller, Graham. "Shots in the Dark: When the stuff dreams are made of turns into nightmares—Movie Column, *The Singing Detective, In the Cut*." *Interview*, November 2003, 12. http://www.findarticles.com/p/articles/mi_m1285/is_10_33/ai_109085145/print

Gristwood, Sarah. "What is This Thing Called *Love's Labour's Lost?*" *The Guardian*, March 27, 2000, 1 of 1. http:film.guardian.co.uk/Feature_Story/feature_story/04120,152536,00.html

Intercourse, B. Alan. "Interview: Agent Orange: John Cameron Mitchell on *Hedwig and the Angry Inch!*" *Movie Web*, July 16, 2001. http://movieweb.com/news/news.php?id=2394

"Interview with Director of *Chicago*." *CNN*, March 6, 2003. http://www.cnnstudentnews.cnn.com/TRANSCRIPTS/0303/06/lt.03.html

"Interview: *Everyone Says I Love You*." *Edward Norton Information Page*, 1 of 1. http://www.edward-norton.org/audio/esilyclips.html

Kaufman, Anthony. "Interview: Lars von Trier Comes Out of the Dark." *Indie Wire*, September 22, 2000, 1 to 5. http://www.indiewire.com/people/int_vonTrier_Lars_0922.html

Kennedy, Lisa. "*Phantom* Unveils a New Beauty, but it Doesn't do Beast Any Good." *The Denver Post*, December 22, 2004. http://www.denverpost.com

"Kenneth Branagh, CrankyCritic StarTalk." *The Cranky Critic*, 1 to 6. http://www.crankycritic.com/qa/kennethbranagh.html

Kim, Ellen A. "Nicole Can-Cans On." *Hollywood.com*, May 13, 2001, 1 of 1. http://www.hollywood.com

Lemire, Christy. "*Phantom* a Bloated Nightmare. Big images, little charm in movie adaptation of musical." *CNN*, December 22, 2004. http://www.cnn.entertainment.com

Leopold, Todd. "Sing a song for movie musicals. Is the venerable genre going to make a comeback?" *CNN*, March 27, 2003, 2 of 3. http://www.cnn.com/2003/SHOWBIZ/MOVIES/03/26/movie.musicals

Minow, Neil. "Writer Neil Minow Sat Down with *De-Lovely* Star Ashley Judd to Talk About the Film." *Yahoo Movies*, 1 of 1. http://www.movies.yahoo.com/movies/feature/delovely.html

Murray, Rebecca. "*Baz Luhrmann Talks Awards and Moulin Rouge*." *About.com*, March 9, 2002, 1 of 1. http://romanticmovies.about.com/library/weekly/aa030902a.html

Murray, Rebecca. "Interview with Keith Gordon, the Director of '*The Singing Detective*.'" *About.com*. http://romanticmovies.about.com/cs/singingdetective/a/sdkeithgordon.p.htm

"Natalie Portman" http://www.natalieportman.com

"Newsweek Interview: Lars von Trier." *Newsweek*, March 28 2004, 1 of 1. http://www.Newsweek.MSNBC.com

"No Longer on Cruise Control." *Tiscali*. Summer 2001, 1 and 2. http://www.tiscali.co.uk

Otto, Jeff. "Interview: Ashley Judd and Kevin Kline. They're *De-Lovely*." *Film Force*, July 1, 2004.

http://filmforce.ign.com/articles/527/527723p.html?fromint=1.

Rausch, Andrew J. "Sure I'll Do It: An interview with Robert Wise." *Bright Lights Film Journal.* http://www.brightlightsfilm.com/35/robertwise1.html

Rawson, Christopher. "The starry cast of *Chicago* follows Rob Marshall's lead in his big-screen directing debut." *The Post-Gazette*, April 21, 2002. http://www.post-gazette.com/ae/20020421chicago0421fnp1.asp

Rayner, Jay. "What a song and dance." *The Observer,* March 26, 2000, 1 of 1. http://film.guardian.co.uk/Feature_Story/feature_story/04120,152666.00.html

Rheinhardt, Bernd. "*Dancer in the Dark*, written and directed by Lars von Trier." *World Socialist Web Site,* October 31, 2000 1 to 3. http://www.wsws.org/articles/2000/oct2000/danc-o31_prn.shtml

Saenger, Diana. "Irwin Winkler's *De-Lovely* Embraces a Lost Hollywood Glamour." *About.com,* July 28, 2004, 1 of 2. http://romanticmovies.about.com/od/delovely/a/delovely062804_p.htm

"Singing to Sundance." *Associated Press*, January 21, 2002. http://entertainment.msn.com/news/article/aspx?news=112776

Steele Bruce C. "John Cameron Mitchell." *The Advocate Online.* http://www.advocate.com/html/stories/843_4/843_4_hedwig_web.asp

Susman, Gary. "Plain Song and Dance." *The Boston Phoenix*, January 16–23, 1997, 1 of 1. http://www.bostonphoenix.com/alt1/archive/movies/reviews/01-16-97/EVERYONE_BAR.html

Szymanski, Mike. "*De-Lovely* Experience: Ashley Judd and Kevin Kline bring Cole Porter's life to the big screen." *Zap2It.com.* http://entertaiment.msn.com/celebs/article.aspx?news=162717

"*The Singing Detective*." Interview with Keith Gordon." *Psoriasis.org*, March 18, 2003. http://www.psoriasis.org/resources/publications/singingdetectiveinterview.php

"*The Singing Detective.*" *Ritz FilmBill*—Showing Movies to Talk About (Philadelphia & New Jersey). http://www.ritzfilmbill.com/editorial/synopses/singingdetective.shtml

Tonguette, Peter. "Off-Key: What the Critics Missed in *The Singing Detective.*" *Senses of Cinema.* http://www.sensesofcinema.com/contents/04/30/singing_detective.html

Index